Bridges to Cuba / Puentes a Cuba

Bridges to Cuba

Puentes a Cuba

RUTH BEHAR, Editor

Ann Arbor
THE UNIVERSITY OF
MICHIGAN PRESS

Copyright © by the University of Michigan 1995
All rights reserved
Published in the United States of America by
The University of Michigan Press
Manufactured in the United States of America
⊚ Printed on acid-free paper

1998   1997   1996   4   3   2

A CIP catalogue record for this book is available from the British Library.

Library of Congress Cataloging-in-Publication Data

Bridges to Cuba = Puentes a Cuba / Ruth Behar, editor.
    p. cm.
    ISBN 0-472-09611-7 (hc : alk. paper). — ISBN 0-472-06611-0
(pbk. : alk. paper)
    1. American literature—Cuban American authors.   2. United States—
Relations—Cuba—Literary collections.   3. Cuba—Relations—United
States—Literary collections.   4. Cubans—United States—Literary
collections.   5. Cuban Americans—Literary collections.   6. United
States—Relations—Cuba.   7. Cuba—Relations—United States.
8. Cuba—Civilization.   I. Behar, Ruth, 1956–
PS508.C83B75   1995
810.8′08687291—dc20   95-34522
                                                           CIP

Gracias

To Juan Leon for being my co-conspirator on the *Michigan Quarterly Review* double issue of "Bridges to Cuba" (Summer and Fall, 1994), where this project first took shape. To Larry Goldstein, editor of the *Michigan Quarterly Review,* for wholehearted support. To Nancy Mirabal, our *MQR* intern, for intelligent assistance. To Doris Knight, the *MQR* administrative assistant, for such amazing patience.

To David Frye for exquisite translations. To Nena Torres for giving me courage. To Nereida García Ferraz for her art. To Rolando Estévez for his art. To Natalia Raphael for being with me in Cuba in 1991. To Alan West and Ester Shapiro for their nurturing. To Nancy Morejón for spirited conversation. To Abilio Estévez for inviting me to see "Pearl of the Sea" in Havana. To LeAnn Fields of University of Michigan Press for making this book possible. And to all the contributors for having faith in our bridge.

CONTENTS

Part 2: RUPTURE / RUPTURA

Part 3: REMEMBERING / RECUERDOS

Nereida García Ferraz, "Regreso." A photograph of her first return trip to Cuba, 1979.

INTRODUCTION

Un puente, un gran puente, no se le ve,
sus aguas hirvientes, congeladas,
rebotan contra la última pared defensiva.

A bridge, a great bridge, that can't be seen,
its boiling, frozen waters
batter against the last defensive wall.

—José Lezama Lima

Las paredes	Walls
vueltas de lado	turned on their sides
son puentes.	are bridges.

—Anonymous. A message on a 1994 New Year's greeting card from Cuba

Once upon a time, Cuba was such a commonplace of the United States's imagination that it was included in maps of Florida. After the Cuban Revolution in 1959 and Fidel Castro's declaration that Cuba would be resculpted as a communist nation, the United States sent the island into exile. A blockade was imposed, cutting off communication with a Cuba that had fallen from grace into the arms of the enemy, the Soviet Union. Cuba, in turn, accepted the blockade as the price of independence. Suddenly, inexorably, a hundred years of connections between Cuba and the United States were severed. Cuba became, in the words of U.S. policy analyst Mario Lazo, a "dagger in the heart" of this country.

Lately that dagger has lost its edge, its ability to wound, even its precise location on the map. A filmmaker from the island, visiting the United States in 1993, told me that when he was introduced to a medical doctor in Grand Rapids, Michigan, the doctor remarked, "Oh, so you're from Cuba? Nice to meet you. I lived in Nepal for five years." Stunned by this surrealistic encounter, the filmmaker didn't know what to reply. The doctor was suggesting that Cuba and Nepal were somehow related to each other. And maybe they are. The longest ninety miles separate the tip of Florida from the island of Cuba. Cuba, it seems, now borders on Nepal.

Only the United States could erase Cuba from its map of the world. Cuba tried but never could manage to erase the United States from its map. The fact is that Cuba and its diaspora are always defined within a U.S. framework, on the right and the left. Indeed, after the revolution the nation split apart precisely between those who stayed, to live with their backs turned against the great power to the North, and those who left and took refuge in the belly of the beast. The powerful and unyielding groups within the Cuban American exile lobby—that not only refuse any kind of contact with the contemporary island but frequently use violence to terrorize those Cuban Americans seeking to forge connections—could not exist without tacit U.S. support. Other players within the North American left, in seeking to highlight the inhumane aspects of the blockade and provide unequivocal support for Cuba's right to self-determination, sometimes impose their own hard line about what can or cannot be said about Cuba, unwittingly closing off possibilities for constructive debates.

Cuba since the revolution has been imagined as either a utopia or a backward police state. Cuba, viewed with utopian eyes, is a defiant little island that has dared to step on the toes of a great superpower and dreamed ambitiously of undoing the legacy of poverty, inequality, and unfulfilled revolutions that has plagued Latin America and the Caribbean. Alternately, as newspaper headlines in the U.S. media like to declare, Cuba is "an island of lost souls," a place where "huddled masses yearn for the comforts of life" and will sacrifice everything to leave, plunging into the "deadly sea of dreams" as *balseros* (raft people) or Cuban "wetbacks." Within this conflicting web of representations born of the Cold War, there is little room for a more nuanced and complex vision of how Cubans on the island and in the diaspora give meaning to their lives, their identity, and their culture in the aftermath of a battle that has split the nation at the root.

Bridges to Cuba, which began as a special double issue of *Michigan*

Quarterly Review, grew out of the conviction that there is another map of Cuba, a map crosscut with contradictory desires and yet luminous, like our cover art by Nereida García Ferraz, whose own quest for a bridge to Cuba is the subject of all her work. The enthusiasm and support of Cuban artists and intellectuals, as well as the quantity and quality of manuscripts and artworks that found their way to Michigan, exceeded our wildest expectations and convinced us that a great many original, brave, exciting, and compassionate Cuban voices, inside and outside the island, had yet to be heard. News of the project spread by word of mouth, here as well as in Cuba. As the chorus of voices and visions grew in strength, it became clear that there is an immense need for a forum such as this, in which Cubans can openly define themselves and dismantle, once and for all, the hurtful stereotypes of the islander as a brainwashed cog of a Marxist state and the immigrant as a soulless worm lacking any concern for social justice.

Given the obstacles to phone and mail communication, it was difficult for work from the island to reach us. After repeated efforts and visits, I succeeded in gathering together something of a sampling of poetry especially, one of the most popular Cuban genres. Manuscripts frequently came on frail or recycled paper, typed with faded ribbons, often in handmade envelopes. On the island, writing is truly a heroic act. With the loss of economic support from socialist Europe, there are continual blackouts and food shortages. The once vibrant publishing world, for which Havana was well known, has withered, as even *Granma,* the state newspaper, has been reduced to a single newspaper sheet folded in half. For most of the island participants, this publication is their debut not only in English but in the United States.

On this side, not all responses were positive. I received an angry and sarcastic letter from a Miami Cuban poet who said my head was stuck in an academic Michigan cloud. Refusing to participate, he wrote, "Tell me, Professor Behar, how would you go about editing a 'Building Bridges' issue focusing on apartheid South Africa, the Argentina of the Dirty War, or Nazi Germany?" All the links he drew seemed to me grossly inaccurate, but the comparison he made between Cuba and Nazi Germany pained me profoundly because it was an undignified manipulation of the massacre of six million Jews and others in Europe. A poet cruel to history, I decided, is cruel to poetry.

Yet this letter foreshadowed other critical responses I would receive from members of the second generation of Cuban Americans who feel it is impossible, even absurd, to build a bridge to Cuba so long as the regime of Fidel Castro remains in power. A flurry of such responses arrived after I published "A Bridge to Cuba," an op-ed essay in the *New York Times* in 1992. In this essay I stated that there is a second generation of Cuban Americans who want to go beyond the Castro fixation and create cultural and emotional ties among *all* Cuban people. I had tried, in the first draft, to get away with not mentioning Fidel Castro, but a *Times* editor insisted that any opinion piece on Cuba must take a stand on Him. Indeed, as Alan West shows in his essay "My Life with Fidel Castro," the charismatic leader has come to embody the rifts in the nation of Cuba, "as persecuted and prosecutor, as hope and desperation, as rigidity and flexibility, as myth and history."

Normally, an essay such as my op-ed would have called forth harsh criticism and ridicule by the Cuban American radio talk shows in Miami. But it happens that the essay appeared exactly when a spectacular dramatic escape from Cuba to the United States took place. My essay was published on December 18. The very next day Orestes Lorenzo, a former Cuban Air Force pilot honored for his bravery in Angola, swooped down near the Varadero coastline with a borrowed plane, picked up his wife and sons, and delivered them safe and sound to the United States. Immediately given hero status, Orestes Lorenzo appeared on the *Tonight Show* to speak about his daring "act of love," which had captured "mid-America's heart." He was appointed grand marshal of the parade at Disneyland, where he communed with none other than Mickey Mouse—the ultimate validation of his arrival on this side of the border.

Orestes Lorenzo undertook his daredevil escapade because the Cuban government refused to let his family go. Raúl Castro had also challenged Lorenzo's masculinity by saying that if he were such a macho he should return to Cuba himself for his family. But Orestes Lorenzo didn't become embittered. Two months into his welcome in the United States, he began to call for a floating "Crusade of Love" from the Florida Straits to El Malecón, Havana's seafront. In their boats, he urged Cuban Americans to take clothing, food, and medicines, not bullets. That way Cubans on the island would know they had nothing to fear from their brothers and sisters across the straits. By making this declaration Lorenzo tarnished his own heroic image within the Cuban American exile community and quickly lost credibility. Soon after, he stopped dreaming aloud.

Like Orestes Lorenzo's vision of the floating crusade of love, this vision of bridges to Cuba will not please everybody. It may, indeed, please nobody. On this side, people may find it too soft on Castro. On the other side, it may seem too heterodox. That is the risk you take with Cuban matters. Freedom of speech in the Cuban community, on both sides, is an ideal that has yet to be fully realized. But, as Marilyn Bobes suggests in her elliptical, self-censored poem, there are dangers both in speaking and in staying quiet. Without being deluded about the failings of their respective societies, the participants in *Bridges to Cuba* affirm, in voices that are earnest, angry, witty, and hopeful, that it is possible to go beyond the polarizations of Cold War thinking.

Now that the Berlin Wall has been ground to dust, the Soviet Union dissolved, and the United States trade embargo against Vietnam recently lifted, the Cold War would seem to be over. Yet even in the midst of so many global shifts, where U.S.-Cuban relations are concerned, the war is still quite *hot*. For the last thirty-five years, while North Americans have been unable to vacation on the island that was once their backyard, this heat has consumed Cuban life on both sides of the ocean wall. Our tables, clothes, and flesh, as poet Victor Fowler Calzada writes, are covered with burn marks. Nothing lost will come back with the rain, but many of us now long for the cleansing waters of mutual understanding and forgiveness.

Bridges to Cuba is a meeting place, an open letter, a castle in the sand, an imaginary homeland. It is a space for reconciliation, imaginative speculation, and renewal. It is a first-time event. "Diaspora, like death, interrupts all conversation," writes Jorge Luis Arcos from the island. After being "enemies," it isn't easy to trust one another. But conversations can begin again. Walls can be turned on their side so they become bridges. It is possible to resurrect ourselves. As Jésus Barquet writes from this side, "Let's think of the bridges peace could bring us."

The work that graces the front and back covers of this book is an effort precisely to envision an artistic bridge between the work of Nereida García Ferraz, who lives in the United States, and Rolando Estévez, who lives in Cuba. The title of Nereida García Ferraz's work, *Es agradable pero no es el correr* ("It's agreeable but it isn't the same as running"), a line of poetry from the pen of Fernando Pessoa, suggests that, despite our best intentions, there are limits to the desire to imagine another map of Cuba. The boat in her painting is much too large to cross under the bridges uniting the islands to the mainland. As a counterpoint to this Cuban American vision, our back cover features the work of Rolando Estévez, *Cuerpo de lágrimas* ("Body of Tears"), who from the island offers us a view not of a bridge but of a wall, on which boats and rafts slip and slide, a wall driven into the body of a man, a body of tears. Estévez was left behind in Cuba when he was fifteen after his parents and sister went into exile in the United States. Twenty-five years later, his work as an artist offers a moving reflection on the wrenching consequences of that family separation. When will the day come, his work seems to ask, when that wall, built of so much hurt, so much loss, will become a bridge? Or is it already too late?

Bridges to Cuba stems from a personal quest for memory and community. As a Cuban Jew growing up in the United States, where you can only check one box for your ethnic identity, I had often been questioned about the authenticity of my Cubanness. How could I, being Jewish, claim to be Cuban? Wasn't my Cuban identity nothing more than an accident of history, another stop in a Jewish diaspora? It wasn't deep, it wasn't in my blood, the Cubanness, so who was I fooling?

In our milieu I never thought of my "mixed" identity as strange or contradictory. Each of my grandparents arrived in Cuba, young, alone, searching for their America across the border, because as Jews from Poland and Turkey their entrance into the United States had been foreclosed by the 1924 Immigration and Nationality Act. My parents were born in Cuba, and they, like the friends in their circle, had constructed a cohesive Jewish Cuban identity for themselves—an identity explored in all its psychological depth by Ester Shapiro in her essay for this book. Reunited after the revolution in New York, we'd eat matzoh for a week during Passover then go with El Grupo to eat black beans, rice, fried plantains, and *palomilla* steak at La Rumba Restaurant. In many ways the Jewish members of El Grupo were no different from non-Jewish Cuban immigrants of the first generation. For that generation, Cuba represented nostalgia, a paradise lost, youthful dreams of social transformation gone sour. We had burnt the bridge back and were not to look behind, lest we turn into pillars of salt.

Like other Cuban Americans of the second generation who left the island as children, when I came of age I longed to return to Cuba and see the island with my own eyes. In 1979 I was finally able to go, with a group of students and professors from Princeton that included only one other Cuban American. At the time I was ignorant of the fact that groups of young Cuban Americans, organized in work brigades named after the Afro-Cuban Independence leader Antonio Maceo, were making pilgrimages to the island in an effort to open dialogue between the Cubans who left and the Cubans who stayed. In my solitude, I began to fear that it was foolish of me to desire a link to Cuba. Twelve years would pass before I would go back again, after a long detour living in villages in Spain and Mexico in the name of anthropology. Not that those years were wasted. From Spain I brought back a lived sense of the pueblos in which so many Cubans (including Fidel Castro) claim their origins; and from Mexico I brought back the concept that the border with the United States is an open wound.

As I prepared to return again to Cuba in December of 1991, I became bedridden with a mysterious illness. My legs were too weak for me to stand on, and my heart beat terrifyingly quickly. I came to realize that my body was forcing me to confront the internalized blockade—my own profound terror about returning. That terror was compounded by intense family pressure. My parents demanded that I write out a will and leave them all the custody papers for my five-year-old son, who'd be staying behind with them. I believe it was the thought of never again seeing my son—who was the same age as I was when I left Cuba—that was most chilling.

With the paranoia of all my exiled ancestors on my back, I set off. To my surprise, I met extraordinary people in Cuba who appeared to be my mirror images. With my island counterparts, I seemed to reclaim not just by childhood but an imaginary adulthood, a parallel existence—the "ghost limbs" of which Teresa Marrero writes. They had been told by their parents to view the bridge to the United States as burnt and broken, just as my parents had told me not to look back to Cuba. On my return to the United States, I came into contact with networks of Cuban American scholars, activists, and artists living in Boston, New York, and Chicago who were also trying to resolve the puzzle of their connection to Cuba. They had distanced themselves from Miami's exile politics, hoping to find breathing space to articulate their sense of Cuban identity, without wallowing in nostalgia or being naive about the shortcomings of the revolution. All of us, Cubans of the second generation, inside and outside the island, had lived through an internal struggle between capitalism and communism, between our need to question inherited dogmas and our loyalty to family and community. We didn't want to wage the same struggles as our parents, yet we were still caught in the frameworks, fears, and silences of their generation.

Bridges to Cuba had been attempted before by members of my generation, most notably in the 1970s. There was a moment of euphoria in 1978 when it seemed as though "the dialogue," involving 140 Cubans living outside the island and the government of Cuba, would heal the divided nation. Cuba immediately began the family reunification program, recognizing the right of all Cubans living abroad to visit their homeland. By 1979, a hundred thousand Cubans residing in the United States had returned to Cuba for one-week visits with their families.

Our suitcases were full of goods that were scarce or nonexistent in

Cuba. Even those of us who sympathized with the accomplishments of the revolution had not sweated out its hardships. The return of *la comunidad*, as Cubans living outside the island came to be called, unloosed repressed desires among many of those who had stayed. The storming of the Peruvian embassy in Havana in 1980 by Cubans demanding political asylum drove a wedge through the romance of "the dialogue." It led to the Mariel boatlift and the departure of 125,000 Cubans, even more than had returned to visit from the United States a year before. Among the "Marielitos" were many gay men who, along with others who left in 1980, were dubbed the scum of the revolution by the Castro regime in a sad effort to save face.

After Mariel, Cuba closed up once more like a clam to those of us who left. The nation continued divided, even more divided than before. It is through informal networks that family, artistic, and academic ties have been maintained. According to U.S. law, only those who have family in Cuba, or are going there to do research or journalism or offer humanitarian aid, may travel to Cuba. According to Cuban law, anyone born in Cuba, even if "naturalized" elsewhere, must return with a Cuban passport, or a reentry permit. For me, that passport, which might be seen as a ploy to extract revenues from those who've left, settled a lot of my postmodern doubts about multiple, inauthentic, and shifting identities. I was born in Cuba, so I'm Cuban, and that's it, case closed.

In the midst of the stand-off between Cuba and the United States, the Marazul ticket counter at the Miami airport became our borderland, that is, until the new regulations of August 1994, which have almost entirely restricted family visits. It was a theater of the absurd, where the concern for things took on obsessive dimensions. The forty-four pound limit on baggage was strictly enforced and every suitcase and carry-on bag going to Cuba got weighed. Women took to wearing several layers of clothing and putting hats on their heads crammed with costume jewelry. On their backs they carried stuffed Panda bears; around their waists they tied rings of sausage. Their huge plastic bags brimmed with bottles of aspirin, enough for an eternity of headaches. At the grass roots, rigid categories like communist or capitalist cease to be relevant. It is there that the wall is bridged daily.

Those of us who continue to travel back and forth are the bridge between the island and the exile. We carry letters, dreams, grief, from one side to the other. Returning from Havana, I brought back the letter-poem that Jorge Luis Arcos wrote for his friend, Jose Luis Ferrer, now living in Miami. On a trip to Havana, I took an actual letter that Teresa Marrero had written to her cousin. I felt I had crossed into a strange limbo by being the bridge between the two cousins of "Ghost Limbs" who in real life had yet to meet. (Now Marrero's cousin lives in Miami.) Communications with Cuba are such a peculiar combination of the near and the far that it is difficult to imagine the day when you will be able to post a letter through regular mail and have it arrive. And yet increasingly Cuba draws closer. Thanks to AT&T, direct dialing to Cuba is now possible. It's no longer necessary for me to go to Havana to catch the film *Strawberry and Chocolate*. I can see it in Ann Arbor, with popcorn on my lap.

Looking back at that first effort to build bridges, I am struck by the central role played by two brilliant Cuban American women. Both Lourdes Casal (who died in 1981) and Ana Mendieta (who died in 1985) were at the height of their creative powers when death claimed them. Both women turned their preoccupation with Cuba into the stuff of art, shaping the worldview of an entire generation of Cuban Americans.

There is no question that the first plank of the bridge to Cuba was thrown into the sea by Lourdes Casal, a woman of middle-class background whose own mix of African, Spanish, and Chinese heritage epitomized the mosaic of Cuban culture. As a psychology professor in the United States, Lourdes Casal conducted scholarship on Cuban immigration and also wrote poetry and stories in Spanish. She helped found the magazine *Areíto*, a predecessor to this project, which published the works of Cubans inside and outside the island. Initially part of a counterrevolutionary group, Casal had a change of heart in the 1970s and became an active supporter of the Cuban Revolution. She was the first Cuban expatriate intellectual to go back to Cuba, and on her return to the United States she urged young people of the second generation to join her. Casal became the "mother" of the Antonio Maceo brigade and in 1977 led the first group of fifty-five young Cuban Americans on their return to Cuba, where they were perceived as the lost children of the Revolution. A film by Jesús Díaz about the group, titled *55 Hermanos*, was widely shown in Cuba and proved heartrending, showing the suffering created by the division of families and the splitting apart of a nation.

Young Cuban Americans who returned to Cuba as *Maceítos* hoped to prove that they were not *gusanos*, the worms of the revolution. This took great courage, for they were often cast out not only by their families and community but by sectors of the North American left. Maria de los Angeles Torres recalls how she was rejected by North Americans involved in the Venceremos Brigade: "These experiences were perhaps the worst. They relished having a connection to Cuba and authoritatively spewed the rhetoric claiming that we could not return for we were 'gusanos' who had abandoned the revolution. 'Yes, but I was six years old!' I'd say. They would respond, 'So what, you were obviously middle-class, and as such your class origins make you unworthy of return.' The hypocrisy of their statements still stings today: none of them were working-class either. We, Cubans in the United States, had become the community of color that white North Americans could discriminate against, ironically with the help of the Cuban government."

Misunderstood in turn by their parents, who'd worked hard to make it in the United States and expected their children to be grateful, the Maceítos struggled to create a new identity on the borderlands. Many of them felt they returned to Cuba with their "hearts in their hands," but their innocence was met with suspicion and intense scrutiny. Lourdes Casal's poem, "For Ana Veldford," with its lines about being "too *habanera* to be *newyorkina* and too *newyorkina* to be anything else," spoke for a generation of Cuban Americans who reclaimed the lost country of their childhood, recognizing that immigration had left them unable to think of home as being in any one place. And as Nancy Morejón makes clear in our interview, Casal's poem, like her return, also spoke to those Cubans who stayed but wanted to reopen conversation with those who had left.

In one of her *descargas,* Lourdes Casal had written about the irony of occupying the position of the *turista político,* the political tourist who returns to Cuba for an academic vacation. Casal recognized, as do the various contributors who tell the stories of their return visits to the island, that those of us who go back must confront not only our traumas and grief but the reality of contemporary Cuba. This means facing the fact that we've grown away from that reality and that with our all-too-brief visits we may, indeed, never fully get to know it. Many of those returning are children from the earliest waves of migration, composed of the white upper and middle classes, who've needed to reorient themselves within a society that now legitimates the African contributions to Cuban culture, such as Santería. Cubans on the island, in turn, must overcome their suspicion that Cuban Americans are back for a re-encounter with their roots that is self-indulgent and ultimately frivolous. If we can get beyond our mutual doubts, we might recognize the creativity and desire for memory and community that is being released on both sides.

Ana Mendieta was unusual in that she did inspire such trust and hope. For Ana Mendieta, the question of reestablishing roots in the soil of Cuba took on a meaning at once spiritual and material. As an art student at the University of Iowa, she gave up painting because it wasn't "real enough." She wanted her images "to have power, to be magic." This led her to use her own body as the primary material of her art and to draw upon ritual elements from Santería. In Mexico, she lay down naked on a Zapotec site, surrounded by flowers; later, she had a firework piece made in the shape of her silhouette and ignited it, so that her body was at once consumed and resurrected in the flames. On her first return trip to Cuba in 1980, all Ana Mendieta brought back was earth and sand from Varadero Beach, where she spent many happy days of her childhood, as her cousin Raquel (Kaki) Mendieta poignantly remembers. In time she would obtain permission to carve exaggerated female figures in the caves of the Jaruco Mountains outside of Havana, fulfilling her ideal of creating sculpture in a natural site, where it could eventually be reclaimed by the earth. And in turn, as Nancy Morejón writes, the rocks and caves of Jaruco also became hers.

Ana Mendieta had written, "There is no past to redeem: there is the void, the orphanhood, the unbaptized earth of the beginning, the time that from within the earth looks upon us. There is above all the search for origin." She wasn't being abstract; Ana Mendieta, who began life in an aristocratic white Cuban family, truly ended up an orphan. Along with many thousands of young Cubans, she and her sister had been sent alone to the United States, ending up in Iowa through the Peter Pan Operation, which sought to save children from communist indoctrination. She never recovered from her sense of orphanhood. Falling to her death from the thirty-fourth floor of a New York City apartment building, she left behind a form of art as evanescent as a sand castle.

And yet her art became a lasting inspiration for Cuban artists inside and outside Cuba. In 1983 she became the first Cuban American artist to have her work exhibited in Cuba. Twelve years later, the Brooklyn-based Cuban artist Ernesto Pujol has become the second artist living outside the island to have his work exhibited in Havana (the Boston-based artist Natalia Raphael exhibited her work in Matanzas in 1994). Using furniture, suitcases, and other objects borrowed from Cuban homes, Pujol set up a series of temporary installations entitled "Los hijos de Pedro Pan" (The Children of Peter Pan) as a way of marking the loss of the island to the whole second generation. This work was dedicated to Ana Mendieta, whose dream of a bridge to Cuba haunts the corn fields of Iowa.

The sexual metaphors underlying U.S.-Cuban relations have never been far below the surface. As Louis Pérez notes, "the North American resolve to possess Cuba and the Cuban determination to resist possession became part of each, an obsession for both." In seeking to free Cuba from its position as a colony of the United States, the Cuban Revolution hoped to redeem an emasculated nation. Manhood and nationhood, in the figure of the Cuban revolutionary hero, were fused and confused. Redeeming the nation required the creation not so much of a new woman but of a new man, as even Cuban films about women such as *Portrait of Teresa* clearly showed. The recent film *Strawberry and Chocolate*, which was nominated for an Academy Award for best foreign film, is another case in point. Nothing has ever seemed to threaten the utopia of new men more terribly than homosexuality.

Manhood is an integral part of the counterrevolution too. As Flavio Risech points out, "neither *revolucionario* nor anticommunist *gusano* can be a *maricón* [queer]." On this side it is unforgiving and scolding father voices, like that of Jorge Mas Canosa of the Cuban American National Foundation, that attain power; the ostentatiously romantic Ricky Ricardo types such as Orestes Lorenzo attain glamour. The voice of a strong-minded woman like Alina Fernández is heard because she is the estranged daughter of Fidel Castro. If national identity is primarily a problem of *male* identity, how are Cuban women on both sides to write themselves into Cuban history?

As a work that reinserts women into the Cuban national narrative, Cristina Garcia's novel *Dreaming in Cuban* is a major historical event. It is the first novel written in English by a Cuban American woman of the second generation that transgresses the border between the United States and Cuba by giving voice to three generations of women divided by revolution and exile. As Garcia says in her interview with Iraida López, "Traditional history . . . obviates women . . . and basically becomes a recording of battles and wars and dubious accomplishments of men. You learn where politics really lie at home." In a situation where there is no bridge linking the two sides of the Cuban community, Garcia suggests that women's dreams can begin to heal the wounds of the divided nation.

Our collection offers several examples of how women's subtle rereadings of Cuban history and contemporary politics can offer crucial insights. In her chronoogically scrambled diary, Coco Fusco imagines herself as a late-twentieth-century Miranda, reclaiming the central female figure of Shakespeare's *The Tempest* as "the Cold War, that modern day tempest, subsides." Patricia Boero, who returned to live in Cuba for five years, tells of how the memory of her deaf cousin Raysa stays with her, as she uses "her eyes to read the world, imagining it sometimes devoid of sound, as she knows it, and free of dogmatic speeches and hurtful words, like *gusano,* and rigid categories like *comunista* or *capitalista.*" The two women cousins of Teresa Marrero's "Ghost Limbs" likewise go beyond the communist/capitalist split as they try to make sense of their lives for each other.

Ester Shapiro, in turn, recalls how when she returned from Cuba her father continued, "resentful and embattled, to insist that I was betraying the family with my communist sympathies." Her mother, aunt, and female cousin instead "pored over the photographs of our old neighborhoods in El Vedado, the intimately known streets of old colonial Habana, surprised and delighted to see the preservation of their lost, once much-loved world." And Nancy Morejón, whose commitment to the revolution has always been strong, nevertheless dedicates two of her poems to Cuban American women who became her friends.

There are, of course, contradictions to being a woman of the border. Maria de los Angeles Torres writes, "I am 'white' when I wake up in Havana, but I am 'other' because of my migratory experience. I am again 'other' when I journey the thirty minutes through airspace to Miami, because I am no longer 'white,' and because my commitment to return to Cuba and have a normal relationship with my home country makes me politically 'other' among Miami Cubans. I arrive in Chicago, and again I am other, now because I am Latina in a city which is defined in black and white."

We should not forget that, in turn-of-the-century Cuban monuments, Independence is often figured as a woman. Zaida del Río, in the drawing she chose to illustrate her poem, shows a woman perched between flowing water and dark marks suggesting footprints on sand, memory, and losses. Perhaps the bridge to Cuba, like Independence, is best imagined in the shape of a woman.

Exile, in Spanish, is a male noun—*exilio.* Curiously too, most writing about the idea of exile is done by men. Is that because women don't have countries to lose? Excilia Saldaña, an island poet, takes on the theme of exile in her long poem, "My Name," an extract of which appears here in translation. The poem is a series of reflections on the meaning of her own name, a feminine version of exile—*excilia.* Excilia Saldaña told me she began to write her poem while traveling in Europe, which opened her eyes to the experience of displacement, an experience she had long avoided. When she was fifteen, she could have left Cuba with her father's family but chose to stay behind with her grandmother, whose name was also Excilia. In her poem she celebrates her grandmother's memory in a way that resonates nicely with Sonia Rivera Valdés recalling the grandmother whose grave she cannot visit; and with Carilda Oliver Labra recalling the grandfather she lost to immigration. But the main theme of Excilia Saldaña's poem is the other exile, the exile of those who stay behind, watching as everyone departs. As she writes, with irony, "They banished my name and banished me. / They condemned me to carry it / from door / to / door / as she who left or she to whom they've gone."

We associate nostalgia with the Cuban American exile sensibility of Miami.

On the island there is also nostalgia. In his play "Pearl of the Sea," which I saw performed in Havana, Abilio Estévez speaks of wanting to go "in search of the Island . . . to find it once more past the line of shadows of rhetoric and confusion." He describes his work as a play that would like to be a ritual or an invocation. It is, in the end, "an act of faith" about the desire for a common language of memory and culture that will reconstruct "the Island of all Cubans, of every time and place." One of the most poignant characters in his plays is Mercedes The Unsatisfied, who exclaims, "I cannot remember being born anywhere. I search and search, but there is no street in my memory." She describes memory as "that piece of old cake without salt or sugar." Yet the absence of memory, she realizes, is hunger.

Estévez's play stylistically enacts the process of remembering by being composed largely of quotations from Cuban poets and popular songs. Jorge Luis Arcos, too, uses a similar literary strategy in his poem. Marilyn Bobes in turn explores the patchiness of remembering by offering a half-erased version of a Quevedo poem.

Remembering is, indeed, the key theme of our issue, as it perhaps must be in any project focusing on the imagining of nationality and homeland. Perhaps that is why personal essays and poetry, both of which readily lend themselves to the exploration of memory's ambiguities, have played such an important role here. José Kozer, for example, reflects on the absurdity of returning to the past in a poem. Emilio Bejel confronts the fact that he has no memory and must invent "a false book of false stories." Mirtha Quintanales writes about traveling in a cardboard box, haunted by "hands without prints" that glide over her body. Flora González Mandri discovers that the Havana she knows is not built of true memories but of the literary imaginings of Cuban poets and writers. And Rosa Lowinger, whose job as an art conservator is "to repair things," lays claim to places like Trinidad that didn't form part of her parents' experience or memory and in that process truly makes Cuba her own.

Eduardo Aparicio's photo essay, parts of which were recently exhibited in Cuba, focuses its lens on the varied ways that Cubans have maintained their sense of identity. People are shown with things they've kept from the past, such as childhood passports, old photographs, and the map and flag of Cuba. But they are also shown remaking themselves in the present. There, too, is Cristina Riley-Lazo, no longer worried, as is her grandfather Mario Lazo, about Cuba being a dagger in the heart of the United States.

René Vázquez Díaz, a Cuban writer living in Sweden, tells Elena Martínez that what unites Cubans inside and outside is that "our grandmother is the same." This book includes two short stories about Cuban grandmothers: a fable by the Cuban writer Senel Paz about a blind grandmother from the provinces who encounters Jesus Christ, and a comical tale by the Cuban American writer Elias Miguel Muñoz about the adventures of a visiting grandmother in the strange planet of the United States of America (Paz and Muñoz are paired up again in the two theatrical Cubas explored by Lillian Manzor-Coats). The grandmother has become a potent symbol within Cuban culture, on both sides, because she represents a figure who has grown old with our century, with the stops and starts of modernity, outliving the eras preceding and succeeding the Cuban Revolution.

Indeed, it is no accident that the Cuban poet Dulce María Loynaz, now 93, has become a kind of intellectual grandmother for Cuban writers and artists of the second generation, who have only recently discovered her. Her selected poems were published in Cuba in 1984 but only after nearly fifty years had gone by without any of her work appearing in print. Since 1992, when she won the prestigious Cervantes Prize for literature written in the Spanish language, all her poetry and fiction has belatedly become available in Cuba. As a hermetic writer who throughout her life has remained within the insular walls of her house and garden in the Vedado neighborhood of Havana, writing of roses, birds, bees, love, death, and eternity, philosophical and transcendental issues far removed from the political battlegrounds of the century, Dulce María Loynaz represents a courageous resistance, a womanist absence from male power struggles, a will to live that is exemplary. Pablo Armando Fernández, the Cuban poet and novelist who has been a bridge to so many Cuban Americans of the second generation seeking to reengage with the island, imaginatively compares Dulce María Loynaz to Emily Dickinson, the great reclusive woman poet of North American literature. Mischieviously, he acknowledges the obvious links between Dulce María Loynaz and other Latin American women poets of her time but remains firm in his vision of "bridges of the heart." Indeed, the poems we include here by authors Reina María Rodríguez, Achy Obejas, Georgina Herrera, Lina de Feria, María Elena Cruz Varela, Yanai Manzor, and Carlota Caulfield are yet further testimony to the vigor with which Cuban women's writing crosses all kinds of borders.

The artwork of Rolando Estévez (featured on our back cover and part pages), bridging the gap between word and image with Blakean splendor, reflects the strong engagement of a younger generation of Cuban writers and artists with the work of Dulce María Loynaz. I take pride in introducing to readers in the United States the work of Rolando Estévez, who has created, with editor and writer Alfredo Zaldívar, the joyful, hopeful, endless publications of *Vigía* in Matanzas, the "Athens of Cuba," as that city of many bridges is known. In María Eugenia Alegría's interview with Zaldívar and Estévez, they recount how they created an independent journal and publishing house that uses stencils, scrap paper, bits of cloth, calligraphy, and a mimeograph machine to produce artisanal books that hark back to the arts and crafts movement of the last century. The desire to make beautiful books—not just functional texts—at a moment of intense economic and moral crisis in socialist Cuba is not simply daring; it is an act of faith in the utter necessity of the cultural arts, without which life itself would become impoverished.

Outside of the island, in the belly of late capitalism, Cuban creativity necessarily takes other forms. Here, we present a range of visions of the remaking of Cuban culture in and around Miami, this city of immense contradictions, which Cubans have turned into their island away from the island. Short fiction by Virgil Suarez and Roberto Fernández offers us well-fleshed portraits of YUCAs (Young Upwardly Mobile Cuban Americans) as well as of working-class Cuban women employed in a southern Florida agricultural factory. Gustavo Pérez Firmat's montage of images of the popular culture of Cuban Miami shows us that being lost in translation is not such a terribly tragic condition, after all. In contrast, Juan Leon, in his bold intertextual reading of Mark Twain, Edmundo Desnoes, and Roberto Fernández, offers a more somber vision of the way underdevelopment and modernity rub shoulders in the twin cities of Miami and Havana.

Cuban American identity is further explored by Eliana Rivero, who charts the process of coming to her Cubanness through interactions with Chicana/o and Nuyorican writers. Refusing to dwell on nostalgia, she concludes that one can be Cuban wherever one is, even on the U.S.-Mexican border. And yet even when one makes peace with one's distance from Cuba, certain compulsions may remain, like Teofilo Ruiz's need to take people to the airport so he can say the last goodbye.

This project would have been incomplete without the voice of at least one of the "children of William Tell," the 1980s generation of nervy intellectuals, artists, and enfants terribles who left Cuba via Mexico at the end of the decade. Now, in the 1990s, artists such as Arturo Cuenca, Consuelo Castañeda, and Quisqueya Henríquez, whose work is featured in our portfolio, are remaking their professional lives in New York and Miami. Madeline Cámara explores this generation's notion of a "third option" and the new conjuncture created by the encounter, in the diaspora, of the children of William Tell and the children of the first wave of Cuban exiles. There is a deep irony to that encounter, for the children of the exiles are welcomed on the island if they want to build bridges, but the children of William Tell are rarely allowed to return home; as "velvet exiles" formed in the bosom of the revolution, their departure is a more stinging betrayal. And yet we must not forget, as Lourdes Gil shows in her essay about an earlier artistic diaspora to Paris, exile and the hope of return are part of the dialectic of Cuban history. Indeed, several of our contributors, who were living in Cuba when I began going to the island seeking bridges, have now crossed over to diaspora.

Blacks and Jews are two of the diasporic peoples who forged a new sense of home on Cuban soil, altering (and being altered by) ideas of "race" on the island. The legacy of the African presence in Cuba is found not only in the collective memory of slavery but in life-affirming music, literature, and spirituality derived from Yoruba, Bantú, and Abakuá influences. Those bridges are given artistic play in the work of Zaida del Río, Yolanda Fundora, Ernesto Pujol, and Osvaldo Mesa, and in the poetry of Miguel Barnet and Minerva Salado. In turn, the legacy of the Jewish boat people of the St. Louis, who (unlike the thousands that became Jewish Robinson Crusoes) were returned to Nazi Germany after being refused entry into Cuba, is portrayed in *Carnaval*, the play by Carmelita Tropicana and Uzi Parnes.

If Dulce María Loynaz represents the will to live, to persist to the end of the century and wherever it takes us, then Reinaldo Arenas represents the other face of the Cuban revolution, of homosexuality taken to the limits of machismo, of vengeance, anger, AIDS, nightfall, and suicide. Here, for what I believe is the first time, a brave writer from the island, Abilio Estévez, offers us a thoughtful and moving review of *Before Night Falls*, the final work of Arenas, an autobiography written in the turmoil of his last days suffering from AIDS. Arenas, who left Cuba unperceived in 1980 through Mariel after being jailed and forbidden to write, has yet to be revindicated in Cuba. When I approached Abilio Estévez about writing a review of Arenas, I almost hoped he'd turn me down, but he replied that he felt it was his obligation. And so, through Abilio Estévez's pen, Arenas at last returns from exile to the "Island-mother who expels us and gathers us in." Despair is transformed into hope, into a bridge, a bridge to and from Cuba.

What, finally, is it that we expect this collection of words and images to accomplish? Cuba continues in the news, and its future is uncertain as ever. Those of us who long for bridges wait, our wings tense. Will the ocean wipe blood off Havana's old, salty seawalls? *Bridges to Cuba,* as it turns out, is less about dreaming in Cuban than about our awakening to a history that has yet to be resolved, let alone absolved.

I have been at a loss for a way to conclude this introduction to a project that marks the beginning, or perhaps the end, of a long process of reconciliation for a nation divided by revolution, the Cold War, and exile. So I turn to José Martí, the leader of the Cuban independence struggle, who is claimed as a hero on both sides of the Cuban border. Pity the nation that needs heroes, wrote Brecht. But fortunately for Cubans our hero had something to say about everything. Martí wrote: *"Los libros sirven para cerrar las heridas que las armas abren."* Such is the hope of *Bridges to Cuba*—that this book will help to close the wounds that weapons have opened.

Statue of José Martí and Liberty. Central Plaza, Matanzas, Cuba. Photo by Ruth Behar, 1993.

PART 1 Reconciliation / Reconciliación

Dulce María Loynaz
del libro Poemas sin nombre -1953-

VII

Muchas cosas me dieron en el mundo:
sólo es mía la pura soledad.

LOURDES CASAL

FOR ANA VELDFORD

Never a summertime in Provincetown
and even on this limpid afternoon
(so out of the ordinary for New York)
it is from the window of a bus that I contemplate
the serenity of the grass up and down Riverside Park
and the easy freedom of vacationers resting on rumpled blankets,
fooling around on bicycles along the paths.
I remain as foreign behind this protective glass
as I was that winter
— that unexpected weekend —
when I first confronted Vermont's snow.
And still New York is my home.
I am ferociously loyal to this acquired *patria chica.*
Because of New York I am a foreigner anywhere else,
fierce pride in the scents that assault us along any West Side
        street,
marijuana and the smell of beer
and the odor of dog urine
and the savage vitality of Santana
descending upon us
from a speaker that thunders, improbably balanced on a fire
        escape,
the raucous glory of New York in summer,
Central Park and us,
the poor,
who have inherited the lake of the north side,
and Harlem sails through the slackness of this sluggish afternoon.
The bus slips lazily,
down, along Fifth Avenue;
and facing me, the young bearded man
carrying a heap of books from the Public Library,

and it seem as if you could touch summer in the sweaty brow of
    the cyclist
who rides holding onto my window.
But New York wasn't the city of my childhood,
it was not here that I acquired my first convictions,
not here the spot where I took my first fall,
nor the piercing whistle that marked the night.
This is why I will always remain on the margins,
a stranger among the stones,
even beneath the friendly sun of this summer's day,
just as I will remain forever a foreigner,
even when I return to the city of my childhood
I carry this marginality, immune to all turning back,
too *habanera* to be *newyorkina*,
too *newyorkina* to be
— even to become again —
anything else.

Translated by David Frye

From *Palabras Juntan Revolución* (Havana: Casa de las Americas,
    1981)

Patria chica: home town or province.
Habanera, newyorkina: from Havana, New Yorker.

"The Woman-Bridge."
Drawing by Zaida del Río.

RUTH BEHAR

PRAYER TO LOURDES

For Lourdes Casal, poet, scholar, bridge

Lourdes, don't bother waking up to hear me.
I wasn't there when you led the brigades.
I was studying at Princeton in those years,
a scholarship girl reading Marx behind ivy walls
where dangerous ideas are kept in cages.
Lourdes, I doubt I would have had the courage
of the other young people who went with you
to look into the eye of that country
where we left behind our childhoods
to grow up without us, dumb and blind.
Lourdes, forgive me, I wasted too much time
worrying whether I was Cuban enough
to claim the loss of that country as my loss.
I claim it now in the name of my Yiddish grandfather
who worked on the railroad in Artemisa,
growing hands as thick as the ceiba,
hands like a map, like memory, hands that never wept.
Lourdes, and your hands, I never held,
those open hands that flew like doves
releasing your African and Chinese ancestors
from the history books about slave emancipation.
Lourdes, I have no right to call to you,
disturbing the lonely river of your bones
which winds around the illustrious men
who lived for Cuba just as much as you did.
Lourdes, I shouldn't be saying this,
but they gave you a grave I found too plain
and etched on the monument words from José Martí.

Good enough words from our national hero,
an exile happy to return to Cuba to die.
Lourdes, it was your words I wanted:
"I will remain forever a foreigner
even when I return to the city of my childhood."
Or do women's words not belong on tombstones?
Lourdes, we are citing you in so many places.
In Miami, New York, Madrid, Mexico City, Ann Arbor,
Tucson, Rome, Chicago, Santo Domingo, Paris, Tulsa . . .
Name a city where a Cuban has not found an island.
Lourdes, I tell you, they are leaving on rafts now.
Some to swallow the ocean, some to scrub floors.
The choice, these days, is capitalism or death.
We don't talk about revolution anymore.
Lourdes, we are children hitting middle age,
the brave ones along with the timid ones,
the generation that inherited this cold war.
We have one country, as Martí said,
Cuba and the night.
Darkness, Lourdes, darkness,
and home a salty pearl lost at sea.

MARIA DE LOS ANGELES TORRES

BEYOND THE RUPTURE:
RECONCILING WITH OUR ENEMIES,
RECONCILING WITH OURSELVES

Rupture

Over thirty years ago, on April 16, 1961, my parents nervously put me and my sister to sleep in the bathtub of our home in La Vibora, a middle-class neighborhood in Havana. In early April, Cuban authorities had warned of a possible U.S. invasion. In case of bombings, bathtubs were the safest part of the house. Out of the ordinary routines had become customary. The Catholic school I attended had been closed for months. I took my classes down the street at a neighbor's house with other children on the block as she ironed clothes and brewed coffee through a stained cloth filter which hung over her kitchen sink. For a few weeks, my uncle slept on the living room couch, and we were told not to tell anyone he was there — an early supporter of Fidel, he had joined the counterrevolution. We were to call him "Pepegrillo," a Cubanization of Jiminy Cricket, Pinocchio's conscience in the Walt Disney production.

The Bay of Pigs invasion materialized. Many families, fearing a second attack, made plans to leave for the United States. We waited in long lines for polio vaccines, passport pictures, passports and visa waivers. Again we were sworn to secrecy. No one was to know we were planning to leave the country. Finally, at dawn on July 30, 1961, my parents and I left my home. At the airport, I remember hundreds of people and children, some crying, others unusually silent. All the children wore name tags with telephone numbers of relatives or friends in Miami. I kissed and hugged my parents. As I walked through the glass doors onto the runway, a guard abruptly stopped me and tried to take away a doll I was carrying. I grabbed it back and held it tight to me. I must have given him a very angry

25

look for he gave up and told me to keep going. (I kept my "Cuban" doll with me until I gave it to my oldest daughter. When I did, I took out a whistle it had in the back and found out it had been "Made in New Jersey.") I boarded a plane full of small children and 45 minutes later arrived in Miami.

At the airport, I was greeted by Americusa, my kindergarten teacher who was living in Miami. She took me to Nenita and Pucho Greer's home, friends of my parents who had agreed to care for me. Their kindness could not alleviate the pain of separation or replace the familiar routines of my home. School in Cuba had been a source of pride and accomplishment for me, but Miami was disorienting and dehumanizing. I sat in a crowded classroom not understanding a word of what the teacher said.

A few months later, Nenita almost miscarried and was ordered to bedrest for the remainder of her pregnancy. Pucho drove me over to the house of one of my mother's cousins, and again the sense of loss and fear set in.

My parents and my two younger sisters arrived shortly after and moved into the house I had been living in. Everything had changed. My mother was chronically sad and worried about the relatives she left behind. My father, in an effort to compensate, even started washing dishes at home. Everything that had held our family together — visits to my grandparents in El Vedado and Matanzas, weekend outings at Santa Maria del Mar, family gatherings in Yaguajay, the park at the end of my block, our neighbors, our pets, our future as had been imagined by my parents — was left in the past.

Lying in bed the early morning sun bathed me; I had to strain to remember the smell of humid red dirt.

Deconstruction/Identity

By the end of my first year at school, I won the spelling bee. I learned to dance "mashed potatoes" on the sidewalk of what later became Little Havana, and memorized the words to Petula Clark's "Downtown." I could not know that kids in Cuba were also singing the song in Spanish and learning to dance "el puré de papa." But my parents refused to stay very long in Miami. My mother was rightfully critical of the pretentiousness and consumerism which early on took form in Miami. So my father applied for "relocation," and we were sent to Cleveland, Ohio. In response to pressure from the state of Florida, the federal government had started a program to disperse Cubans throughout the United States – a program white North American sociologists argued would hasten the assimilation of Cubans.

The trip to Cleveland was the second time I was on a plane. This time, I was with my mother and two younger sisters. Cleveland proved difficult for me in another way. The cold and the racism were so severe. The incident I remember most clearly occurred the day after Kennedy was assassinated. By this time, my two first cousins had come to live with us. Every morning we would walk about two blocks to catch the school bus. The kids on the block started following us and yelling at us that we had killed Kennedy. Their taunts grew louder as we got on the bus. "You dirty Cubans, You dirty Cubans, You killed our President." I screamed back that we were not those kind of Cubans, that we had fled the island. But the geographic and political boundaries which had so restructured our entire lives and redefined our realities meant little to those who only saw "dirty Cubans." The next day, we found our bicycles smashed and so my father gave us a lesson in self-defense.

I remember thinking to myself that these people see us as enemies, they also think that the Soviets are bad and are their enemies; I know that I am not bad, therefore, the Soviets are probably not bad after all. I could not extend this logic to include Cubans on the island. I was not ready to even imagine crossing the political boundary which divided us.

Even so, a sense of nostalgia gripped me as I entered the third grade. In a notebook I wrote poems and practiced writing Spanish by copying other poems. All the entries in my notebook made reference to goodbyes, to the darkness of winter, to the sun I yearned for. The last entry was a sonnet written by Gertrudes Gómez de Avellaneda as she parted the island for Spain centuries before, entitled "Soneto al Partir."

The next relative to come – not leave, because by this time my point of reference was the United States, not Cuba – was my grandmother, who had been waiting in Spain to come to the States. For several years there were no commercial flights between Cuba and the United States and Cubans leaving would go to third countries first. She showed up with a present for me, an album by a new hot band: *Meet the Beatles.*

After two winters, we decided to head south. My father got a job in Dallas. My mother and sister flew to Texas while my grand-mother, two cousins and I drove with my father. I remember stop-ping at a gas station somewhere in the south where we were not allowed to drink water. There were two water fountains, one for "only whites," the other for "coloreds" (which had been scratched out and replaced by "niggers"). We didn't fit into either of the cate-gories. We left thirsty.

Texas is almost a separate place in the universe. After a year in Dallas we took off to one of its furthest corners, Midland, the land of oil and Larry King's *Confessions of a White Racist*. The racist hatred I had felt in Cleveland was awaiting us there as well. My best friend was a black Cuban, whom I recently learned was killed by her pimp in Dallas. We attended a Catholic school that six years earlier was still excluding Mexicans. Kay and I felt we had a strong bond as Cubans. She was a gifted pianist and my father loved music. We were also bound together by the graffiti we frequently found in the bathroom stalls, "niggers and spics."

When I was in seventh grade, the John Birchers started to orga-nize the parish. A young priest had been sent to Midland after the death of an older priest. His sermons were based on the books of St. Paul and often made references to love and peace — words that in the sixties had political connotations. The Birchers accused him of being a communist and with the help of my father ran him out of town.

But my father's newfound political friends were racist. We already knew that for the average white Texan there wasn't much difference between a spic and a nigger. North American anti-communists had no use for us either. The world-view that was sup-posed to explain the dislocation from our homeland and rationalize the distance shattered before our very eyes as the champions of anti-communism also wanted to run us out of town. Our windows were shot up and there were threatening phone calls telling my mother that her daughters would be killed if we did not leave the country.

Yet what was our identity? The angry diatribe we heard when the phone rang, "Go back to where you came from," had no meaning for us. Even if we had wanted to, we could not go back. Now and then we would receive a letter from my mother's relatives. Or some-one would come to the States. The only other Cuban family in Midland had supported Batista and since my parents had been Fide-listas, we did not have much contact with them. I was busy, not thinking about Cuba, but sneaking around dating behind my parents' backs. They wanted me to go out with chaperones as they had in Cuba.

It wasn't until the early seventies, while watching the evening news, that my unconscious past started to erupt. I watched — in an inexplicable panic — images of hundreds of Vietnamese children being loaded on planes taking off to the United States. I remembered being in a plane full of kids and I started to question why I had been brought to the United States. I later learned that my coming to the United States had been part of a State Department/ CIA operation code-named "Peter Pan." The origins of the "Operation" are still open to speculation but unquestionably U.S.-backed propaganda scared parents into thinking that the Cuban government was going to take their children away from them. Once here, the United States government took us to camps in Florida, Iowa, and another 35 states. While the expectation was that our parents would meet up with us soon, relations between the U.S. and Cuba quickly deteriorated. It took about four years for many of the 14,000 "Peter Pans" to be reunited with their parents. Some never were.

As young Cubans became aware of the discrimination they faced in their adopted country and grew increasingly critical of the role of the United States in Vietnam, they came to question what really had happened in their home country. For me, this process of politicization took place via the Chicano movement. I started college in 1972, in the heat of the grape and lettuce boycott, the Raza Unida governor's race, and a waning antiwar movement. But the Chicano movement had a very exclusive definition of identity. I was, after all, a Cuban. I always introduced myself as Cuban, quickly adding that I was not like the rest (whatever that meant). Members of CASA on the other hand, a radical organization of Mexican political refugees who had fled the repression of 1968, had a more inclusive definition of Latino identity. They had a Latin American perspective on the world and, together with the Puerto Rican Socialist Party, maintained close ties to Cuba. They became supporters of my journey back.

At first I was ambivalent about returning. For a while, I justified not going back to Cuba by thinking that there was nothing left to do — the revolution had taken care of social ills, my social responsibility had to be articulated in other parts of the world, such was destiny. My radical views increasingly alienated my parents and my family in Miami. Traveling back to Cuba would be the definitive break.

The further I got from Cuba, the more I wanted to return. On a long excursion through Mexico and Central America, I sat outside the van in which we traveled, watching bats dance in the moonlight, and flipping the radio dial until I connected with a Cuban radio station. I started to listen to Silvio Rodríguez and Pablo Milanés, songwriters of La Nueva Cancion Latinoamericana. I read everything I could get hold of about Cuba.

I started talking to North Americans who were part of the Venceremos Brigade. These experiences were perhaps the worst. They relished having a connection to Cuba and authoritatively spewed the rhetoric claiming that we could not return for we were "gusanos" who had abandoned the revolution. "Yes, but I was six years old!" I'd say. They would respond, "So what, you were obviously middle-class, and as such your class origins make you unworthy of return." The hypocrisy of their statements still stings today: none of them were working-class either. We, Cubans in the United States, had become the community of color that white North Americans could discriminate against, ironically with the help of the Cuban government.

It was the years of feeling the sting of this contradiction that finally made me start looking for other Latinos who traveled to Cuba. Unlike radical white North Americans who to this date continue to discriminate against Cuban exiles, they understood the need to connect immigrant communities to their homeland. The doors, little by little, were opened.

Return: (Re)constructing Identity

In December 1978 I returned to Cuba, for the first time after having been sent alone to the United States by my parents in 1961. I was part of a delegation invited to Havana to engage in a dialogue with the Cuban government. I went as a member of the Antonio Maceo Brigade, a group of young Cubans who, like myself, had been radicalized in various antiwar and civil rights movements.

The relative calmness of the Carter years had allowed for a rapprochement between the U.S. and Cuba. A political opening on the island was taking place, including a change of policy toward "the communities abroad." My sister Alicia and I received an invitation from the Antonio Maceo Brigade to spend three days in Cuba. A Cuban airliner was to pick us up at the Atlanta airport, the same airport through which we had started our journey north. We were part of a delegation that negotiated with the Cuban government the release of 3,000 political prisoners (a phenomenon I did not understand until much later) and the right of Cubans to visit their homeland. More than that, we wanted to be able to go back and live in Cuba, and participate in political and military organizations. We wanted to be part of the nation. But, in the end, we were denied this right.

I didn't understand the reason or the implications of this denial back then, for my first trip home was charged with memories and emotions. I spent three sleepless days crying. Like the sunlight that comes pouring into a bedroom when the shades are pulled, memories of smells, colors, and faces broke through the layers of distance. Everything looked beautiful, even the young military guards poised with shiny rifles, whose job it was to guard the Palace of the Revolution from us.

In one year alone more than 120,000 Cubans returned to visit the island. It was a time of optimism in Cuba. Elections were being held, peasant and crafts markets were flourishing, and revolutionary governments had recently come to power elsewhere in the Caribbean.

Since then, I have journeyed across the longest ninety miles of ocean in the world, the Florida Straits, over thirty times. I have returned in almost every conceivable way and at times under threat of death. I have organized work brigades of U.S. Cubans to construct schools and apartments. I have picked coffee beans, I have harvested citrus fruits. For years I thought it was my patriotic duty to gather for the nation all those young children who had been taken away. I believed that Cuba wanted us back. At the same time, the exile community reacted to our returns with violence and terrorism. One member of the Brigade, Carlos Muñiz, was killed in Puerto Rico.

Returning has always been vulnerable to politics and to internal bureaucratic warfare in the United States and in Cuba as well. The brief period of détente—which even then was taking a turn toward a lucrative money venture for the Cuban government, and not a humanitarian thaw of relations—ended abruptly with Mariel and the rise of the Reagan administration. The Reagan administration's understanding of the power of symbolic politics nurtured a group of Cuban exiles and their hardline policies toward Cuba, while at the same time allowing them to claim they were bringing Latinos into foreign policy positions in the federal government. The Cuban government, having fewer cards to play, took its wrath out on the entire Cuban community when Radio Martí was launched, reversing its policy of allowing family visits. Even the Antonio Maceo Brigade was not allowed to return that year.

I decided I would continue to return even if it meant returning with North Americans. For a while, Cuban officials tried to keep us from doing this, but finally reason gave way and many of us began to be included as "the Cuban-American" on delegations of North Americans. Although we return with a Cuban passport, we are categorized in a strange category called "of Cuban origin," which segregates us from the population as well as from foreigners. In this border zone we have no rights, no official links to the nation. We can only spend our money, and even that is subject to restrictions and a unique ritual in which we have had to convert our dollars into government-issued coupons marked with a "B", a monetary category invented for "la comunidad." There are also constantly changing regulations which determine in which stores and hotels they can be used.* We are Cubans and we are not Cubans at the same time.

In the late 1980s, some of us were able to professionalize our relationship. In my case, I forged a link to the University of Havana, which made perfect sense for me as a professor in the States. It was also the place my mother had taught at and flourished for a time in her life. To this day, I am committed to academic exchanges and the struggle to strengthen and professionalize higher education in Cuba, a battle I am convinced will be waged regardless of what political and economic destinies await the island.

These exchanges are not easy. There are few of us who have managed to continue returning throughout the eighties. I feel fortunate, for I have shared this experience with one of my best friends, Nereida García Ferraz, with whom I have traveled and with whom I have waited days in Miami for reentry permits that sometimes didn't arrive. They are also difficult because for all practical purposes we do not exist on the island, and those who do work with us are few in number as well, and vulnerable to the political winds. I conducted a research project with a colleague who lost her administrative job in a political purge. Together, we were reconstructing the history of the Peter Pan Operation. In so doing, we were trying to

---

*Editor's Note: In July 1993 these restrictions were lifted and the possession of dollars was depenalized in Cuba, but that law has now been reversed.

understand the moment of rupture. It was a personal journey for both of us. While her parents made the decision to return to Cuba after the revolution, mine decided to leave and did so by first sending me out. Students from the island and Cubans from the U.S. worked with us; they also felt an urgency to understand the past which continues to define their realities.

But politics permeates the search for history. Topics perceived to affect the country's national security are always difficult to navigate. In Cuba, the "communities abroad" are a topic of national security concern, for they are a result of emigration which has been equated with treason. Most of us have ended up living in a host country which is not only antagonistic toward our homeland, but has used émigrés to fight its dirty war.

The CIA recently denied my request to view documents about the origins of the Peter Pan Operation. "The CIA may neither confirm nor deny the existence or nonexistence of records responsive to your request," the rejection reads. "Such information — unless, of course, it has been officially acknowledged — would be classified for reasons of national security under Executive Order 12356." We are, as Cubans, trapped in a national security war that seeks only to manipulate needs for political ends.

I sometimes break through the veil of secrecy and suspicion on the island. My relationships and contacts with people there are varied and multiple. I have had long discussions with both high-level officials and dissidents. I have relatives in Yaguajay and Havana. I have relished some love affairs and been devastated by others. I have friends who have triumphed. A very close friend committed suicide when his father hung himself in despair after his daughter left through El Mariel.

And two spiritual fathers, both sensitive, loving human beings who are also great poets, have always opened their homes to us (those living in the United States), for they insist that we too are part of the nation. Poets of a very special generation who hold the keys to the nation — one Eliseo Diego, a member of *Origenes*; the other Pablo Armando Fernández of *Lunes en Revolución* — crossed over their own factionalism to expand the frontiers of the island to embrace us. They understood our need to connect, and they trust our motives for return. They have constructed bridges with us and, perhaps most importantly, opened doors and windows into the soul of our nation to welcome us back.

Thanks to Pablo, his wife Maruja and their children, my daughters have a home in Miramar, en la Calle 20. In fact, my oldest daughter, Alejandra, tells her friends she has two homes, one in Chicago and one in Havana. They have nurtured me through the most difficult times of my life, including my marriage and near-separation from my husband, a Chicago-born child of World War II Jewish/Catholic refugees, who has not always understood my passionate love for an island in the Caribbean.

Returning has always been difficult, but it is made increasingly easier by close friends who have either been to the United States or who are touched by our experiences. More and more people have someone close to them, a brother, sister, cousin, best friend, daughter or son, who has left or may soon leave. More and more professionals, writers and artists are finding they cannot work on the island. Therefore emigration is as much a part of the national experience today as it has always been. We are a nation of immigrants and emigrants.

I find people in Cuba who fail to recognize those of us living outside of Cuba as part of the Cuban nation to be narrow — as narrow as Cubans in the United States who fail to see that Cuba after 1959 is part of our experience. I have come to think that they are also denying the nation important resources for the future. For despite the hybrid nature of our day-to-day cultural practices, we who live outside often have more of a need and desire to maintain our culture than those who have never left the island. Given the potential cultural disintegration posed by accelerated economic integration, those of us living in the United States have something to bring to our homeland in this regard.

With each trip I find more similarities between myself and my friends on the island, although increasingly I also understand how two very different and feuding societies have marked us. Cubans on and off the island are all in search of a new context, one we can call our own. In part it is a search for memory, our memory. We are worried about our future. We are redefining what it means to be a Cuban. For me this includes being able to have a normal relationship with the nation of my birth; for my friends in Cuba it is a redefinition of nation. We coincide. A normal relationship to my homeland means that there must be a redefinition of nation which includes those of us who have left and those who will yet leave. From 1959, all who left have been categorized as traitors on the island and heroes in the United States. For Cubans on the island, a constructive definition of nation means casting aside the "official interpretation" of history and collecting those parts of the past which have been erased, including the story of émigrés. We are united by the shared urgency to take the great leap from the middle of this century to the next.

Nevertheless, our political cultures are very different. I am an activist. To survive in the United States and to lay claim to my identity as a Cuban and as a Latina, in fact to return to Cuba, I have to fight for political space every day. My friends on the island shun activism because within their context it is the opportunists who participate in politics. My countercultural experience was about changing the world; theirs is about the desperation and frustration of not being able to change theirs. I am part of a broader Latin American community in the United States, for I live and struggle with Mexicanos, Puertoriqueños, and Centro-Americanos who are also in search of coherence. Despite the official rhetoric on the island which portrays Cuba as part of the Latin American family, many of my close friends there do not see themselves as Latino Americanos. In this sense, they are closer to Miami Cubans than I am.

Increasingly economics, not just politics, divides our experiences. When I am in Havana, I can invite island friends to eat out at a restaurant, but they cannot reciprocate, for more and more restaurants in Cuba are now only accepting U.S. dollars. I do not worry about feeding my children, or about finding medicine for my daughter with asthma. Their daily lives are increasingly consumed by these preoccupations, and there are few prospects that the situation will improve in the near future.

Nonetheless, we are curious about each other. Many of them, or their close friends, may soon find themselves in the United States. This blurs the great divide which has defined our personal realities for the last thirty years. But regardless of where we find ourselves, we are inevitably tied by a common past: the place where we were born. And we have been marked by a period of history when our people sought to create an independent nation. We continue to share this historical commitment.

Yet we have few words or concepts with which to understand or act upon what we are experiencing. Everything about us, our past, our identity, our loyalties, has been prey to the larger forces of world politics. We not only have categories of "us and them," with reference points of north and south, "lo Americano y lo Cubano," but in our case, they have also been cast in terms of east and west, communism or democracy, the Cold War.

Every time I return across time and space, between cultures and economic systems, I am more convinced that I do not want or need to accept the either/or definition of my identity which demands that you choose sides. My identity is far more complex than this. I was born in Havana. I was raised in Texas. I was radicalized with Chicanos. I returned to Cuba and thus was ostracized from my community. Now I live in Chicago, but I also live in Havana, emotionally and professionally. I am always returning.

I am "white" when I wake up in Havana, but I am "other" because of my migratory experience. I am again "other" when I journey the thirty minutes through airspace to Miami, because I am no longer "white," and because my commitment to return to Cuba and have a normal relationship with my home country makes me politically "other" among Miami Cubans. I arrive in Chicago, and again I am other, now because I am Latina in a city which is defined in black and white.

I am always a woman and a mother, I am always Cuban. I will always have been born in Havana, of a mother who was born in Meneses and a father who was born in Matanzas, and of grandparents born in Meneses and Matanzas. My great-grandparents were born in Meneses and Matanzas to parents who were born in Spain, the Canary Islands, or still others in Caibarien and Meneses. These multiple identities and experiences make up my identity. My search for coherence is my politics. While for years I felt that I had neatly put away pieces of my identity in different parts of the world, I now understand that I do not have to accept categories which split who I am. Instead I must construct new categories, new political and emotional spaces in which my multiple identities can be joined. Returning has been part of this healing journey.

(Ex)change & (Re)contextualizing

Even though returning was a political statement, officials in Cuba did not let us arrive. As the years passed, it became more evident that the policies toward the communities abroad were closely tied to the closed political space in which Cuba has evolved. It seemed crucial to do everything possible to help normalize our relationship and struggle to change policies in the United States and in Cuba which created obstacles to our ability to reengage. This is also a moment in which our presence may make a difference. With the collapse of an entire economic system, and a subsequent power struggle, a new ideological struggle is being waged on the island to redefine the revolution and the nation.

A key component of this redefinition is the relationship to those who have left. While officials have renewed the rhetoric against those who live abroad and in fact have christened the latest generation of critics with the term "new gusanos," those at the vanguard of radical thinking in Cuba say that those who have left are part of the nation and should be brought into discussions about the future of the island — economically, politically, and culturally. This call is echoed by every major internal opposition group. These sectors call for an easing of U.S. pressure on the island. They also applaud the departure of Soviet troops from the island and have demanded that the United States respond in kind and retrieve its troops from Guantanamo. They understand that a process of demilitarization will open up political space. It is interesting to note that growing numbers of Cuban exiles are calling for the same.

Generational pressure is a growing reality in the Cuban community in the United States as its younger members are not necessarily inclined to support attempts to take over the island. Most believe that change will occur in Cuba through internal processes. Many want to heal before they reengage. They are also concerned with establishing a democratic culture in their own community — yet they would like to have a normal relationship to Cuba.

But both in Cuba and in the Cuban community in the United States, debate about the future of Cuba or U.S.-Cuba relations is fraught with problems. In Cuba, while broad discussions took place within the process initiated by the Party several years ago, publicly people were rallied to unify in favor of an ever-hardening official position which makes debate or dissent difficult. Human rights activists are accused of being agents of the U.S. government and jailed under laws which prohibit the right to assembly. And important institutions which have been islands for free thinkers have been swallowed up by vicious turf fights which may end up destroying many of the programs worth saving.

In 1989, the FBI named Miami the capital of U.S. terrorism, as eighteen bombs went off in the homes and businesses of Cuban exiles working to better relations with Cuba. Hardline organizations such as the Cuban American National Foundation accuse those who sup-

port better relations with Cuba of being agents of the Castro government. They stage marches in Miami to unify the exile community
under the banner of an end to Fidel and no dialogue with the Cuban
government. Their plans for the reconstruction of Cuba do not
include people living on the island.

But there are cracks in both empires nonetheless. In the last few
years in Cuba, artists and professors at the Ministry of Culture's Art
Institute have fended off a rather amateurish attempt by Young
Communist Party functionaries to take control of the Institute, and
have defended their right to create freely — and to include, in their
definition of culture, that which is created by Cubans abroad. In the
communities abroad a realignment has occurred in the political center of the community which includes "dissidents" from the right and
the left as well as recently arrived immigrants. They are also fighting for a more democratic culture in their communities and a reconceptualization of their relationship to the island. They publicly call
for an easing of U.S. pressure on the island, support the internal
movement for a national debate, and condemn a U.S.-imposed solution to Cuba.

There is, then, a space in which to develop a more productive
alternative to the right-wing Cuban exile and U.S. project of hard-
ening policies toward Cuba and tightening the economic embargo,
an alternative which could open up relations and encourage
exchanges. The hardliners in Cuba have always been opposed to
these changes. Their position of no negotiation is mirrored by hard-
liners in the United States. Yet what is certain is that any positive
future resolution will have to include a constructive and respectful
relationship between those who stayed and those who left and will
continue to leave.

A creative approach would be to initiate negotiations on a series
of bilateral issues which deeply affect the one million Cubans living
in the United States, such as free travel, immigration and business
and cultural exchanges. The resolution to these issues would have
profound implications not only for U.S. policies but also for the
internal reordering of ideology, politics, and economics in Cuban
society. For instance, for Cuba to develop a humanistic and compre-
hensive policy toward its "communities abroad" would mean that,
for starters, the government would have to give up the notion that
all those who leave are traitors. For this to happen, there would
have to be meaningful forms of dissent within Cuba beyond leaving
the country or risking jail. And this would be a major step toward a

more democratic political system on the island, which in turn would allow the Cuban community to normalize its own politics.

In some ways Miami is the closest place to Havana. Miami is a place in which 10 percent of Cuba's population lives; a place that could become home to another 10 to 20 percent of the island's population. It is a border town, a place in which immigrants from the island arrive daily. A place in which the political and cultural discourse revolves around the question of homeland in ways not found in other cities of the United States. It is a site in which foreign and domestic policies are played out constantly.

In other ways, Miami is the furthest point from Havana. From this perspective, it is a place in which Kafkaesque metamorphoses occur daily as persons who were defined as traitors forty minutes airspace prior to their arrival are transformed into heroes — human beings into "gusanos" from the Cuban vantage point. It is a place in which world politics and local power groups prey on people's most intimate desires and identities. And it is a city in which an immigrant's natural desire to relate to the homeland is treated as an act of betrayal.

Miami is a city in which antagonistic chapters of Cuban history coexist in the same geographic space. It is one of the few places in the world where Batistianos (those who were part of the pre-revolutionary regime) cohabit with disillusioned Fidelistas who were once their opponents, as well as recent immigrants who were part of the revolution and today critique it from a leftist perspective. It has become a depository of the island's political memory.

Miami is also a place in which U.S. and Cuban policies have fueled a political culture of intolerance. Miami emerges as a product of a standoff between two superpowers at the brink of a nuclear war. It is a city held in the clutches of international national security interests. However, Miami is a place in which this extreme politicization has created human needs at the same time that it has not permitted the political structures to resolve them. Therefore, the search for solutions to needs unmet by either home or host country is extending beyond the established political structures and in this unclaimed space a new language is emerging for all Cubans.

This new space is inhabited by friends I knew in Cuba who now live in Miami, and by our friends who live in Havana and sometimes visit the U.S., some of whom may someday stay. It is a circle of friends, not divided by the old political boundaries which prohibited even a daughter from writing to her father if he had left, or in which a son who attempts to return to see his mother who had stayed on the island would be terrorized. We have a new context, one which exists outside of the established power structures.

We speak the same emotional language. We exchange books, we are critical of the postmodern paradigm, we are reading Gaston Bachelard, Jurgen Habermas, José Martí, Fina García Marruz, Michel Foucault, and contemporary Latino writers and thinkers. Jesús Diaz and Milan Kundera have become textbooks. We also listen to a wide range of music including John Lennon, Cat Stevens, Enya, Silvio and Pablo, Lecuona, Bach, Thelonious Monk, Amuary Prada, Gloria Estefan, Willy Chirino and Juan Luis Guerra. We all dance to Celia Cruz.

Surprisingly, we even share a similar political vision: of a Cuba that is democratic and economically viable, in which social justice and sovereignty coincide and are not seen as antagonistic to each other. So far no one listens, for there is little room for negotiations between the power structures in the exile community and those in Havana. One does not let you go back because the act of returning is treason; the other does not let you return because the act of leaving was treason. Yet there is a process underway, most visibly in the arts, in literature, in private conversations, and in new social networks which sometimes become public, of recontextualizing the past in order to explore options for the future.

Deep Wounds, Desires, and Haunting Dilemmas

As my oldest daughter turned the age I had been when my parents sent me to the United States, I began to understand the depth of the wounds. I also became convinced that the healing process would not be initiated by those who had benefited from the divisions. Therefore, new voices needed to emerge on the island and abroad that could develop a more respectful relationship. Although some Cubans on the island seemed willing to engage in discussions and many Cubans outside joined the process, the questions remained: Why did U.S. policies discourage a constructive resolution and why were Cuban officials so willing to participate in closing off the island?

As a small nation in the Caribbean which sought its independence and waged a radical nationalist revolution, we became a threat to the most powerful country in the world in the hysterical climate of the Cold War. Emigrés became the yellow ribbons of the 1960s with which common folk could fight communism by adopting a Cuban child or sponsoring an entire family. In the meantime, the besieged revolution became bureaucratized and power became concentrated. Leaving or staying became a litmus test to ascertain where one's loyalties resided. Throughout more than thirty years, people, families, and children have been manipulated politically to feed the growing power structures on both sides that became so similar that they started acting in unison, yet so far apart that they could not understand that they now, more than ever, needed each other.

I will continue to return; Cuba is my home. But while the circle is larger and more coherent, there is a new conflict which I have not resolved. Those who have left recently cannot return. Those who are "inappropriately" critical of the government are sometimes denied reentry permits or their passports are not renewed, even if they are equally critical of the hard-liners in the exile community. I am morally conflicted because, for now, I am able to return while others who would like to do so cannot. But even as I write, I do not know if things I say will offend those who determine whether or not I receive a reentry permit. But still, I know we must continue the dialogue, however painful it may be.

Midflight between Miami and Havana, it doesn't matter much which way, I feel that I can hold both sides together. There is increasingly a possibility for a coherent perspective, for an imagined future which flies beyond the rupture without denying the pain, or without compromising the ethics and principles which in the long run make a difference in history. Ninety miles — today the longest in the world, but only ninety miles.

I arrive in Havana, the smell of humid red dirt surrounds my soul, I feel so far away from Miami, I feel so close to my daughters, they can reside in both spaces; they have not lost a home, they have gained a heritage. I converse with friends in Havana, pick up the letters they wish to send. I arrive in Miami and continue the conversation I started in Havana. We drink a bottle of Coronilla, like the one they used to drink when they partied in Varadero during the summers, as I do now — not daring to think of what life was like on the other side of the Florida Straits, where we now sit watching the moonlight cast an eerie light, the same light I saw the night before from the other side. I suddenly feel very far from Cuba; I miss my friends Kaki and Maruga, I miss the intensity, I miss the familiar context.

When I return a few months later I start a new conversation, in Miami. About an hour later I am sitting on a rocking chair upon the porch of my home on La Calle 20; Josesito comes by, and we pick up the same conversation I had started in Miami. Somehow the time between this and our last conversation has been suspended. We are creating a third persona, one that watches as both sides struggle alone and away from each other, that brings our lives together even as our day-to-day life is separated by hostility and fear. It is the persona of friendship and shared passions. We return to the place where we parted and we feel the connection.

I don't know how long political structures can survive while impeding the tremendous human desire to belong, to construct, to have a coherent existence which for all of us in Miami, Chicago, Havana and Varadero includes all these places. Our lives have all been marked by the rupture. It is our nation, it is *our lives*, after all. I am comforted by the fact that no matter how hard states try, they cannot control the nation or legislate identities; they cannot erase our history. Our identity is multiple, for power struggles have fragmented who we are. A collective understanding, recognition, an *areito* to heal, may still be the way to continue searching for coherence, to begin reconciling with our enemies — ourselves.

"Pedro Pan Operation." Drawing by Alejandra Pier-Torres, daughter of the author.

Tony Mendoza, "Lydia, who had just turned three, wanted to be a bride,"
Halloween, 1992.

TERESA MARRERO

MIEMBROS FANTASMAS / GHOST LIMBS

12/1/90
Santa Monica, California

Dear Prima:

Lately I have been feeling out of control. I dream that I am at sea,
maybe the Caribbean, and I am full-throttle on a high-speed boat
with photos, old photos, spread out on top of the deck . . . they have
the sepia cast of time; they lie in an orderly fashion, some kind of
order that I should understand but don't . . . mostly they are childhood pictures. Who is that serious little girl with the large brown
eyes staring back at me? And suddenly, a delicate breeze causes a
faint tremor on the surface of the water, and the sea begins to pucker
little crests and soon the one who trembles is me, as I shout out,
"Please, someone, give me a hand so that the wind will not carry the
small memories out to sea. . . ." But it is too late and there are no
hands, except mine, and they are not enough to stop the wind and I
sit, immobile, watching the irreversible scraps of time float away on
the water, like fallen leaves.

In the same dream I wake up in the arms of a man and I say to
him: "Darling, I don't know what's wrong with me; lately I keep
dreaming that things are out of control, out of my hands, why is
that?" And he responds: "Don't worry sweetheart, it's just a dream.
Just forget about it. Let's get up and have a cup of coffee." And I get
out of bed to the smell of café Bustelo and search for the newspaper
and read the date: December 30, 1959. And then I wake up and
realize that I have been dreaming in Spanish, yet my husband's
conversation is in English, and I think, Oh my god, that is completely anachronic. . . . How could I have a husband "in English" in
Cuba in 1959?

44

I'm always at a loss to answer the question "¿En qué idioma piensas?" I have no idea if I dream in color or black and white. Primita, you hadn't been born in '59, and I was a little girl. There was no reason to have had a husband "in English" then, like I have now. Do things like this happen to you?

Bueno, ya no te doy más lata, que vas a pensar que tu prima aquí en la USA está tocada del queso. Dale un fuerte abrazo a mi padrino, y a mi abuela. Muchos saludos a mi primo y tu mamá, a tu esposo y niñitos. Write to me soon. Your loving cousin,

Isabel

La Habana, 25 de enero, 1991

Querida Isabel:

As you can see, I have not waited long before answering your letter. It takes so long for communication to travel between our two countries. As it turns out, I had already mailed you another letter just before receiving yours.

I was filled with emotion reading your letter. I too have much to tell you. Please write to me the date when my letters arrive. If I could project upon a white wall images from your life and moments of mine, I am sure it would make one of those movies that everyone would think was fiction, instead of real life. While I was reading your words, I kept commenting to the others: "Isabel and I have gone through similar things in life." After finishing your letter I had the distinct impression that we have led parallel existences, or you know, like when a limb is amputated and the person still feels like it's there: miembros fantasmas. I hope that God will permit us some-day to be able to sit down quietly and talk, and drink coffee, and walk the callejones of this little island we call "nuestra patria." (Because you know, prima, los cubanos are deeply patriotic, whether we are in agreement with the government or not. For bet-ter or for worse, I think the Cuban people are fiercely like that by nature!)

Prima, I have understood very well your sense of longing. It is for that very reason that I want to explain to you certain things, which may be impossible for you to perceive, no matter how hard you try. First of all, I would like you to know that the only persons with whom I shared your letter were my parents and brother. Our other family here does not approve of our communication. And although I know Abuela wants to hear everything about you, I couldn't bring myself to tell her the details because she is in very delicate health, and such strong emotions are not good for her. I am telling you this because one of the virtues that I love most in a human being is that of honesty, and whenever I establish a relationship I always place honesty first. For this reason I want you to know that our grandmother is not in good health. She is almost blind and very sad and beleaguered, like a little candle losing its light in the long night. I am the one who battles with her daily, and it is very sad, my cousin, but no one can go against the law of life, and Abuela has lived 85 years, and they have not been in vain. She holds on to the Bible you gave her in California, the one with the picture of that Mexican Virgin with all of the bright rays shining from her back. She told me in California it is difficult to find statues of La Virgen de la Caridad; instead, it is the Mexican Virgin who is on all of the holy items. Well, I don't think that those things really matter to God, a Bible is a Bible, and here they are impossible to find, so we treasure this one.

There are many persons here who do not believe, and those of us who do cannot do so in public. But I don't want to talk about that. Tell me instead about your life. You have done so much with your life! You have traveled all around the world and you have studied, and now Tío Mongo tells me in his letters that you are about to finish your doctorate. I am so proud of you! I could tell by your letters how poetic you are, and what a refined sensibility you possess. I have studied too, you know, my field was economics. I say "was" because I have never really practiced my career, due to political constraints. As you may know from your readings, as I was growing up many positions of privilege were conditioned by one's affiliation to the party, and I have refused to participate. I have never been able to think one thing and do another. It is not in my nature. Consequently my opportunities have been greatly reduced. But I have my children who are very lovely, and I try to educate them the best way I know how: I teach them to have an open mind and to reflect upon things, rather than to parrot their elders. They are both quite intelligent and, with all modesty, I think it runs in our family.

Well, dear cousin, this is enough for now. I have a million things to do. Right now I must walk ten blocks to the bodega to get meat. It may seem crude to you, but here one must always be thinking about food, where to get it, how much it costs, how to get more. We are very primitive in this island. I don't know when we will learn. Mami y papi, y los niños y mi hermano te mandamos nuestro más sincero y profundo cariño. Y tú recibes un fuerte abrazo de tu prima,

Caridad

P.S. I am sending you a picture of me and my two children. Idiana is seven and Andresito is five.

2/28/91
Kailua-Kona, Hawaii

Primita:

I am writing you from paradise and sending you a postcard also so that you can appreciate this beautiful island. Maybe it looks a bit like Cuba, I have always felt it does. I am here visiting some dear, dear friends; as you may know, I lived here for seven years, and made some very deep friendships.

You don't know how many hours I have spent gazing at the picture you sent me (I brought it with me). Really, I prize it almost as much as your beautiful words. I think first that you look like your father, my godfather, but then again I pull out my old Cuban album and see pictures of your mother and then I think, no you are the very image of your beautiful mother. And then I look deeper into your eyes, and I think: Caridad is right, I cannot fathom all that she has lived and seen. There are deep circles under your eyes, and a kind of sadness difficult to put into words. I believe that I am capable of such deep feelings, but then I look again and realize it is not so much the depth but the duration of that sadness. And there I stop, because when I look into the mirror I cannot find that in myself. It is strange, but I have just realized that for the past few years I don't think I really saw myself at all, in spite of putting on make-up every morning. This thought just came to me here, on this island.

I had to return here for the first time after having left ten years ago to attend the university in California. I had a dance teacher, a very wise Hawaiian lady who is today declared a national treasure, Auntie Edith Kanaka'ole, who said to me then: "If you leave here now, you will never return to live here again." And I shrugged it off, responding: "Of course I'll return, Auntie, I'm just leaving for a little while." I have this incredible capacity for blindness, mi prima. Sometimes, it is as if I were so interested in the movement of things, in going and doing, that I cannot see the gravity and consequences of a situation until much, much later. Why is that? I now know she was right.

I used to think that my fondness for this piece of lava in the middle of the Pacific Ocean had to do with my longing for Cuba somehow . . . or at least those close to me reflected this idea — even if unspoken sometimes. But I wonder if Polynesia wasn't already in my blood, in some other time and place before this one, because the way I experience this place is as though I have always known it. It is oddly familiar, and the people here have accepted me as theirs "because once an island girl, always an island girl." It is this sense of being an islander that they perceive as a bond . . . and maybe they are right. There is something that happens to a person's mind upon the realization that she is surrounded by water, and that the only straight line in sight is one distinguishing heaven and sea.

I cried when I got off the plane, and I fell on my knees to kiss this black, volcanic earth. (You know this is the same thing that Cubans do when they arrive in Florida after being picked up adrift from those balsas out at sea?) I wanted to rub my belly to the earth and let the hot volcanic magma filter through my skin directly into my heart, and have the lava flow through my veins. I wonder if such a strong feeling will emerge from my insides for Cuba? Is it a futile question? Not knowing the answer is the worst part.

Prima, I hope that you will take my words in the spirit I feel them. . . . I sometimes wonder if it is harmful to you when I share my impressions of other places I have been. I do not want to sound "demasiado fina" or snobbish. This would never be my intention. I realize that part of your sadness is dealing with the role in life that history has dealt you. My mother tells me that it was your father who never wanted to leave Cuba, and that your mother did, and that this has been a source of pain between them (please don't read this part to them). If I can talk you into it for one moment, consider this: I have spent many hours and years now wondering what would have happened to me had I stayed there. Sometimes I wish we had. You may find this crazy, but sometimes I think that staying behind and knowing who you are, to have a place, a culture, an identity, would have been worth all the rest. I am ashamed to even think this sometimes because of the great sacrifice that my parents underwent coming here, but inside somewhere I am angry. I am angry that I could not make my own choices. I am angry that history has played with our lives with the force and arbitrariness of a hurricane. I am even angrier now that the Soviet bloc has disintegrated, because it makes the whole damn thing seem even more ironic and futile. Thirty years is most of my lifetime and all of yours. In thirty years one "yo supremo" has held the hearts of people both inside and outside of the island. Because, believe me primita, he is just as influential here as there. Here, we are defined in degrees of "Cuban-ness" according to how much we hate the man. Never mind histori-cal antecedents and causes for the revolution, because while I don't want to scare you by using words like "manifest destiny" or "Yankee imperialism," it *is* an historical fact around the world, including this little island where I now stand and the one there under your feet.

So, I want you to open your eyes wide and not fantasize about life in the United States, because it can be very cold and very lonely here. And while capitalism has its undeniable advantages, it is also ruthless in its treatment of those who cannot or don't want to play the game well. In San Francisco, in New York, in Los Angeles, there is nothing like walking the streets during a wet, cold winter day and seeing indigents begging for food and shelter. Some of them have hand-painted signs that say "Viet Nam Vet. Homeless. Will work for food." I am not telling you stories, I have looked into these people's eyes and was made to feel genuine shame to be an "American." Coño! It is an outrage, in this "great" land. So, primita, don't be fooled by exile dreams in the land of plenty. Aquí todo cuesta, y bien caro. Sometimes the price this country asks you to pay can only be paid with your identity, your language, your self. The way I've figured out to deal with it is a little bit like these new contact lenses that the doctor prescribed: with one eye you have a lens that helps you see far away, with the other eye you see close-up. Somewhere in the brain all of this gets worked out so that the person can see both close-up and far away without bifocals. It takes a while to get used to it, a person feels disoriented at first. When I look out my right eye only, I can see far away, but not up-close; and vice-versa. Well, I figure being Cuban here is a little bit like that: each cultural eye sees what it is capable of seeing on its own, yet somehow they work it out in the brain when they are both experiencing things simultaneously. Yet each maintains its internal domain paradoxically: separate/ together, equal/unequal, different/the same.

Bueno, chica, I don't want to depress you, but I got inspired. But as you say in your letter, honesty comes first in any friendship. What I have just said would cause a big fight in my house. Mami y Papi would get furious that I say such things . . . "don't you know that with all its defects this is still the best place on earth?" Is it? My Tía Clara in Miami would simply dismiss me with light sarcasm: "Oh, those words coming out of her mouth are the things they teach people out there in California, because there they let the leftist radicals say and do whatever they want." Anyway. How did we get on this subject? It's the same way at Mami y Papi's house, we never quite know how the discussion starts, but we always seem to end there, in politics.

Mami is fine and she is very pleased that we are writing. She says they have all of the letters you have written, because they are so beautiful and you express yourself so eloquently. Tell my godfather that the medicines he needs are on the way, we sent the money to Tío Mongo and he is taking care of sending the medicines from Miami. Tell my godfather that I never forget him, and always remember him as a young and handsome man in my childhood birthday party pictures or in those great big "comelatas" that Abuela would have for Nochebuena in the patio. (Maybe you haven't seen those photographs, because Abuela was able to get them out of Cuba and bring them to us . . . they are all I have left of my first ten years. I will show them to you someday so that you can see your handsome father).

Bueno, mejor no darte más lata. Muchachita, take care of yourself, my love to your parents and to your children (please write me their names again) and you receive a warm hug from your cousin,

Isabel

8 de abril, 1991
La Habana

Dear Isa:

First of all let me explain why I have waited so long to reply to your last letter. Things in my life have been changing quite rapidly, and I have barely had enough time to reflect. I didn't mention it to you before, but my husband and I have been separated physically for six months now. Spiritually, this thing has been falling apart for years. I have much to tell you, cousin. This marriage didn't have heads or tails, and I am in the process of a divorce. (Tío Mongo told me that you had been divorced too, but have remarried. You have never said anything, so I hope I am not putting my nose where it doesn't belong.) Since I have separated from my husband I have begun to work within my field, as an economist, in a housing development project here in Arroyo Naranjo. I got the job through a good friend whose sympathies are like mine, but she has learned to hide them better. Anyway, everybody knows that people here don't say what they really think and everything is a charade. The weeks passed and I began to feel quite wonderful: I was earning a decent income, had shaken myself loose from a crude and jealous husband who didn't let me breathe. I suppose all of this new radiance showed, because soon thereafter I met a fellow compañero on the project, an architect. Isa, I tell you honestly, I felt as if I had been living on another planet all of these years. It is difficult to put into words the feelings I began to experience as our friendship developed along the most harmonious of avenues. We decided to reach deeper levels of intimacy, and with this decision we both feel very satisfied. Our friendship gave birth to passion and a bond we both want to endure. My family, however, began to put obstacles in our way, and soon it became clear to me that I would have to leave the house. (He has a nice house in El Vedado). It is a very difficult decision to make, prima, because Abuela needs me to be her eyes and feet, yet my heart tells me to run to this man. What would you do in my place, prima? I know the correct thing, and the desires of my heart. I am in the middle of a crisis and things are not so clear.

Now to address the things you tell me in your last letter, I must let you know, first of all, that nothing is left of those grand family reunions during Nochebuena or other festivities. That is over, or better yet, I have never experienced them in my lifetime. All that's left are your and our parents' memories of them. I have heard them speak of those big parties at Abuela's house, with all the relatives, and music and lechón asado y congrí y plátanos fritos y el arroz con leche that Abuela is so great at making. Between the family that is left here, none of that remains, not even the custom of wishing each other a Happy New Year, or of coming over and sitting around in the patio to drink a coffee. It is all very sad, but it is, as you say, the cold reality we live here in Cuba today, and I imagine it was the same or maybe worse thirty years ago: families divided because of political ideologies. I don't want you to misinterpret me, please, but I do want to make you aware of the realities that we live by daily. Unfortunately our family here is divided and don't think that it is because of physical distance. It is the opposite for me: I feel close to you and yours living in a distant place and I feel very distant from those right here a block away. Do you understand me? The society here has distanced us, but I also think it is due to a kind of spiritual poverty, a lowliness of spirit that prevails here. I know lots of people would disagree with me, but this is the way I feel. Please don't think that with these words I am judging people, let alone people of my same blood. Each person has her own conscience and must respond to herself. And also don't think that I spend my life bickering or arguing with my relatives here. That is not so, on the contrary. But it is a very superficial relationship, very little uplifting. We do not speak of important things . . . only about the eggs and the beans and the sugar. It is bad enough having to think all the time about getting food, let alone having it be the main topic of conversation constantly. It is as if we have learned to think with our stomachs instead of our heads.

You mustn't ever think about having stayed here, although I can sense your longing for a place in the world. Maybe this is why you are always traveling, I don't know. But the sacrifice your parents made was not small, and just imagine if you, who grew up in the United States and can speak the language, feel so disconnected, imagine how your parents must feel. And just as you tell me not to dream about the idyllic life there, you must do the same and not let memories of things which no longer exist rule your life. I agree with you on one thing: history has dealt us a difficult hand. But then again, no one ever promised that life would be fair, or beautiful or long.

I love you, mi prima. Keep writing to me. I need it more than air.

Caridad.

28 de mayo, 1991
Arroyo Naranjo

Dear Isabel:

It is with the saddest heart that I send you this telegram to inform you that our Abuelita died two days before her 86th birthday. She died in her sleep and I was the last to look into her eyes. I know she wanted me to tell you first. Please let the family know. We are burying her tomorrow in Arroyo Naranjo, next to Abuelo. They are together now and she can rest. She gave me the Bible you gave her. I hope you don't mind.

With all my love,

Caridad

6/30/92
Santa Monica, CA.

Cari:

You don't know how hard the news of Abuela's death hit all of us, but particularly Papi. He is a laconic man, but the pain was visible all over his face. He has always revered his mother because of her strength. He would tell me stories of how "mujeriego" Abuelo was in his early years, because he was so handsome and with blue eyes, you can imagine, the women went crazy for this isleño. You know, Cari, when Abuela was here in the United States to visit in '85, it was the strangest sensation, because when I saw her get off the plane in Los Angeles I thought: "Dios mío, I have this woman's face, this woman has my face." And that is really very odd for me, because in our family it was always said that I was supposed to look like Mami's side of the family. But my sensation was different, and when I saw her feet I knew. We have exactly the same toes. Isn't that strange? When Abuela was here I took her to my apartment—after a big battle with Mami, because Mami somehow thinks that even though I've been married, divorced, and later remarried, that I can't really take care of myself, let alone Abuela! She would ask me: "And what are you going to feed your grandmother?" And I would always reply, laughing, "Comida!" Anyway, I'm sure Papi had something to say about it to Mami in private, because finally Mami gave in and let me take her for a night to sleep at my apartment. Cari, we had so much fun . . . first we went to the supermarket, and I thought we'd never leave! She was amazed at the variety of "stuff" here. And I kept telling her: "Abuela, no seas guajira." And she would smile and tell me of things as they were in Cuba. Anyway, once I finally got her to my apartment I lit the fireplace and sat her in my wooden rocking chair while I prepared some spaghetti with chicken, lettuce, avocado, onion, and tomato salad with Italian olive oil, pan cubano and chocolate cake (her preference, and I'm glad, because I'm not much for cooking Cuban desserts). Bueno, I had this idea to tape-record her stories, and particularly I was interested in listening to family things, how she and Abuelo met, where they're from, etc. . . . Well, she began to tell me how Abuelo was actually quite older than her, and how he had "been around the block a few times already and she was just a young girl with her eyes closed to the world." She told me a story that she said none of her five sons knew, because she was embarrassed of what they would think: as it turns out whoever was fixing the papers for Abuela and Abuelo's marriage did some kind of "maraña" that she didn't know about until it was time for her to fix her papers to come visit us here. They were never really legally married, because the guy who was supposed to have been the notary public was a crook and he never filed the papers, but told them he did and kept their money. So, she said, here she was "una vieja" (Abuelo was already gone by then) when she found out that she had been "living in sin" all of these years. As she burst out laughing, mischievously pleased with the idea, she said "Caramba, if I would have known this I wouldn't have put up with so much from your Abuelo!" and then I heard a sharp shout and I ran from the kitchen to see that Abuela had fallen backwards "patas pa 'riba" on the rocking chair. And as I was trying to get her out of this embarrassing position we laughed harder and harder until, prima, I really did pee in my pants. (I think she did too, but she was laughing so hard she couldn't talk!) I still have that conversation and laughing on tape. I'd love to share it with you someday.

This is the way I will always remember Abuela. Some days, when I walk into my bedroom I have the distinct impression that her scent is lingering in the air.

I am very proud that you have the Bible. You, she and I form an irrevocable triangle. She is gone, but now you and I are left to nurture the ghost limbs, blood ties on pieces of paper and in our hearts.

Tu prima,
Isa

3 de enero, 1993

Estimada Isa:

Thank you for your beautiful, long letter. It gave me and my family a great deal of comfort. I think we have much in common, I love to write too. Often when I walk (everybody here these days either walks or rides a bicycle, have you heard about the Chinese bikes they've imported? They've become "un objeto de lujo" for heaven's sakes. Good thing Cubans have a sense of humor about life.) As I was saying, often when I walk things around me register in a special way, I call it the "bichito," and when it bites, I must write.

Things are very tough here right now, you know it's the "special period." We have very little in the way of food and other essentials. Where to get things and how much they cost continues to be on everyone's minds. The younger generation has taken to openly criticizing some of the government's economic policies, and there are many here who would like the US embargo to end, so that our economy can gain some currency in the world market. If the artery with the US was big prior to 1959, the one we've had with the Soviet bloc was even thicker. We have felt the dissolution of Eastern Europe in our skin and bones. I don't know where we will go from here. Some say that Cuba has many friends internationally, but I know that we are isolated, this little defiant island. Like you, my feelings are confusing sometimes, because on the one hand I hate the absolutism here, and on the other I admire our strength. I think this has played a big role in Cuban politics for a long time, the rhetoric of the regime appeals to our sense of national pride.

In the middle of all of this, my life continues. I miss Abuela terribly, but I can feel her presence close to me. Oh wait, I must tell you that Daniel (the young man I had told you about) and I were married late last year. Mami and Papi were making things very difficult for us, so we decided to get married and be autonomous. The children and I are well adapted to our new situation. (I'm sending you another picture. This one is a much happier one. It was taken while the four of us were on vacation in Varadero a few weeks ago.) We live in Daniel's house in El Vedado now, and as I said previously he's an architect and has very good taste in design. Actually, we agree on most things, and our home is very pretty. We like a very rustic and natural atmosphere, so we have several walls with the bare bricks. The patio is my favorite, he built wooden shelves into the bare brick wall, and in there we have some valued objects, among them a picture of our great-grandparents (on Abuelo's side). You can imagine the color-tone of the photograph, it is very antique-looking, and I am saving it so that you can see it when you come to Cuba. Cousin, if you ever have the chance to come, take it and don't worry about anything, I'll take care of everything here. Things are loosening up here a bit, and they have lowered the age of people who can visit relatives in the United States. Maybe I'll end up visiting you first. I am only twenty-seven, so I still have to wait a while.

I think we'd have many things to talk about. My tastes are very simple, as it is in simplicity that I find beauty. We are not very materialistic (we couldn't be even if we wanted to, so I guess it's wise to make a virtue of necessity, ¿verdad?)

Bueno, mi prima, cuídate. And remember, I am saving family pictures that *you* have never seen before . . . don't worry, they are well-protected from the wind. Between us we can complete the panorama. Y recuérdate de seguir escribiéndome, que lo necesitamos más que el aire. Saludos a todos por allá, y tú recibes todo el cariño de tu prima,

Caridad.

"The Woman-Bridge."
Drawing by Zaida del Río.

FLAVIO RISECH

POLITICAL AND CULTURAL CROSS-DRESSING: NEGOTIATING A SECOND GENERATION CUBAN-AMERICAN IDENTITY

> *Cuba is a peculiar exile. . . . We
> can reach it by a thirty-minute
> charter flight from Miami, yet
> never reach it at all.*
> Cristina García[1]

My parents fled Cuba at the end of 1959, crossing the Florida Straits in a Pan American DC6. I was five years old and had no idea of the profound impact that short flight would have on my life, no inkling of the way it would forever affect the very essence of who I am. I lived with my family in Miami for the next sixteen years. In 1976, I crossed another kind of border, the more subtle and complex one between the Cuban community of southwest Miami and the rest of the U.S., and settled in Massachusetts, where I have lived since. In 1982, I returned to the island for the first time; I have traveled there a number of times since then, often passing en route through my family's home in Miami's *la sagüesera*. I see myself as having lived in three very different countries, and have found that my movement through each demands a different way of presenting myself, a different way to "dress."

In the metaphor of cross-dressing, I suggest that we of the Cuban-American second generation have at our disposal a wide array of identity "garments," the specific cultural, political and social attributes that we have acquired by virtue of having lived in the distinct communities of Cuba, exile Miami, and other U.S. cities, and that taken together make up who we are. As we continually cross and re-cross the boundaries between these communities, we find we cannot wear all our "identity wardrobe" simultaneously, since it can make us too "hot": there are strict taboos or high costs associated with presenting oneself in certain kinds of "garb." For example, how can a politically progressive gay or lesbian Cuban-American display leftism in Cuban Miami or queerness in Havana? Each time we cross these boundaries, then, we must in an important sense "cross-dress," making coded decisions as to how to present ourselves, about what part of our identities to wear proudly or keep closeted.

Cubans have for many years benefited from unique and far-reaching U.S. immigration policies designed to encourage mass emigration from revolutionary Cuba.[2] However, for close to twenty years Cubans could only cross the border in one direction, and despite the expectation of many of the early emigrants that they would soon return, the crossing proved over time to be irrevocable and necessitated a reconceptualization of the meaning of leaving Cuba for the U.S. For those of us who were children when we came, or who were born here in the 1960s, this question is extraordinarily complex. Two decades after the revolution, when it became possible for Cubans to travel back to Cuba, this "second generation" began to come to terms with its origins and its identity.

What would it mean to go back? What could we seek to gain from (re)establishing contact with a country most of us knew only from hazy childhood memories or family and community mythology? How do we present ourselves in each of these communities, now that changing political and legal conditions over the past decade have allowed many of us to cross and recross the divide between the U.S. and Cuba, even while the "border" itself, the ideological chasm for which that ninety-mile stretch of sea serves as an apt disjunctive metaphor, remains as fixed as the Berlin Wall? For many Cubans of the second generation, this border is not merely the political frontier between two countries, but a kind of frontier of identity between images of ourselves as Cubans and as hyphenated Americans.[3]

For those of us born on the island and raised in the U.S., the return to Cuba offers answers to many transcendent questions as to who we are, though we may find that paradoxically we neither feel nor are perceived by cubanos there as being quite as Cuban nor as American as we imagined ourselves to be. Those like myself who are light-skinned bear a particular burden, as we return to our *patria* to find that we are perceived not only as not fully Cuban but as whites in a society now over half composed of darker-skinned people. In a sense I and others like me change race when we cross this border:

only a profoundly coded *cambio de piel* — a kind of cross-dressing involving shifting between two very different social constructs of race — could make it possible for me to be a *blanquito* there and a latino and therefore something of a "person of color" here.

These borders, moreover, are not solely those that separate communities from each other. They are internal as well, separating us in critical ways from each of the communities in which we move. We thus cannot merely construct uncomplicated and stable understandings of ourselves as assimilating immigrants. And perhaps most critically, these "interior" borders balkanize our own images of who we are, mandating our ongoing interrogation of our national, political, cultural, racial, and even sexual identities.

I

As I walk across the Parque Céspedes in Santiago, a small boy calls out after me, "*¡Oye, Boris!*" I retort in my best Miami-inflected Cuban Spanish, "*¡No soy ruso, chiquillo de mierda!*" His eyes widen for a second before he scurries away, visibly shaken. It is 1983, and Russians are still commonly seen in Cuba. I am infuriated that I am mistaken for one of them, and it happens several more times during this trip. I wonder whether it is the style of my clothing or my eyeglass frames that causes it, until I slowly realize that it might be my skin color, my New England-in-midwinter pallor, that inspires kids to call me "Boris" and beg me for cheap Russian ball-point pens.

But it is more than my skin, it is the combination of the complexion, the clothing, and the foreigner's demeanor which triggers the Cubans' perception of me as other, as someone from another country. *I am not seen as Cuban.* I had not expected this on my first return trip. I had envisioned a prodigal homecoming, not a major crisis of identity. But the prodigal return is in fact the resolution of an identity crisis, as the prodigal son repentantly surrenders his deviancy from the normative family and is reincorporated into it. Such a resolution, I now understand, was and is impossible for me, for each of my communities demands as the price of resolution that I surrender certain parts of myself — the "garments" I wear comfortably in one but not in the others — and I will not part with any article of my identity "wardrobe," deviant or passé though it may be.

And yet being in Cuba makes me feel profoundly at home in certain ways. The look of Havana, the faces of the people I encounter, the music, the jokes, the accents I hear all tell me I am among my people. I rejoice in my experience of my *cubanía*; I revel in the knowledge that living most of my life in the U.S. hasn't stripped me of it. I even come to terms with the fact that I am a clumsy dancer: after all, my first cousin has lived here all of his forty-five years and he's a worse dancer than I am. He tells me it runs in the family.

Then an acquaintance in Havana tells me I speak Spanish with a Puerto Rican accent. I am shaken, for how can I claim to be Cuban if I neither look nor sound Cuban? Later I stop in Miami for a few days on my way back to Boston, and find with some annoyance that Cuban store clerks and waitpersons answer me in English when I address them in Spanish. I adopt a new strategy in responding: "*¡No hablo inglés!*" They scrutinize me impassively, and respond appropriately in Spanish as though nothing were amiss. They probably think I'm a tourist from Uruguay or Venezuela. At least they don't think I'm Russian.

Back in the Cuban capital I irrationally wonder whether everyone is looking at me as I ride the bus to my uncle's house, though as I look around I see a number of fair-skinned women and men, unmistakably marked as Cuban by their polyester pants, too-tight shirts and Eastern bloc shoes. My uncle and three of his four sons have light brown hair and skin that reddens and burns easily in the sun, like mine. I notice as they greet me that all of them have my nose, my father's wide, almost African nose (*¿y tu abuela, dónde está?*). I think about how good it feels to be *entre familia*, being among people who knew me before I was born, who had cried with me, that first time I returned, over the twists of fate and politics that divided our family, my father from his brothers, me from my homeland and from them, for more than twenty years. But of course, I am not home. I have only temporarily crossed the chasm that separates me from them, from Cuba. I will go back to the place I now call home; they will stay here, home, in Havana.

II

The feeling of *belonging* was what I most had wanted from my trip, but my sense of belonging in Cuba is ambiguous at best. Though our experiences differ, most significantly in that she left

Cuba as a young adult of 22, Olivia M. Espín's account of her first return resonates deeply for me:

> What I learned . . . from this trip is that who I am is inextricably intertwined with the experience of uprootedness . . . entailing an awareness that there is another place where I feel at home in profound ways[.] That place, however, is not fully home anymore. And this reality is, precisely, the most powerful reminder of my uprootedness. My daily routine is not the daily routine of people in Cuba; their way of life is not my way of life; . . . I have learned new things about myself—and what is important for me—that do not fit in Cuban life anymore.[4]

But was my place then in the U.S., or in Cuban Miami? As a Cuban child in early-sixties Miami, I was a foreigner to the Anglos, who forbade me to speak Spanish in school and for whom even pronouncing my name was a major linguistic challenge. Conversational Spanish was one of the subjects in my second grade class. The teacher gave each pupil a Spanish name for the half-hour lessons: Arthur became Arturo, Mary was María, and, strangely enough, she insisted on calling me Pablo. She did not see the *difference* between the other kids and me that I felt so acutely, or perhaps she did not want them to notice it. Her implicit denial of my reality in dressing me up with a Spanish name that was not my own told me *I did not belong*, and so deeply did I experience it as such that this incident, occurring one morning early in my eighth year of life, remains as clearly inscribed in my memory as if it had happened yesterday.

As I grew older the gap between the Anglocentric environment of school and the world of *arroz con pollo, dominós* and the music of Lecuona grew increasingly difficult to negotiate, but in the end it was politics that made it unbridgeable. Initially, I had only the knowledge of Cuba that I had received from my family, and it only slowly dawned on me that there were other perspectives to account for. I date my major political break with my family, and by extension with Cuban Miami, to May 1970: once I knew it was possible for my relatives to approve of the massacre of unarmed students at Kent State ("four less communists," they said), I began to question all of their political positions, including those on Cuba.

It was not long before I had read enough to realize that they knew very little about the real Cuba, the post-1959 Cuba that they had fled en masse. The more I read, the more alien I felt in Miami, as I found that even though I had reservations about their policies, I did

not hate but rather admired Fidel and Che Guevara for their courage in the face of implacable U.S. aggression and for their efforts to
improve living standards for most Cubans. The very fact that I read
the things I did set me apart from Cuban Miami in ways I did not
fully grasp at the time. Though I still felt in certain profound ways
at home in Cuban Miami, in others I knew I was no more one of
them than someone from another planet.

The fossilized rhetoric of *Añorada Cuba*, the lament for a pre-
Castro Cuba that never really existed, a mythical Cuba where
everyone had wealth, health and high culture, where there was no
racism, was the constant refrain at the dinner table. Always in
counterpoint was the theme of the communist evil which had
despoiled our island paradise, often punctuated with allusions to
Fidel's perfidiousness and his brother Raúl's supposed homosexuality. From these representations I drew the following lessons: it was
bad to be a communist, it was worse to be a *maricón*, and it was *el
colmo* (the ultimate sin) to be both. It would be some years before I
would discover that being a *maricón* had anything to do with sex,
but the link between communism and queerness—then defined for
me as effeminacy—was clear enough.

My first awareness of homosexuality came from reading my
grandparents' copies of *Zig-Zag*, a satirical exile tabloid that often
ran cartoons depicting a limp-wristed Raúl Castro dressed in
fatigues, high heels and a ponytail. The flies which buzzed around
him in the frames symbolized not only his imputed *falta de aseo*
(poor hygiene) but his deep moral decay, for to cast the communist
Raúl as a *maricón* was to reduce him to an effeminate, stinking
wretch posing as a real man. It mattered little whether he supposedly had sex with other men, for the essence of *mariconería* in Latin-
American culture is being womanly or insufficiently masculine-
appearing,[5] and in the specific context of Cuba effeminacy is the
antithesis of true patriotism. The *maricón*, like women, can be neither *revolucionario* in Havana nor anti-communist *gusano* in
Miami, because both of these identities require unambiguous and
unquestioned masculinity for their constitution.

As an adolescent and young adult, I understood these rules well,
and therefore cloaked my emerging sexual desire for other men
beneath an intricately tailored suit that read unequivocally as het-
erosexuality. Though I also felt erotically drawn to women and
eventually acquired the ultimate accessory of heterosexual
couture—marriage—I lived in constant fear that a little lisp, a

barely discernible bend of the wrist or saying "*¡Ay!*" with a slightly wrong intonation would give the secret away and I would be stripped of my straight clothing, a *maricón* standing naked for all to see. As my politics continued to drift leftward, moreover, I knew I was becoming, like Raúl, *el colmo*. Leaving Cuban Miami seemed like the best solution to my sartorial/identity dilemma, for though it would take me many more years to fully come to terms with my sexuality, at least outside of Miami I could wear the left political styles I thought I looked good in.

III

Some years later, I arrive in Miami at five a.m. after a two-week stay in the island. I wait in the humid, yellow glare of the deserted airport arrivals level. My mother's car materializes at the far end and comes toward me. I wonder who she sees, what she is thinking as she spots my plastic tote bag emblazoned with "Habana Club Rum." She is in her nightdress and *bata de casa*. I pile my things in the back seat and get in. Lack of sleep and a few cups of Cuban coffee have loosened my tongue, perhaps too much. She asks how my trip was, and I rattle off my eager account of the benefits socialism has brought to Cuba despite the limitations on personal freedoms. She will not concede even that little, so I counter that she should see it for herself and reach her own conclusions. "And give Fidel $2,000 for the privilege? Forget it. *Además, no tengo nada que ver allá*," she says sharply. "You've been brainwashed!" she continues, "Don't you know they only let you see what they want you to see?" And finally, "*¡No comas tanta mierda!*"

As dawn breaks over the endless flat expanse of Miami's suburban sprawl, we are in the midst of yet another argument about my "leftist" politics, a fixed feature of our family life since I was sixteen and began protesting against the Vietnam War. I am thirty now, returning from my third visit to Cuba in as many years. She understood why I needed to go the first time, to find my roots, as she put it, but with every subsequent trip her worst fears seemed to her to be coming true. She begins to cry. "If I had known you were going to turn out to be a communist, I would have left you there in the first place." The c-word rolls off her tongue with the special venom Miami Cubans convey so exquisitely. I cannot believe I am saying what I say next, half to myself: "I wish you had." Her Pontiac cruises

like a boat down the empty concrete river of the Palmetto Expressway. Our angry and hurt silence gives way as we both cry and call a
truce, a tacit agreement that Cuba will not be discussed any further
today. Soon we are at her house, a pastel bungalow in Westchester.
Flowers sprout around a large ceramic *tinaja* in the front yard,
recalling the gardens of Camagüey. I understand that she is home,
here in Miami, in ways I can never be.

Though Miami's hot weather invites the shedding of one's garments, my wearing of my essentially Cuban cultural trappings without my tailored left political "accessories" is tolerable only for short
periods. It's not that I am shy, but I have learned the hard way the
futility of arguing against the right-wing grain, of presenting myself
in Miami in the political "drag" that has become so much a part of
my being in my life in Massachusetts. To paraphrase Espín, I simply
do not fit in Cuban Miami life anymore.

IV

Despite the freedom to "dress" politically more or less as I choose
that I have enjoyed in my nearly two decades in Massachusetts, I
found that as I became actively involved in progressive solidarity
work with Cuba, I had to negotiate a political minefield. The fervent anti-communist cant of my Cuban relatives and neighbors, the
U.S. pro-Cuba left's sometimes insufficiently critical, single-minded
defense of the revolution, and the frequently impenetrable "party
line" positions of many revolucionarios on the island all pulled me
across the terrain in different directions. At the same time, I must
reconcile all these with the realities of life in Cuba which I experience when I cross the border. I often feel like a billiard ball on the
highly polarized pool table of U.S./Cuba/Cuban-American politics,
ricocheting off the bumpers of the contending discourses but never
quite landing comfortably in any of the ideological pockets.

I find myself on a panel on human rights at a college conference
on Cuban socialism. It is 1988. I am looking out at an audience of
perhaps fifty, among them many North American solidarity activists
for Cuba and Central America. A number are Cuban-Americans,
some of whom I know, others new to me. I have always found it
fascinating to observe, even while I engage in it, the ritual of two
Cuban-Americans who know little about each other meeting for the
first time. We always ask each other what part of Cuba we are from,

and in what U.S. city we grew up. Then we do a kind of rhetorical dance to divine each other's political persuasions without asking directly. Discovering that the new acquaintance is from Miami is for me a "red flag," if you will pardon the expression. I tend to assume that he or she is a *gusano* until proven otherwise, and I am initially very guarded about revealing much about my own politics. But in this setting I don't have the luxury of being coy about where I stand. I rustle my papers nervously and glance about the room, now filled to capacity.

One man stands out: he is perhaps sixty, well over six feet tall and completely bald. He takes a seat directly in front of me and I feel his eyes burn into me. Three suspiciously clean-cut young white men sit near him, taking notes on crisp yellow legal pads (I later learn that they are members of Young Americans for Freedom). They interrupt my admittedly abstract discussion of the socialist versus bourgeois liberal conceptions of human rights: they do not like that I have used the modifier "bourgeois" to describe their cherished liberal democratic values. Some of the North American activists demand that I be allowed to finish my presentation. I have only spoken for about two minutes so far.

Then the tall bald man leans over the little student desk he is spilling out of, points a long finger at me, and launches into a diatribe about the horrors he suffered as a political prisoner for eighteen years in Cuba. He inveighs against our academic posturing and claims that the only honorable course is to oppose communism in all its manifestations, especially Castro's version. The three Yaffies nod supportively as they scribble furiously on their legal pads.

I am sweating, not knowing how to control the situation, angry at the organizers for not including a moderator or a security detail for this panel on such a sensitive issue. This man came here to disrupt the panel and to red-bait and intimidate the participants. I am most angry at the fact that he succeeded.

I felt threatened, not so much because of any direct statement he made but because I inevitably interpreted his comments, his demeanor and his very presence in the context of the long history of exile violence against those within the Cuban community who publicly dissent from refractory and dogmatic anti-Castroism.[6] I was only too aware of the possible consequences of being read by right-wing exiles as a Cuban-American apologist for Fidel's tyranny. As such, I was crossing a coded political boundary at a potentially high price, for most intolerable to this exile mentality are *Cubans* who think differently. The still-unsolved terrorist murders of such dissenters as Luciano Nieves and Carlos Muñiz and dozens of bombings such as the one in which radio commentator Emilio Milián lost both legs serve as grim and lasting warnings to those who would ideologically transgress. Perhaps my feeling of dread is not fully rational but I cannot deny that these images cross my mind when I am publicly presenting myself suited up as a "Cuban-American progressive."

Finally my interlocutor is finished, and he and his three flunkies stage a dramatic exit from the room. I resume my presentation, which, though it takes issue with the rather narrow U.S./liberal democratic conception of human rights, is also critical of Cuba's policies and of the revolution's general lack of channels for supportive dissent. I am careful to point out that UN and other nongovernmental observers have found the human rights situation there much better than that in many other Latin American nations supported by the U.S., but now some of the pro-Cuba activists are enraged. They cite the tedious and familiar statistics about Cuba's advances in health care and education, the lack of unemployment and the low infant mortality, as if these ends justify all means, as if human rights entailed no more than attending to these social welfare issues.

The unspoken epithet *gusano* hangs heavily in the air, and the other Cuban-American progressives in the room risk being tarred with that label too as they argue for a more complex understanding of the situation than these particular activists seem willing to contemplate. They seem to feel that to criticize Cuba is to add fuel to the already raging anti-Castro fire. While I may disagree with them on this point, I also know that they are among the few in the U.S. who steadfastly defend Cuba's right to self-determination, and as such, Cuban-American progressives for whom Cuban sovereignty is the non-negotiable bottom line must continue to work to improve communication with this sector of the left. They, in turn, are increasingly recognizing that Cuban-Americans are not monolithically counter-revolutionary and that our nuanced second generation perspectives on Cuba are worth serious consideration. My sense is that over the five years that have passed since the incident I recount above, there has been a great deal of movement in a positive direction.

V

For many progressive Cuban-Americans, especially those of us who are lesbians or gay men, a particularly difficult intersection to negotiate is that between support for the social advances of the Revolution and revulsion for Cuban homophobia. It is at this juncture that even many committed leftists have turned down the path of condemnation, as our assumptions about the basic humanitarianism of the Cuban socialist system collide with the lurid narratives of re-education camps, officially sanctioned discrimination and expulsion of thousands of supposed *maricones* during the 1980 Mariel crisis. Gay North American activists and intellectuals, such as Allen Young, the very title of whose book *Gays Under the Cuban Revolution*[7] symbolically presents gay Cubans as "bottoms" to communist macho "tops," reconsidered their pro-Cuba positions. In the process, they often failed to grasp the full nature and depth of homophobia in Cuban culture, which certainly predates and is likely to survive the revolution.[8]

In the early eighties, Cuban émigré gays and committed exile Castro-bashers became strange bedfellows in a campaign to discredit Cuba by denouncing Fidel's homophobia. This occurs most visibly and effectively in the film *Improper Conduct*, made by émigrés Nestor Almendros and Orlando Jiménez-Leal, in which non-Cuban intellectuals such as Susan Sontag are presented as strategic allies not only of oppressed Cuban homosexuals but of right-wing straight male Cuban exile leaders, perversely positioning themselves as defenders of gays and lesbian rights in Cuba.[9] By its silence on the existence of homophobia in Cuba before 1959 and in contemporary exile Miami, the film implies strongly – and misleadingly – that Cuban homophobia is the product of socialism.

Given this exile strategy of blaming Fidel for gay oppression, it should not be surprising that these self-styled crusaders never addressed the virulent homophobia of Cuban Miami. The ravages of the HIV epidemic in Miami, which has the fourth-highest city total of reported AIDS cases in the nation (over 7,450),[10] have also been met with a deafening silence in the enclave, which persists in viewing HIV disease as someone else's problem. The epidemic, however, has played a crucial role in reconfiguring the Cuban-American conception of homosexuality, as many men who few suspected of homosexuality were forced "out" by an AIDS diagnosis. The AIDS crisis in Miami thus precipitated a crisis in Cuban-American sexual taxonomy, for how could one tell whether a man is gay if he doesn't look or act like a *maricón?* The old categories have been destabilized, the boundaries of sexual identity blurred. As Cuban Miami enters its fourth decade, *maricones cubanos* have become gay Cuban-Americans; queen culture is becoming queer culture.

This taxonomic crisis has its roots in the butch or "clone" style of dressing up male homosexuality which emerged in North American gay enclaves in the late 1970s and early 1980s, which gay Cuban-Americans, especially those of the second generation, often emulated. Cuban-American queers, like other gay and lesbian Latinos in the U.S., increasingly "dress" their sexual identities in the styles in fashion in the North American gay communities in which we have lived, and in turn, these fashions have had increasing influence in queer Cuban Miami, as more of us leave the formerly *de rigueur* identity apparel of effeminate *mariconería* to molder at the bottoms of our closets.

Hatred of homosexuality, whether dressed as Cuban *mariconería* or as American style queerness, pervades the Cuban communities on both sides of the Straits of Florida. Yet as I cross the border, I see incipient cracks in the edifice of homophobia, as a Cuban gay and lesbian culture manifests itself against the odds and even achieves a level of unofficial tolerance. I sip tea at *la Casa de las Infusiones* (literally, the Tea House) on Havana's busy Rampa and overhear a lesbian couple loudly arguing about each others' infidelities, and learn later that at Cuba's *sidatorios* (mandatory HIV residential treatment centers) gay couples are permitted to live together in the small but comfortable private apartments. I read a short story about a gay middle-aged man's desperate search for love,[11] which was published by the state despite shortages of paper which severely limit all printing on the island. Of course, the character ends up trying to kill himself, but what is crucial here is not the denouement of the story but the fact that the Ministry of Culture chose to put it in print at a time when less controversial manuscripts go unpublished.

Clearly, though gay identity in Cuba may be changing slowly, it is in fact changing. Partly this is due to the increased contact over the past decade or so between the island and Miami, where Cuban-American gay identity is rapidly undergoing a much more radical transformation. I notice the prominence of Cubans in the Miami gay and lesbian communities and in AIDS action organizations, and begin to see that Miami's ascent to world-class-city status has allowed many Cuban-American gays and lesbians to transcend the narrow parochialism of Little Havana, though I wonder whether the price they pay for crossing that border is the loss of much of their connection to their own *cubanía*.

Can we proudly "wear" our Cuban identities along with our Levis, tight tee-shirts and workboots in the U.S. gay world? To which group do we owe our primary allegiance? Many Latinos have found that admission into American-style queerness requires that they leave at the door the garments of their *latinidad*, acquiring in the process a deracialized status. Latino gays and lesbians are, in Charles Fernández's phrase, "undocumented aliens in the queer nation," homogenized in the melting pot of a presumptively universalized gay and lesbian community which simultaneously denies our differences and tokenizes us as examples of its colorful diversity.

Yet things have not changed sufficiently in Cuban Miami to allow us to comfortably "dress" as gay Cubans there, nor has its exile political ideology allowed a space for safe occupancy for those professing political orientations of any degree of leftist persuasion. And there is no doubt that things have not changed enough in Cuba to permit my presentation of myself as gay on the island without incident. I must continue to be careful about what I wear when I am in either place. Ironically, my coming to terms with my sexuality has not made my wardrobe selections any easier. Instead, I have become more aware of the complex requirements of cross-dressing.

Perhaps the conflict I and others like me feel when crossing the borders is irreconcilable, yet I wonder whether owning these multiple and shifting identities is really an asset rather than a problem. There is a constant tension between passively accepting the ways in which others define us—racially, culturally, politically, and sexually—and actively staking out our own terrain, contesting simplistic definitions, and carving out what Guillermo Gómez Peña would call a new "border identify."[13] We are, after all, the *atravesados*, "those who cross over [boundaries], or go through the confines of the 'normal' ",[14] for whom crossing the border at once means defiance, reconciliation, return to a place where one has never and does not now fully belong. In short, the crossing itself is a profoundly and inescapably political act.

Because the very fact that I "cross-dress" is what defines me as transgressive, suspect, not "normal," perhaps I will never feel entirely comfortable negotiating the shifts of identity which occur as I transport myself across the external and internal borders—or rather the ideological, emotional, and cultural chasms—that separate Cuba from Miami, Cuban Miami from Anglo-America, and myself as an individual from all of these. Rather than traversing the boundaries to become either a "hyphenated American" or a political exile looking to go home, I stand astride many frontiers, belonging fully to none of my communities yet paradoxically deeply and irrevocably connected to all of them.

NOTES

[1]Cristina Garcia, *Dreaming in Cuban* (New York: Alfred A. Knopf, 1992), 219.

[2]For a full analysis of U.S. policy toward Cuban emigrants, see Félix Masud Piloto, *With Open Arms: Cuban Migration to the United States* (Totowa, NJ: Rowman and Littlefield, 1988), 32–110. This legally facilitated access to the United States has set us apart from many other Latin Americans, who have been at least as much in need of asylum but who have found their respective paths to refuge in the U.S. to be fraught with legal obstacles and the danger of deportation.

[3]I do not mean to suggest, of course, that similar issues of identity and borders do not arise for Mexican, Puerto Rican or other Latin American peoples living in the United States. See, e.g., Richard Rodriguez, *Hunger of Memory* (New York: Bantam, 1983) and *Days of Obligation: An Argument with my Mexican Father* (New York: Viking, 1992), Sandra Cisneros, *Woman Hollering Creek* (New York: Random House, 1991), Nicholasa Mohr, *Rituals of Survival* (Houston: Arte Público Press, 1985), Cherrie Moraga, *Loving in the War Years: lo que nunca pasó por sus labios* (Boston: South End Press, 1983).

[4]Olivia M. Espín, "Roots Uprooted: Autobiographical Reflections on the Psychological Experience of Migration," in Fernando Alegria and Jorge Rufinelli, *Pardise Lost or Gained? The Literature of Hispanic Exile* (Houston: Arte Público Press, 1990), 160.

[5]See e.g., Tomás Almaguer, "Chicano Men: A Cartography of Homosexual Identity and Behavior," in *differences: a Journal of Feminist and Cultural Studies* 3(2):75 (1991).

[6]For an in-depth look at the issue of the lack of freedom of expression, especially for Cuban-American dissidents, in Cuban Miami, see Americas Watch/Fund for Free Expression, *Dangerous Dialogue: Attacks on Freedom of Expression in Miami's Exile Community* (New York: Americas Watch, August 1992).

[7]Allen Young, *Gays Under the Cuban Revolution* (Boston: Lexington Books, 1979). Young's book, based primarily on the testimonies of a handful of men, assumes a U.S.-style paradigm of sexuality in which one is either straight or "gay," and thus misses the nuances of a culture in which such discrete categories do not exist, in which sexual identity is framed in terms of masculinity or lack thereof rather than strictly on the gender of one's sexual partners. See, e.g., Almaguer, note 5 above.

[8]Lourdes Argüelles and B. Ruby Rich, "Homosexuality, Homophobia and Revolution: Notes Toward an Understanding of the Cuban Lesbian and Gay Male Experience," in Duberman, Vicinus and Chauncey (eds.), *Hidden from History: Reclaiming the Gay and Lesbian Past* (New York: New American Library, 1989), 443–445.

[9]B. Ruby Rich and Lourdes Argüelles, "Homosexuality, Homophobia and Revolution, Part II," *Signs* 11(1):132–134 (Autumn 1985). For a detailed critique of

Improper Conduct, see B. Ruby Rich, "Bay of Pix," *American Film* 9(9):57–59 (July-August 1984).

[10]Cumulative total of AIDS cases reported to CDC as of December 31, 1992. Centers for Disease Control, *HIV-AIDS Quarterly Surveillance Report*, December 31, 1992.

[11]Padura Fuentes, "Leonardo," *El Cazador* (Habana: Ediciones Unión/UNEAC, 1991).

[12]Charles Fernández, "Undocumented Aliens in the Queer Nation," *Outlook* 12:20 (Spring 1991), 23.

[13]Guillermo Gómez Peña, "Documented/Undocumented," in Simonson and Walker (eds.), *Graywolf Annual Five: Multi-cultural Literacy* (St. Paul: Graywolf Press, 1988).

[14]Gloria Anzaldúa, *Borderlands/La Frontera* (San Francisco: Spinsters/Aunt Lute Foundation, 1987), 3.

RAQUEL (KAKI) MENDIETA COSTA

SILHOUETTE

To Ana Mendieta, Artist

—My saint's day is July 26: Saint Ann . . .

My brother and I had taken the boat from Dupont to La Casa Vieja to spend the day together with the whole family. Summer was at its peak, and you and I had acquired that mulatto hue which made us targets of the stupid phrase, "you're so black, they'll be asking you for your papers."

Upstairs, in the patio of the great house, the grownups poured themselves drinks and spoke in whispers about "the situation."

You were the indisputable leader among the younger cousins. Your sense of authority came from being two years older than me, and from your infinite capacity for inventing games and stories; but most of all, from your strong, dominating, authoritative character.

—But this year they're not giving me a party, because my papá says that things are real bad. If we play rebels, I'm the captain, and you'll have to draw to see who'll be captain of the soldiers.

I knew that we wouldn't be playing, because nobody wanted to be the soldiers, and you knew it too. That's why I felt relieved when you thought of playing at burying ourselves in the sand. You lay down and started to tell us about the dinosaur movie you had seen at the Varadero Theater the night before, while my brother and I busied ourselves covering your whole body with sand.

Soon afterwards we heard the bell ringing from the north patio of the house, calling us to lunch. You moved, and the sand which covered you began to crack, to break open, as if that monstrous body which we had made you into and which imprisoned you, that strange chrysalis formed by diminutive, insignificant bits of colored

72

seashells, were pushing to give birth to you. Finally, suddenly, the sand gave way and you stood. We ran to the sea to rinse ourselves off. Back, in the wet sand, stayed your silhouette, arms and legs extended.

PROFILE II

In the last year the old house had gone through quick and constant changes. Sound and light seem to have been the defining traits of the status of the house and its inhabitants: an almost blinding clarity, declarations made in shrill or low and resonant tones, during the first few months of the "triumph"; darkness, muffled conversations, restrained footsteps, toward the end of that year; and now, surprisingly, almost without a transition, a feeling of strangeness, a dense texture which kept the soul from moving forward, and which we did not feel there for the first time — rather, we had met it earlier in the house of our children's games. It was a peculiar feeling, as of swimming upstream, slowly, through a river of oil.

Sunday lunch was charged with a strange tension. I remember my anguish when I saw how you swallowed your food with a lack of appetite, while they wouldn't let you drink water "because it swamps your stomach." Facing you, also with no appetite, I set to drinking all my water plus all the water I thought you might need.

Then the words. Tall words, excessive words, inaccessible words: communism, religion, paternal authority. At first we couldn't understand. Neither of us. Only later did they begin to acquire profiles and then, slowly, rounded forms: dark, terrible ones, some of them; all of them aggressive. "Mine stay with me. For good or for bad," said my father. "This is communism and nobody's taking my children away, and no 'paternal authority' either," said yours. "The Church, the Church will save them" — your mother spoke, and it was as if a dam had broken. "Hell with the Church, coño. That stuff about the priests is just a bunch of propaganda. You're going to ruin your daughters." Our last family reunion had ended.

I would never see you again. Nor your sister. Two weeks later they sent you *up North* with the priests, "and if things don't go well they can come back. No matter what, it will help them perfect their English." They didn't let us know you would be going.

Only with time did I come to understand what that meant: they had split your soul like the wing of a dove, and you could never

again come home to roost. But you would retain forever the mysterious carnival images of the Museum of Cárdenas: the sword of your
mambí great-grandfather, the shell collection, the flea circus, the
bote in which Maceo crossed from Júcaro to Morón, the death mask
of Máximo Gómez, the embalmed lioness, the live cayman in the
fountain of the central patio.*

Years later you came back to recuperate them.

PROFILE III

They were placing a call to the United States. My grandfather
paced excitedly. Since he was fluent in English, he would have to
speak with the American priest. Your grandmother, as if watching
the scene through a window of amber, disconsolate, held in her
hands the letter from Father Francisco: "We are well aware, from
the reports of Father Antonio of the parish of Cárdenas, of the good
habits and the religiosity with which they have been educated. But
the family that took them in, with benevolence and charity, has
accused them of stealing." What had happened? You were all so
certain . . . (Or weren't you, since "the master's eye wasn't fattening
the horse"?) "Now that we were so happy that the girls had left the
orphanage . . . sorry, I mean the school, to go live with a Catholic
family."

Then the ringing phone, the explanations, the recommendations,
cutting too close to the bone. "But the girls come from a Catholic,
educated, well-raised family." "But they are incapable of such a
thing." "But their education would not permit it." And what good
would all that do them? They were suspiciously Latin.

After a few months, the clarifications: "No. They say it wasn't
them. That it was the daughter of the North Americans who had
taken them in." And everyone was happy, because the good name of
the family had been cleared. But what of the anguish, the humilia-
tion, and the feeling of helplessness? No, not that! It was better to
sleep calmly, satisfied with the good education they had given to *the
girls.* "*This* will soon fall, and everything will go back to the way it
was before."

But it didn't happen. *This* didn't fall, and you began to lose the
color and the light, faces became blurred, and the phrases repeated
in ever more distant letters were no longer enough. You searched in
your instinctive, ancestral memory, and you became the Artist,

because you could be nothing else: you laid your body down on the earth, on the white sand, on the black, on the red, on the multicolored water and on the green grass; you covered it with blood and flowers, with mud and rock, with gunpowder, fire, and gnarled bark, and you traced your outline, your silhouette of indefinite, detached profiles.

PROFILE IV

Years later you returned. First by television: "Yes, since I look Latin, I was always '*la putica*,' the little whore, to them." And we all cried: you, in front of us; we, feeling that you had already arrived. But your arrival came later. You came with your Art, and we waited for you in the lobby of the hotel.

Those were nights of painful conversations, nostalgic memories, anecdotes forgotten and reconstructed. Nights of non-stop partying, especially for you and for me. We roamed the streets of the city, the Apostolado school, the old house in El Vedado. Then Cárdenas, grandparents, our roots and history, the *mambí* great-grandfather. You searched for the old museum, but it wasn't there any more; it had changed, but you could recognize yourself in the new one, too. In the sand on Varadero beach you recovered the detailed profiles of your silhouette, and you left your definitive outline in the small caves of the southern coast.

You left and you came back several times. You were still the same little girl, passionate and argumentative. But now your soul was hard, as if covered with calluses.

Still it was not enough. Again your emotions betrayed you, and one day the news reached us: your silhouette had been carved, forever, indelibly, into a New York street.

Translated by David Frye

---

*Translator's Note: *mambí*: rebel fighting for Cuban independence from Spain under Máximo Gómez and Antonio Maceo, 1868–1898.

FLORA GONZÁLEZ MANDRI

A HOUSE ON SHIFTING SANDS

Arriving from my family's home in Camagüey to the hotel in Miramar, on the outskirts of Havana, I started to feel uncomfortable. I
had come to Cuba with an American group and I would be leaving
with them. That meant I'd have to spend my last night in Cuba
speaking English. My friend Tania wasn't staying at the hotel, but
she had left me her telephone number at her mother's house so I
could arrange to meet her at the airport in the early morning hours.
I felt imprisoned by the English language. For the time being, I had
no alternative but to belong to the small group of people traveling
with me. I met up with Tim and Peter to pass my last night away.
Both men had been in Cuba on several occasions and knew Havana
much better than I. It seemed totally incongruous that someone
could get to know a country without being able to communicate
with its people. Tim had done it through the lens of the camera,
Peter with music.

Late that night, we sought shelter at the Hotel Nacional where a
band from the Vieja Trova was playing. They were on a large balcony facing the Malecón. Tired of the noisy crowds, we took refuge
behind some glass jalousie windows so we could see out but block the
sound. Since the blinds were shut, the couples on the dance floor
resembled little wind-up dolls dancing to a silent beat. Someone
opened the windows so that the air would circulate better and the
tune invaded us with its melody. Here in Havana, listening to Caribbean music, could bring back the sound of my mother's voice to me,
along with the sound of the Old Wave Song:

Though I may want to forget you
it would be impossible
because you'll always have
a lasting memory of me.
My caresses shall be

the terrible specter
of how much I suffer
of how much I suffer
when I'm away from you.

Aunque quiera olvidarte
ha de ser imposible
porque eterno recuerdo
tendrás siempre de mí.
Mis caricias serán
el fantasma terrible
de lo mucho que sufro
de lo mucho que sufro
alejado de ti.

Even though I lived in La Víbora, in Havana, just before we left, my childhood memories are in Camagüey, the land of the earthenware jugs. On subsequent trips to Cuba, I discovered the city of Havana as I have discovered so many other Latin American cities — through the eyes of literature. The Old Havana that I know is Alejo Carpentier's *City of the Columns*. The same goes for the University of Havana, which I got to know through my father's stories about when he took part in the student government during the time of Machado (a period depicted by Lezama Lima in *Paradiso*). Just as memorable is Eliseo Diego's *Calzada de Jesús del Monte* or a stroll by the waterfront with Lezama Lima. I need to return to Cuba in order to be in Camagüey, in order to walk down the streets of my childhood once again, but I need to return in order to really get to know the byways of the Havana literature. When I'm at the university, I think that I could have learned in those classrooms, walked those steps, but you can't live off the nostalgia of something you never lived. That's why when I return to Havana I'm already returning to my present. Each time I return I get to live a little more in the present and less in the past.

Tania and I met at the José Martí airport and we both had the look of having lived intense moments with our families. She was the only one in her family to have left the country and her farewell, especially to her mother, was very difficult. Her mother was there on the other side of the glass. Tania introduced me through signs. We opened our hands, and with our sweaty palms we touched the glass, trying to shake hands in an impossible gesture of human contact. Tania and I went through the passport control booth and were lost on the other side of the glass. Tania knew her mother would be waiting there until the plane took off three hours later.

We shared our regret that better relations couldn't exist between the two countries so that this coming and going would be less painful. After sitting down a while, they called my name and Tania was startled. For a second, we could hear echoes of the voices of those who refuse to return: "You travel there with a Cuban passport? What happens if they don't allow you to come back to the U.S.? All the American passports in the world won't help you then." A young man in military garb checked my papers and everything was in order. But if everything *is* in order, why do we have to enter and exit through different gates, why are we subjected to those thorough searches, why so much fuss? We have to justify ourselves on one side and the other. How many times do you have to return in order for the Cuban government to leave you alone? How long do we have to pay for having left? What do you have to do so that Miami Cubans won't despise you just because you want to return to the country where we all were born? I return because I need the warmth of my family over there, because I need to walk down the streets of my childhood and have the feeling of being at home. I'm tired of roaming, of acquiring perennially interrupted histories. For the time being, I don't want to live in Cuba but I do want to be able to know that I can return without inconveniences, without aggressions, without having to justify everything.

Already on the other side of the puddle, forty-five minutes into the flight, you feel the shock of the jump from underdevelopment to the outrageous overdevelopment of Miami. We can't hear our footsteps because of the thick, blue and red carpet covering all the floors as you get off the plane. The walls are draped with modern paintings, tapestries made with the finest taste and artistry of a well-fed people. Soon, we overtake an older woman who is traveling to the United States for the first time. She says she feels overwhelmed by so much splendor. She tries to hold back the tears but they well up in her eyes.

"Don't worry, ma'am, your family is waiting on the other side and we will help you with the paperwork at customs."

Tania and I take her by the arm and the three of us feel better. The young man who asks for my passport, obviously a Cuban, does so in perfect English as if to let me know that he doesn't accept me as a Cuban. I've been speaking Spanish but he insists on establishing the difference between himself and we Cubans who travel to Cuba.

I answer him in the most Cuban Spanish from the heart and stare at him proudly, coldly. Beyond customs, there is a metro rail waiting to transport us to the twenty-first century. With the sound of an electronic bell, a computerized voice requests that we hang on to our bags and be careful getting off. The older woman takes leave of us after the baggage search. I'm returning with books and nothing else.

"I've got to rush," says Tania. "The flight I had booked has already left. I must be in New York at noon, I have a rehearsal with the orchestra."

We begin walking quickly. We look at each other, surprised at the transformation that is beginning in us. We go from one booth to another finding out on which airline she can leave soonest. She finally gets a flight; we are already speaking English. How strange our intonation is in that language! Our bodies are already tense, anticipating a new pace of life. I grab one of her bags and we start running. Her plane is leaving in fifteen minutes. As we approach the gate we look at each other and hug tightly. When will we see each other again?

I retain the inexplicable emptiness of all farewells. I feel like a young girl, alone in an airport, in search of adventure. I carry with me the fragile but portable house of a mother tongue. Instructions to build and rebuild it are easy: take sand, add water, and build a castle.

Translated by Jaime Martínez-Tolentino and
Flora González Mandri

FROM *EL LIBRO REGALADO*

I

Godmother
I remember well that afternoon when
smaller and bigger than ever
you shouted "Down with Batista"
at the civil guards that were passing by
    on their giant, sweaty horses
From that afternoon on, I realized that you had
    supernatural powers
    that let you transform yourself
    into the passionate goddess
    that I had seen in paintings
    of the French Revolution

You've always been the strongest of all
always guided by a sharp distinction
    as if cut by a razor blade
    separating the just from the unjust

That strength and that sharp edge are what kept me alive
    beyond natural life
but, don't get carried away
I also am about to leave and join up with them

You're already leaving, godmother, and you barely say good-bye?
I'm here, you know
always with my puzzled voice
I wish I could talk with you in another way
to transform into spoken flesh the question mark
    that you represent

a letter
    an image
        a dream . . .
and my solitary and clouded voice
your body grows like a shadow
and another loss approaches
will you join up with them?
will you chat again with them
        on the rocking chairs of the living room?
I wish I could talk with you in another way

Don't be sad
I have to leave like the rest
and like the rest I will rot like a cashew
        buried in the swamplands
I keep my eyes open
        a few minutes more just waiting
        for the poem you promised me
        when I lent you a stool
        so you could kiss me on the forehead

I've finished it before you vanished
        so you can take it to her
        as proof that I'm always
        in the promised place:

"I have no memory to recall what happened
I have no home to keep the memories
in the closely guarded drawer
In passing I always pass by the *barrios*
        where the prostitutes ply their trade
        in the corner alleys
I have no memory to know your name
I invent it all
A story told by the rough hide
        with hairs like palm trees
To remember! I have no memory
I don't know where you're from
        nor the fever that made your lip bleed
        nor how to stitch the distance in the abyss
        with a golden needle or a fish bone

I invent it all for me and for you
A false book of false stories
and a huge quilt
    woven with a fish bone
One last mistake and one last hope
    to tie up with sailors' knots
    the intermissions or interruptions
    the crossroads that announce
    either death or new births or terrors
I have no memory to tell your story
even if I dream myself picking petals
    from amongst the ruins of the revolution
even if I barely remember the day
    when Godmother offered me a stool
    so I could kiss her on the forehead
even if I almost remember when mother
    returned from the North dressed in mystery
    like in the Ava Gardner movies
even if I hardly remember when grandfather
    used to take me to the park with the Moorish gazebo
    that opened up like a destiny spilling over
I don't even have a memory to remember
    what happened
    on the most important night of my life
    when you. . . ."

II

To return to the place of origin
is a perfectly serious thing
to gather or to try to gather the little pieces
    of the shattered mirror
is to invent a story that evades us
and it evades us like fine sand through our fingers
but we must take that path through the woods

Godmother was still waiting for me with her lips wrinkled
    by wisdom
withered and wise
wise and tired

a teller of tales which I translate
    with a precise pen
and she was showing me the pink shells
    on the true beach
as we were going to build
    a wicker throne for the good ones
but stubborn death was biting
    and multiplying a heaven bigger than her skin
and we had to hurry to escape the concrete
    and the cold platform
and return to the familiar or unfamiliar countryside
The small building of our journey
    was crumbling
while I insisted on rebuilding
    with butterflies and palm trees the land almost ours
The revolution and godmother
godmother and the revolution that were tiring out
sharp and wise and withered
where the whites and the blacks
the poor and the rich
once hoped for the same place amongst the gods
and I arrived alone
with the memory on my back
and a burning desire
    to continue writing what my godmother was telling me
but while the revolution was emerging and disappearing
    in the middle of a poem
the sparkling store windows of Miami
    were winning the battle
    with their tumultous and shiny novel
it was a melting or a crumbling
    of any sense of stability
And the Americans were starting
    to raise their flag again
and shamelessly urinating
    on the statue of Martí
Then I said to myself: I have two countries
and I told myself: actually nothing was planned
    with rulers and compasses
actually I didn't know what was happening

nor did I tell grandfather that I would draw graffiti
in other lands
nor did I imagine the planet hanging from a ladder
which godmother pointed at
I knew nothing or almost nothing
when the revolution came in
full of berets and songs
nor did I imagine that madness brought to me
by the memory of the fishermen
who wove prayers with fish bones
I was unaware of the star or the forest
which wrapped me up in the glass
of a new universe that spoke in tongues
and shrank me and enlarged me like a Tom Thumb
from Alice's stories
I didn't know which fruit to hang on to
when you emerged from the middle of the sea
with seaweed like hair and skin of shells
I didn't know when I read your poems
that I would tremble on my island
endless and furious
spreading budding jasmines
nor did I know that I would write
that I would write. . . .

Translated by Stephen Clark

ESTER REBECA SHAPIRO ROK

FINDING WHAT HAD BEEN LOST
IN PLAIN VIEW

Dreaming of Bridges

As an adolescent in Hollywood, Florida, of the late 1960s, captive in the confining cocoon of my Cuban Jewish Polish shtetl family, I longed to enjoy the greater personal freedom so taken for granted by my unencumbered friends and peers. At that time I began to have recurrent dreams of bridges. In one of these series of dreams I would be driving or walking on a road and would reach a body of water traversed by an apparently sturdy bridge of metal pilings and cement connecting to land visible on the other side. Sometimes the body of water seemed small, like the tributary of a modest-size river, and my destination seemed near. Sometimes the waterway seemed like the passage to a more distant island, an expanse spanned by a long bridge similar to the one we crossed weekly to visit Abuela Adela across the Miami Beach Causeway. I am partway across the bridge, certain of my destination and my footing, when the ground underneath me suddenly shifts and I am standing on a precarious swinging bridge made of rope and planks. I struggle to maintain my balance, but my efforts only increase the sway of the bridge underneath my feet. I wake up as I am about to hit the water. In these adolescent dreams I never make it to the other side.

During my twenties I interpreted the dream in narrow, only partially accurate terms of separation from my controlling, overprotective immigrant family. Only many years later did I realize that the place beckoning me on the other side was Cuba, within view but unreachable. The image of an apparently secure connecting bridge which suddenly shifts beneath my feet to become the shakiest of foundations exposes the illusion of wholeness about my own life experience and highlights the fragmented sense of identity which I

85

constructed and carried with me, baggage in my Gypsy's pack, from the time I left Cuba on October 21, 1960, until my first return on January 8, 1990. For nearly thirty years I did not step across that bridge nor test its ability to carry my weight except in nostalgic dreams of a hauntingly familiar yet always elusive landscape. I can now better understand the many obstacles, both externally imposed and internalized, across the path of my return: the disavowed aspects of myself and my diasporic family legacy, which I needed to retrieve in order to find my way back to Cuba.

Weaving a Whole Life From Multiple Cultural Strands

I have traveled much further on the path of my life's work since my conflict-ridden adolescence, the work of weaving one whole life out of the scattered fragments of exile and immigration, bridging the multiple worlds of my Cuban Jewish Eastern European cultures which at one time had seemed to me utterly impossible to retrieve, connect, and make a coherent whole. I have made a professional career as a clinical developmental psychologist out of the personal and intellectual work required to understand my own life course and lived experience as responsive to events in historical, cultural, political, and intergenerational family development. As a clinical developmental psychologist, I have generated a dialectical, systemic theory of family development which redefines the individual as a collaborative creation (Shapiro, 1988, 1994). This theoretical model has evolved directly from my need to create coherence out of a shattering personal and family legacy of politically motivated traumatic immigration.

Immigration tears apart a familiar landscape and community, an intimately known language rooted in childhood learnings, a whole social fabric out of which we construct a sense of self and gain support and affirmation. The world lost to traumatic immigration becomes frozen in time, sometimes idealized, sometimes disavowed, but of necessity contained, encapsulated, while individuals and families struggle to re-establish a shared sense of coherence and stability in an unfamiliar new world. The frozen image of the lost world interferes with the freedom of genuine, full, multifaceted remembering which permits us to face, bear, and learn to live with loss and grief. Only when we can face the anguish of uprootedness can we regain access to a past that enriches our present and future, restores the forward movement in developmental time, permits the creative integration of a multicultural identity.

For many unexamined years I considered my Cuban identity an exotic appendage to my true Jewish American self. I spoke Spanish exclusively with my Hollywood and Miami family, but only rarely after leaving home in the outside world of school and friends. In my professional life as a psychologist, my bilingual, bicultural experience was a substantial resource, and I cherished the occasions when I could join a Spanish-language working group. Yet I never made this work the center of my professional life. I didn't think I remembered very much about Cuba, and was surprised when I encountered a flood of dreams and memories in my twenties, during the course of my psychoanalysis. As I turned thirty-five I began to plan my return to Cuba. This followed almost immediately upon the personal crisis precipitated by my divorce in 1988.

At that time, my patients suddenly wanted to talk to me about problems of translation. The study of family development had convinced me that our patients, like our children, struggle with us in those areas of our own lives that we have inadequately explored. Our systematic avoidance along with our greater power and their vulnerable dependence can lead to the shared creation of an impenetrable barrier across the path they need to explore. From two schizophrenic patients, exquisite attention to the deep implications of language for both capturing and failing to capture our complex lived experience, I learned that I placed a naive faith in my ability to put feelings into the words of the English language. One multiply traumatized and self-mutilating young woman whom I pseudonymously call Susie would insist on speaking only romance languages when she wanted to speak of her most inchoate feelings. She began to study Spanish, and I Italian, so we could find words in common that might begin to articulate her painful childhood history of terrifying abuse. At times when she was mute during the course of therapy, we were able to talk together on safer ground of her losses and mine in being uprooted when we were eight years old, she when her parents moved across the country, I when I left Cuba.

In reaching deeply into myself to construct the shared relational bond that might provide Susie's emotional lifeline, I began to consider, for the first time, what the use of English obscured of my life's full texture. I had not wanted to recognize the obvious, that in spite of my facility with English, it had always felt two-dimensional to me. I found myself unmoved by poetry in English, and realized how much the words lacked the resonance and multiple meanings of a childhood language. Already an avid reader in English, I began to read novels and poetry in Spanish, discovering even in my limited literary vocabulary a depth which English simply never held for me.

Exploring further, I began to reclaim my most precious possessions, the memories and desires which we immigrants are often forced to jettison by the emotional imperatives of coping with overwhelming tasks of transplantation. Many of these cherished memories and ideals still resided within my own directly lived experience, stored in the twilight world between worlds — what Bollas (1983) calls the unthought known — where we save the necessary and forbidden.

The Politics of Personal Identity

Our family's flight from Cuba to the United States was an extension of its ancestral Jewish struggle for freedom from political and religious persecution. Intimately familiar with the Bolshevik revolution which had destroyed my paternal grandfather's Jewish bourgeois family, my kin were alert to the first sounds of Marxist rhetoric. We left Havana when I was eight years old, in October of 1960, when travel between Cuba and the United States was still permitted, and it was possible to vacation in Miami — as long, of course, as one planned to return. Afraid the children might spontaneously reveal the true nature of their plans, my parents told us that we were going on our customary vacation to Miami. The secretive circumstances of our departure began a process of dislocation made terribly complicated by the discrepancy between my direct, lived experience and my parents' instructions as to what I should see, believe, and feel. My parents' words — that we were taking our usual Miami vacation — were belied by the air of barely suppressed panic and the thoroughness of our packing. One indelible image captured the contradictions of my new life and divided consciousness: my parents' open clothes closet, totally empty except for a row of stiff little-girl's petticoats, useless and decorative.

On the way to the airport, we made one stop at my Tía Consuelo's home, where all the little girls, my sisters and cousins, as well as the grown-ups, were loaded down with all the gold jewelry we could possibly wear without arousing suspicion. When we got to the Tropics hotel and my parents stated the new reality, that these were not gifts but belonged to Tia Consuelo who needed them back, I watched silently while my beautiful gold bracelet jangling with gold coins was gathered up with all the other jewelry. My 3 year-old sister Miriam, too little to comply with the shifting definitions of our lives, wailed inconsolably when her golden toys vanished along with all that was familiar and reassuring in our lives.

One month into our "vacation" at the seedy Tropics hotel, my cousin Edith corrected me during the course of play when I mentioned Castro as we always had, in reverential, heroic terms. Edith commented casually, with her customary older cousin's air of condescending superiority: "You are wrong, Ester Rebeca, Castro is bad, *es malo*, it is because of him that we have left Cuba and can never go back." That moment joined the secret collection of shattering and unexaminable contradictions which I began to hoard during my life as an exile.

I remember the air of impermanence about our leaving Cuba, and the Miami Cuban community's excitement about the Bay of Pigs invasion. Once the hope of Castro's immediate collapse was thwarted by Playa Girón, my family stopped dreaming of return and initiated the tedious, self-depriving, insecure yet ancestrally familiar work of reestablishing ourselves in a new language and a new land. At first we joined the majority of Cuban immigrants in Miami's Little Havana who tried whenever possible to minimize their dealings with their neighbors in the rest of the United States. When I entered third grade in a Miami elementary school in November of 1960, the only Cuban boy in my class had come with his family years before the revolution and seemed well acclimated to his new environment. Within six months, my classroom would become half filled with the children of Cuban immigrants.

My well-meaning teacher placed me in a classroom for the retarded part of the day to facilitate my learning English. I imagine I set a speed record for acquisition of a new language, since I was terrified of the retarded children and adolescents with whom I was placed. Did my new language ignorance make me more like these children, so limited in every way, so frighteningly mature yet peculiar? I showed off my quick mastery of English in the classroom to my teacher, in the playground to my peers. Sometimes stumbling over a sentence I reached for the unfamiliar English but retrieved a muddle of familiar Spanish and Yiddish words.

A few years later my family moved to Hollywood, Florida, in order to reestablish the hardware business they had operated in

Cuba. I remember leaving our apartment building in Miami. Carrying luggage and wearing my father's canvas hat, I was determined to be a good sport even though I was once again facing the need to reestablish myself. Abuela Berta, my father's mother, looked at me and out spilled an amused, almost exuberant laugh, as she remarked: *"se parece exactamente a Nachemie cuando salimos de Polonia"* (doesn't she look *exactly* like her father Jaime the day we left Poland). Pleased at the comparison to my father, and pleased to be a source of pleasure to Abuela Berta, at the same time I felt an almost uncanny sense of unreality at her incomprehensible laughter under our sad and difficult circumstances.

I remembered that moment for years as one of many instances of vertigo, when the members of my family treated me not as myself in the present but as a match to a template from the more significant, painful past. Only now, as I retrieve this image, do I see how much Abuela Berta was drawing on her historical connection to an earlier image of terrifying yet ultimately successful immigration, in the voyage from Poland to Cuba. She was laughing the survivor's laugh of triumph in the face of adversity. After successfully evading the demonic Hitler, wasn't our arrival in the United States remarkably easy? Out of love and loyalty, I accepted Abuela Berta's view of my experience and used it to disqualify the importance and value of my own memories of immigration.

For years, I used to turn over in my mind the legendary images from my father and his family's harrowing flight to Cuba. By borrowing money from Tía Anita and selling everything they owned, they pieced together the funds for the long train trip across the European continent and the long trip in steerage across the Atlantic ocean. They were almost prevented from leaving when my then five year-old father Nachemie accidentally stabbed himself in the eye while playing with a rusty umbrella. To this day, my father holds the panic of a five year-old at separations, so directly do they resonate with his child's conviction that if he didn't get better the family would surely leave without him. Perhaps the more terrible truth, one which I'm sure was hovering in the anxious family atmosphere and transmitted through the family air waves, was that had he not recovered quickly they all would have stayed with him and perished together.

In our family psyche, leaving and losing Cuba was unremarkable in many lifetimes of diaspora, moving like Gypsies wherever we might not be punished for being ourselves. On the rare occasions in my childhood when I mentioned to my family my profound sense of loss, of intense curiosity and deep longing for Cuba, they would inevitably reply: you don't have any idea how easy you had it as an immigrant, compared to what we endured in leaving Russia and Poland. We would have gladly come to the United States, where so many of our relatives found economic prosperity and religious freedom, except that United States immigration had already closed its doors to us. Cuba was a brief stop in our many journeys during centuries of exile, and now we have finally arrived where we belong.

I was always silenced by such admonishments. My private longings went underground. Listening to family stories of life in Poland, imagining the hardships of their lives and the constant threat of even more violent persecution that darkened the atmosphere, I could understand how my relatives might not miss cold and dark Polish shtetl life. But why didn't they miss Cuba, with its warmth and generosity and vitality? There, our difference as Jews was only the smallest part of a patchwork of New World cultures. I struggled inwardly with the conflict between my secret, forbidden attachment to Cuba and my family and ancestral loyalties: after all, where do we belong as Jews if not in Eretz Yisrael, the land of Israel?

I found the Jewish people's fight for a homeland profoundly moving, and was deeply drawn to images of kibbutz life with its communal values and rejection of materialism. But that, too, was a source of confusion, since our families had chosen Cuba at a time when Palestine was receiving European Jewish immigrants. When her own religiously observant mother had refused to immigrate anywhere but Palestine, Abuela Berta had fought her mother for the right to determine her own fate and that of her family, choosing the economically hospitable if heathen and unfamiliar Cuba. Why had we never exercised the now well-established freedom, mentioned at least once a year in our Passover service, next year in Jerusalem?

As a young person I had accepted the Miami Cuban community's official political line, incorporating it into my own passionately held vision of emancipation from my family: I would never choose to live in a country which interfered with my precious freedom to speak my mind. Unspoken though not forgotten were my early childhood memories of hearing my family, like many others, speak of Fidel Castro as a hero who would restore Cuba's proud heritage as a nation committed to social justice. At times in my adolescence I felt grateful that our family had left Cuba, as I feared their control over my life would have been more total. I went back only in my dreams, in which my longings for Cuba were satisfied, like my equally forbidden sexual curiosities, in the disguised form which would permit me access without transgressing my family's rules. In my line of work as a psychologist, we call my experience "dissociated," that is, known at one level but hidden from view at another because to weave back together the once fragmented connections is to feel fully the pain of loss.

Finding What Had Been Lost In Plain View

In 1990, in the teeth of my family's fervent objections, I went back to Cuba after twenty-nine years of absence, twenty-nine years of loss and negation of loss. My first trip to Cuba only began a slow and profoundly meaningful process of weaving one whole life out of the fractured fragments of immigration. It helped, in a surprising way, that Cuba of the 1990s is so recognizably like the Cuba of the early 1960s, complete with the dinosaur American cars that have been lovingly tended by people whom necessity has made the world's most inventive auto mechanics. Unlike my experience of Miami, where tall buildings block the landscape of my childhood and obscure my retrieval of memory, the Cuba of my return in many ways matched the Cuba of my childhood memories and enduring dreams. I found the densely green undulating landscape dotted with improbably tall palms, the labyrinth of small shops jammed together in fanciful colonial buildings, the constant currents of talk and people, the pungent perfumes permeating the air, part seawater, part fragrant flowers and foliage, part moist musty sweat and humidity that never quite dry out.

To my surprise, I also found the family I had always yearned for. I had thought I had no family at all in Cuba, as most of the Cuban Jewish community including a few of my holdout great aunts and uncles had long ago left to grow old alongside their children. I had been told that our entire family left Cuba as soon as they possibly could, building one more assertion in the unified family story that no reasonable person could find anything worth having in Castro's Cuba. Shortly before my planned trip I heard Pablo Armando Fernández, a Cuban writer and cultural ambassador, speak at a Boston College conference of Cuba's enormous loss in losing the children of my generation to immigration and mutual political enmity. Having braced myself for the contempt I expected most Cubans to have toward the "gusanos" like myself and my family, I felt enormous relief at being accepted into a community which could tolerate the complexities and contradictions of our shared history. I began to tell him how grateful I was that he appreciated our shared loss as a Cuban people, that he welcomed my return instead of reprimanding me for so long postponing it. Then I broke down weeping. Knowing I could go back and be welcomed rather than hated was essential in order to tolerate the grief which would surely accompany retrieval of my lost memories, with full realization of my enormous losses.

As I waited in Miami for the visa which seemed might never come, my father's cousin's wife, Tía Anita's daughter-in-law Sofia Rozenswaig Garmizo whispered to me, furtively (as if the thought police might be listening), "Let me give you the address in Habana of my cousin Xiomara Rozenswaig Yelin. Just don't tell your father I told you about her. She's a communist." I will be eternally grateful to Sofie for defying the family injunction to keep Xiomara a secret. Sofia had left Cuba in 1961, at the age of twenty-three a young mother of three little children, without saying goodbye to her cousin Xiomara, as close as a sister to her, because she was certain that Xiomara would turn her in to the communists for treason.

Although my widowed cousin Xiomara and her three children Karen, Aaron, and Yoanna are not blood relatives, they would have been as integral a part of our family in Miami as the other Rosenzwaig relatives. I was shocked to find that when I knocked unexpectedly on their door, my socialist cousin Aaron Yelin greeted me looking just like my Hollywood cousins Gustavo and Jaime Garmizo. He and his family were equally shocked that there was actually a Miami cousin who appreciated their political commitments, respected their personal sacrifices to remain in Cuba, and yearned as much as they did for bonds of kinship which would bridge our political differences.

The Yelins are cultured, educated, politically committed without being at all doctrinaire. Meeting them immediately punctured one of the polarizing myths perpetuated by the Miami Cuban community to maintain ideological distance, perpetuated by my family to make their own choices seem like the only viable alternatives for living a moral life. Sitting in their apartment near my old neighborhood in El Vedado, I felt at home with family in ways I had known only with my sisters, who moved from Miami to Boston with me, in search of an education and some freedom of movement. Xiomara told me of her now seventy-five year-old mother's singleminded commitment to communism, which had made her a notorious figure in the Eastern European Cuban community with their fanatical devotion to financial security.

Like many other diaspora Jews, my family stopped their Jewish observance when they left the shtetl for Cuba, retaining as central values the closest devotion to family togetherness (with remarkably little real intimacy, by my standards) and the strongest commitment to accumulating and self-indulgently spending lavish sums of money. Unlike the at least ostensibly stated ancestral values of Jewish life, which emphasize study and charity, my family considered an education a dangerous invitation to rebellion — how could I be a loyal daughter if I permitted myself to entertain thoughts which my parents had never considered and therefore were not in a position to evaluate for me? Look where all my independence had gotten me; I was flirting dangerously with communism. From my viewpoint, plagued as my parents were by the anxieties and insecurities of their immigrant experiences, fearful of travel, hostile to my love of reading and study, the small world which they considered safe and familiar seemed like prison to me.

Suddenly, in Xiomara Yelin's living room, I experienced the extraordinary, longed-for and forbidden pleasure of being a smart, independent-minded woman who could see herself reflected and appreciated, confirmed by enduring ties of kinship, reconnected to an ancestral community. While the Boston community where I have made my home represents my most inclusive compromise embracing Rybishevish, La Habana, and Miami, my choices had always been shadowed by my loss of homeland and compounded by my family's unyielding demands for loyalty. You are either with us, or you are not one of us. Out of their own vulnerabilities, they barred me from direct access even to my own traditions, as both a Cuban and a Jew who wished to live a socially committed life.

While visiting in Varadero with my cousin Karen Yelin, as we tried to cram a lost lifetime of shared activities and feelings into our few remaining hours, I broke my ankle while running for a bus. I left Cuba with my ankle in a cast, and had to spend three weeks in my parents' home in Hollywood, recovering from surgery and letting my fractured bones heal. The surgical repair was successful, and became a metaphor for my psychic healing, the knitting together of severed ties. My long, enforced stay at home made it possible and necessary to review my experience with my parents and their generation (my cousins were distinctly uninterested). While my father continued, resentful and embattled, to insist that I was betraying the family with my communist sympathies, my mother, Tía Elsa, and Sofia pored over the photographs of our old neighborhoods in El Vedado, the intimately known streets of old colonial Habana, surprised and delighted to see the preservation of their lost, once much-loved world.

When I was first preparing to leave, my mother insisted that she remembered almost nothing about Cuba. After my return, she too reviewed the photographs with the bittersweet pleasure of recovery and loss, acknowledging that it made her much too sad to think about Cuba. My photographs brought forward undeniable evidence of the reality of Cuba, which my family had lost to ideological enemies and to unexamined grief, sorrows now found again through my contrary actions. No wonder they had put all their collective weight behind the barriers to my return, no wonder it had taken me so much of my adult life to find the courage to return, to make both the Cuba of my memory and of a current complicated reality a part of my own life story.

REFERENCES

Bollas, Christopher, *The Shadow of the Object.* New York: Columbia University Press, 1987.

Shapiro, Ester R. *Grief as a Family Process: A Systemic Developmental Perspective.* New York: Guilford, 1994.

Shapiro, Ester R. "Individual change and family development: individuation as a family process." In Falicov, C. (Ed.), *Family Transitions.* New York: Guilford, 1988.

VICTOR FOWLER CALZADA

NOTHING LOST WILL COME BACK
WITH THE RAIN

Nothing lost will come back with the rain.
The voices, the gestures of those
whom we longed for
and that now are a pause in our breathing.

The eye sees the burn marks on the edges of tables,
on clothes, the burn marks on the flesh.
The eye looks for the water that will cleanse
but it won't let us return.
What is absent has to be absent to be.
Neither things nor sounds come back
nor events that once had meaning
or that unravelled on their own.

There is only one way to understand the rainfall,
once it passes tree trunks rot away.

Maybe, while we stare at the enormous wall
of water crashing down on us, what is lost moves on,
no longer recognizable:
memory has redrawn it as a pastoral.

The hand that knotted up my hair,
the mouth I once touched.
Maybe in front of our eyes
everything will repeat itself in broken forms
like in a witch's Sabbath.

What is there behind a witch's Sabbath of rain
that had no beginning?

Burn marks: on the edges of tables,
on our old clothes, under our eyes.

I see it rain.
To make comparisons with water
is dangerous in this country where the rain
cannot recall how long ago it began.

Translated by Ruth Behar

"Un puente entre mi cielo y estrella" (A bridge between my sky and star).
Painting by Nereida García Ferraz, 1984. Oil on paper.

REPAIRING THINGS

Before I went back to Cuba, I had little idea of what there was in the way of art, architecture and museum collections, the things that form the basis of my work in the United States. For me, Cuba was the place we left when I was a child. It was a place of sadness, of loss, a place once beautiful and full of promise that was now in a rubble of disrepair. As an art conservator my job is to repair things. Yet Cuba was my parents' domain, part of a distant past they did not long for anymore. In the mid-eighties, I decided that I had to visit Cuba, to see the country for myself, to form an opinion of it based on my own observations and not the painful memories of my family. My profession gave me the entry ticket. In 1992 I was invited to a conference on the preservation of cultural patrimony sponsored by Cuba's national conservation center, known as the Centro Nacional de Conservación, Restauración, y Museología (CENCREM).

On the day I arrived, I took a taxi to Vedado, the stylish district in Havana where I was born. I wanted to walk down the streets my parents had loved, to photograph the apartment building my grandparents had owned. The taxi from Miramar went along the Malecón, the famous boulevard that arcs along the northern coast, separating Havana from the ocean. Everyone who left Cuba remembers it with longing. Over the years I had seen countless pictures of the Malecón in the still summer heat, in winter storms when the ocean waves come spraying over the sea wall. It looked dilapidated now and there were barely any cars due to the current shortage of petroleum. The taxi dropped me off at the Hotel Riviera; once a glittering resort, it is now just another late fifties structure that has seen better days. I walked the rest of the way, not wishing to seem too conspicuous. It was bright and windless and there were many people on this stretch of the Malecón—lovers on the sea wall, swimmers beyond. Music blared from loudspeakers in a plaza across from the Riviera hotel. The sound was tinny, not pleasing to the ear. Nor were my surroundings pleasing to the eye. I had expected to see a general state of disrepair, but the extent of it was dismal—columns were cracking, paint peeling, walls crumbling. Focusing on the greying gardens and rusty iron gates, I missed seeing that the buildings were spectacular—Spanish architecture next to Deco and fifties modern. I pined for what this once was, for bright clean buildings along broad leafy avenues, the constant sound of the sea in the background. I saw things through my parents' eyes, not those of an art conservator. I walked around for a few minutes, conspicuous with my camera, acting like yet another exile disappointed by the rubble of loss.

The conference began the following evening, at a cocktail reception at the Convento de Santa Clara in Old Havana, a former seventeenth-century convent that now houses the national conservation center. Earlier in the day, I joined a couple of Venezuelan architects on a walk through the cobbled streets of the historic center, an area designated by UNESCO as a monument belonging to the world's patrimony because of its architectural and historic significance. Cuba has two of these world patrimonies: Old Havana and Trinidad, a resplendent eighteenth and nineteenth century city, a jewel on the Caribbean coast. I didn't know that then. I'd worked for fifteen years as a specialist in preservation of sculpture and monuments, but my knowledge of art history ended on this side of the Malecón. The only thing I knew about Old Havana was that my mother grew up on one of its streets, not far from the Convento. She had always described this area as poor and rundown, calamitous, some place best forgotten. Her nostalgia was reserved for the more upscale neighborhood I had visited the day before, a place that would now surely look even more rundown to her than it had to me.

Two years later, now that I am so closely involved with the Cuban conservation community, it seems odd that at the time I had no idea of what there was to preserve. I didn't know about the narrow cobbled streets of Old Havana, the rows of ancient stucco buildings, the iron grillwork of the eighteenth-century balconies. I didn't know that my mother grew up almost in view of a grand Baroque cathedral, a structure so perfectly proportioned that the architects I walked with that first day stood in front of it for a full half hour, marveling over its massive, unfinished facade. My head buzzed with a sudden recognition of a place that held something for me beyond memory. I turned wide circles in the Baroque plaza so I could absorb it all at once, like a panoramic photograph—broad buildings of coral and limestone, stained glass as bright as the sky, the narrow noisy streets that fanned out from the Cathedral Plaza in all directions, poor and rundown, to be sure, but laden with historic treasures that link us all, the people who still live there and those who are dedicated to their preservation, the architects, conservators and historians on both sides of the ocean.

*   *   *

On my second visit to Cuba I went to see Trinidad. For architects, conservators and history students all roads eventually lead to Trinidad. It is a special place, notable for its exquisite location between the Escambray mountains and the sea, for its historic importance as the Caribbean center of sugar production in the eighteenth and nineteenth centuries, for the magnificence of its period architecture, and most important, at least to me, because it is a place where preservation of the past links everyone.

The vast conservation activity in Trinidad is coordinated by the department of restoration, which is located in the nineteenth-century mansion that once belonged to Don Mariano de Borrell, one of Trinidad's most illustrious former citizens and one of its most infamous sugar barons. I climbed the steep hill to the office on a blazing August day in order to meet the head of the preservation department, Roberto Lopez Bastida, an architect and scholar of Trinidad. Nearly everyone in Trinidad knows Roberto and everyone calls him Macholo. He has lived there his entire life. A man of my generation, he is articulate, kinetic, with dark hair and a bristly moustache, passionate on many subjects, particularly the preservation of Trinidad. On my first trip we walked for hours through the hot city, along ancient cobbled streets lined with tile-roofed buildings, through museums with frescoed walls and collections that spanned hundreds of years, the Spanish and African artifacts that tell the story of Trinidad and the valley of sugarcane fields that gave rise to it. As we walked, he pointed out the sites—churches, mansions, monuments, all the while peppering me with technical questions to problems they had. "How could we get these fungal stains out of this marble sculpture? What can be used to get rid of termites in the church archives?" These were not difficult issues from a conservation standpoint. But I had already seen that obtaining the materials would be a problem. At the Museo Romántico, a nineteenth-century mansion that houses a decorative arts museum, I had noticed a honeycomb drying out in the courtyard. There was a bee infestation in one of the galleries that was being allowed to flourish so the hives could be harvested to make beeswax, not an ideal material for conservation, but it was all they had.

As we toured, people stopped us constantly to ask him questions. "Oye, Macholo, don't forget that my roof is leaking, my front door won't close properly, what can I do to fix the plumbing?" I wondered why everyone was coming to him with their domestic repair problems. "It's because almost every house is historic," he answered. "Every major repair has to be approved and often carried out by our department." This conservation department is responsible for museum collections, monuments, architecture, and everyone's leaky pipes.

At the end of my first day in Trinidad, we climbed the tower of a bright yellow mansion that had once belonged to the Canteros, another family of sugar planters. The rich families of Trinidad used to compete with each other in the construction of their houses — they vied for the tallest towers, most ornate frescoes, grandest houses. The Palacio de Cantero, which now houses the city's history museum, affords one of the best views of the city, the blue green hills that surround it, the sparkling Caribbean on the other side. Almost without thinking, my guide continued to point out the sites of the region he knows by heart, the place he says he could never leave no matter how difficult life becomes. "That river in the near distance," he said, "That's the one Cortés used when he left Trinidad to conquer Mexico. And that one, further out, that's where the sand for our mortar comes from." Earlier, in the courtyard of a ruined house, he had shown me the raw materials used for making restoration mortar, great pits of aggregate and lime. The aggregate is a coarse mix of beach sand and river stones collected from a spot along the river. It is the same material that was used by the builders of Trinidad. As Macholo said to me, "At least we don't have to worry about a shortage of that material." Although he laughed, I could tell he was worried about his city, his country in general. Yet I thought about how amazing it must be to live in a place where you are so closely tied to your own history. That sense of place is something I have lacked in all the years I have traveled around the world, gaining my technical knowledge of conservation. It was something my family forgot to pack when they left, something I didn't know I had lost until I found it in Old Havana, Vedado, and Trinidad.

IRAIDA H. LÓPEZ

"... AND THERE IS ONLY MY IMAGINATION WHERE OUR HISTORY SHOULD BE": AN INTERVIEW WITH CRISTINA GARCIA

Cristina Garcia was a finalist for the 1992 National Book Award for *Dreaming in Cuban*. Michiko Kakutani described it in *The New York Times* as a "completely original novel. It announces the debut of a writer, blessed with a poet's ear for language. . . ." Thulani Davis called it "a jewel of a first novel" and welcomed her work as "the latest sign that American literature has its own hybrid offspring of the Latin American school."

The novel focuses on the lives of three generations of Cuban women. The matriarch of the family, Celia del Pino, fully supports the revolution. For twenty-five years she has been writing a monthly letter to the Spanish lover of her youth. Celia and her husband, a Cuban businessman, have three children, Lourdes, Felicia and Javier. The exiled Lourdes, a fervent anti-communist and the owner of the Yankee Doodle Bakery, communicates with her dead father in Brooklyn and makes her punk daughter's life miserable. Felicia, a "Santera," stays behind in Havana, mad and unhappy. Javier leaves for Czechoslovakia but returns to the island after his wife and daughter abandon him. After many years of separation and yearning, Lourdes' daughter, Pilar, decides to visit her grandmother Celia, with whom she has always had a special relationship. At her father's urging, Lourdes returns to Cuba with Pilar.

Cristina Garcia was born in Havana in 1958 and raised in New York. She lives in Los Angeles with her husband, Scott Brown, and her baby girl, Pilar. After her first trip to Cuba in 1984, Cristina tried to return to the island but was unable to get a visa.

This interview was conducted in the Winter of 1993.

. . . "But sooner or later I'd have to return to New York. I know now it's where I belong — not instead of here, but more than here . . ."
Dreaming in Cuban, Cristina Garcia

LÓPEZ: Clearly and understandably, Latina/o writers in the U.S. continue to raise questions of ethnic identity in their writing. You share this concern with Latina/o writers, Cuban-Americans included. How important is it for you as a writer, this issue of ethnic awareness?

GARCIA: It is very important to me even though I didn't grow up as part of any Latin or Cuban community. For me, being Cuban was very much a family affair. My life was bifurcated in that sense. At home I felt very Cuban and that identity was very much instilled in me. Culturally and temperamentally and in every way I felt very Cuban. This element was a very strong part of my identity.

On the other hand, this Cuban identity wasn't that relevant as I moved through the rest of my life. It was a schizophrenic situation without the negativity that this implies. I grew up with Irish, Italian, and Jewish kids. My family used to live in a Jewish neighborhood in Queens and I took a bus to Catholic school. Then we moved to a mixed neighborhood in Brooklyn Heights. I went to high school in Manhattan and all my classmates were Irish and Italian. I knew virtually no other Cubans except for cousins, and a couple of Puerto Ricans.

LÓPEZ: Given the lack of a Cuban social context, how were you able to nurture and maintain your well-defined Cuban identity?

GARCIA: I have to give full credit to my mother. She always insisted that my brother, my sister, and myself speak Spanish at home and instilled in us a sense of tremendous pride. I didn't grow up sensing that I was inferior or that Spanish wasn't as good as English. My mother was very adamant about language and understood how language and culture go hand in hand. She made a very strong effort to make sure we knew we were Cuban.

My father not so much. He was away a lot of the time working. And he is not technically Cuban. My father was born in Central America of a Spanish father and a Guatemalan mother who is half Indian. He was raised in Cuba but was sent to boarding schools in Canada, so he grew up speaking French and English. He had a more worldly upbringing whereas my mother is Cuban, Cuban, Cuban . . . all the way! Her roots go very deep.

My parents had retail businesses when I was growing up. Sometimes you'd get people coming into the store and making some kind of ethnic remark or slur, like: "Go back to your country!" My mother always fought them to the nail: "You don't have to shop here if you don't want. This is my country too." She'd never let anybody push her around. I grew up with that attitude.

I always thought of myself as Cuban.

LÓPEZ: Did you ever go back to Cuba?

GARCIA: I went back to Cuba with my sister in March of 1984 for two weeks and I visited all of my mother's family there. I spent my time between Havana and Guanabo, where my aunt lived. She had a little house on the beach which I had in mind when I was writing *Dreaming in Cuban*. My mother spent some of her childhood in that house. It was the family's summer house.

LÓPEZ: How did your family react?

GARCIA: They were immediately welcoming and embracing. Right away they accepted me and observed everything I did and made fun of me. There was no sense of formality, no barriers whatsoever. For the first two or three days everyone was very curious about me, my mother, everything from the mundane to the ridiculous. And then I began to hear their stories. They would come out slowly one by one; and a lot from my grandmother in particular.

It was during this trip that I got a larger sociopolitical context for being Cuban. For me, Cuba had been a black and white situation up to that point. Half of my family came here, half stayed there, and most of them didn't speak to each other for twenty years. There was very little shading, very little room for gray or for interpretation. Though I never bought that, it wasn't something that I worried about every day; it was something *de familia*. I didn't think about it in much larger terms . . . until I went back and met the other side of the family. I started synthesizing things more for myself and ingested them and they became part of me, on a deeply emotional level.

LÓPEZ: What happened after that?

GARCIA: About two years after that trip, I was sent by *Time* magazine to be the Miami Bureau Chief covering Latin America and the Caribbean. I went to Miami and met the Cuban community for the first time in my life. It was a shock, it really was. I felt extremely alienated. I was given a tremendously hard time by my peers and family. They frequently called me a communist and attached all kinds of ridiculous labels to me just because I was a registered Democrat.

Things can get pretty extreme. Here I was feeling comfortable being Cuban all along, taking it for granted, and suddenly I became a black sheep. I had never had to confront that intolerance outside of my immediate family, which is very conservative. I used to think: "They're just my parents. . . . They're crazy." When you multiply that by a million, it's overwhelming. I feel that I'm not a welcome daughter in the community. I feel part of it and yet somewhat rejected. It's very hard to reconcile.

LÓPEZ: Do you find it difficult to speak out in the community?

GARCIA: Yes, although I think that the people who purport to speak for the large community are not speaking for as many people as they think. However, they tend to dominate the airwaves and the news and they have a stranglehold on the debate about Cuba. A lot of people and opinions are muted and shouted down. I also think there is a generational difference. My generation and probably even younger Cubans are more apolitical than their parents and grandparents. But right now, the Cuban community is not a tolerant exile community. That's not healthy for any community.

LÓPEZ: When you think about Cuba these days, what comes to your mind?

GARCIA: I think of it as an island in transition right now. What it will transit to, I really don't know. But it seems like Cuba needs to be moving somewhere else. I hope it won't go the way of the Cuban-American National Foundation, which has set itself up as a leadership in exile and expects to fill what it perceives will be a vacuum after Castro goes. I hope that the changes will come from within. I'm also very concerned about the U. S. policy of continuing to isolate Cuba in a world where everybody else has been accepted and dealt with. Cuba continues to be ostracized in a way that makes no political or economic sense. Finally, I have a tremendous empathy for the hardships that the Cubans are undergoing now in the wake of what's happened in Eastern Europe.

LÓPEZ: Are you aware of the fact that *Dreaming in Cuban* is being read and liked in Cuba? Generally speaking, intellectuals in the island are interested in the artistic production of Cuban Americans and try to follow it closely.

GARCIA: That's nice. I didn't know that other people besides my grandmother had read it in Cuba. The Spanish translation, which will come out next spring, will make it more accessible.

LÓPEZ: Given the Spanish regional variants, how are you handling the translation?

GARCIA: The person who's translating the novel for the Spanish editors is a Puerto Rican from New York. I feel more comfortable with that than having a madrileño translating it.

LÓPEZ: *Dreaming in Cuban* deals with separation, antagonism, misunderstanding, betrayal, lack of communication, intolerance, obsession. . . . Can the microcosm of the del Pino family serve as a symbol of the discord of the Cuban people on both sides of the Straits?

GARCIA: I didn't set out with that in mind. My aim when I started writing the novel was to stay very close to the characters themselves. I wasn't trying to make any of the women emblematic of something larger than themselves. I tried to stay very close to their lives, their idiosyncrasies, their individual obsessions. It so happens that they are diametrically opposed politically.

If it were somebody else's book and I happened to be reading it, I probably could interpret it in that fashion and see them as symbols. But when I was writing, I was thinking very specifically about Felicia and her madness, her obsession with Santería and her children; I was thinking about Lourdes and what she had gone through and her struggle to make a success for herself in America . . . I tried to inhabit each of the women as much as I could and let them do the work, lead the way.

LÓPEZ: There's obviously more to your novel than a sociopolitical symbol for Cuba's most recent history. For one thing, the novel goes back to 1934. Yet, there are comments that make their way into the novel which lead the reader to attach a political interpretation to it.

GARCIA: There is a context for these women. I wanted to examine very closely the personal cost of what happened in Cuba after 1959. And I wanted to very specifically examine how women have responded and adapted to what happened to their families after 1959. I also was very interested in examining the emotional and political alliances that form within families. There is a larger backdrop to it all, but in the writing itself I just stayed very close to the women. There wasn't any attempt to have everyone pick a point of view on the revolution.

LÓPEZ: The need to remember and record events is a thread that runs through the novel and is related to your feminist concerns. In a way, Celia's letters and Pilar's diary fulfill this need. At one point, we find Pilar asking herself: "Who chooses what we should know or what's important?" The writing, then, becomes a way of salvaging what's meaningful to these women: their history, their identity. . . . Do you agree with this interpretation?

GARCIA: Absolutely. Traditional history, the way it has been written, interpreted and recorded, obviates women and the evolution of home, family and society, and basically becomes a recording of battles and wars and dubious accomplishments of men. You learn where politics really lie at home. That's what I was trying to explore on some level in *Dreaming in Cuban*. I was trying to excavate new turf, to look at the costs to individuals, families, and relationships among women of public events such as a revolution.

LÓPEZ: Is this why you decided to focus on women?

GARCIA: In retrospect, I think so. When I tried to give shape to the novel, which was the more analytical part of writing, I think I definitely had that in mind.

LÓPEZ: How autobiographical is your novel?

GARCIA: Emotionally, it's very autobiographical. The details are not. I was not like Pilar at all growing up. I was very much a dutiful daughter. I never talked back to my mother . . . so Pilar is a kind of alter ego for me. In retrospect, it would have been fun to be the punk, extremist artist that Pilar is. A lot of the seeds for the characters were based on people I know, but in the writing they became quite transformed and led me down very unexpected paths.

LÓPEZ: What is the role of Santería in the novel? Is it in the book because of its relevance in Cuban culture?

GARCIA: Felicia led me to it. Suddenly she started going to these Santería meetings with her friend Herminia. I knew very little about it, just a few odds and ends from an aunt who grew up in the countryside. My family was Catholic and thought that Santería was mumbo-jumbo African rites. They were very disdainful of it. So I had to send away for books on Santería to Miami, and read as much as I could. Once I became exposed to it, I was completely fascinated. It's part of our cultural landscape and, as Pilar says at one point, it makes a lot more sense than more abstract forms of worship.

LÓPEZ: Probably something similar happened to you with the music; with salsa, Celia Cruz, Beny Moré. . . .

GARCIA: I didn't grow up with much of that either. My family used to listen to Perry Como. It wasn't until the mid-'80s, when I had a Puerto Rican boyfriend, that I learned how to dance. I first heard Beny Moré from my boyfriend's vast collection of salsa and Latin music.

LÓPEZ: You were saying that Felicia had led you to Santería. How do you explain the relationship that develops between you and your characters?

GARCIA: Celia was the one that hit me with the most force initially. She is the backbone and the strength of the novel. She is its spiritual guide. Slowly and gently, she introduced me to Felicia and facets of Lourdes and Pilar that I didn't understand. My relationship developed at first by being guided spiritually by Celia and then as I got to know the other characters better, they revealed themselves to me layer by layer. And often I would be sent scurrying to find out about one thing or another. For example, for Pilar I had to find out quite a bit about punk music because that was not part of my upbringing.

Dreaming in Cuban didn't come in one big flash; the book was done in the rewriting. The initial inspiration got everything down, but it was like an archaeological dig, each time I went a little deeper and found something new that would somehow change everything that I had previously found, and then things couldn't be written quite the same way again. Even things I said had to be said in a different way. There are parts of the book that I wrote over a thousand times.

So it was a process of discovery. Sometimes it would happen all of a sudden, like when you're having a conversation with somebody and they reveal something to you that is utterly devastating and you can't believe it and it changes the way you look at them forever. This happened to me. I remember distinctly the day Lourdes got raped, and as I was writing how the events were leading up to the rape and then the inevitability of it, the horror of it, and how I never saw Lourdes the same way after this incident. That was quite a shock. So things like that would happen, small things and big things. I didn't know that Felicia was going to go into this long amnesia. It just sort of happened. That came gradually. But the idea of pushing her third husband off the rollercoaster came very suddenly. And I was surprised: "Oh, my God. This is what she is capable of."

LÓPEZ: Celia's letters are the most lyrical parts of the novel. How did you arrive at the decision to include letters as a literary form in the novel?

GARCIA: I didn't quite know how to work so much history into the novel. I tried to judiciously fit it in, but the novel bulged with the weight of Celia's history. It was a "python swallowing the elephant" situation. The first short letter she wrote to her lover came as part of the narrative and I guess it just occurred to me: "Why not do more of these letters?" I had no idea what shape they would take or how many I would do. The letters started coming out naturally, not following any kind of order. It was later that I organized them.

They came in bits and pieces, like poetic fragments. They were more language-driven than story-driven. The letters were the least edited part of the book. The other parts were rewritten maybe hundreds of times. But the letters came out almost intact. They came from another well entirely.

LÓPEZ: Your ability to use poetic language doesn't come from your training as a journalist.

GARCIA: Nor from political science! I was as surprised as anybody! I didn't read much poetry growing up and it wasn't until shortly before I started writing the novel that I began to read poetry intensely. Poetry caught me off guard, and I became enthralled with language itself. At the same time, I was always interested in foreign languages and had studied French, German, Italian, a year of Russian, and a little Portuguese. The musicality, the expressions, the idiosyncrasies of language gave me sheer pleasure.

LÓPEZ: The 1990 Pulitzer Prize for *The Mambo Kings Play Songs of Love* by Oscar Hijuelos helped bring about a "mini-boom" of Latino literature in the U.S. More recently, *How the Garcia Girls Lost their Accents*, by the Dominican Julia Alvarez, and your own *Dreaming in Cuban* have had strong reviews. How do you account for the fact that these works have been so well received by the mainstream?

GARCIA: I would add another person to that list, Sandra Cisneros. Her short story collections have also been very well received.

There are probably a number of factors at work. I think that the more educated and the more comfortable Latino writers feel writing in English, the better literature we are going to get. Immigrants have to make their way into the U.S. Eventually, English becomes the first language in terms of social interaction, of education. Those of us who kind of straddle both cultures are in a unique position to tell our stories, to tell our family stories. We're still very close to the immigration, we're in the wake of that immigration, and yet we weren't as directly affected by it as our parents and grandparents were. So we are truly bilingual, truly bicultural, in a way the previous generations were not.

All of us are in a unique situation. Julia Alvarez came when she was about ten years old. So Julia had the experience of immigration and yet she writes in English and was educated in American schools. Oscar is second-generation Cuban; he was born and raised in the U.S. I came when I was two-and-a-half.

I think it's a matter of time before Latino writers are recognized. Even though our literature is now called "minority" writing, population studies show that we're really becoming the mainstream, and the literature of the future will be what has traditionally been called "the margins." We're part of American literature, and what's keeping it vibrant and dynamic these days.

LÓPEZ: So you think that these novels will eventually make their way into English literature departments at universities and will no longer be confined to ethnic studies departments?

GARCIA: I think so. This is what happened to Jewish writers in the past. This will be what American literature is about; it will not be defined by a white male sensibility. It's inevitable.

LÓPEZ: What you're saying seems to imply that Latinos will integrate into the mainstream culture, following the theory of the melting pot. Yet, Chicanos and Nuyoricans have been around for a while, and not only have they resisted assimilation but many Chicano and Puerto Rican writers define their art and literature as a form of cultural resistance and protest. How do you view this process?

GARCIA: What I mean is not that we'll become part of the melting pot nor that our identity and culture will become diluted, but that the mainstream itself will be redefined to include us. We'll.be part of the mainstream not by becoming more like "them" and less like "us," but by what it means to be an American in the twenty-first century. This is changing and its definition will be necessarily broader and more inclusive. I don't think this means leaving our culture in the dust.

LÓPEZ: And the more recent immigration waves have been very different.

GARCIA: Absolutely, since the '60s. It's a whole different influx of people and cultures from Asia and Latin America.

LÓPEZ: Now that we're referring to other minorities, let's focus for a moment on the incident with the Puerto Rican woman, the Navarro woman, in the novel. The reader meets her when she tries to steal some money from Lourdes at the bakery and is fired. Later on, we learn that her son is involved in drugs. Isn't this portrayal reinforcing the stereotype of the Puerto Rican people in certain discourses?

GARCIA: I had Lourdes very much in mind. In the Cuban community there is quite a bit of racism. Moreover, in some sectors of the community there is a superiority complex. Growing up I definitely sensed that the Cubans felt they were better than the Puerto Ricans and the Dominicans. I was thinking very close to Lourdes, how she, as part of her generation and her experience, would view it. Obviously, that's not how I see it. I abhor racism in all its forms. In no way does this incident reflect my own point of view. I thought about that very carefully.

LÓPEZ: It's pretty clear that García Márquez has had some influence on your perspective and sensibility as a writer. What other authors have had an influence on your work?

GARCIA: I had three books that always stayed on my desk while I was writing *Dreaming in Cuban* and one of them was *One Hundred Years of Solitude*. The second was Toni Morrison's *Song of Solomon*. The third was a Wallace Stevens selection of poems. That's quite a mix. Oddly enough, they all contributed the same thing: a sense of limitlessness with language and imagination.

LÓPEZ: In *Song of Solomon* there is an incestuous relationship between one of the characters and her father, just as there is more than one of this kind of relationship alluded to in your novel. Is this one extreme way of exploring the manner in which alliances form within a family?

GARCIA: I'm certainly interested in the subject. There is quite a bit of ambiguity in terms of Felicia and her son.

LÓPEZ: And even in the relationship between Lourdes and her father. . . .

GARCIA: That element is definitely there, although I meant to keep it very ambiguous. I'm not sure myself what happened with Felicia and her son, if anything. It was definitely not your typical mother-son relationship, nor was Lourdes' with her father. I think I was trying to explore the different levels of closeness and identification between a parent and child. Also, the kind of domination a parent can have over a child. At the time I was just writing, but now I'm thinking of it in terms of themes of domination and power within the family. That would be the ultimate domination, an awful domination.

LÓPEZ: What Latin American and Caribbean authors have you read in addition to García Márquez?

GARCIA: I've read all the Latin American writers and loved them. But they were the writers I came to last, in my twenties, after I had read a lot of European writers, a lot of Russian writers, and a lot of American writers. For some reason, that was the way I was educated. It wasn't until I came of age in my twenties that I really discovered the Latin American writers and then in translation, interestingly enough, not in Spanish. But they were a revelation when I came across them. It was a literature that I identified with very heavily and continue to enjoy today.

LÓPEZ: What about Cuban writers?

GARCIA: They came later: Carpentier, Lezama Lima, Cabrera Infante. . . . I read them in my late twenties. I enjoyed them, but I wouldn't say they were that much of an influence. My reading of them was more sporadic than other Latin writers like García Márquez, Vargas Llosa, Jorge Amado (I've read everything of his), and Borges (my favorite!). Part of it had to do with the way women were portrayed by the Cuban writers. It was hard to find a place where I could get comfortable in some of these books, much as I loved the language and the scope of the novels. For instance, *Infante's Inferno* really turned me off after a while; I found it so overwhelmingly male. I didn't get that impression from other Latin writers.

LÓPEZ: Cristina, tell us about your education and training.

GARCIA: I went to Barnard College in New York and majored in Political Science, with a concentration on International Politics. I studied French, German, and Italian. I hoped to get into the Foreign Service. For my graduate studies, I went to the School of Advanced International Studies at Johns Hopkins University, where I got a Masters degree in International Relations with an emphasis on European Politics and Economics and Latin American Politics and Economics. I graduated from Barnard in 1979 and from Johns Hopkins two years later. As part of my studies at Johns Hopkins I spent a year in Italy.

Most of the people I went to graduate school with went into International Banking or the Foreign Service. With a Republican administration in Washington, work at an international agency didn't appeal to me. What I got was a part-time job as a "copy-girl" at *The New York Times* while I was in graduate school. The atmosphere appealed to me, but even then journalism wasn't necessarily the career for myself. I was earning some money for school.

My first real job was at Procter & Gamble in West Germany as a marketing person, but I only lasted about three months. I hated it. After I came back, through some connections I had made working at *The New York Times* I got a very entry-level reporter position at a newspaper in Knoxville, Tennessee, called *The Knoxville Journal*. That was after a brief stint at *The Boston Globe* as an intern. I was there for a while and after that I went to United Press International in Atlanta. In 1983, I got a reporter-researcher job at *Time* magazine in New York. I used to research articles for the writers in the Business section. I did that for two-and-a-half years.

I was then promoted and transferred to San Francisco as a technology correspondent for *Time*. I covered the Silicon Valley, and did medical and biotechnology reporting. That was my entrée into becoming a correspondent for *Time*. I was in San Francisco for a couple of years and then got transferred to Miami as Bureau Chief in the summer of 1987. I was responsible for news and feature coverage in the Caribbean and Florida. In November of 1988 I moved to Los Angeles because my future husband was there. He was also a correspondent for *Time* then. Shortly after I moved to Los Angeles, I began writing fiction. About a year-and-a-half later, in the summer of 1990, I quit *Time* and began writing fiction full-time.

LÓPEZ: What did you do for a living?

GARCIA: I had a lot of savings which I used up very rapidly. Then my husband got a fellowship to the University of Hawaii. The two of us were able to live on the fellowship. That's how I ended up finishing my novel. Since then, I've done OK because of the advance on the book. And now [1992–93] I have a fellowship at Princeton.

LÓPEZ: What are you currently working on?

GARCIA: I'm working on a second novel about more Cubans. This is going to take longer to write. *Dreaming in Cuban* came in a white heat, I worked on it furiously and consistently. This book is coming a lot more slowly and the characters are still largely unknown to me except for the main character, an 82 year-old man, an ornithologist who leaves Cuba for the first time in 1985, after one of his sons dies in New York. I'm not quite sure yet where it's going.

LÓPEZ: Let's talk about the commercial dimension of publishing a book. How did you get a major publisher? Latina/o writers often complain that only little-known or small, specialized presses become interested in their work because major publishers believe there is a very limited market for Latino literature. Elsewhere, Oscar Hijuelos recalls being told when his novel came out: "Minority novels don't sell. Period. . . . Forget it, baby." What can you say about this?

GARCIA: So much has happened in the last few years. My sense is that publishers are very eager to see new work by Latinos. Sandra Cisneros' work has such a wide audience; also Julia Alvarez. . . .

LÓPEZ: And Nicholasa Mohr. . . .

GARCIA: Yes, all women! There has been a lot happening in the last two years. I'll tell you what happened with me, but I don't think it's illustrative of anything. As soon as I quit *Time*, I went to a writers' colony in upstate New York. I was there for one month. In the second half of that month, I was in a writing workshop with Russell Banks, whose work I admire very much. He suggested that I contact his agent when I finished my novel—he'd read about fifty pages of it. About three or four months later, I finished it and sent it to Banks' agent who took the book and sold it within a month. I think this is very unusual. It just landed in the right hands at the right time. Russell Banks is fascinated by the whole cultural milieu of the Caribbean. He was able to convey his enthusiasm for the novel to the agent who in turn sent it around. One of those who got it is Sonny Mehta, who's editor-in-chief of Alfred A. Knopf and is fascinated by fiction from the "other." So it was a series of incredibly lucky steps. If I hadn't met Russell Banks, and I had just started sending my manuscript out cold, I don't think I would have gotten the ears. It would have been harder to get to the right people. I don't know what to say to others, except to get as good an agent as they can or to write to people whose work you admire and see if you can interest them.

I do think there is a greater receptivity to work by Latino writers. For instance, Joaquin Fraxedas, a Cuban lawyer from Florida, just published a novel, *The Lonely Crossing of Juan Cabrera*, that was accepted by St. Martin's Press. And they've published the book both in an English and Spanish edition. I do think it will get better.

López: What audience do you write for? Do you think there is a subtext in your novel that Cuban-Americans will understand but others will have trouble getting?

Garcia: I don't know. I so little allowed myself, when I was writing, to think about where it might end up. The only little fantasy I permitted myself was the vision of my reading at "Books and Books," in Coral Gables. I spent many happy hours at this great bookstore when I was in Miami. My office was just a few blocks from this bookstore. I went to many readings there. It was at a time in my life when I was on my own although I had a boyfriend, my husband now. I had a lot of time to read. Also, it was the first time I'd lived among many Cubans, and I think something congealed during that period in terms of the fictional future.

López: Did you get to give a reading at "Books and Books"?

Garcia: Yes, I did! It was wonderful.

López: How did you experience the reception of the book?

Garcia: I wasn't prepared for this. Now it's a lot more terrifying to think about writing. Then it was a labor of love and obsession. I'm still astonished that so many things could come from that. I've been so lucky.

PABLO ARMANDO FERNÁNDEZ

BRIDGES OF THE HEART

Ever since the appearance in 1984 of Dulce María Loynaz's *Poesías escogidas* (*Selected Poems*; Havana: Letras Cubanas), I have been tempted to review this long-awaited yet unexpected first Cuban edition. Only one of her books, *Versos*, had been published before in Cuba, in 1938. Two new generations of Cubans now have in their hands the work of one of our most illustrious poets.

I first encountered her work in the anthology compiled by Cintio Vitier, *Cincuenta años de poesía cubana, 1902–1952* (Havana, 1952). But it was in 1956, on a visit to Cuba and charged with bringing the writer an English translation of one of her poems by Norman Di Giovanni, that I truly became acquainted with Loynaz's poetry. I remember sensing then a certain intimate resonance with something I couldn't quite identify. Was it a taste of Spanish Golden Age poetry, of the Cuban Romantics, of José Martí? Every attempt at recognition led me to further fruitless searches, and all led back to her delicate, humbly wise personal voice, replete with knowledge revealed to her by her own blood, her own breath. I felt that I was acquainted with a similar poet—or with her poetry that manifested to us, albeit in silences, in pauses between verse and verse, a rich vein of wisdom only transmissible to those past the threshold of initiation.

Dulce María Loynaz (1902-) is customarily compared with other great women poets of her generation: Delmira Agostini (1886–1914), Gabriela Mistral (Chile, 1889–1957), Alfonsina Storni (Argentina, 1892–1932) and Juana de Ibarbourou (Uruguay, 1895–1979), an Olympian group with whom she certainly belongs. In my youth, before I knew the poetry of the Cuban poets, I read widely in these other poets of our America, and I still read with delight the work of Gabriela Mistral, who more than once in her talks in Cuba brought up the name of Dulce María Loynaz, her friend, at whose house she stayed in Havana. It is no secret that Juan

115

Ramón Jiménez, too, visited the Loynaz family when he stayed in Havana, as did Federico García Lorca and every other man and woman of letters who passed through Cuba; yet hers is a voice which has nothing to do with the influence that Juan Ramón Jiménez had on his contemporaries, much less with the poets of the Generation of '27, nor the Cuban poets Emilio Ballagas and Eugenio Florit.

It is not my aim to sew discord among scholars of Loynaz. These influences have become accepted, perhaps through repetition, and they give continuity and order to the history of poetry. The lineages of great writers always strengthen and extend. The forms of lyric poetry in the Spanish language, the meters to which it lends itself, in themselves create resonances. The use of formal combinations — quatrains, *serventesios*, ottava rimas, *espinelas*, and so on — requires the poet's personal authenticity, a clearly differentiated language which obeys her own form of expression and distinguishes her among the choir of voices harmonizing in song or elegy.

I write this to explain what caused my almost spontaneous recognition of the voice of Dulce María Loynaz when I first read her poems. Was it, perhaps, the surprise that her poem "Eternidad" (Eternity) produced in me? The explicit juxtaposition of life, nature, love, time, and eternity in this poem, its pattern of meter and strophe, make it kin to the poetry of Emily Dickinson. Roses, birds, bees, love, death, eternity: are these not the insistent themes of the recluse of Amherst? Are not both poets obsessed with questions of good and evil, life and death, the essence and the fate of human beings?

Eternity

In my garden roses unfold
but I will give you none:
no roses, for tomorrow . . .
tomorrow they will be gone.

In my garden there are birds
singing crystal lays.
I will not give them to you,
they have wings to fly away.

In my garden labor bees
in their fine beehive:

the sweetness of a moment . . .
to you I will not give!

For you, the infinite
or nothing; the immortal
or this mute sadness that
you will never understand. . . .

This sadness without name
of having naught to give
to one who wears upon the brow
signs of eternity. . . .

Leave, then, leave my garden. . . .
Do not touch the rose:
the things that are to die
should not be touched by you.

This poem of Emily Dickinson almost seems to be a reply:

It's all I have to bring today —
This, and my heart beside —
This, and my heart, and all the fields —
And all the meadows wide —
Be sure you count — should I forget
Some one the sum could tell —
This, and my heart, and all the Bees
Which in the Clover dwell.   (#26)

My surprise grew when I read "Miel prevista" (Anticipated
Honey):

The bee returned to my rosebush.
                        I said:
— It is too late for honey; for me it is still
winter.
              The bee returned. . . .
                      . . . Go find
— I said — some other sweetness, other freshness
more innocent. . . .
                (The bee was dark
and would not leave the hollow bloom. . . .)
It thrust its thirst upon the dried-up rose!
And left me, filled with sweetness. . . .

We can find numerous correspondences between these verses and Dickinson's. The final quatrain of the poem which begins, "It makes no difference abroad":

> Auto da Fé— and judgment—
> Are nothing to the Bee—
> His separation from His Rose—
> To him— sums Misery— (#620)

Or the last lines of the poem "The nearest Dream recedes— unrealized":

> Homesick for steadfast Honey—
> Ah! the Bee flies not
> That brews that rare variety!   (#319)

Or this one:

> The Pedigree of Honey
> Does not concern the Bee—
> A Clover, any time, to him,
> Is Aristocracy   (#1627)

And this delicate jewel:

> To make a prairie it takes a clover and one bee,
> One clover, and a bee,
> And revery.
> The revery alone will do
> If bees are few.   (#1755)

In my memory, the hard-working, tropological bees of Emily Dickinson, constants for establishing similes of varying attributes, set off the search which ended by associating the North American poet and the Cuban. For the moment I seemed to have discovered that both identified themselves through incidental coordinates in a kind of common sensibility. Finding an affinity between them did not seem absurd or pretentious to me. Their poetry was informed by an inconsolable feminine lyricism. Dickinson's poems are miniatures, as John Malcolm Brinnin notes, which within their "microscopic structures" enclose a macrocosm.[1] The same could be said of the short poems of Dulce María Loynaz.

It must be admitted that my first impression, founded in metrical structure, might have thrown me off course. Dickinson's technical reach is modest, built upon the meter of church hymns and school songs, with eight syllable verses, or frequently alternating verses of six and eight syllables, in iambs, trochees or dactyls, with a similar uniformity in the strophe design. Even in her first book Loynaz is much more complex and ambitious, adjusting the range of her versification to different registers, which she continues to amplify in later books. Nonetheless, in *Juego de aguas* (*Watergame*, 1947) simpler verses of seven and eight syllables reappear, and they coincide with one of Dickinson's recurrent motifs: the waters of the sea, the river, the rain.

Loynaz:

> How shall I watch the river,
> which seems to flow
> from me. . . .
> ("Integrity")

Dickinson:

> My river runs to thee —
> Blue Sea! Wilt welcome me?
> My river waits reply —
> Oh Sea look graciously —
> I'll fetch thee Brooks
> From spotted nooks —
> Say — sea — Take *Me*!   (#162)

In these poems the lyrical subject adopts the condition of water by lending it human characteristics, emanations of the subject's self. In the collection of Loynaz — one of the most handsome, sensitive and intelligent in our literature, a book filled with mystery and grace — the turmoil of the soul and conciliating reflection are harmoniously balanced. Dickinson, for her part, finds in nature a symbol of death. Who will pacify their spirits? Women of faith in God, they are obsessed with death and immortality. They pay homage to all that breathes — fish, bird, steed, or human — yet do not slip into pantheism. Loynaz invokes the creations of nature generically; Dickinson, on the contrary, seems to know them almost individually, domestically. Each poet draws symbols and metaphors from nature, the essence of things and the human condition, with analogous clarity.

Much is symbolic in each poet, but when Loynaz takes on the themes of family and country, she incorporates, embodies it: she becomes the Island, her hills and streams. She writes of the river Almendares:

> I will not say what hand draws him from me,
> Nor from which stone in my breast he is born:
> I will not call him handsomest . . .
> But he is my river, my country, my blood!

There is no point in looking for parallels between their lives. One hides away between the walls of her house and gardens, confesses she acquired her knowledge of the outside world in her geography classes: "Volcanoes be in Sicily / And South America / I judge from my Geography. . . ." The other travels the world, visits Turkey, Syria, Lybia, Palestine, Egypt, Spain, the Canaries, Mexico and South America. Yet each in her own fashion searches for company in solitude:

Loynaz:

> The world gave me many things: all that is mine is pure solitude.

> (*Poemas sin nombre*, VII)

> Solitude, solitude, long dreamed of. . . .
> I love you so that I fear at times God
> Will punish me one day, filling my life with you.

> (*Poemas sin nombre*, XXX)

Dickinson:

> The Soul selects her own Society—
> Then—shuts the Door   (#302)

And these moving, terrifying lines:

> I tried to think a lonelier Thing
> Than any I had seen—
> Some Polar Expiation—An omen in the Bone
> Of Death's tremendous nearness   (#532)

I think now that the impulse behind this youthful discovery of correspondences came from the differences between Dulce María Loynaz and her South American contemporaries. Perhaps I have not read enough or scrutinized enough, yet I still find a greater spiritual sympathy between Dickinson and Loynaz. I am struck by all that seems to unite them, their twilight silences, the tender gaze fixed on the minuscule, the familiar, the domestic, on all that goes on, leaves traces, and becomes memory: wings beating, the wheels of a carriage, dust . . . their love, their pity, their courage, and their words.

Says Loynaz:

> From this, my bow, I blindly
> loose an arrow unto the world:
> The word goes flying . . .
> and does not return.

("Noé")

And Dickinson:

> A word is dead
> When it is said,
> Some say.
> I say it just
> Begins to live
> That day.   (#1212)

NOTES

[1]John Malcolm Brinnin, "Emily Dickinson, the Legend and the Poet," *The Laurel Poetry Series* (1960), 7–21.

Translated by David Frye

ANA MENDIETA

Ana was fragile as lightning in the sky.
She was the most fragile girl in Manhattan,
lit up always by the autumn rains,
her story burnt to ash upon the saddest lattice shutters.
Up on a balcony, Ana opened the windows
to lean out and watch the multitudes pass.
Like silhouettes of sand and clay
they walked by, on foot. Like a silhouetted
army of silent ants they were,
scattered in the constant wind of Lent
or burrowed into glass.
Ana loved the extras on that set
because they brought her remembrances,
old, resonant, sweet remembrances
of some side street in the South, in El Vedado.
Ana, cast into space.
Ana, our lady of despair,
yourself sculpted in the hostile cement of Broadway.
A desert, like the desert
you found in the orphanages,
a desert, yellow and grey, reaches you
and holds you tight, through the air.

Under Ana's balcony the trains rush past,
as the water flowed in some other time
through the gutters of that strange small town
of green aspens and the burning lamp.
Above the balcony of Ana, of noble Havana calling,
fly tutelary butterflies,
fly simple swallows, which emigrate,

as always, as usual, as everyone knows,
to vast cities aflame with comfort and with fright.

Ana, a swallow is fluttering above your black hair
and the simple purity of that flight presaged your death

       Ana

A swallow of sand and clay.

       Ana

A swallow of water.

       Ana

A swallow of fire.

       Ana

A swallow and a jasmine.

A swallow that made the slowest of summers.
A swallow that scores the sky of Manhattan
towards a fictitious North we cannot quite see
or imagine, even farther North than so many vain illusions.
Ana, fragile as those vivid little crosses
that nest in the domes of certain medieval churches.
Ana, cast upon the mercy of the elements of Iowa, once again.
A black drizzle falls on your silhouette.
Your sleeping silhouettes lull us
like supreme goddesses of inequality,
like supreme goddesses of the new pilgrims of the West.
Ana simple. Lively Ana.
Ana with her enchanted orphan's hand.
Sleeping Ana. Ana, goldsmith.
Ana, fragile as an eggshell
scattered over the huge roots of a Cuban ceiba,
darkleaved, thickly green.

Ana, cast into space.

Ana, gliding like a kite
above the red roofs of the great houses of the old Cerro.
Ana, what radiant colors I see,
and how they resemble certain paintings of Chagall
that you loved to follow through all the galleries of the Earth.
Your silhouettes, sleepy, calm,
tip up the multicolored kite
which flees Iowa, skirting indigenous cypresses,
and comes to rest on the sure clouds
of the mountains of Jaruco, in whose humid land
you have been reborn again, wrapped in a celestial moss
that dominates the rock and caves of that place,
yours now, more than ever.

Translated by David Frye

From *Paisaje Célebre* (Caracas, Venezuela: Fundarte, 1993)

"Rupestrian sculpture" carvings in the
caves of Jaruco by Ana Mendieta.

NANCY MOREJÓN

BEFORE A MIRROR

To Sonia Rivera Valdés

Should you decide to leave this city,
your city,
in search of new horizons,
fortune,
or perhaps a love without precedent,
then the city, this city,
as yet unaware of its ruins,
will be on the watch,
following your steps.
On some hot afternoon
(you, atop the bridges
of some deeprunning river: not this one)
our city will bury
beneath a rare aroma
all the years that have passed
before and after Christ.
No other country, no other city is possible.
There may be dawn, but no twilight.
If parks fill with flowers,
are flush with firm tulip blooms,
the boulevard will bring you the smells
of those who are close to you,
and above all, of your dead.
Should you decide to leave,
the harbor and the bays
and the Garden of the Queen
will accompany you with their fumes.
You will roam the same passageways,

the din of archaic neighborhoods
and the indolence of their bars;
not a single verse of Blaise Cendrars will help,
and the very rooms of your sealed-up house
will hem you in with the anguished cadence of deceit.
Wherever you might move
you'll hear the same streetcry every morning,
be on the same boat crossing the same route,
the route of eternal emigrants.
Nothing will put you in place, anywhere.
Though you scavenge the world over,
from castle to castle,
from market to market,
this will always be the city of your phantoms.
You will have spent your life rather fruitlessly
and when you are an old woman
before a mirror, as in Cinderella,
you will smile half-sadly
and in your dry pupils
will be two faithful rocks
and a resonant corner of your city.

Translated by David Frye

From *Paisaje Célebre* (Caracas, Venezuela: Fundarte, 1993)

A CHRONICLE THAT SWOONS BEFORE
THE IMMIGRANT TREE

Frangipanis matter to me.
Never asking where we're going,
they offer shade for the adventurous
who make a path through this invulnerable Vedado
refuged in its own spiral
of passing years and comfortable latitudes.
It's taken me a long time until now
to understand why
I give myself up to frangipanis.
A poet of my generation told me all about their migratory history
and the strangeness of their flowers
and with what boldness they reach for space.
In a chronicle written up in a city newspaper
someone spoke with affection
of those trees called frangipanis
which regale the passerby
with Chinaesque, modernist, elegiac shade.
I love frangipanis and don't need to know where they come from.

Translated by Ruth Behar

From *Paisaje Célebre* (Caracas, Venezuela: Fundarte, 1993)

Nancy Morejón, Havana, 1994. Photograph by Ruth Behar.

RUTH BEHAR AND LUCÍA SUÁREZ

TWO CONVERSATIONS WITH NANCY MOREJÓN

Nancy Morejón, one of Cuba's most prominent poets, was born in 1944 and studied Language and French Literature at the University of Havana. In addition to being the author of several books of essays and poetry, she has also worked as a journalist and translator of poetry from French and English. Her poetic works include *Mutismos* (Silences), 1962; *Amor, ciudad atribuida* (Love, Attributed City), 1964; *Richard trajo su flauta* (Richard Brought His Flute), 1967; *Parajes de una época* (Parameters of an Epoch), 1979; *Elogio de la danza* (In Praise of Dance), 1982; *Cuadernos de Granada* (Grenada Notebook), 1984; and *Piedra Pulida* (On Polished Stone), 1986. Her most recent book of poetry, *Paisaje Célebre* (Famed Landscape), 1993, received a finalist award at the International Poetry Competition "Pérez Bonalde." The poetry in this text explores the lyrical beauty and complexity of Cuba as a geography of identity and of remembering. English translations of her work have appeared in *Ours the Earth*, published by the University of the West Indies in Kingston, Jamaica (1990), as well as in *Where the Island Sleeps Like A Wing*, published by The Black Scholar Press (1985). As a prose writer, Nancy Morejón is well known for her work, *Nación y mestizaje en Nicolás Guillén* (Nation and Racial Mixture in Nicolás Guillén), 1982. She has traveled widely in Europe, Africa, the Caribbean, Latin America, and the United States, and her poetry has been translated into many languages.

Until recently Nancy Morejón directed *Ediciones PM* of Pablo Milanés Foundation (the Ministry of Culture took it over in June 1995). A multimedia, nonprofit center, the foundation's objective was "to promote and support projects in all fields of artistic expression that contribute to the preservation of the cultural identity of the Cuban nation."

As an Afro-Cuban writer with strong links to the arts and letters of both the Caribbean and the United States, Nancy Morejón has opened bridges in many directions. The following two-part interview is the result of separate conversations held in 1991 and 1994, which explore her literary opinions and the possibilities for reciprocal understanding among Cubans on the island and in the diaspora.

The first interview, with Lucía Suárez, took place on July 8, 1991 in Casa de las Américas, Havana, Cuba. The second interview, with Ruth Behar, took place on February 12, 1994 in the Pablo Milanés Foundation, Havana, Cuba. Both interviews were conducted in Spanish.

I

SUÁREZ: I'm curious to know if you think that being a woman affected the type of intellectual encouragement you received from your parents?

MOREJÓN: My parents always encouraged my studies and intellectual development. My education was a major family concern. Neither my mother nor my father were able to get a formal education, but they were people of great awareness, and understood the importance of knowledge. We received many journals and newspapers at home and my father had a modest library. He saved books of poems by Nicolás Guillén — which were published in Argentina at the time because he was living in exile and was publishing with *Editorial Losada*. Actually, I think my first readings of Nicolás Guillén came from my father's library. My literary inclinations were welcomed and enthusiastically encouraged. I wrote my first pieces at the age of nine. When I showed these to my parents, they agreed I had talent. By the time this talent began to be cultivated into a literary vocation, I was already attending the university. The revolution had taken place, and a series of social advantages were made available — for example, free education. My father never had to pay the university registration so I could pursue my studies. The social climate in the country at the time stimulated literary creativity, and the literacy campaigns eventually created a large audience of readers.

SUÁREZ: Could you discuss your religious background?

MOREJÓN: I was raised in a mostly atheist atmosphere. Theoretically, we declared ourselves Roman Catholic and Apostolic, just like everyone else did, more or less. That is, I was baptized and I received my first Holy Communion. But religion didn't have any other impact on us. As an institution, the Catholic Church didn't have any power in the world in which I grew up. My father was a relatively atheistic man; he cursed religion in every sense. Yet religion in Cuba, in its popular sense, is fundamental — Santería, Spiritism, the religious beliefs which are now called magico-religious systems. These practices were so commonplace that they existed in and around the world within which we moved. Not exactly in our house, but where I lived and went to school. I have always said that these religions constituted a focus of cultural resistance for the slaves. That shaped me. It was a world I could enter and exit, in which I could feel a song, listen to a chorus of slaves, listen to a *guaguancó*, a *rumba*, a *guaracha*, or a *toque de santos*. This is the world that, many years later, I realized I had not learned about from anthropological sources, or in lectures by Fernando Ortiz. This was a reality that belonged to my uncles, my distant uncles. It was seen as a religion, but at the same time it was a form of cultural expression. For example, in my house we often put out flowers for the dead; yet my mother's act of putting flowers out for her dead mother didn't always represent, necessarily, an act of religious resistance.

My parents didn't think it was healthy for me, at the age of seven or eight, to participate in a *toque de santos* or go to a *rumba*. These things were not supposed to shape me; but at the same time, since they were practiced so frequently and it was everywhere around me, it was what I saw. One time, an uncle of mine upset my parents without intending to or even knowing that he was undermining my parents' authority. He took me to see a *rumba*. And I will never forget that. For me, it was an extraordinary experience. I began to scream and my uncle had to take me home. Yet the event left a positive impression. At the time I didn't understand, but later I realized that I loved those practices, and that this feeling was rooted in my childhood. I have written a chronicle about this, about what I could hear in the sonorous world of my neighborhood at night. Especially late at night, you could hear the percussion improvisations on the human body. People would play all the percussion with the palms of their hands.

All of this shaped me. It was a world I have been able to understand better in large part because of the revolution, which dismantled all the prejudices against such practices and provided a legitimate space for exploring the African roots of our culture. Those things which at one time were practiced in the neighborhood, and therefore devalued, became part of the larger culture. They were no longer seen as atavistic and taboo.

SUÁREZ: Given that religious experience is an important part of your writing, I wonder how you reconcile that with Marxism, which considers religion a kind of opiate?

MOREJÓN: Some years ago, I listened with much interest to a lecture in Buenos Aires. Darcy Ribeiro, a great defender of classical Marxism, commented that Marxist texts are not to be held responsible for later interpretations and changes in politics, thought, philosophy, and economics. Then Ribeiro said, "Well, gentlemen, the problem is that Marx never saw a car." For us, a car is something very natural. You don't need a book to tell you what a car does. A car is a car. You know what it is used for, you use it, and that's it. To the extent that Marx didn't see or live certain experiences, he has his limitations. He foresaw that revolutions would take place in industrialized countries. Yet those revolutions occurred in a medieval country like the former Soviet Union, which was almost feudal. Marx never foresaw a revolution such as ours on this side of the Atlantic, in the colonies. In that sense, we have contributed something. One of the most marvelous things about the Cuban Revolution is that it is original and independent. Our revolution has its unique history, stemming from the wars of independence to our present day. The texts of the Cuban Revolution don't have to be derivative, carbon copies of the thought of the great German thinker, Karl Marx, because then we'd be ramming our heads against the wall.

SUÁREZ: How do you view your writing?

MOREJÓN: I think that my literature is a bit like myself. I think it is sincere, and it has its unreasonable and irrational zones. In other words, I think that there is an irrational side to the creative process that is inexplicable, though one has to have a technique, one has to work. My literature is like that, open, and it is open to many things. I don't aspire to reproduce the thinking of a certain literary school. I respond to various literary movements and to generational dynamics, which are valuable for establishing the chronology of literature, but at the moment of writing they all take a secondary place. The important thing is to know where one is, what world one belongs to, and offer a testimony.

SUÁREZ: Can you tell me what it means to you to be a woman who writes? Does it make a difference that you are a woman writer?

MOREJÓN: Yes, I think it makes a difference and I've said so in the past. That doesn't mean I'm a strident feminist. I don't tend to be strident about anything. But I do believe that had I not been a woman, born where I was born, into particular circumstances, I would not have been able to write the things I've written — it would be absurd to think otherwise. Women also have a special vision that is born of pain, and pain smartens one up a great deal.

SUÁREZ: When writing do you choose a theme or do you allow yourself to be inspired?

MOREJÓN: I believe in inspiration and I reject the idea of defining poetry or even of defining the process of writing. I believe there are irrational factors in the creative process. I would never be able to explain the need I have to write. One's text, one's poem, the page that one writes — that is born from a mystery, a mystery that later becomes a habit. I don't know what happens to me; it is something that visits me. I never force it, either; it comes and I write. Of course, then one has to tighten the screws, add your knowledge, because one has to shape it. I don't always know why I used a particular word — -that word came, I found it, I improved it, I removed it, I substituted it, but that word leads you to the one you need, the true one. This career is like a shoemaker's in that it has its techniques and formal elements. You must know several languages because that gives you the opportunity to see other literary worlds and compare different methods of doing literature. Yet the need to write is born of a mystery that cannot be defined or explained.

Translated by Lucía Suárez and Ruth Behar

II

MOREJÓN: It was my mother who got me to start studying English. When I was nine years old, in 1953. By the time I was thirteen I could speak it. My cousin was going to get married to a Protestant pastor, in a North American church, so I was the interpreter.

BEHAR: And that's why you speak English so easily.

MOREJÓN: Naturally — children are made for learning languages. So I feel very committed to my parents. I only have my mother left now, and I won't abandon her in the name of a career which they launched themselves, which they built with their own efforts, because they were from very humble backgrounds. And they were very concerned about my education. That's why in my poetry readings I cite Virginia Woolf so much, because Virginia Woolf said that behind every *escritora*, every woman writer, there is the ghost of her mother. I always read a poem dedicated to my mother, which is called "Madre."

There are so many reasons. For example, my mother was a friend of Ana Mendieta. She knew Ana well. Ana was my friend. When Ana would come to Havana — I live in a very modest house, a little neighborhood house — , Ana would always come over to eat. I'll never forget one time that Ana came, out of the thousands of times that she came to visit me, it was so *simpático*. My uncle El Chino was there, the husband of my mother's sister. He's a carpenter, a marvelous person; I wish you could see how Ana talked with him. She was someone who became very close to me. And all the people who have been my friends, who have been important to me, have been connected with my mother, with my parents. No matter who came over to visit me, if it was a friend of mine, they would receive them with open arms, just as they would if you were to come over now.

BEHAR: I'd like to hear more about Lourdes Casal and the role of women in the re-encounter of Cubans inside and outside.

MOREJÓN: Look, the fact is that we all got to know each other through Lourdes. Lourdes is the main inspiration in this moment of re-encounter and dialogue. Lourdes was the first to talk in those terms, of dialogue. In the broadest sense, not the way that many political factions that move around Cuba use the term. Nowadays it's very easy to talk about "the dialogue," in quotation marks. But Lourdes arrived, creating the miracle that we could hold a conversation. That we could confront each other. Without imposing exile as a precondition, and without us imposing the precondition of being revolutionary islanders. And all this happened at the end of the 1970s — I think it is an extraordinary chapter in the cultural history of Cuba. That's why I maintain that without Cuban culture there is nothing, there is no Cuban identity, no Cuban history, because it was only through culture that we could establish those links, recognize each other. And for me that is why we can now consider each other compatriots. Many times I have done poetry readings in the United States and young people who don't even speak Spanish have come up to me and told me, in English, "I was born here," or, "I came here when I was very small, and I came to your lecture to buy your book." And I ask them, "What's your name?" "Well, González. Eugene González."

BEHAR: But in the 1970s not everyone was so receptive to the idea of a dialogue.

MOREJÓN: No! No, imagine, if even today there are still so many problems, after the Berlin Wall has fallen and so many things have changed, back then it wasn't easy at all. They really put themselves forward. I think you have to recognize the bravery of those women and those men: they opened up new paths, and they faced up to terrorism. Nowadays it's easy to talk, but back then there were bombs and threats and more threats and more bombs, and anonymous notes, "I'm going to cut your tongue out," and "I'm going to kill you because you went to Cuba." I remember that time perfectly well. A lot's happened since then — and here, naturally, time passes, nothing stays the same, because otherwise there's no movement, no evolution. And there have been so many positions taken since then. But they were the ones who opened a path that is so wonderful that I don't think we should ever abandon it.

BEHAR: But it was cut off, in part because of the Mariel exodus and in part because of Reagan's policies.

MOREJÓN: Yes. If you look at it from the point of view of the official circles, yes. But I always maintained good relations with Ana and Lourdes, who were my best friends. And it was never interrupted, that dialogue was never interrupted, never, we've kept right on inventing new journals, coming up with new things to do. Because after you've done so much to open up a new path, you just can't go back.

BEHAR: It seems to me that Lourdes's conflict was to understand why she had left.

MOREJÓN: It was so interesting. But in any case, in Lourdes's family they were professionals, they were doctors and all that — she studied in a private university, the only private university that existed here, the University of Villa Nueva. I got confused myself, because I was in the same circle as the students of the University of Villa Nueva and I couldn't understand what happened. I assumed the values of a class that I didn't belong to. And it was only in the United States that Lourdes noticed what color she was, what kind of hair she had, that she was a woman, do you understand? But in the University of Villa Nueva she didn't, because sometimes in our little countries people can create little bubbles and then they don't notice what's going on, they just have no idea.

BEHAR: Bubbles?

MOREJÓN: I mean she lived inside a bubble because, for example, she had no contact with her own origins because they had taught her to forget those origins. And when she gets to the United States, the bubble bursts and she notices that they've put her in her place. "You go over there, you can't go here, you can't enter here," and so on. And that radicalized her in the United States, and then she noticed the mechanisms that kept her from understanding what was going on here.

And at the same time I think she had a critical sense of this gesture. She wasn't submissive. Lourdes Casal never groveled. As she said in her marvelous poem, the one "To Ana Veldford," you know: "Too much a New Yorker to be from Havana, too *Habanera* to be *Newyorkina.*" She understood that she already had a new skin that hadn't been formed here, because everyone lives their own reality. But hers wasn't that reality, either, understand? So that struggle, that vivacity, that interest in saying "This is what I am, I'm betwixt and between," is so important. It's an extraordinary problem.

BEHAR: I also wanted to ask you about what you think of the possibilities of bridges today. Earlier, we spoke of Cristina Garcia's *Dreaming in Cuban* as another kind of bridge.

MOREJÓN: Look, I think these are very important facts. That there is now a Cuban literature in English, written by Cuban-Americans, people who were born here, by people who didn't necessarily go to the United States of their own will—that's an important fact to remember. Naturally, those are things that literary historians should decide on, and not poets—minor poets like myself. But my own perception is that we shouldn't fall into the error of focusing too much on language. Culture is transmitted through language, but language isn't the same thing as culture itself. Nobody can tell me that I am Spanish just because I speak Spanish and write in Spanish—in that case, all of Latin American literature would just be Spanish literature. In Latin America we speak and write Spanish—and so what? From my own experience, the world of the Caribbean is a Tower of Babel: we have a common historical experience which we have shared throughout our existence. There are so many similarities between the city of Fort de France in Martinique, and the city of Havana of my childhood. The differences are even greater, and one of the differences is language, but nevertheless the experience of slavery has created so many points in common that it doesn't matter that I speak Spanish and that in Fort de France they speak French, or that they speak English in Kingston, to understand that we all have the same skin. So when you speak of the fact that there is a Puerto Rican literature in English, Nuyorican literature or whatever they wish to call it, we have to treat this subject from the point of view of literary history with a lot of respect, because these are processes that express social conditions. It's a fierce history—it goes way beyond the personal decisions of the authors of that literature.

So something is happening in Cuban literature, because in those novels written in English, like that one, there is a substrate, there's a likeness of Cuba, of Cuban problems and the problems of Cubans and of the Cuban character. And that is where I would situate the literature of Cristina Garcia and other writers, such as Oscar Hijuelos and so many others. There is an anthology now, *Iguana Dreams*, that collects not only Cuban works but the whole Latin American phenomenon in the United States.

BEHAR: What they call the "Latino Boom."

MOREJÓN: We have to go very slowly, very deliberately, in relation to all this. Not let ourselves be carried away by presuppositions established in this chaotic world we are living in, where no one knows what's going to happen. I remember at the Strasbourg writers' conference, where someone confronted the great Martinican philosopher Jacques Coursil, and the two of them debated Derrida. Jacques Derrida was hitting himself in the head trying to explain the end of the twentieth century. And they finished off Derrida: they told him, "Look, your problem is that you're the savage here, and we're the philosophers: we've switched places. What lies can you tell us about the future of humanity in this era, after the fall of the Berlin Wall, in which that fierce, burning point, the war of Sarajevo exists, or the Cuban embargo? Who can have the last word about anything?" Our values have been turned upside down and things have changed so much, and we are at a critical point, in which we have our feet up above our heads and our heads down under our feet. Who am I to determine what's going to happen? I'm speaking in terms of the world of ideas and of art and literature, because in terms of social conflicts—the Los Angeles riots, or what's happening in Chiapas right now—these are things that weren't in anybody's plans, just like Moncada wasn't in anyone's plans either. So, it's not a matter of whether I agree or disagree. I might disagree with Cristina Garcia on many issues, but I can't question the legitimacy of Cristina Garcia's writing on this experience, and of transfering to her literature all the likenesses, the sweat, the dust, that come from this island. I can't, and no one can say, "Cubanness goes this far and no farther."

BEHAR: What is it that attracts you to people in the United States who are trying to build bridges?

MOREJÓN: Because I have visited the United States many times and that has made me aware, the way people come to find me, how desperate people feel to get a letter, how desperate they feel if they have a sick relative and they don't know what's going to happen to him, since there is no communication, there's no way to get a message through. And I was there like a kind of magician, someone who could—not load myself down with everything, but just give them a bit of news, tell them, "Your grandmother is still alive." It made me feel very useful, in the middle of that difficult conflict. And I'm a good messenger, too. For example, there was someone who hadn't heard from a relative for years and years, and I went and found out from someone I know from Santiago de Cuba, and I was able to bring them the news: "Look, in your family so-and-so has died, and this person and that person are still alive." Sometime I would like to write some of those experiences. The famous story of the family that ate their grandmother.

It was when the people were starting to come to visit. The grandmother had died in the United States, because she had left; but she had always said, "I want to be buried in Cuba." You can tape this, but I don't want you to put it in the written interview because I want to write this story myself someday. It is such a cruel story. It sounds like an Alvarez Guedes joke. So, the old woman always said, "You have to bury me in Cuba, I want you to bury my ashes in Cuba." She dies in New York, and then a Cuban shows up, from Cuba, and they tell him, "We want you to carry this to our family. This is illegal, but look, our grandmother died and we want you to carry her ashes back because she always wanted to be buried over there. Here's a letter that explains everything." And the man comes back here, but he forgets the letter, and he carries the grandmother's ashes in a stewed-fruit jar to camouflage it. And then, what are the relatives supposed to think when this jar arrives without any letter? They thought it was some kind of oatmeal or spices or something. And then about six months later the letter finally arrives: "At last, dear cousins, we are sending your grandmother's ashes in this oatmeal jar," and so on. "Ay! We ate Grandmother!"

I have to reconstruct that story.

BEHAR: It's a popular tale?

MOREJÓN: No, it's a true story. It does sound like a popular tale, though.

BEHAR: Can't we put the story of the grandmother in the interview? I love it!

MOREJÓN: Well, put a note that no one else can have it. As long as no one takes it: put that down, okay?

Translated by David Frye

"The Woman of the Unicorn." Drawing by Rolando Estévez, 1993.

JESÚS J. BARQUET

VERRAZANO-NARROWS BRIDGE

once joined the seas and the prairies.
Vladimir Mayakovski

Think of the bridges that brought us peace.
Think of the peace the bridges brought us.
Cornered by the world
Made drowsy by truth
we were searching for each other
through cobble-stones of dreams
which dawn would break
like crystal when kissed.
Rebelling at the precise
moment of a hope
we beat our temples
where blood demanded
its motives with screams.
That was the time to cross the river
of rivers:
to reach the shore
where the self is completed
with the eyes of the soul's eyes.
Death: Open book: Faith
of a deserted gallows
and of a rampant night:
a calm and obscure night
of glowing darkness.
The river was evaporating, the humidity
of the valley was on your body
while I was in it.
The two hostile shores,
of medieval hatred,

are today wings of a descending bird
rising as if it were Harmony.
And this is the peace
of biting your hands
while they rewrite the entire universe.
So that nothing is oblivion
but rather founding and lasting.
So that the entwining legs
of our philosophical sexes
appear at the banquet
where Truth is momentarily
fulfilled: and this is the peace
of the wanderer
who boldly walks
onto the arms of the bridge
not intending to jump.
Let's be fair:
Let's think of the peace the bridges brought us.
Let's think of the bridges peace could bring to us.

Translated by Jeff Longwell and
the author

FRAGMIENTOS DE NARRACIONES CUBANAS

FOTOGRAFÍAS DE EDUARDO APARICIO

FRAGMENTS FROM CUBAN NARRATIVES
A portfolio by
EDUARDO APARICIO

Artist's Statement

The personal history of each Cuban living in the U.S. is mostly unknown, unspoken, and often lies buried under a thick layer of inaccurate assumptions. Every Cuban knows that we do not constitute a monolithic social or ethnic group. The people who have agreed to be photographed for this series are a small indication of the great diversity among us, based on differences of generation, class, and political views. They also represent different waves of migration and regional origin.

Although it's true that as Cubans outside of Cuba we may feel united by a set of shared historical and cultural preocupations, my interest has been to investigate our subjective differences. On my first return trip to Cuba this year, I began to photograph people who have loved ones living outside of Cuba. The people I've photographed have touched me deeply with their willingness to open up and share their feelings.

A camera is much more than a device for making mute decorative pictures to hang on the wall; it is a tool for observation and investigation. These photographs are observed details, fragments, of a much larger picture. The accompanying texts bring forth the thoughts of these Cuban, making it possible that not only their faces be seen, but also, that their voices be heard.

Eduardo Aparicio
West Palm Beach, Florida, March, 1994

Declaración del artista

El historial personal de cada uno de los cubanos que vivimos en los Estados Unidos es mayormente desconocido, no se ha hecho escuchar y, por lo general, yace sumido bajo un manto de presunciones erróneas. Todo cubano sabe que no formamos un grupo social o étnico monolítico. Las personas que se ofrecieron a ser fotografiadas hacen ver, a pequeña escala, la gran diversidad de la población cubana en los Estados Unidos, según diferencias de generación, clase social y opiniones políticas. También representan diferentes olas migratorias y diferentes regiones de origen.

Si bien es cierto que como cubanos fuera de Cuba podemos sentirnos unidos por un repertorio común de preocupaciones históricas y culturales, mi interés ha sido investigar nuestras diferencias subjetivas. En mi primer viaje de regreso a Cuba este año, empecé a retratar a personas que tienen seres queridos viviendo fuera de Cuba. Las personas que he fotografiado me han conmovido profundamente por su disposición a compartir sus sentimientos abiertamente.

Una cámara es mucho más que un aparato para fabricar imágenes mudas y decorativas y colgarlas de la pared; es un instrumento de observación y de investigación. Estas fotografías son detalles observados, fragmentos, de un panorama mucho mayor. El texto que las acompaña pone en evidencia el pensar de estos cubanos, haciendo que no sólo se vean sus rostros, sino que se escuchen también sus voces.

Eduardo Aparicio
West Palm Beach, Florida, marzo de 1994

Mis padres me criaron ajena a mi cultura y a mis raíces, con el propósito de que fuera una buena americana. Eso me creó un vacío. Por eso tomé la decisión de irme a Puerto Rico, porque sentí que era lo que más se parecía a Cuba. Pero también crecí aquí desde los siete años. Eso es también parte de mí, lo cual explica mi regreso a Nueva York. Para mí Cuba es un mito, casi.

No hay nada más liberador que una buena carcajada, especialmente cuando uno se está riendo de uno mismo.

Yolanda Fundora
Artista
Nueva York, 1992

Translation: My parents raised me out of touch with my culture and my roots, to make me into a good American girl. That created a wanting in me. That's why I decided to move to Puerto Rico, because I felt that it was the closest thing to Cuba. But it is also true that I was raised here since I was seven. That's also part of me, which explains why I returned to New York. For me Cuba is a myth, almost. There's nothing more liberating than a good laugh, especially when you're laughing about yourself.

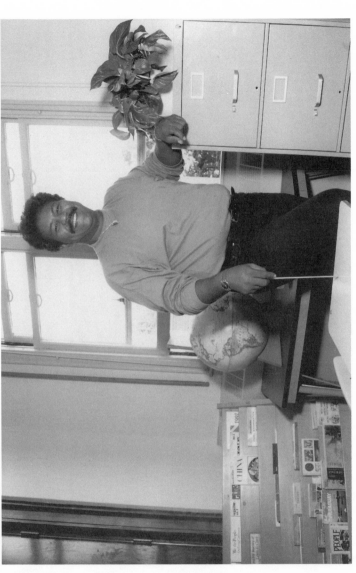

Salí de Cuba hace más de 25
años y prácticamente me siento
tan cubano como la caña de
azúcar. Ser cubano exiliado es
una ventaja amarga puesto que
el destierro nos ha enseñado a
querer a nuestra patria aún más.
Siempre pienso en el regreso a
ver a mi familia. Pues aunque
hayan pasado tantos años, el
amor y la relación familiar jamás
se han perdido. ¿Qué les diría?
¿Cuál será la relación de ese
momento en adelante?
Verdaderamente es difícil tratar
de recuperar el tiempo perdido,
pero el cariño puede vencer.
Los años pasan y mi juventud
se va marchitando y el miedo de
llegar viejo a Cuba y no poder
disfrutarla me entristece. Nací
en La Habana, Cuba, procedente
de una familia de clase media y
me crié en Nueva York. Hoy día
soy maestro de educación
especial en la misma escuela
intermediaria donde fui
estudiante hace 25 años.

Rubén D. Jiménez
Maestro
Nueva York, 1992

Translation: I left Cuba more than 25 years ago and I practically feel as Cuban as sugarcane. To be a Cuban exile gives you a painful advantage: it has taught us to love our native country even more. I'm always thinking about going back to visit my family. In spite of all the years since I last saw them, love and family ties have never been lost. What would I say to them? What will our relationship be like from there on? It is truly difficult to try to make up for lost time, but love can conquer. The years go by and, as I lose my youth, the thought of arriving in Cuba as an old man and not being able to enjoy it makes me sad. I was born in Havana, Cuba, to a middle-class family, and raised in New York. Today I am a special education teacher in the same middle school that I attended 25 years ago.

Mi familia emigró a los Estados Unidos en los años 30. Mi abuela me enseñaba en los libros de National Geographic dónde estaba Cuba, porque después de la Revolución en los partes meteorológicos no aparecía; la habían borrado. Yo nací en Nueva York, pero desde pequeña mi madre y mi abuela me inculcaron la cultura cubana. Ellas no tenían idea, en ese entonces, que después de grande escribiría un estudio de la cultura literaria cubana, publicado en La Habana.

Pamela María Smorkaloff
Escritora
Nueva York, 1992

Translation: My family emigrated to the United States in the 1930s. My grandmother used National Geographic books to teach me where Cuba was, because after the revolution it was not shown in the weather forecasts; it had been erased. I was born in New York, but from childhood on my mother and grandmother instilled Cuban culture in me. Back then, they had no idea that as an adult I would write a history of Cuban literary culture, published in Havana.

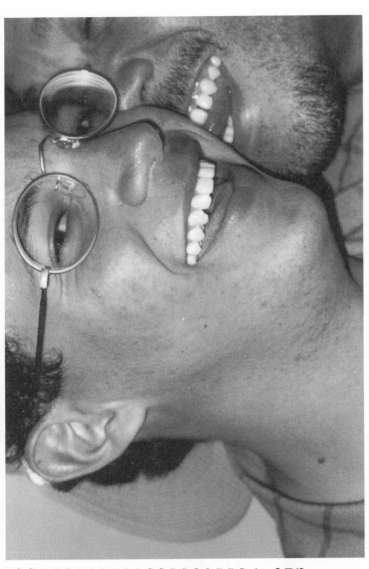

Ignacio Agramonte fue mi bisabuelo materno. El origen de mi familia en cierto punto parte de España hacia Cuba. Varias generaciones después migró a la República Dominicana y luego a Puerto Rico. Yo fui a Cuba en el 30 aniversario de la Revolución. Fue un descubrimiento porque pude confrontar lo que me habían enseñado de Cuba con la Cuba que yo estaba viendo. Al momento trabajo como activista en Chicago por los derechos de los homosexuales y de las personas que viven con VIH/SIDA.

Cecil Romano
Trabajador social
Chicago, 1995

Translation: Ignacio Agramonte [19th century Cuban patriot, killed by the Spaniards in 1871] was my great-grandfather. My family originated from Spain and then at some point migrated to Cuba. Several generations later, it migrated to the Dominican Republic and then to Puerto Rico. I went to Cuba on the 30th anniversary of the Revolution. It was a revelation for me, because I was able to confront what I had been taught about Cuba with what I had in front of my eyes. At present, I work in Chicago as an activist for gay rights and the rights of people with AIDS/HIV.

©Eduardo Aparicio, 1994

"Soy balsero y trabajo por comida. Ayúdame."

Yo llegué aquí el 14 de noviembre. Un hombre ahí me dijo que eso era un mal ejemplo para los cubanos porque yo estaba pidiendo trabajo por comida. Yo le dije que yo no sé hacer otra cosa. Yo no sé robar. No sé quitarle la cartera a una vieja. No sé vender drogas. En Cuba yo trabajaba en abono químico. Soy de Regla y no tengo familia. Allá yo no podía vivir porque el régimen está muy malo.

Julio Ramírez Marques
Desempleado
Miami, Florida, 1993

Translation: "I arrived in a raft and I work for food. Please help me." I arrived here on November 14. Some guy there told me that I was setting a bad example by asking to work for food. I told him that I wouldn't know anything else. I wouldn't know how to steal. I wouldn't know how to snatch a purse from an old lady. I wouldn't know how to sell drugs. In Cuba I worked with chemical fertilizers. I'm from Regla and have no family here. I couldn't live over there because things are so bad with the regime.

Cuando yo llegué a los
Estados Unidos, Inesita, la
suegra de mi hija, me dijo:
p"Ana, usted diría que con
los años que tenemos
nosotras dos lo hemos
visto todo en la vida,
¿verdad? Yo le dije que,
bueno, que yo creía que sí.
Y me dice ella: "Pues ahora
que está aquí, espérese
Ana, espérese porque usted
no ha visto nada".

Ana Baldó
Madre de familia
West Palm Beach, Florida,
1983/1993

Translation: When I first arrived in the United States, Inesita, my daughter's mother-in-law, said to me: "Ana, you would say that given our age, we have seen everything in life, right? I said that I would kind of say so. And then she added: "You wait then, now that you're here, you just wait, because you haven't seen anything yet".

Yo soy de Banes, Oriente.
Nosotros nos fuimos de
Cuba el 26 de septiembre de
1961. La lancha era de
catorce pies y medio, con
un motor fuera de borda de
15 H.P. Salimos para las
Bahamas en un viaje como
de 18 horas. Éramos cuatro
en la lancha. Cuando
llegamos a Nassau, el
cubano que atendía a los
cubanos recién llegados,
por esas cosas del destino,
¡se llamaba Fidel Castro!

Hilde F. Cruz
Capataz
Washington Heights
Nueva York, 1992

©Eduardo Aparicio, 1994

Translation: I'm from Banes, Oriente. We left Cuba on September 26, 1961. The boat that we used was 14 and 1/2 feet long and had an over-board 15-H.P. motor. Our journey to the Bahamas took about 18 hours. We were four in the boat. When we got to Nassau, there was a Cuban guy in charge of processing incoming Cubans. By one of those acts of fate, it so happens that his name was also Fidel Castro!

Yo soy de allá. Ésta es la segunda vez que vengo. Ojalá pueda venir de nuevo. Yo no me quedo. Aunque quiero mucho a mi hermano y al hijo y los sobrinos que tengo aquí, yo quiero mucho a Cuba y no dejaría a los seres queridos que tengo allá. Pasé unos días muy buenos aquí, pero adoro mi patria. Aquí también adoro porque tengo parte de mi corazón. Ojalá un día podamos estar todos juntos. Yo estoy jubilada. Trabajaba limpiando en La Dependiente.

Concepción Gil del Real
Trabajadora jubilada
En el aeropuerto de Miami
rumbo de regreso a
La Habana, Cuba, 1994

Translation: I'm from over there. This is the second time that I've come here. I hope I can come back again. I'm not staying. Although I love my brother and my son and all the nephews and nieces that I have here, I love Cuba a lot and would not leave my loved ones there. I spent some wonderful days here, but I love my country. I have a lot to love here too because part of my heart is here. I hope that some day we can all be together. I am now retired. I used to work as a cleaning person at the clinic "La Dependiente."

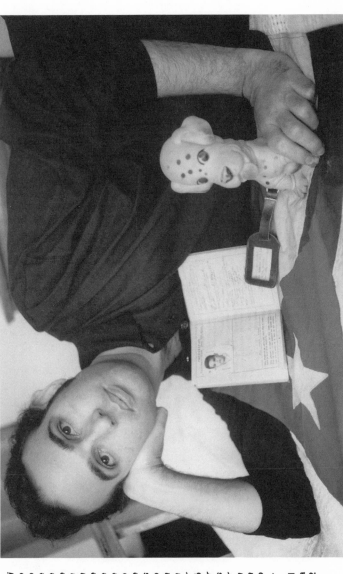

©Eduardo Aparicio, 1994

Conservo varias cosas de mi salida de Cuba a los cuatro años, en 1961, cuando lo perdimos todo: un pasaporte de niño inocente, un perrito de goma que aún chilla tristemente cuando lo aprietas, y una bandera cubana manchada. Sin embargo, el objeto más terrible que conservo es la etiqueta de identificación de la maleta de mi abuela paterna, Amparo Pino Dueñas. Ella, que fue quien me crió, tuvo que quedarse atrás sola y salir más tarde. El exilio fue particularmente duro para los viejos cubanos. Mi abuela siempre se arrepintió de haber salido de Cuba y murió deseando en vano ser enterrada allá. Treinta años más tarde volví a La Habana por primera vez y pensé mucho en ella. Nunca la olvidaré; la extraño como si hubiera muerto ayer. Para mí, ella era Cuba.

Ernesto Pujol
Artista
Nueva York, 1992

Translation: I have kept several things from the time I left Cuba in 1961, at the age of four, when we lost everything: the passport of an innocent boy, a rubber doggy that still whines sadly when you squeeze him, and a stained Cuban flag. However, the most terrible object that I still preserve is the name tag from my paternal grandmother's suitcase. Her name was Amparo Pino Dueñas. She was the one who raised me, but had to stay behind and leave Cuba later. Exile was particularly harsh on older Cubans. My grandmother always regretted leaving Cuba, and she died wishing in vain to be buried there. Thirty years later I returned to Havana for the first time and I thought a lot about her. I will never forget her. I miss her as if she had died yesterday. For me, she was Cuba.

©Eduardo Aparicio, 1994

Mi abuelo, Mario Lazo, escribió Daga en el corazón: Cuba traicionada. *Mi mamá se crió en Cuba pero no nos enseñó español a los hijos acá en los Estados Unidos. Yo aprendí español a los 16 años porque quería hablar el idioma del lado cubano de mi familia, como para reclamar esa parte de mi ascendencia. Yo soy lesbiana y trabajo con gays, lesbianas y bisexuales en solidaridad con Cuba para quitar el bloqueo. Yo fui a Cuba en noviembre del 92. En mi familia, yo fui la primera de mi generación que fue a Cuba.*

Cristina Riley-Lazo
Investigadora clínica
San Francisco, California
1993

Translation: My grandfather, Mario Lazo, wrote *Dagger in the Heart: American Policy Failures in Cuba.* My mother was raised in Cuba, but she did not teach me Spanish. I learned Spanish when I was sixteen because I wanted to be able to speak the language spoken by the Cuban side of my family, as a way of reclaiming that part of my extraction. I'm a lesbian and work with gays, lesbians, and bisexuals in solidarity with Cuba to remove the blockade. I went to Cuba in November of 1992. In my family, I was the first one of my generation to go to Cuba.

Salimos de Cuba en 1955 y 1956 por razones económicas. Nuestra madre, sobre todas las cosas, amó a Cuba. Ella decía que no había santo a quien no le hubiera rezado para que las madres pudieran volver a ver a sus hijos en Cuba. Debido al amor que mi madre siempre tuvo por su patria nos sentimos en el deber de tratar de hacer algo por Cuba en su memoria. Nosotras supimos de una organización en Miami que se dedica a enviar medicinas a Cuba, ayudar a la reunificación familiar y trabajar por el levantamiento del bloqueo. Fue así que fundamos una filial aquí en Chicago. Este trabajo es muy agotador y lleno de frustraciones, pero sentimos que nuestros hermanos cubanos nos necesitan más y con más razón hacemos nuestra obra. Somos optimistas y nos sentimos llenas de esperanza.

Gisela López
Técnica de computadoras
y Gilda López de Martínez
Oficinista, Chicago, 1993

Translation: We left Cuba in 1955 and 1956 for economic reasons. Our mother loved Cuba above all things. Our mother loved Cuba for economic reasons. We feel that mothers could see their children again in Cuba. Because of our mother's love for her country, we feel that we have a duty to try to do something for Cuba in her memory. We learned of an organization in Miami that sends medicine to Cuba, helps with family reunification, and works towards the lifting of the blockade. So, we formed a branch here in Chicago. This work is exhausting and full of frustrations, but we feel that Cuba and our Cuban brothers and sisters need us more now, and that gives us even more reason to do our work. We feel optimistic and full of hope.

Yo tengo a mi jefe que se
fue para allá también. A él
lo quería todo el mundo
mucho—una persona joven
y muy cariñosa. Él vino aquí
de visita en diciembre. Yo
lloré mucho cuando se fue.
Mira... aquí tengo unas
fotos de él. Se casó allá con
una cubana.

Migdalia Rodríguez Rocabruna
Técnica poligráfica
La Habana, Cuba, 1994

Translation: I have my boss who also left. Everyone loved him very much—a young and very loving person. He came to visit in December. I cried a lot when he left. Look.... I have some pictures of him here. Over there he married a Cuban.

Yo nací en Oriente, Cuba, el 13 de abril de 1966. Mi niñez fue feliz aunque con muy pocas riquezas. En 1980 emigré junto con mi familia a los Estados Unidos. Soy el producto de dos culturas y de dos naciones. De mi hispanidad estoy muy orgullosa y es por eso que representé a la comunidad latina de Nueva York en un concurso internacional. Por otro lado, amo a este país y, aunque todo aquí no es perfecto, fue la mejor decisión que tomaron mis padres al traerme a este país para garantizarme un mejor futuro. Hoy en día, mi vida es como la de cualquier hispano neoyorquino y no la cambiaría por nada en el mundo.

Ofelia Cobián
Agente de publicidad
Nueva York, 1992

Translation: I was born in Oriente province, Cuba, on April 13, 1966. I had a happy childhood, even if without many riches. In 1980 I emigrated to the United States with my family. I am the product of two cultures and two nations. I am very proud of my Hispanic heritage, that's why I've represented the Latin community of New York in an international contest. In addition, I love this country and, although everything here is not perfect, my parents made the best decision when they brought me here to secure a better future for me. Today my life is like that of any other Hispanic person in New York and I wouldn't change it for anything in the world.

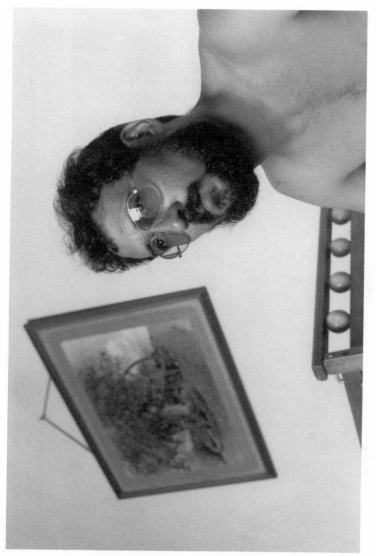

En esta casa vivieron mis abuelos hasta que se fueron del país en 1969. Cuando me casé, mis padres hablaron de la posibilidad de permutar esta casa por dos. Yo dije que no, que ésta fue la casa de mis abuelos y que yo de aquí no me iba.

Ricardo Herrera
Trabajador de los muelles
La Habana, Cuba, 1994

Translation: This was my grandparents' home until they left the country in 1969. When I got married, my parents and I talked about the possibility of swapping this house for two. I said no, that this was my grandparents' home and that I wouldn't leave here.

©Eduardo Aparicio, 1994

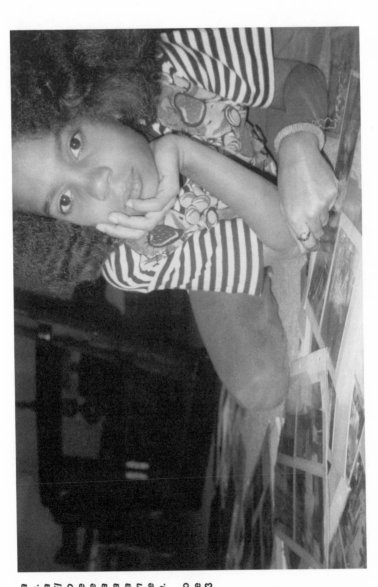

*Ésta es mi tía Silvia. Ella
siempre nos cuidaba.
Después de la escuela
íbamos a su casa a jugar. El
otro día yo tuve un sueño
con tía Silvia y la mamá de
todas ellas que ahora tiene
90 años. le decíamos tía
Amparo. Soñé que fuimos a
su casa. Yo vine de Cuba
hace un poco más de un
año. Cuando la veas dile
que estamos muy bien.*

Ana Laila Pedro
Estudiante
Chicago, 1993

Translation: This is my aunt Silvia. She always took care of us. After school, we would go to her house and play. The other day I had a dream with her and the mother of all of them, who's 90. We called her aunt Amparo. In the dream we went to her house. I came from Cuba a little over a year ago. When you see her tell her that we are fine.

PART 2 Rupture / Ruptura

Rolando Estévez, *"El Cuerpo de Lágrimas"* *(Body of Tears),* ink on paper,
1994.

LOUIS A. PÉREZ, JR.

THE CIRCLE OF CONNECTIONS: ONE HUNDRED YEARS OF CUBA-U.S. RELATIONS

In the days just after the war of independence, Liborio was alone in the cane field, still cutting as others ate their meager lunch. He chopped through a row of cane to discover God, sitting in an expensive white suit on a little stool, the type colonos used when they stopped to survey their property.

"Buenos días, Liborio," said God. "I have come to see how my cubanos are doing."

Liborio stood with his clothes soaked with sweat, his hands cracked and bleeding, his feet bare and filthy. He stuck his machete into the ground, spit out the piece of cane he had been chewing on, and thought for a long time about what he should say to God.

"First of all, Señor," he said, "we are no longer subjects of the King of Spain. We are free men."

"I can see that," said God, looking at Liborio from head to foot. "The difference is astounding."

"But I wonder sometimes," Liborio continued, "why life is still so hard."

God smiled at him. "My son, nothing on this earth can be perfect, or nobody would want to go to Heaven. Sugar is sweet, but man has to labor to take it from the ground. The ocean is wide and bountiful, but it has sudden storms and dangerous currents to pull you under and drown you. This Cuba is so beautiful, the pearl of all my creations, so I had to make the pests, the mosquitos, the sea urchin, the thorn of the marabú, all so life here would be less than Paradise. Nothing can be perfect in this world."

Liborio pondered this, trying to fathom the wisdom of God's ways. "But nothing can mar the beauty of freedom," he said finally. "Surely freedom is perfect?"

161

God smiled again, "For that," he says, "I created los yanquis."

— Adapted from John Sayles, *Los Gusanos*

God created the United States, envisioned as one of the great nations of the world, endowed with power hitherto unimaginable and wealth previously unknown. But God understood too the perils of such power and wealth and the ease with which confidence could be transformed to arrogance. God wanted to teach humility, most of all to underscore that the exercise of power and wealth, even on such an unprecedented scale, was not without limits.

And to this end God created Cuba, certain to be coveted by the North Americans, described by the first European as "so beautiful . . . so lovely that my eyes could not weary of beholding such beauty." And God deliberately placed the island near North America, only ninety miles away, so close, in fact, as to give the appearance of Divine sanction for possession.

But God also endowed Cubans with the moral resources and the collective will to resist possession. North Americans could not understand that while they could possess almost anything they wanted, anywhere they wanted, they could not have Cuba. And the more they tried, the more the Cubans resisted.

For nearly two centuries this continued, so that the North American resolve to possess Cuba and the Cuban determination to resist possession became part of the national character of each and something of an obsession for both.

I

Cubans and North Americans came to know each other well, early, through frequent contact and close encounters, both here and there, sometimes in pursuit of common needs, but just as often in defense of conflicting interests. They lived among each other, and early developed the types of familiarities with one another usually reserved only for a people of the same nation — which meant, too, that they began to imitate each other, to become somewhat like one another. They occupied, too, a place in each other's imagination, and in their fantasies about one another, both public and private; in ways that were continual and reciprocal, efforts to interpret each other served to give shape to the cultural forms of both. It has been thus for more than one hundred years, and the past thirty-five years of estrangement have not in the slightest diminished the legacy of this connection.

Trade was one important link and early established the basis from which familiarities developed and contacts expanded. Access to North American markets made the expansion of Cuban sugar production possible and profitable, and the decision to pursue economic development through sugar exports early assumed a logic of its own, driven by expansion and more expansion: expanded cultivation, expanded production, and expanded exports in pursuit of expanding markets.

Nor was it simply a matter of producing more sugar, more efficiently, more profitably. Cuban success was very much derived from a strategy of specialization: an export economy organized principally around sugar production, increasingly to the exclusion of other products, increasingly to the exclusion of other markets. It was indeed more cost effective to rely on food imports for the local market than sacrifice sugar exports for the foreign market. That the United States could meet these needs, from comparatively short distances in relatively short periods of time, at reasonably low transportation costs, and provide Cuba with necessary industrial and manufactured supplies, served early to give Cuban development its distinctive and definitive characteristics.

II

North Americans began to contemplate Cuba early in the nineteenth century, mostly in the form of musings on possession. The vision of possession derived inspiration from a combination of faith and reason, driven by an arrogant and aggressive self-confidence that early shaped North American assumptions about the New World and their place in that world. Cuba dawned on the North American imagination during a time of national formation, and was thus incorporated early in the emerging national consciousness. The acquisition of Louisiana and Florida, and later Texas, projected the United States into the Gulf and directly onto Cuba, and, of course, beyond: borders beyond borders that implied the possibility of hemispheric preeminence, in which control of Cuba was at once prelude and prerequisite. Possession of Cuba was an end, to be sure, but it was also a means — a way to act out North American presumptions of primacy in the Western Hemisphere.

Much of this was related to geography. Cuba was so near — "almost in sight of our shores," John Quincy Adams exaggerated to make the point. That Cuba could be this near and not be part of the Union was inadmissible to the North American logic of the nineteenth century. Proximity did indeed seem to suggest destiny, and about destiny there was unanimity: it was manifest.

Cuba thus early became implicated in North American meditations on power. Almost from the outset, even as North Americans began to think of themselves as a nation, Cuba was a presence, a means of fulfillment. Cuba was subsumed into the collective national identity, a prism through which North Americans saw themselves and their future, and linked directly to the North American sense of security and well-being. For Jefferson possession of Cuba portended control over the Gulf of Mexico, as well as influence over all the countries in the region in order to "fill up the measure of our political well-being." The solvency and, indeed, the very survival of the North American nation was soon associated with Cuba. President James Buchanan predicted that Cuba promised to "strengthen our bond of Union" and "insure the perpetuity of our Union." Adams insisted that Cuba was "indispensable to the continuance and integrity of the Union itself." It was only a matter of time, and perhaps inevitable, for North Americans to determine that the well-being of the entire world depended on U.S. possession of Cuba. "The future interests not only of this country," argued Senator James A. Bayard at midcentury, "but of civilization and of human progress, are deeply involved in the acquisition of Cuba by the United States."

Early in the nineteenth century, and all through the nineteenth century, Cuba became enmeshed in the North American preoccupation with security as a people, as a nation. It was not always certain that these concerns were wholly rational, but it is clear that Cuba eventually was transformed into an obsession, one that extended deep into the ways that North Americans defined their interests and the sources of their well-being. The preoccupation remained long after the need — as part of the national character. That the North American nation took form around the expectation of possession of Cuba implied that the idea of national completeness remained unfulfilled without Cuba. If possession of Cuba was to have made the United States stronger, more secure and indeed, as Buchanan insisted, insure the perpetuity of the nation, that Cuba remained outside the union must have raised a specter of vulnerability and uncertainty.

III

It happened, too, that North American musings on well-being and security were more than adequately reciprocated by Cubans. The nineteenth century was a time of far-reaching change in Cuba. Market forces were transforming sugar production into the dominant economic activity of the island, and in the process changed everything else. Production modes, labor systems, race relations, class structures, colonial relationships, credit institutions, and commercial linkages were only some of the more important facets of Cuban life undergoing change. Prosperity arrived to the island in dramatic, sometimes ostentatious, forms and the taste for the materials that wealth brought in its wake and the demand for guarantees to expand wealth posed new challenges to existing colonial structures.

Cuba at midcentury had crossed a threshold into dynamic capitalist development. It had established vital linkages to world markets, organized around new production technologies and modern transportation facilities. Cuba was a presence on world markets, and the engine of its economy was modern, in almost every sense: integrated into international finance, dependent on science and technology, and employing modern industrial organization.

Cuba was in transition for much of the nineteenth century. Market-borne change was constant, at work always and always working to change everything else. Expectations changed, so too did the ways that Cubans defined their needs and defended their interests. Change created the circumstances in which the ordinary assumptions of colonial relationships were increasingly called into question, and increasingly lost credibility—all of which created readiness for more change and suggested the possibility of faster change.

Many changes were apparent. They could be measured and quantified, in a variety of ways through a variety of means. Increased sugar production was weighed and its value calculated. Rising land values were appraised and assessed. Expanding trade revenues were tallied in the form of customs duties, sales taxes, and import fees.

Change arrived in Cuba in waves, and as the nineteenth century wore on, the waves increased both in frequency and in reach. By the middle of the century, the issue was not merely change, to which Cubans had already become accustomed. The question had become the pace of change. And it was increasingly clear that the nature of change itself had changed. It was no longer measurable, and in some instances it was not even visible, but it was at work always — inexorably, relentlessly, governing the lives of vast numbers of people in ways not always comprehensible, or even recognizable.

Expanding familiarity with practices and procedures from the North contributed to this process. Indeed, North American presence served both as a source of change and the measure of change, which was in any case assuming increasingly institutional and structural form inside Cuba. Not all of this was new, of course, nor was it all from the outside. The rhythm and requirements of sugar production had already made for a regimen of planning, organization, and efficiency. Sugar did indeed engender a "time is money" economic environment and more than adequately lent itself to North American production methods. What was different was that adjustment to market forces necessarily implied changes in attitudes and values, a process that expanded in several directions at one time and in varying degrees affected all of Cuba. Part of this involved greater Cuban familiarity with business techniques and commercial practices of the North, increased participation in those ways, and inevitably accommodation to if not acceptance of those ways. This created new possibilities, new opportunities for Cubans to expand contact with the North, new ways through which Cubans were integrated in North American normative patterns.

Change also assumed new forms, much of which implied discontent and disaffection. Most immediately, and most of all, change served to expose the contradictions of colonialism and set in relief the many and varied ways that continued Cuban development could no longer be contained within existing colonial structures. On all counts, and all at once, Spanish colonialism was straining to accommodate the changes driving the transformation of Cuba — and increasingly revealing itself as incapable of doing so. Spain could not furnish adequate shipping to handle Cuba's growing foreign trade or provide adequate markets for Cuba's expanding production. Nor could Spain provide the capital to finance Cuban economic expansion or furnish the technology around which Cuban production systems had organized.

The implications were not ambiguous. The importance of Spanish participation in the Cuban economy was diminishing, in almost every sphere, and with far-reaching consequences. Spain could not adequately meet Cuban needs simply because it lacked the material resources and technological knowledge required in Cuba. Cuban development had been swift, in some instances spectacular, and production advances and industrial innovation had transformed key sectors of the colonial economy.

Cubans discerned promise and possibility in the United States. These were years of travel by Cubans, in great numbers, and they traveled mostly northward. Many arrived as immigrants, in flight from uncertain economic conditions and unstable political conditions. Periodically and repeatedly, during revolutionary upheavals of the nineteenth century, most notably in 1868–1878, and in 1879–1880, and again in 1895–1898, Cubans by the tens of thousands, young and old, often as entire families, sometimes as shattered households, took refuge in the United States, often for years at a time.

They arrived all through the nineteenth century, in vast numbers, an exodus that assumed fully the proportions of a diaspora. They represented all classes, the planter bourgeoisie and the working class, merchants and manufacturers, artisans and professionals, and settled across much of the United States.

Prosperity also served to stimulate Cuban travel to the North, more of them, more often. Expanded trade produced increased travel — for business, for pleasure, for education. The auguries did not please all, and especially displeased colonial officials who sensed uneasily the implications of this connection. "With increased wealth and expanded trade relations," Governor General José Gutiérrez de la Concha warned authorities in Madrid at mid-century, "the Island's inhabitants not only travel frequently, but infinitely worse, they have their children educated abroad, especially in the United States, and they return to their parents' homes with habits contrary to the institutions that govern us, disseminating among members of their family, their friends, and neighbors the prejudicial doctrines that they have learned."

Vast numbers of Cubans came into close and prolonged contact with North American culture and institutions. Their experience guaranteed that U.S. influences would penetrate Cuban society deeply and indelibly. This experience in the United States took a variety of forms, many of which were taken back to Cuba. Many were educated and trained by North Americans. Thousands acquired U.S. citizenship, and citizenship passed on to their children. Many abandoned Roman Catholicism, associated with Spanish rule, and became Methodists, Baptists, and Quakers. Some returned as Protestant ministers, to carry glad tidings of salvation in the hereafter, and in the process posed another challenge to the then and there. Spanish Catholicism, identified with colonialism and tradition, was under assault from North American Protestantism, associated with freedom and modernity.

The nineteenth century, almost all of it, were years of transition and transformation, of realignment and reorganization, and, in the end, of revolution. Cultural forms were in flux, and the effects of proximity to the United States and distance from Spain were taking their toll, inexorably and irreversibly. Geography and economics combined to change Cuban orientation away from Madrid and Barcelona and toward Washington and New York—and with far-reaching consequences.

In habits, in tastes, in preferences—in other ways perhaps too many to appreciate fully, with consequences impossible to measure, Cubans partook freely of North American culture. That so many traveled so often between Cuba and the United States provided a myriad of ways by which U.S. influence was diffused through the island. Cubans returned to the island clothed in North American attire, with tastes for things North American. Many decorated their homes with North American furnishings. The houses of *Habaneros*, observed William Cullen Bryant as early as 1850, "are filled with rocking-chairs imported from the United States." No self-respecting well-to-do Havana household was without the fashionable New York coupe. North American bicycles appeared on Havana streets in growing numbers. The best horses in Cuba, for transportation and sport, for work and pleasure, originated from the United States. Woven wire mattresses, postal lock-boxes, calendar clocks, cameras, and plated cookware were only some of a vast array of North American consumer goods that found widespread popularity and a ready market on the island.

Thus, Cubans were present and participants in the dawning of the consumer culture in the United States. And they learned early to adapt and adopt to the convenience and utility of things, and learned too of the ways in which things served to define and delineate social status. The implications of these developments were indeed far-reaching for they occurred as Cubans were assembling the distinct elements by which they were to distinguish themselves from Spaniards and define themselves as a national community.

It would be difficult if not altogether impossible to assess fully the impact of these developments, the myriad ways in which Cubans responded to North American society and how those responses influenced behaviors and attitudes in Cuba. Cubans came to know the United States intimately and were shaped by this knowledge. Several generations of Cubans were educated in the United States, many others were born and raised there. Contacts of this kind, and often decades in duration, could not but have affected the way Cubans came to take the measure of their own society and contributed to shaping their values and influenced the meanings they gave to their lives. The process spanned fully the second half of the nineteenth century and, indeed, the transformation occurred so gradually as to become part of the pattern of daily life.

Progress arrived to Cuba in the form of things North American: technological advances great and small, innovations lasting and ephemeral, the newest and the latest. Cubans could not help but stand in awe at the prodigious accomplishments of the North, many of which were already transforming the way Cubans were living in their own country. United States companies operated the utilities in the principal Cuban cities. The Santiago Gas Light Company provided gas lighting to the eastern capital. The Spanish-American Light and Power Company of New York illuminated the nights of Havana with gas light to the wonderment of *Habaneros*. C. & A. Beatty of New York provided Havana its fleet of new omnibuses. Runkle, Smith & Company constructed the modern water works of Havana in 1890. Havana hotels were transformed as elevators of North American origin were introduced. Telephone service was inaugurated in Havana in 1889, only a decade after the establishment of the first fast commercial exchange in the United States. Electric lighting arrived in the early 1890s.

These developments profoundly shaped the way Cubans thought of themselves. All these things had become theirs, a part of the material culture that Cubans claimed as their own. Cubans derived much satisfaction in these displays of material progress, all of which seemed to confirm the position of Cuba as a modern and civilized place. Cuba assumed the appearance of modernity, it exuded progress: steam-powered mills in the 1810s, railroads in the 1830s, telegraph service by early 1850s, telephones in the mid-1880s, and electric lighting in the early 1890s.

To be a part of the North, many Cubans reasoned, was not an altogether unwelcome turn of events. Cubans in vast numbers were familiar with the United States, and perceived in union the possibility of redemption and fulfillment. Such an arrangement promised to resolve some of the more anomalous features of colonial structures that threatened to obstruct continued economic development. Producers saw markets, technology, and capital — accessible, and so near. For other Cubans union promised lower prices on imports, lower living costs, and raised living standards. Liberals were heartened by the prospects of democratic institutions. Conservatives welcomed the promise of political stability and social order. The United States represented modernity and progress, and most of all the promise of unlimited economic development. The United States was the future, many concluded, and Cubans could not afford to remain in the past.

These were years of decisive importance to the formation of Cuban notions of nation and the development of nationality. Much in Cuban identity, and sense of future and place in that future, were related to the United States. Important elements in the development of Cuban nationality were shaped by or derived from nineteenth-century contact with North Americans, in Cuba and in the United States. So much of the enduring process of change in Cuba during these years involved North Americans, as cause or as effect, or both, as the source of change or as a means. Cuban well-being, specifically economic expansion and prosperity, which is also to say social peace and political order, depended on the United States: entry to its markets, use of its capital, and access to its technology. At some point in the nineteenth century, it became all but impossible for Cubans to contemplate their future, and especially their future well-being, without pausing first to consider the North American factor.

IV

Through all of the nineteenth century the North American presence in Cuba expanded, in all directions, in the capital and in the provinces, and into all sectors of the economy. North Americans took up residence in Cuba, and as their numbers increased, and their roles expanded, so too did their importance. The U.S. presence presaged the new order of things. They arrived to operate the sugar mills, to build the railroads, to work the mines, to farm. North

American capital expanded early into the local economy, including sugar plantations, mines, commerce, cattle ranches, and coffee estates. North Americans organized trading companies and established boarding houses. They were money lenders and shippers, buyers and sellers, engineers and machinists. They arrived in growing numbers to operate and service the industrial equipment imported from the United States, especially modern steam-powered mill machinery, the steamships, and the railroads. And as the century came to an end, they arrived as an army of occupation, to rule and, in the end, to seek anew possession of Cuba.

The colony ended in January 1899, ambiguously and perhaps even anticlimactically. Spain had been defeated, to be sure, and at least that part of the Cuban purpose had been achieved. But it was not certain that the Cubans had triumphed. The U.S. intervention in 1898 changed everything. Cubans and North Americans may have had a common enemy but they had not shared similar objectives. The North Americans arrived in the guise of allies and in the name of Cuban independence, as self-proclaimed liberators, but through a mixture of dissimulation and deception devised the pretext to remain as conquerors.

The expulsion of Spain in 1899 opened the island to new forms of contact with North Americans, and deepened the impact of old forms. Gradually the United States became reconciled to control as a substitute for possession, and it was thus arranged in the Cuban constitution of 1901 and later by formal treaty.

The cost of ending Spanish rule had been frightful, and across the island property and homes lay in ruins. Economic devastation during the war and military occupation after the war served to open Cuba to vast numbers of North Americans in search of opportunity and profits. Cheap rural land and urban real estate, bargains on indebted farms and plantations, mines, factories, and retail operations were only some of the opportunities that attracted carpetbaggers, land speculators, investment brokers, and countless numbers of small farmers and settlers from the United States. In the years immediately following the end of the war, North Americans of all social types swept across Cuba, with projects and schemes of all kinds, who looked upon Cuba as a place to make their fortunes. The island filled with U.S. agricultural colonists as thousands of North American homesteaders established new communities, and across the island appeared new Cuban towns with such improbable names as McKinley, Ocean Beach, Riverside, Garden City, Palm City, Omaja (Omaha), and Bartle.

The end of Spanish colonial rule eliminated state defense of Roman Catholicism and instantly the island was open to waves of Protestant missionaries from the North. Hundreds of North American Protestant missionaries arrived in Cuba, representing the principal North American denominations, and established churches, chapels, and schools, in the cities and in the countryside, from one end of the island to the other.

The end of Spanish rule also allowed the thousands of Cubans who had spent years in the North to return, and they returned to a new country, with new possibilities, in which the dominant cultural forms, political structures, and economic organizations originated from the United States. They enjoyed unique if unforeseen advantages. They returned to an island ruled by North Americans, to an economy dominated by North Americans. They knew English and were familiar with the ways of the North, and they fit in at home, in a world defined increasingly by North American standards, in which decision-makers, property-owners, power-wielders were increasingly North Americans. The new Cuba of the twentieth century emerged as an environment of limited opportunity and even fewer possibilities in spheres not related to the needs of North Americans.

The U.S. presence in Cuba after 1899 changed profoundly the character of the Cuban economy and the role of Cubans in that economy, no less than Cuban attitudes, social values, and habits. It was a presence to which vast numbers of Cubans were obliged to acquiesce, as a means of security and mobility, in the role of employees, debtors, renters, and customers. These relationships served to place Cubans in a new cultural context and within new ideological structures. The pursuit of security and success necessarily obliged Cubans to adapt to those forms that most promised to provide a measure of well-being for themselves and their children. This relationship served also to influence psychological needs, suggest new economic possibilities, and shape normative structures, both private and public, individual and collective. Increasingly large sectors of the Cuban population were incorporated into North American cultural forms: in recreation and leisure, in education and religion. Tens of thousands of Cubans were bilingual and, in varying degrees, bicultural. Consumption patterns and life-styles, no less than personal definitions of self-fulfillment and public perceptions of success, were derived from North American standards. That Cubans came in such close contact with U.S. society guaranteed that vast numbers of them would think like North Americans, act like North Americans, look like North Americans, and generally derive their cultural, social, and ethical orientations from North American sources. In the end, Cubans would construct many of their expectations and aspirations around these experiences.

All through the early decades of the twentieth century, Cubans and North Americans expanded contacts, and continued to cast spells on each other. These were two peoples who seemed to possess the capacity to meet each other's needs well, finding in one another fulfillment of their fantasies, a kind of complementary co-existence in which each had something to offer — something each seemed to lack and could find only in the other. The connection seemed to promise completion to both. North Americans could act on libidinous impulses, without restrictions and without guilt. Cuba became then and thereafter a place of exotic promiscuity and license, where the illegal was permissible — a place, one travel writer exulted in 1923, where "conscience takes a holiday." Cubans could fantasize about "making it" in the North — as a film star in Hollywood, or professional ball player in the major leagues, or artist in a New York art gallery: the North was the ultimate source of validation, "*las ligas grandes*" in every respect. North Americans found in Cuba relief from work, Cubans traveled North in search of work. North Americans arrived in Cuba seeking a tropical adventure, to lose themselves in the primitive and the exotic. The Cubans traveled north to find modernity: for business, for an education, to guarantee themselves a future, to learn English, to master technology, and to learn to compete and prevail in a world — their own world, dominated by North American structures, and from which they could not escape: not in Cuba, not in the United States.

North American travel to Cuba began immediately at the end of the war in 1898, and continued through the sixty years that followed. Recreational travel and tourism on a large scale began in the 1910s, and gained momentum. Cuba offered North Americans release from repressive morality, and in the years that followed World War I hundreds of thousands of North Americans traveled to Cuba and almost all came for the same things: rum, rumba, romance, roulette, and racing. Many came for the gratification and release they could not obtain at home and, if only briefly, to live beyond their means and outside their morality. Havana became a

Two postcards. Top: "Tropicana. Lefty Clark's new casino where you can try your luck at the most fascinating games in a distinguished atmosphere," 1959. Bottom: "Sloppy Joe's Bar, first port of call, out where the wet begins," 1952.

place for North Americans to enjoy themselves, to do the kinds of things they would not do—or could not do—at home, a place to flaunt openly the moral and sexual taboos that shaped the character of North American public life. Cuba was fun, a good time, a place to let loose, and Cubans were there to assist North Americans achieve these goals, in whatever form desired. This was a particular type of tourism, organized largely around commercialized vice. Goods and services North Americans were denied in the United States were patronized in Cuba: alcoholic drink, gambling, prostitution, and drugs. These were the years of Prohibition, and North Americans swarmed to Cuba in the pursuit of drink. Bars in Havana multiplied prodigiously, to more than 7,000; so did prostitution, as did drugs—and opium, heroin, and morphine became only slightly more difficult to obtain than rum, scotch, and gin.

These developments were central to the images both people developed of each other, the way Cubans functioned in their own society, the ways North Americans thought about Cubans. Cuban influences worked their way at all levels of U.S. society and nowhere more than on popular music and dance: the rumba and the conga during the 1930s and 1940s, as well as the mambo and the cha-cha-cha during the 1940s and 1950s. Cuban influences appeared in the compositions of W. C. Handy, Aaron Copland, Irving Berlin, and George Gershwin. Cuban rhythms pointed to new directions in U.S. jazz, and in increasing numbers Cubans—Machito, Mario Bauzá and Chano Pozo, among many others—worked with leading North American orchestras and bands, including Cab Calloway, Dizzy Gillespie, Duke Ellington, and Stan Kenton. Sports, and particularly baseball and boxing, were factors that contributed to the further incorporation of Cubans into North American life.

The linkages between material culture and political culture were telling and Cuban participation in an expanding and dynamic consumption culture as consumers from within a contracting and stagnant export economy served to create unrealistic expectations and in the end contributed to releasing the forces that led to revolution. Cuban society in the 1950s contained deep tensions and frustrations, as Cubans of all classes were experiencing economic stagnation and downward mobility. The cost of living was increasing, unemployment was expanding, and the aspirations of tens of thousands of Cubans were in jeopardy. An uncertainty existed, and was increasing, as the realization took hold among Cubans that they could not keep up with the standard that they set up as the measure of their own well-being. Large numbers of Cubans, middle class and working class alike, despaired of solutions within existing institutional structures, many of which were derived from and integrated into North American ones.

From the beginning of the century, the United States had set out purposefully to "Americanize" Cuba, but never considered the consequences of success: a First World frame of reference within Third World structures, and no way within the latter to fulfill the former.

Cuban identification with ways and things North American was unabashed and unambiguous, but it was not untroubled and certainly not without its anomalies. They had linked both worlds sufficiently to cross between each, with frequency and familiarity. But frequent and familiar crossings also — and inevitably — invited invidious comparisons, and almost at every turn Cuba came up short. They created a world of borrowed forms and imported structures, around which they adapted as a means of mobility and security, requiring in the end a redefinition derived from North American models. This was an illusory world sustained principally by a mixture of dissimulation and self-deception. Enormous effort and energy went into an endeavor that proved to be imperfect and, in the end, impossible.

And therein lay the source of the Cuban angst. Cubans had fashioned a version of the North in the tropics that created high expectations but without any capacity to deliver. Structural ties to the U.S. economy, no less than the psychological ones to U.S. cultural forms, served to create expectations in Cuba that were as unrealistic as they were unattainable. It simply was not possible for most Cubans to sustain a consumer economy of this magnitude within dependent capitalist structures of a sugar export economy. Few Cubans could keep up, at least keep up for long. The Cuban discontent ran deep and wide — and deepened and widened as conditions worsened. Cubans had become accustomed to a higher standard of living than they could sustain. At the height of years of presumed affluence and prosperity, even as national per capita income raced ahead of Latin America, Cubans were actually experiencing a decline in living standards and an increase in the cost of living. These were years of raised expectations and lowered possibilities, and expectations were rising higher even as possibilities were declining further.

Vast numbers of Cubans had redefined themselves and in varying degrees identified with ways and things North American. But it would be facile to suggest that these were positions without ambivalence and ambiguity. Certainly no other attribute characterized large sectors of the Cuban upper and middle classes more than their identification with the United States. Emulation did not, however, bring acceptance. In fact, hard as Cubans tried, they never obtained parity with their patrons. Imitation was suspect and ridiculed, and resulted largely in an indulgence that was both patronizing and mocking. North Americans demanded emulation and adaptation, but rejected the finished product as inauthentic. In its final form, emulation was the most complete form of submission — something North Americans understood and Cubans could only suspect. No amount of acquired forms and adaptive behaviors could offset factors of race and ethnicity. The willingness with which Cubans sought to integrate into North American capitalist structures, adopt U.S. cultural forms, and assimilate elements of the normative system from which they were derived, could not, in the end, deliver to Cubans control of those forces that most directly governed their lives. And the harder they tried, and the more complete that adaptation, the more difficult it became for Cubans to preserve the integrity of the nation, of the culture, and of themselves.

Many Cubans had indeed become, more or less, "Americanized," but in ways that Americans could never have foreseen. Cubans acquired sufficiently the values, and methods, and the expectations to allow them to identify and articulate the malaise of dependent capitalism in ways that most directly challenged the premises of North American hegemony in Cuba — on its own terms.

And more: Cubans in growing numbers were arriving at the realization that emulation could not produce authenticity, that North Americans could not deal with them on any terms other than instrumental ones: without a past, without a future, only a means, and that the meaning of "Cuban" had come to imply displacement and dispossession. Many soon found themselves with no alternative other than to make a virtue of necessity: to proclaim the supremacy of nation and affirm the primacy of nationality.

Cubans of all classes, in varying degrees, had grievances against the status quo, and much of that condition was a function of ties — historic and actual — with the United States. For one critical moment in 1959, all Cubans — men and women, black and white, of all ages, of all classes — participated in a joyful nationalist celebration, without being aware that the exaltation of things Cuban had profoundly different origins and radically different objectives. The revolution contained many diverse and divergent tendencies, central to which was the expectation that nationalism offered all a means of collective upward mobility. But when forced to choose, many used mobility as a means to nationalism. The demands of the revolution in 1959 for the primacy of Cuban interests as the principal consideration of national policy struck a responsive chord from all classes in Cuba, and more than adequately opened the way for radical change.

North Americans were unprepared to accept and unwilling to acknowledge the depth and breadth of Cuban grievances. The failure to take Cuba seriously, indeed—given the structures and relationships through which North Americans derived their perceptions of Cubans—the inability to take Cuba seriously, had far-reaching policy implications. Cubans meant to be taken seriously in 1959. The remarkable triumph of arms and spirit over the U.S.-backed Batista government served to confer on Cuban demands a heightened sense of confidence and expectation. The affirmation of national sovereignty and self-determination, the demand for control—control over their resources, control over their lives, control of their future—were not accepted at face value by North Americans. This demand for parity, this insistence upon equal opportunity, this appeal to fair play—very much formulated in North American terms—was incomprehensible in the United States, coming from Cubans. North Americans could presume familiarity with Cuba on many levels, and commonly did—as another tropical island, another vacation site, perhaps with a history, perhaps without—who cared, it really did not matter. "You Americans will never understand us," Blas de la Peña in John Sayles' novel *Los Gusanos* concludes ruefully. To which the American responds: "We don't really need to, do we?" At a February 1959 National Security Council meeting on Cuba, CIA director Allen Dulles expressed the view that "the Cuban leaders had to be treated more or less like children"—precisely the treatment Cubans set out to change.

These circumstances produced among Cubans their own version of familiarity with North Americans, and resulted in a love-hate relationship with a people Cubans were having difficulty living with but understood the greater difficulty of living without. That many chose, ultimately, to live without must be understood as a purge that reached deep into the psyche of the nation, and perhaps more than any other single development seemed to set Cuban against Cuban—between those who stayed and those who left. The revolution changed the terms of that relationship in dramatic terms, driving one portion of the population into the United States with the other against the United States. Cubans all, they continued to define their world as a function of their relationship with the North.

As for the United States: North Americans had accepted the exercise of control as an adequate substitute for outright possession. And when control was lost, after 1959, memory's vulnerability revived. Not unlike Cubans, North Americans defined their world in relation to the other.

"Visit Cuba." Postcard, circa 1930s.

EPISTLE TO JOSE LUIS FERRER
(FROM HAVANA TO MIAMI)

Jose, I am dazzled less often with every passing day
It is the child heading off toward an incomprehensible classroom
A time in which one begins to mistrust appearances
So that a young woman's beauty seems intolerably suspicious
"It is the voice of Satan, weeping over the world," says Hallach, a
    Muslim theologian
"Satan is condemned to love what will pass away, therefore he
    weeps," comments Louis Massignon
Now I understand that the past that I mythify was a threshold
We didn't know how to read it, and all we have left now is the
    belated melancholy of rereading
Diaspora, like death, eternalizes emotions
But we are all cast upon a deserted beach
Because we all live on an island
We all carry an island within
Looking at the night, knowing it is the same for everyone, is a
    strange solace perhaps, or an intimate dread
Sometimes, like the Indians of Cuba, I get nostalgic for tobacco
    smoke:
as in Lezama's *tokonoma*, there we would meet each other again*
Diaspora, like death, interrupts all conversation
As Enriquito Saínz says: "Listening to music, reading a book,
    conversing with a friend or two. . . ."
And Eliseo: "The parties that once lit up deep corridors have
    ended"
But my memories keep on my tongue his other verse: "Like the
    hurdy-gurdies of winter"
And an unfathomable melancholy fills me
In the shade of flowering mangoes or beneath inconceivable stars,

Kaki and I play checkers, play Parcheesi, play Chinese
checkers, roll and smoke a cigarette, drink coffee, herb tea,
bitter orange, sometimes a bottle of homebrewed wine (too
bitter to be our wine), on exceptional or absolutely trivial
occasions a bottle of hooch
This summer, in Varadero, we picked up many shells!
("little bones in the sand")
Where is passion, eternal adolescence?
It too, like childhood, passed without our notice
Diaspora, like death, interrupts all conversation
We are as if bewitched, ecstatic before these high walls
Of History? Now we hear tell that History has ended. . . .
One passes from hate to laughter but in the end a melancholy
    smile always wins out
One would like to shout and, as in fairy tales, for the ogre to turn
    to stone
One misses certain feelings — the savage, barbaric, primitive ones
All power is abominable
One needs something to air out the soul — I was going to say: "like
    springtime. . . ."
Will you come to think in English? Every language has its music,
    they say.
"Do you know what country it is turning into?" asks Fina in her
    "Song of Autumn," paraphrasing Goethe
What a melancholy gesture, to stretch your hand out to so many
    books already read
But it is worse to stretch it out to what does not exist
I wanted to be an astronomer, an argonaut, an obscure voyager
    through cities of gold, a shipwrecked sailor on a floating isle.
Ah, yes, I wanted to be so many things!
How did you do with the Hurricane? That certainly wasn't "a
    little breeze from Cojímar"
The other day I wrote a poem that I called "Thoughts in Days of
    Uncertainty"
This is a fragment:
". . . there is an unsettling kind of pause, a silence, an interval
One would like to assert: 'But action saves'
Suddenly you remember that 'Art is long and life is short'
And the dizziness gets worse, like certain depravities
Something almost Roman emerges in your consciousness
A universe without God is terrible

A strange clarity augments your perception of the unknown or the
    invisible
As Cavafis would say: 'Yet what the future may bring, wise men /
can know. Sometimes their ear, / in hours of deep meditation, /
becomes alarmed. And from the march of strange events / they
perceive the hidden meaning.'
Like a distant water that paints a landscape in a dream, I would
    add
But living through the impossible is the supreme uncertainty"
What do you think of these letter-poems?
If only I could write one day an epistle like that of Darío to
    Madame Lugones!
But for now I can only send you this embrace, as the only
    certainty

Diaspora, like death, interrupts all conversation.

Havana, 23 August 1992

Translated by David Frye

---

*Author's Note: José Lezama Lima uses and recreates the Taoist concept of
tokonoma, emptiness, in his poem "*El pabellón del vacío*" (in *Fragmentos a
su imán*, 1977), to refer to a kind of creative point or vacuum through
which humans can gain access to resurrection, to spatial and temporal
ubiquity.

Drawing by Zaida del Río.

Excilia Saldaña with a photograph of her grandmother, Ana Excilia Bregante, Havana, 1994. Photograph by Ruth Behar.

EXCILIA SALDAÑA

FROM *MY NAME*
(A FAMILY ANTI-ELEGY)

. . . .

I am guilty of everything and I accept it.
She who I am not—but who usurps me out of habit and fear—
bites
                              the sophistication of the bread
                              like a caress:
Crushes the serpent.
                    Swallows the sword.
                              Opens the forbidden
      lattices:
God entered my body of ten years.
Ah, vanity of vanities, vainglory of theophagy;
neither my mother nor the mother of my father could devour
an entire, round, white soundless god.
It is not I—but how well I pretend to be, under a tender smile—
who now sits,
                    not at the right,
                                        not at the left,
                              But in the middle:
                    In the throne of tinsel and tin cans
dictating the future of her race for ever and ever, world without
      end.
And chooses to save you, Ana Excilia Bregante,
                    affectionate *mulata* of Atarés,
                    keeper of the oranges,
                    lady of coral and *canistel*,
                    mistress of *flan de calabaza*,
                    grandmother and martyr,

while the country is torn to pieces
                              in bombings and killings.
I save you
                    and I save my name from oblivion and from hell,
today,
                    December 8, 1956.
· · · · · · · · ·

A slow finger traces the circle of my eternity:
seven letters
                              my name, a way of saying yes,
                              my name that fills the space,
                              my word-name,
                              my poem-name.
The Word that remakes chaos. The prophecy that creates order.
Only ripe fruit is humble enough to kiss the ground.
Go find yourself a legend, and therein let join together who I am
      not
and who you'll be forever.
Fifes and panpipes in the secret of the *monte*, in the hump of the
      yerbero.
Play the flute, accompany yourself
                              like the elves
with the whistling that awakens the yagruma or the anemone.
Sit in the crown of the ceiba.
Dilute yourself with the sunflower or the black prince.
Take revenge on the compassion of the flamboyant.
Blow indifferent,
blow mischievous,
blow ingenuous
now that the dementia of words is yours alone,
the firebird and crystal of wisdom.
Blow until the moment before it bursts in flames
now that the island is a bonfire.
· · · · · · · · · ·

                                        I await you
with the bed laid out,
                              scented with vetiver and mint,
with *leche ahumada*,
                              with my hands and my puppets.

Excilia,
          you,
                    always Excilia:
                    name of my name:
                    granddaughter,
                    guardian:
                    companion.

I did not inherit this confusion.
They banished my name and banished me.
They condemned me to carry it
                              from door
                              to
                              door
as she who left or she to whom they've gone.
Sleepless in my bed, fasting at my table.
The house does not exist:
                    No one watches over it;
in the eye of the hurricane
only windbags by vocation are allowed:
I am free in the space
                    of the first freedom
to find my origin
                    in the son who will engender me.
The oregano branch humbly perfumes
                    the hand that breaks it off.
A child laughs and steals the leaf from me.
And I smell it.
                    And I give it to him to smell.
                                        And he laughs.
I have a bird's belly
                    because I have given myself to the world
in the happiness of the earth.
Grow swiftly,
          my son's breast;
grow hard,
          my son's hand;
grow strong,
          my son's back;
rise up now,
          my son's height;

my name awaits you.

But not the tiny and strange name
in the official papers.
That talisman already out of date,

that old watchword,

that bastion of family,
who should care, but me?
Or the one they say I am

out of pure intuition or ill will.

I don't speak of the name they gave me
so I could speak with the stars.
For my name with its seven letters

made of fear and more fear

I don't want posters nor headlines nor interviews nor sighs nor
    editions nor
        homages nor marquees nor soirées nor royal audiences nor
        jubilees
— I don't miss what I've never had

I don't aspire to what I don't have — .

Rather for that other thing:
            My name
of the foot and the path,
    my name.
        My name
of palm fiber and mire,
    my name.
        My name
of fat and smoke,
    my name.
        My name
of cotton and fire,
    my name.
        My name.
of alcohol and night,
    my name.
        My name
of boiling pan and thunder,
    my name.
        My name
of river and honey,
    my name.

My name
of cave and sky,
    my name.
            My name
of the open laugh,
    my name.
            My name
of bow and wind,
    my name.
            My name
of grain and wound,
    my name.
            My name
of sea and iron,
    my name.
            My name
of moss and petal,
    my name.
            My name
of glass and steel,
    my name.
            My name
My name
        in the name of those who've recently chosen their name and
                                                their memories.
My name
        to hurl it down like rain over the pitcher
                                    of my archipelago.

                Translated by Ruth Behar and David Frye

---

coral: a flowering bush or its decorative seeds
canistel: a tree and its fruit, similar to zapote or mamey
flan de calabaza: squash pudding
yerbero: seller of medicinal herbs
yagruma: a small tree
ceiba: a large tree
flamboyant, or royal poinciana: a tropical tree with scarlet and orange
    flowers

PATRICIA BOERO

CUBANS INSIDE AND OUTSIDE: DIALOGUE AMONG THE DEAF

My first memory of Cuba was probably drawn from a 1953 photograph I saw of myself surrounded by my Cuban aunts and grandfather on a hot Havana afternoon. I was too young to remember, barely one year old. That was the last time my mother saw her family. After the revolution, she could not go back. She had married a foreigner in 1948, but after 1959 all those who lived outside automatically became suspect and could not obtain visas or passports easily. Also, my father was a diplomat from Uruguay, a country that broke off relations with Cuba, as did the rest of Latin America, with the exception of Mexico. Cuba was a place to be remembered, but off limits to us.

When I was six we moved to Sweden. My parents would fight the darkness and the cold of those long Stockholm winters with a steady dose of music: nostalgic tangos and recordings of Lecuona's "Siboney." We also ate *plátanos fritos*, and *arroz con frijoles*, and sprinkled our vocabulary with words like *calato* and *molote*. Even from the safety of our gilded cage in Stockholm it was easy to understand the pain of exile contained in José Martí's verses: "What I want when I die, without a homeland but without a master, is flowers on my grave, and the flag. . . ." ["*Yo quiero, cuando me muera, sin patria pero sin amo, pongan en mi tumba un ramo de flores, y una bandera. . . .*"] My mother would recite to us Martí's "*Los Zapaticos de Rosa,*" a moving account of a rich girl's first encounter with poverty and death: "there is sunshine at the seaside, and fine sand, and Pilar wants to wear her new feather hat. . . . " ["*hay sol bueno y mar de espuma, arena fina, y Pilar quiere salir a estrenar su sombrerito de pluma. . . .*"]

There were also amusing stories from my mother's Havana repertoire. (She had only ventured into the countryside on one occasion,

189

when some *guajiros* had loudly criticized her for wearing trousers.) She had grown up in Centro Habana's San Lázaro Street, amidst an extended family we only knew through occasional clues: I had asthma, like her cousin Georgina; my sister had a temper like her Tía Josefa's. We loved to hear about my mother's *paseos* along the *Malecón*: her sisters attracted many *piropos*, but my mother's skinny legs — an unforgivable defect in Havana's code of beauty — were dismissed as *bacalao* — fish bones.

My mother's recollections always ended lamenting her sisters' bad choices in marriage: Mercedes, the eldest, to a jealous violinist in the symphony orchestra, who forced her to wear black, long-sleeve dresses in the sultry summers. He forbade her even to pluck her eyebrows, so that other men would not find her desirable. The husband finally left my aunt Mercedes after their baby son died. "*Se fue con una rubia*" ("He took off with a blond"), was the lapidary explanation. Mercy was left pining and pregnant (and hairy, as I imagined her). Her second child, a girl named Cecilia, was saved from dying when my mother discovered ants in her diapers, and diagnosed diabetes. The other sister, Mirta, married a tall, handsome *mulato* — she barely reached his waist — and he turned out to have an obsession with tidiness. Mity had to wash and iron his *guayaberas*, so he could change three times a day. Little wonder then that my mother worshipped my father, who made no such demands.

My mother — Rosa — had the sunny character I attributed to the Caribbean: a crystalline, spontaneous laughter that broke all sense of protocol during the ambassadorial cocktail parties we often hosted, and the soft consonants that replace the harsh J's and LL's of Spanish as it is spoken in Uruguay. She was never angry, she never sulked. The only time I saw her crying was when a phone call arrived, unexpectedly, from Havana. Her sister Mity was explaining that there was a shortage of insulin in Cuba, because of the U.S. blockade. Our cousin Cecilia was going blind and would soon die without her regular injections. She was thirteen years old.

My father, in his usual calm and authoritative way, took control of the situation. He asked his Canadian colleague to supply Cecilia with the insulin through diplomatic channels. My cousin was saved, but for a long time we sat by the telephone, shaken, waiting for the news. I was eight years old and already I understood the word *bloqueo*. How many children in Cuba died from medicine shortages? How many Cubans in exile were not able to see their dying relatives because of the reciprocal *bloqueo* Castro imposed on those who left? Those were the cheerless questions Cubans and their families were forced to face wherever they might live.

Other world events eventually displaced the Cuban Revolution from the headlines. The Missile Crisis and the Bay of Pigs invasion were soon forgotten by the world media, and I sat down to watch, in astonishment, the murder of JFK on our first black and white television set. A couple of years later, I succumbed to Beatlemania and concentrated on memorizing their lyrics in English. I no longer read Becquer or Martí, Juana de Ibarbourou or Alfonsina Storni. Cuba faded from my interests—only the occasional letter from Havana would spark my dormant curiosity. Mity always graced her envelopes with patriotic messages: *"Patria o Muerte!"*, *"Viva Fidel!"*, *"Cuba Libre!"*, *"Venceremos!"* My mother dismissed the envelopes and avidly read the contents. The remote names of my cousins were quoted to me: Orlandito, and later, Raysa. Mity had named her only daughter after my mother, and in tune with her passionate admiration for Lenin's homeland, had Russified Rosa to Raysa.

My family returned to Uruguay in the late sixties, in time to live through the most militant years of the Tupamaros urban guerilla movement. My sister, brother and I were sheltered from the chaos of Montevideo in a British school, where we sang "God Save the Queen" in honor of the British Ambassador. He had been kidnapped by the *Tupas* and was unable to attend the graduation ceremonies. I led the cheers, in a proper Oxford accent, for His Excellency's prompt return: "Hip, Hip . . . Hurrah!" I also wore white gloves to carry the British flag, while outside our school other students were erecting barricades and burning the American flag in protest over the CIA training Uruguayan police in torture techniques. In my school, however, we remained isolated and aloof, reading *The Prisoner of Zenda* and memorizing Rudyard Kipling's *If*.

It wasn't till the 1972 elections in Uruguay that I was faced with a political choice. By then I had transferred to a state-run high school, its windows broken by rocks from the demonstrations, and classes often cancelled by ardent rallies and speeches from *"los compañeros de la FEU."* I was swept up by the rhetoric and admired the self-assurance of *las compañeras*. I decided it was more glamorous to be a communist than a *traga*—a nerd—and I discovered a new world of ideology, of commitment, that had been lacking in my life. The key words that drew the loudest applause in those rallies were Cuba and Fidel. To the rebellious middle class students in Montevideo, or the dispossessed sugar-cane cutters from Uruguay's northern provinces, *La Revolución Cubana* was a shining dream, an example to follow, a source of hope and comfort in the violent struggle tearing Latin America apart in the seventies. I understood, at last, what *Che Vive* meant, painted on the walls of the rich houses in my neighborhood. I voted for the Frente Amplio, a left-wing coalition formed only a year before the election, and led by Uruguay's Communist Party.

Other changes occurred in my life. I married, and traveled to Australia, where my husband was working. I was in the distant city of Hobart, in Tasmania, when I read the news of an attempted coup in Montevideo. By the time the military had taken full control of Uruguay, in June 1973, I was separated and living in Sydney. I had not decided how long I would stay in Australia, but I realized I had better not return to Uruguay. I started working in factories and later enrolled in the University of New South Wales in Sydney. I met Latin American refugees from the other dictatorships, and we formed solidarity movements that united us against the military juntas. It was a logical conclusion that our enemy's enemy had to be our friend: Cuba was the country that welcomed our exiles, and supported their struggle. I continued writing to my aunt Mity, who encouraged me to visit her. *"Cuba es tu casa,"* she would say; *"Cuba tambien es tu patria."* Her words moved me, her love for Fidel and the revolution was contagious, joyful, fresh.

In 1981 I landed in José Martí airport in Havana. My telegrams had never arrived, and there was nobody there to greet me. Bewildered, I registered as a tourist and was assigned to the Hotel Sevilla in Old Havana, a glorious, dilapidated hotel where Hemingway once stayed—or so the cigar-smoking, opera-singing elevator operator told me. I opened my bedroom window and breathed in the salty, sunny air. "This is the blue sky my mother always pined for," I thought. *"Por ti, mami, estoy aquí."*

I took a cab to my Aunt Mity's apartment. I had so often written Belascoain, entre Sitios y Peñalver, on my envelopes, that it felt like breaking a spell actually to find the street and number. It was a flaking, dirty street, lined by columns and shaded walkways, and I loved it: smoky, noisy Centro Habana. I climbed the dark stairs to the first floor and rang the doorbell. Nothing. I knocked on the door, my heart pounding. No answer. I knocked again. Finally a neighbor opened her door and yelled *"No te oye, es muda."* At first I did not understand or make the connection. Mute? Then I understood. My cousin Raysa was deaf, not mute. Tía Mity was out, and Raysa could not hear my knocking. But Cuca, *la vecina*, had a key and she let me in. Raysa was sitting down, writing her homework. She looked remarkably beautiful and calm. I started saying *"soy tu prima, Patricia, de Australia,"* and gesturing like an airplane. Her eyes lit up. *"P-rr-i-ma,"* she said, and we embraced. I have never felt so helpless, so tender. Raysita took my hand and led me to her mother's room. It was a replica of my own mother's room, with the same portrait of our grandmother surrounded by candles and roses, and my postcards of kangaroos and koalas lined up along the mirror. Under the bedside table's glass surface, the smiles of my Uruguayan family greeted me. Raysa opened a drawer and pulled out my letters. She opened her closet and showed me the red leotard I had sent her for her gymnastics competition. She had been expecting me, after all.

I continued traveling to Cuba, and created the first Brigades from Australia, which we named "The Southern Cross." Many Latin American exiles participated. We climbed the Sierra Maestra mountains and camped at the historic guerrilla headquarters of Che and Fidel. We picked oranges and we worked in construction sites, visiting schools and factories, hospitals and crocodile farms. We listened for hours to lectures by *combatientes* from Angola and Granada, and believed fervently in *"el internacionalismo proletario."*

Cuba influenced and inspired people as far away as Australia, and the labor leaders, lawyers, and students that joined our brigades would return home filled with revolutionary determination. Only the more skeptical would ask discomforting questions, and be dismissed by us as cynical capitalist stooges, or even suspected of CIA affiliation. Many Aussies were equally moved by the passions of the tropical life style, and hot romances flourished in the *Campamento Internacional Julio Antonio Mella*. This, our Cuban hosts would patiently explain, was also normal. *Brigadistas* were a major headache for the security around the camp, as couples furtively escaped to the infamous "mango lane" behind the segregated sleeping barracks. As long as the sex involved only foreigners, it was just a source of benign jokes; but Cubans showed little tolerance for inter-racial liaisons if it meant that one of their cadres might end up deserting to Australia, albeit for an appropriately internationalist cause. Some hearts were broken, but other romances survived, leading some *brigadistas* to abandon Australia and settle down in Cuba instead.

My mother got to know her niece and namesake for the first time in 1984. Uruguay had just emerged from the dictatorship into democracy, and one of the first initiatives of the new president was to re-establish diplomatic relations with Cuba. We traveled via Mexico, where we entered the Cuban Embassy to collect our visas. My mother paused to look up at the Cuban flag, and cried. She could not believe she was so close to seeing her country again. Her father had long since died, as had her brother, more recently. Her niece Cecilia had finally died of diabetes, but she still had her sisters, and the rest of her nieces and nephews. When we arrived at José Martí it seemed to take hours to clear the airport bureaucracy because my mother had no Cuban passport. Finally they came, my aunts with wilting flower bouquets. Everyone called my mother "Royal," her childhood name derived from the baking powder. At Raysa's house, the sisters began singing tangos and boleros a cappella, in perfect harmony. It was their way of defeating time, and distance: thirty years had not passed; it was truly a triumph of memory.

The neighbors came in to look at *las extranjeras*, and my aunts would reassure them that we were *familia*, that my mother had left in 1948 and was no *gusana*. My aunts had long since divorced their husbands and were now, to my mother's surprise, assertive Marxist-feminists. My mother went for long walks in Old Havana, and visited her parents' graves at the Colón Cemetery. She even attended *misa de gallo* on Christmas Eve to make sure Catholicism was still alive in Cuba. She swam at the beaches in Varadero and played dominoes and danced on New Year's Eve. To me she looked younger and happier.

I had the good fortune of living in Cuba from 1985 to 1990; of seeing my cousin Raysa blossom from the shy fifteen year-old I met behind that door, to the confident professional she now is, drawing up plans for houses and even a sports stadium in Alamar. I was there for her graduation, and for her wedding. I learned to understand her sounds and some of her signs, and she learned to read my lips, off-screen and on television, where I sometimes appeared in a documentary or a talk show, to her delight. Raysa still uses my sheets, my pots and pans, and all the clothes I left behind. I still use her eyes to read the world, imagining it sometimes devoid of sound, as she knows it, and free of dogmatic speeches and hurtful words, like *gusano*, and rigid categories, like *comunista* or *capitalista*.

In those five years I learned a lot more about Cuba. I feared the cliché would come true: Cuba was not only the socialist model I had shown the brigadistas, or my nostalgic mother; it was also the dreary reality of bureaucracy and petty corruption. As the years passed, my own ideological intransigence gave way to pragmatic compromises. I too, reluctantly, began to buy food in the black market, and bribed my car mechanic with bottles of rum in the hope of obtaining a spare part for my collapsing "Polski" car. Soon I was also paying for drinking water with rum, and securing a room in a hotel in exchange for three bars of imported soap. I appeased my "supervising officer" at work with an electric fan and several pounds of coffee in exchange for her cooperation in helping me move out of a cockroach-infested apartment into a slightly less decaying neighborhood.

My Cuban journalist colleagues gradually confided their worst paranoias and fears. I saw many of them *sancionados* for writing the wrong thing, or failing to censor the right story, even by mistake. The punishments were mild but humiliating, usually involving transfers to boring and menial clerical jobs. Some went off to Angola in order to rediscover their revolutionary commitment. Those decisions and transfers would happen overnight, and were accepted as part of everyday life by those who remained in their jobs, aware of how tenuous their positions were.

General Ochoa's trial and execution changed that passive acceptance. Fidel was seen up to then as the aging, *chocho* grandpa who knows best and must be humored. A year and an *autocrítica* later, you would have your job back, all being forgiven. Ochoa, however, was killed. There have been many speculations about his participation in drug trafficking. I believe it was minimal and authorized from above. I also believe that he was sufficiently loyal to Fidel to accept being a scapegoat. He willingly took the blame. "*En silencio ha tenido que ser*" ("In silence it had to be") had been replayed on television often enough to create the cult of secrecy and martyrdom for the revolution. The *telenovela* glorified Cuba's double agents who died in the line of duty while even their families believed they were traitors. Ochoa's execution was a sobering reminder that everyone was disposable; that no matter how many merits you had earned—and General Ochoa was an official Hero of the Cuban Revolution—you could be sacrificed to maintain Fidel and Raul *en el poder*.

Cuba remains in my memory as the magic place of my mother's childhood, even if it no longer has the *batidos de mamey*, and Coppelia rarely offers more than two ice-cream flavors. *El Malecón* is still there, with couples making love by the sea, and children are still named Lázaro and Caridad, after the saints. Cubans are the same sentimental nation, wiping tears after a Brazilian *telenovela* or yet another speech by Fidel reminiscing of heroic battles like Girón. But I have changed. I can no longer cheer a May Day parade, or defend the one-party state with the same conviction. I feel a loss of faith, a loss of innocence, that is a kind of slow burning bereavement, and leads to what a friend of mine calls *el exilio de baja intensidad*. Many of us have left Cuba quietly, regretfully, and live elsewhere, carrying the sorrow deep inside for what Cuba was and could have been. We have not joined the loud opponents of Castro because we detect in them the seeds of tyranny, and recognize the same rhetoric of intolerance that made us decide to leave. We have, in some ways, become "*mudos.*"

I left Cuba repeating my mother's words, like incantations; promising not to forget, *nunca*, and to remember, *siempre*. It is true, I have never forgotten, and I will always remember. That first conversation I had with Raysa, improvising signs and guessing meanings, is the perfect metaphor to illustrate that dialogue is possible between *los cubanos de acá, y los de allá*. Thirty years of mistaken policies, of war games, and of pride, have widened the distance between us, and made dialogue all but impossible. Yet growing numbers of Cubans want to reach past the old exiles, recalcitrant in their resentment, and past the old rulers on the island, arrogant in their splendid isolation, and open the locked doors, and talk, and touch, and trust each other again, like the cousins, and sisters, and neighbors that we are.

I am in Chicago now, and I listen to rumbas and mambos to dispel the sleet and snow. As I look around my room I see portraits of all the Rosas in my family, including my sister, María Rosa, and my cousin Raysa, with her baby daughter, whom she named Patricia after me. I cannot call my aunts on the telephone, because the blockade does not allow enough lines between the countries, so I still have to rely on Mity's letters to tell me that her grandchild just took her first steps, and to keep me up to date on other news of the family. Her words have the same soothing effect as Martí's verses, telling me that, as soon as the Cold War is finally over, and the blockade is lifted, *habrá sol bueno y mar de espuma*. We'll walk together along the *Malecón*, and the baby will be wearing her *Zapaticos de Rosa*.

MARILYN BOBES

DANGERS OF SPEAKING AND STAYING
QUIET. LANGUAGE OF SILENCE*

Since it is   fierce
if   I say
what excuse
if I stay quiet, who will be able to

But   without speaking to you
        sight   semblance
   in the silence
           they say

and whoever makes them happen
and whoever orders silences, understands them

Translated by Ruth Behar

---

*Translator's Note: This poem is one of a series of "Quevedianos," poems
that Marilyn Bobes borrows from the Golden Age Spanish writer Francisco
de Quevedo; she erases words from the originals to create new poems.

COCO FUSCO

EL DIARIO DE MIRANDA /
MIRANDA'S DIARY

Americans often ask me why Cubans, exiled or at home, are so passionate about Cuba, why our discussions are so polarized, and why our emotions are so raw, after thirty-four years. My answer is that we are always fighting with the people we love the most. That intensity is the result of tremendous repression and forced separation that affect all people who are ethnically Cuban, wherever they reside. Official policies on both sides collude to make exchange practically impossible. Public debate is extremely limited in the United States and on the island. Only extreme positions get attention; any other stance is recast as the desirable extreme or ideological "diversionism." Travel is severely restricted by the American and Cuban governments, making contact difficult and encouraging exaggerated rumors to pass for truth. Communication, when it does happen, is often strained.

The main players in this game—the Cuban govern-

Coco Fusco as a babe in the arms of her mother (at bottom of stair), 1960.

An earlier version of this essay was published in *The Subversive Imagination*, edited by Carol Becker (Routledge, 1994).

198

ment, the Miami-based Cuban right, and the Cuba supporters among the American left—are all suspicious of Cuban border-crossers, people who allow ethnic, kinship, and emotional ties to override ideological difference, people whose intellectual and political perspective is less nationalist, and less invested in fictions of separate development. The Cuban government has no official policy vis-à-vis the liberal/progressive sectors of *la comunidad*, which allows the prejudices of individual bureaucrats to determine action and allows for easy erasure of any real distinction between extremist anti-Castro terrorists and proponents of dialogue. The Cuban right wing uses its economic clout and political ties to the U.S. government to proclaim that it speaks for all Cubans. Pro-Cuba intellectuals of the international left, or *cubanólogos* as some of us lovingly refer to them, can use the convenient stereotypes about Cubans outside Cuba—*gusanos, colonizados,* and *fanáticos*—to maintain a paternalist attitude toward all exiles and Cuban-Americans, reject all their criticism of the Cuban government and justify not sharing power with them. None of these sectors has effectively dealt with the complexities of the situation; the revolution and the Cold War created a separate nation, but never completely succeeded in dividing a people.

I am the daughter of a Cuban who emigrated to the U.S. in 1954, and who was deported in 1959, shortly after the triumph of the revolution. My mother hid from the I.N.S. until after my birth. Then, she returned to the island with me. The fact that I was an American citizen secured her permission to return to New York within weeks, while the lines of Cubans at the American Embassy in Havana who sought visas to leave the country grew and grew. In the decade that followed, my mother's sisters, brother, parents, nieces and nephews all emigrated, and my home became a way station. At the age of eight, I was teaching English to my cousins and translating for older relatives; at school I would hide this side of my life to downplay my difference from the rest of the children, and look embarrassed when adults asked me what I thought of Fidel Castro. Yet, as a child among foreigners, I grew accustomed to living with the presence of an imaginary country in my home; it spoke to me in another language, in stories, rhymes, and prayers; it smelled and tasted different from the world beyond the front door. Still, unlike other immigrants who could return and replenish their repertoire of cultural references, we could not. For many exiles, the real Cuba had died with the revolution, and would only live on in their minds.

The Cuban children of my generation didn't choose to leave or to stay — the wars that shaped our identities as Cuban or American are ones we inherited. There are those among us who have made quiet pilgrimages back to the island as a way of reconciling ourselves to the paradoxical familiarity and distance that mark our connections to our origins. That decision to reestablish contact with Cuba is often looked upon as an act of treason — we are traitors to the exile community's extremists, and ungrateful to our parents, who saved us from the Caribbean "gulag." When I began to travel to Cuba in the early '80's, I was naive enough to believe that I could slip past the watchful eye of *la comunidad*. I was soon forced to realize that my decision defined me in ways that went far beyond my power to determine my own life. It also opened the door to understanding myself as a child of diaspora, of the Cold War, of the Civil Rights movement, of the Black Caribbean, of Cuba *and* the United States.

None of this would have been possible were it not for the fact that Cuban culture hadn't died with the revolution, as the exiles would have had it. The neo-colonial world of the middle and upper classes had simply diminished in importance, as different notions of the popular moved into the foreground. I went to the island ostensibly to confront Cuban culture in the present, but returning enabled me to face and come to know my counterparts, the children (now grown) who also hadn't had a choice, but who had stayed. Although history had intervened to separate us, we shared a healthy skepticism toward the nationalist rhetoric of our parents' generation, and a growing curiosity about one another.

What follows is a collection of my reflections on my experiences traveling to Cuba during the last eight years. I chose to write it in diary form because of the fleeting, momentary nature of those encounters; I also wanted to stress the subjective dimension of those experiences, rather than "speaking for Cuba," as I had to do as a journalist to gain entry into the country. The account is not chronological — instead, I piece memories together to find the logic that links disparate events. This way of thinking reminds me of the kinds of conversations I have had late at night on the island; with so little information circulating "officially," our favorite pastime was to drink coffee and chew over details each member of the group could provide to figure out what the government was up to.

I call my piece *Miranda's Diary*, making reference to Prospero's daughter in Shakespeare's *The Tempest*, and to a host of allusions to the play in Latin American intellectual history and postcolonial thought. Shakespeare's drama, set on an island, is considered to have been inspired by accounts of voyages and shipwrecks during the early colonial period. Among the drama's many characters, the patriarchal magician Prospero, his indigenous slave Caliban, and his ethereal assistant Ariel have become symbols of colonial relations and of struggles to forge identity in nineteenth and twentieth century Latin American thought. In 1900, following the transfer of Cuba, Puerto Rico and the Philippines to the U.S. as "protectorates," the Uruguayan writer José Enrique Rodó published *Ariel*, an essay that depicts an allegorical conflict between two versions of modernity; in it, the U.S. is a chaotic and materialistic Caliban whose influence threatens a Latin American Ariel envisioned as a neo-classical, orderly and ideal world.

In the postcolonial period, Latin American and Caribbean intellectuals began to recast this allegory, shifting their identification from Ariel to Caliban. In 1960 George Lamming champions Caliban's ability to reshape his master's language in *The Pleasures of Exile*; in 1969, Aimé Cesaire writes *A Tempest: An Adaptation of Shakespeare's "The Tempest" for a Black Theatre*. Then in 1971, the Cuban writer Roberto Fernández Retamár publishes his *Caliban: Notes on a Discussion of Culture in Our America*, transforming the slave into an admirable combination of defiant Carib and New World Man, and identifying him with the island, the revolution, and even Fidel. These writers concentrate little attention on Miranda, *The Tempest's* only significant female character. They only take note of Caliban's attempt to seduce her shortly after she arrives on the island with Prospero. Psychoanalytic theorists O. Mannoni and Frantz Fanon underscore the implications of this erotic situation. In *Prospero and Caliban: The Psychology of Colonization*, Mannoni coins the term "Prospero Complex" to describe the psychology of the colonial patriarch whose racism is made manifest in his obsessive fear that his daughter's virginity is threatened, especially by the hypersexualized "New World man."

Miranda's name literally means wonder. She is a young woman whose arrival on the island marks the beginning of a process of self-discovery. In the opening scenes of the drama as Prospero reveals to her the secret of her birth, she confesses to having already been haunted by the memory of belonging to another family. Her initial attitude toward the island is one of compassion and curiosity, and it is actually she who teaches Caliban the language of the master. That relationship is immediately sexualized, which provides the pretext for Prospero's intervention to save her "purity"; and this results in her redirecting her attention to a more "appropriate" form of courtship. It would seem, then, that the knowledge Miranda gains in her symbolic loss of a father figure is too dangerous for her to possess — it makes her too independent, or too vulnerable, depending on whose perspective one takes. It was traveling to another place that allowed the original Miranda to understand her identity as different from the fiction that had been propagated by her symbolic father. The Mirandas of the present, myself among them, continue to undertake these journeys, straying far from the fictions of identity imparted to us by the rhetoric of assimilation into American-ness. What was once a potential sexual threat is now a matter of political transgression. As the Cold War, that modern day tempest, subsides, it seems logical that Miranda's story would emerge.

November, 1991: While hundreds of international visitors flock to Havana to attend the country's fourth art biennial, the passports of two art professionals waiting for visas to attend the event sit on desks at the Cuban embassy in Mexico City and the Cuban Interests Section in Washington D.C. Despite frequent phone calls, faxes, and letters, no official move was ever made to accept or deny these visa requests. The biennial passes and neither of them can attend.

January, 1988: After weeks of waiting, I receive the news that two Cuban artists I have invited to New York for the opening of a group exhibition in which they are participating will not be able to attend because they do not have visas to enter the United States. American-based Cuba supporters urge me to lodge a formal complaint against the U.S. State Department.

December, 1990: I am walking down the street with a relative of mine I've just met in a provincial city in southeastern Cuba. I have a new electrical fan in my hand that I have bought from a *diplotienda*, a hard currency store for foreigners. My relative looks uneasy. Outside Havana, that fan is like a red flag. *What will I say if I get stopped with you?* he asks. *Tell them I'm your cousin*, I say. *No*, he says. *Then they'll know that the fan is for me. Ok, tell them I'm a journalist and that I asked you for information about music. No good*, he says. *They'll say I should have taken you to talk to my professors. Look*, he finally says, *if I walk away at any point, just meet me in a half hour in the main plaza, ok?*

No one in Havana has ever expressed such worries about being seen in public with me, or about owning appliances from the *diplotienda*.

January, 1986: My first radio program about Cuban film airs on a community radio station in New York. The next day my mother receives a phone call from a Cuban colleague who tells her that I should try living in a Cuban prison for a while before talking "Communist propaganda" on the radio.

July, 1991: I receive a letter from a friend telling me that an article I published in *The Nation* in which I criticized an exhibit of art from Cuba in the United States for occluding the current complexities and political tensions in the art world there has caused quite a stir in Havana. According to the letter, a faculty member at the Higher Institute of Art was brought in to make an official translation for Wifredo Lam Center director Llilian Llanes and members of the Party leadership.

November, 1987: I stop in Miami to see old family friends before traveling to Havana. The father of the family, a Cuban exile, takes me outside to tell me that it's a bad idea to go to Cuba. He says I will be kidnapped by the secret police and forced to be a prostitute for visiting Russians. His oldest daughter asks me to visit their old house and take pictures. She says she'd like to go with me, but can't because she might get fired from her job for doing so.

November, 1991: One of the professionals whose visa was held up is Nina Menocal, a Cuban-born Mexican resident who owns and manages Ninart, a gallery promoting Cuban art in Mexico City. For exhibiting and selling the artwork of Cuban nationals she has incurred the ire of sectors within the Cuban cultural ministry (for not splitting the profits with the Cuban government) and the Miami-based Cuban right (for allegedly aiding the island "regime" by supporting the artists). The other person whose entry to Cuba was effectively blocked is me, a Cuban-American writer and media artist who has spent at least one month a year there since 1984.

January, 1992: Sufficient confusion was created by conflicting reports so as to obfuscate the deep-rooted causes of my visa problem. Cuban artists who ask about me during the event receive blank stares from the biennial organizers. A biennial committee member who enquired on my behalf was told definitively by Llilian Llanes that "there simply were no more visas to give out." A Cuban-American political scientist who sought information about my case in Havana received the explanation from a local specialist on Cuban relations with the exile community that my request was trapped in a temporary visa war with the U.S., in which Cuba stopped giving press visas because the U.S. had denied entry to two Cuban journalists.

This does not explain why Nina Menocal's visa never arrived. When Nina Menocal questions Luis Camnitzer, a U.S.-based Uruguayan artist and critic who had a solo exhibition at the 1991 biennial and has served as adviser to two previous ones, he told her that it was logical that our visas would be denied since we "both have problems with Cuba." This response expresses a not unfamiliar double standard: the same leftists who defend Cubans' right to enter the U.S. often find many a reason to justify the exclusion from the island of those deemed undesirable to Cuba. None of the Americans who attend the biennial make any public statement of their dissatisfaction over our having been denied entry.

November, 1991: In Mexico City, the first exhibition of art by Cuban nationals and exiles to take place since 1959 opened in mid-November at Ninart, entitled *15 Cuban Painters*. All the Cuban nationals in the exhibition have established temporary residence in Mexico, while the exiles were from the United States. On the island, there were no Cuban-American participants in the biennial exhibition, although there were some other diasporic and ethnic minority populations included, such as Chicanos and Canadian artists of color. American art historian Shifra Goldman delivers a paper that touches on work by Cuban exiles that was well received. Several cultural ministry officials publicly express regret to biennial visitors that an initiative such as Nina Menocal's to join nationals and exiles in one exhibit had not been organized by Cuba.

December, 1991: In Miami, the Cuban exiles who participated in the Ninart exhibition are criticized for aiding the "Castro regime" through their collaboration. One of them had already been counseled by his American gallery representative that such activities would lower his prices. On the other side, the Cuban government sends the Vice-minister of Culture to Mexico to proclaim that the show is a "Miami plot" to compromise the young Cuban nationals politically.

In Mexico City dozens of Cuban artists tighten their belts and enjoy the pleasure of painting to pay the rent. Those in Spain, France, and Germany get a taste of racism from the new xenophobic European Community, a confusing experience for those Cubans who are, at least visibly, white. They are living what artist Arturo Cuenca calls "low-intensity exile," living abroad without defecting.

Several Cuban cultural ministry officials announce their intention to visit Mexico City to interview Cuban artists and determine how these artists can contribute (financially) to the revolution from abroad.

January, 1992: One month after the biennial, a rally takes place in New York City to support ending the U.S. blockade against Cuba. Several thousand people who pack Nassau Coliseum are joined by several thousand more who form a counter-rally led by Cuban right-wing leader Jorge Mas Canosa. The morning of the rally my mother receives a phone call from a Mas Canosa supporter threatening that if I show my face at the rally I will be severely beaten. I had just published an article in the *Village Voice* about Ninart's show in Mexico City last November.

August, 1991: At the Festival Latino opening in New York City, a crowd of anti-Castro protesters who are frustrated because they can't find Gabriel García Márquez, known to be a friend of Fidel's, hurled curses at me as I entered the theater. *Coco Fusco! Puta! Traidora!* they yell and push toward me, and then physically attack the two male friends who try to protect me. The police intervene to break up the struggle.

August, 1989: I arrive in Brasilia on a U.S.I.A-sponsored lecture tour and am taken to the home of the U.S. cultural attaché, where I am questioned for over an hour in an intrusive manner about my trips to Cuba, my activities there and my relatives on the island. My head is pounding from trying to resist his questions. He tells me with a smirk at the end of our discussion that he is going back to the States to run Tele-Martí. A few days later, his Brazilian assistant lets me know that my FBI file was scrutinized carefully by the embassy because I was labeled "sympathetic to leftist movements" and "travels to Cuba."

December, 1986: After working as a co-producer of a documentary shot during the 1986 biennial, I am brought to the office of Wifredo Lam Center director Llilian Llanes, where she and her assistant Jorge Ayala question me for two hours about the material that was shot. They demand copies of all rushes, which I do not provide.

November, 1987: During a phone conversation between myself and a U.S.-based Cuba supporter, he criticizes the video documentary for depicting Havana as run-down and unattractive. I explain to him that the permission to shoot outside was only granted two days before our departure, limiting our ability to capture the variety of the city's landscape. *Oh*, he says, *I didn't know you needed permis-*

sion to film outside. This person has been an official guest of the Cuban cultural ministry several times and is writing a book about contemporary Cuban culture.

December, 1987: At the Havana Film Festival the second screening of the documentary about Cuban artists for which I served as co-producer is mysteriously canceled at the last minute. During a screening of a rough-cut several months earlier, several Cuban artists defended the piece in a closed meeting with officials from the cultural ministry and the Wifredo Lam Center. A Cuban friend who accompanies me to the airport is questioned by police after I leave.

March, 1988: The video master of the documentary on Cuban artists for which I served as co-producer sits locked in a secret vault in Budapest, Hungary, where it was edited. A letter was sent from Cuban officials to the Hungarian minister of culture denouncing the material and demanding that it be confiscated as a gesture of socialist solidarity. We succeed in bribing someone to remove it from the vault and have it sent to the United States, where it is sold to public television.

February, 1992: A recently emigrated Cuban artist is yelling at me on the phone in disagreement over the article I have written for the *Voice* about the Cuban artists in Mexico. *You weren't critical enough,* he says. *I can't write based on speculation,* I retort. *I have to respect people's right to represent themselves as they choose.*

Of course people don't really tell you how bad things are, he screams. *They think you're from the CIA, no matter what they tell you to your face.*

April, 1989: A *Marielito* completing graduate work in the Midwest comes to see me at my office. As soon as I shut the door, he begins to speak with tears in his eyes. *I saw your work and I know you can go to Cuba,* he says. *I want to go home. I made a mistake. I can't stand not being in my country. Can you help me?*

March, 1993: Two Cuban-American colleagues call me from Miami, where they have been waiting for entry visas to go to Havana for four months. *The head of the interests section called early this morning,* says one of them. *He told me there was another delay, but not to worry, because that doesn't mean I'm being rejected. Who is he kidding?* We laugh, uncomfortably.

April, 1991: One of the artists I invited to the U.S. in 1988 who was not able to enter is now living in Miami. He learned before processing his visa that his first request three years ago was never completed in Cuba, though the cultural ministry had told him at the time that his visa had been denied by the U.S. State Department.

June, 1992: I've waited a good six months since my visa was denied to write anything about Cuba. I think I was afraid of becoming a knee-jerk "counterrevolutionary," or at least feared that people might see me that way if I complained. Putting my own dilemma into a broader context becomes my way of depersonalizing a rather painful experience of rejection.

Global politics have changed since the fall of the Berlin Wall and Cuba's future is uncertain. Cultural debates on postcolonialism, and about the relationship between other U.S.-based Latinos and the populations and cultures of their homelands have matured significantly in the last decade. These factors, together with the new migration of '80s generation artists and intellectuals, and the existence of a post-exile generation of moderate Cuban-Americans contribute to conditions that demand a paradigm shift in the way we think about Cuban culture, Cuban cultural identity, and "revolutionary" cultural activity. We must rethink our priorities and define alliances not on the basis of territoriality but shared interests. Nationality has been a Cold War game. Identity, for Cubans, goes far beyond it.

Cuba still operates in the American imagination as the last great mythical terrain of the Cold War. American efforts to isolate Cuba have stepped up and are conveniently justified by "evidence" of intensified repression on the island: i.e., the execution of Arnaldo Ochoa, the quarantining of AIDS patients, the frequent use of physical violence by police against protestors, the arrest of human rights activists, the execution of Cuban exile infiltrators and the United Nations declaration that put Cuba on the human rights violators list. On the other hand, the U.S. government's sabotage efforts are continuously frustrated by Cuba's maintenance of a higher standard of living than most of her neighbors despite crippling food and energy shortages, the island's growing tourist and bioengineering industries, the commercial and critical successes of several Cuban artists and entertainers who *do not* defect, and Fidel Castro's uncanny ability to maintain international media popularity even after communism went out of fashion.

In such a politically charged context, artmaking for Cubans in Cuba is like walking in a mined desert. Supplies are hard to come by. Anything that might spark unrest or a public manifestation of discontent is considered dangerous. The above-mentioned economic and political factors have led to the silent exodus of many of Cuba's best and brightest artists and intellectuals. Over sixty visual artists and writers are in temporary residence in Mexico. Others have recently moved to the United States. More are scattered throughout Spain, France, Belgium, and Germany. The majority of them have opted out of the Havana vs. Miami conflict, and look instead for neutral territory to wait out the last gasp of the Cold War.

In the 1980s, a growing number of younger Cuban-Americans express interest in open engagement with Cuban nationals. Many of them are post-*dialogo*, post-Antonio Maceo Brigade types, less interested in the revolution, and more concerned with multicultural activism, cultural identity, Santería, Caribbean culture, contemporary Cuban art and cinema, etc. Some of them organize activities to bring Cubans to the United States or to help support them during their visits here. Some visit Cuba and begin collaborations with Cuban artists and writers. Most of their activity goes on through unofficial channels, although official bureaucratic demands must occasionally be met to justify travel and stay out of trouble. Some, like Nereida García Ferraz and Raúl Ferrera Balanquet, have developed an entire body of work around their status as displaced Cubans. Others, such as Ricardo Zulueta, Ana Maria Simo, Carmelita Tropicana, Felix Gonzalez-Torres, and Eduardo Aparicio, might refer to Cuba in their work and maintain varying degrees of political "neutrality" with respect to the revolutionary government, but they are also engaged with gay and lesbian politics and culture in the U.S. Still others, like Cesar Trasobares, Gonzalez-Torres and Luiz Cruz Azaceta, have stuck their necks out and broken taboos by exhibiting with Cuban nationals.

Not only have attitudes toward Cuban nationals begun to change, but the exile community itself has evolved to the extent that monolithic descriptive models simply do not work anymore. A class and cultural divide becomes increasingly apparent in Miami. Most of the recent immigrants from Mariel and its aftermath are not accepted by the Cuban aristocracy. Like the Cuban-American second generation intellectuals and artists, many are more politically moderate. Many are gay and lesbian and are out. Many are not white. Together with the first and second generation moderates who reside for the most part outside Miami, they make up an informal support network for visiting Cubans and information exchange with the island. They assist in obtaining visas, provide housing and extra money for visitors, take mail and medicine back and forth from

Cuba, organize receptions, assist the recently arrived in finding employment, etc., etc. The most famous story about this network comes from the Tropicana Nightclub's visit to New York, when the same *Marielitos* who picketed the entertainers from "Castro's Cuba" would run around to the dressing rooms to greet old friends and bring them *pastelitos*.

June, 1992: At a party in New York, Carmelita Tropicana laments that her work is not well received by the Cuban upper crust in Miami. *They tell me I must be Puerto Rican*, she says, *because they don't think that Cubans could be into kitsch*.

June, 1992: Over the last six months I have made dozens of lists in my mind of the conditions for rapprochement between two sides of a divided population. Culture is at the center of this issue, since it is precisely that which has bound a people otherwise split by geography and ideology. Art is also a symbol of the Cuban people's creative possibilities, a barometer of "freedom," that ideologically charged word.

For three decades, two forms of "liberty" stood at odds—on the one hand, the opportunity to have access to free art education and a state infrastructure that allows an artist to carry out his/her métier—with occasional strings attached. On the other, the unlimited availability of an art market open to those who can afford to educate and produce artwork with practically no hope of subsidy. Cultural politics on both sides determine the value of the artwork produced. Until recently, the differences were easy to define: if you lived in Cuba and made art about identity and popular culture, that was very likely to be supported and receive critical attention, and if you made non-figurative art that was also fine but might not benefit from the Euro-American interest in third world exoticism. If you lived in Miami and made non-figurative or surrealist work, you might sell to the local market, but you would not receive a tremendous amount of critical attention. If cultural or sexual politics entered into your work, you would probably have to move to another part of the country, where you would be likely to receive some degree of support—but not from Cubans. Now there are Cubans making art about the island from a variety of political perspectives and locales. Some travel with Cuban passports, others with American or European ones. The majority do not live on the island. Who can say whose is more or less Cuban?

December, 1992: I visit Nina Menocal at her gallery in Mexico. She is making preparations to take a group of "her" Cuban artists to the

Art Miami fair in January. She is extremely worried because she has been receiving calls from Miami warning her that someone is going to give her an unpleasant surprise.

January, 1992 – March, 1993: I have reviewed several articles and catalogue essays by the newly-migrated young Cubans. These are the same people who put spirit and intellectual rigor into their arguments against reductive nationalism in the conceptualization of Cuban identity, who posited a cultural politics of "appropriation" based on Cuban cultural history, and who explained the role of popular culture and ritual in the reclaiming of public space for personal expression in the 1980s. New arguments emerge: if these Cubans could make whatever they appropriated Cuban by virtue of that act, then they can also take their culture to another place. Cuban culture throughout history, they argue, has been influenced by contact with other countries; Wifredo Lam, Alejo Carpentier, Amelia Pelaez, Raul Martinez, José Martí – even Fidel – spent time abroad. Pérez Prado created an entire genre of Cuban music – in Mexico.

A new chapter in the theorization of exile.

July, 1992: I'm in Mexico City, having lunch with a Cuban art critic now living there. *It's one thing to talk about broadening notions of identity on the island*, I tell him. *It's quite another to redefine exile when there are at least three decades of exile culture preceding you.*

We're just beginning, he says.

That's fine, I say, *but you might want to consider getting to know all the other Cuban artists out here if you're going to continue using national paradigms to define the work you're talking about.* I have the feeling he's not really listening to me.

December, 1990: I'm sitting in a conference room at UNEAC in a meeting with Cubans, Cuban-Americans, and American foundation representatives. UNEAC president Abel Prieto starts off by suggesting "that the Cubans introduce themselves." He means the islanders. Raul Ferrera-Balanquet, a *Marielito* exile and video artist, immediately interjects that Prieto's suggestion only enforces polarization, and that he (Raul) considers himself Cuban too. Cuban-American Roly Chang concurs. Prieto clears his throat and begins discoursing on the "inauthenticity" of Oscar Hijuelos' novel, *The Mambo Kings Play Songs of Love*.

January, 1993: I meet up with a Cuban painter friend who has lived in Chicago since she was a teenager. She has just come back from the Miami art fair. *I saw all our friends from la colonia cubana de*

Mexico, she said. *I couldn't help noticing their surprise at the fact that my work was selling like mad. I think they respect me a little more now.*

June, 1992: Is there any difference, I wonder, between the fights Cubans and Cuban-Americans have and the ones Chicanos and Puerto Ricans have with their homeland-based populations? Because of the upper and middle class composition of the mass Cuban migration of the 1960s, and because of the ideological tone of the derogatory terms for exiles, the homeland's image of the immigrant community has a different gloss on it. The problematic, however, is fundamentally the same. It's real identity vs. fake identity, original vs. copy, upper class vs. working class, good Spanish vs. bad Spanish.

The '80s generation in Cuba made enormous contributions to politicizing debates on appropriation and postmodernism, and created an internal critique of the iconography and rhetoric of the Cuban revolution that had been entrenched since the 1960s. There are, however, several aspects of progressive cultural politics that developed in other parts of the Americas during this same period that Cuban artists have not been a part of, and toward which they still display suspicion. I am thinking here of critical social and political movements in North America in which culture has played an enormous role: black cultural politics, the Chicano movement, multiculturalism, feminism, gay and lesbian rights, and AIDS activism. From the point of view of leftist traditions within Latin America, with their deeply ingrained universalist rhetoric and patriarchal and authoritarian tendencies, these movements could easily be dismissed as sectarian and inconsequential. But underneath the frequent knee-jerk rejection of these politics is an old-school brand of Marxism rearing its head. That and some old-style *machista* and Catholic resistance to taking radicalism into the privacy of the bedroom.

Cuban artists for whom the celebration of cultural identity was experienced as official policy of the State, and for whom radicalism could be measured in terms of one's distance from official policy tend to look upon the identity politics of the "New New Left" with skepticism, if not disdain. Multiculturalism more often than not spells manipulation of art for political ends to them. While their evaluations of mainstream institutional paternalism and exoticizing attitudes toward marginal cultures are often prescient, they have difficulty acknowledging the grassroots dimension of efforts toward cultural pluralism in the North, and do not recognize the advantages of an alliance based on shared interest in cultural democracy.

May, 1992: A Cuban artist in Spain shows me a letter from another Cuban artist who is living in Europe: *It's incredible,* writes the artist, *that when I am in Cuba, the Europeans who visit us love my work because it's made on the island, "dentro de la revolución", even if the materials are lousy. Nobody's interested in what I make as a Cuban in Europe.*

June, 1993: An old-time American Cuba supporter calls me, and I share with her the news that another Cuban artist has won a Guggenheim Fellowship. *We're in a very difficult situation with these artists,* she says. *There are a couple of us who are very angry, because some of these artists are asking us for letters of support and then they're defecting. Now I still support Cuba's right to exist. . . .*

I listen, quietly. I've learned to say nothing.

March, 1993: UNEAC continues to send messages expressing their interest in organizing cultural exchanges between Cubans and Cuban-Americans. And yet not even Abel Prieto, who in addition to being the president of UNEAC is a member of the Central Committee of the Cuban Communist Party, seems to be able to guarantee a visa. There will be those on both sides who will not see this dialogue as a priority, or who find any kind of politicized cultural gesture suspicious. It would be naive to think that after over three decades of psychological warfare, everyone would jump at the opportunity to convene with the enemy. And it would also be naive to think that a little individualism on the part of the artists might not be a necessary antidote to an overdose of revolutionary sacrifice. Many artists are startlingly candid about their objectives: some want the comfort that money brings, not just the honor that critical acclaim offers. Others want peace and distance.

May, 1993: I'm in Cologne to give a lecture, and unexpectedly run into a Cuban artist who is opening a show there the same evening and then driving back to his home in Belgium, where he has lived for three years. Over coffee we swap stories and I watch his eyes widen as I list all the peers of his who have ended up in Miami. He confesses that he's glad to be far away from it all. *I saw it coming, and I knew it was time to go. You know what that means, Coco, because you saw us when we were living that utopian moment. At least growing up amidst underdevelopment teaches you how to survive. You'll see how we all manage.*

July, 1992: I receive news from Mexico: the Museo del Chopo is planning an exhibition of Cuban artists. The curators, one Cuban, and one Mexican, intend to include works by Tomás Esson, Florencio Gelabert Soto, Arturo Cuenca, and Dania Del Sol, four recent defectors to the U.S.. They receive word from the Foundation for Cultural Goods (the marketing arm of the Ministry of Culture) that all works promised from Cuba will be pulled from the exhibition if the defectors participate.

In mid-June, the Club Ateneo de Fotografia in Mexico sponsored an exhibit entitled *150 Years of Cuban Photography*, to be donated to the University of Guadalajara. In the show was a piece by Arturo Cuenca. Just before the opening, Nina Menocal was informed by club president Jesus Montalvo that Cuba had threatened to withdraw the entire exhibit if Cuenca's work was included. Cuenca's photo was promptly returned to Ninart.

August, 1992: I receive word from *Third Text* in England that they cannot publish this piece as I have written it. The editors send me a fax stating that all the names must be removed, and that all personal information about my experiences in Cuba must also be excised. I argue by fax for weeks and only succeed in getting them to include a line explaining that Nina Menocal and I were both denied visas to attend the 1991 biennial. I have also sent this piece (in an earlier form) to *La Jornada Semanal* in Mexico, where it is published with no significant editorial changes.

March, 1993: *There's a guy from the island visiting who you have to meet*, says a Cuban artist living in Massachusetts. We're sitting down to dinner, and in walks a man of no more than twenty-five. He entertains us throughout the meal with stories about the new tourist complexes in Varadero Beach. The Fondo de Bienes Culturales has installed a gallery/ boutique in every hotel where tourists buy Cuban art with dollars. Fondo representatives with budding entrepreneurial leanings (like himself) could seek out and contract local artists for exclusive representation at one store or another. *I've got five new artists from Matanzas who'll do anything on order*, he announces proudly. I ask him how he thinks that these marketing strategies will affect creative output, but he doesn't answer. *And if you come down, I can also make arrangements for you to have a driver, and maybe take you to a real toque de santo. Here's my card.*

February, 1993: I'm sitting in the living room of a New York apartment sublet to a Cuban artist for the duration of his Guggenheim fellowship. *What I saw in Miami was so depressing I can hardly talk*

about it, he says. *The chusmeria that we wanted to get away from —
the paranoia, the accusations — it's all been brought over to Miami.
Everybody's accusing the next guy of being an "infilitrado" just to
damage them professionally.*
April, 1993: An American woman comes up to me at a Cuban
artist's opening in SoHo. *Coco Fusco? I wrote to you last fall to tell
you about the Cuban artist* (she gives his name) *who's in New York
and you never answered.* I apologize awkwardly, but am wondering
who this artist is. *Well,* she says, *here he is.*

A young man steps forward with a broad smile, offers me his
hand and then gives me a business card. The woman hands me a
photo album and asks me to look at pictures of his work. Under
duress, I flip through and see baskets. Glancing at his card, I notice
that he gives folkloric dance classes. We chat for a moment. *Did you
study at the Art Institute?* I ask. *Well, no, actually, I didn't,* he
admits, without missing a beat. *In Cuba, I used to be an engineer.*

May, 1993: At the Barcelona apartment of two young Cubans who
have been in Spain for over a year on mysterious scholarships, a
group of us sit on the floor eating pizzas, drinking wine, smoking
cigarettes, and arguing. We take photos and make jokes about
which archives they'll end up in. At one point, one of the women
turns to me and says, *Ay Coco. I remember when you used to come
to Havana. Whenever people from outside would arrive, we would
look at them and notice how pretty they looked. When they would
say they were going to Paris or Rio next I would think, oh what nice
lives they have. Now I just came back from Paris, where I spent a
month washing dishes. We're even thinking about running a Cuban
food stand on the weekends to make money. I didn't know what
things were like out here.*

June, 1993: I'm standing in the ground-floor passageway of the
Museum of Modern Art, at the opening of *Latin American Artists of
the 20th Century.* There are Cuban artists and art lovers of all kinds
around me, ranging from American-raised YUCA's (Young Urban
Cuban Americans) to about-to-defectors. We're laughing and hug-
ging, and everything feels very euphoric. Cuban-Americans I've
never seen or heard of before come up to me and tell me that they're
writing articles about Cuban art or opening galleries to show it. *The
Miami Herald,* a friend whispers, is still trying to foment discord by
attempting to pit José Bedia and Luis Cruz Azaceta, the two living
Cuban artists in the exhibition, against each other. Ironically, the
Cuban government's undisputed "art star" and one of the exile com-

munity's finest painters are represented by the same New York gallery. Their sales are booming and they make a point of being photographed together.

I can't help but notice that Llilian Llanes is standing at the other side of the passageway, staring at us all but unwilling to join our little party. Strange, I think. She's jumped on the bandwagon, and is now pushing for an encyclopedic "Cuban art inside and out" exhibition, for which the preliminary proposal has just been mailed to me by friends on the West Coast. But the sight of us mingling is still shocking enough to keep her at a distance.

*   *   *

This story goes on and on. As Cuba's uncertain future unfolds, Cubans everywhere continue to argue over which direction things will take. In the post-Cold War era, the American press is approaching the Cuba question from every possible angle, singling out potential converts to capitalism among young party officials, casting an occasionally skeptical glance at Mas Canosa while giving space to views of moderate dissenters, and chiseling away at views that cast the exile community as monolithic. As usual, however, the politicians on both sides still lag behind, evincing unfailing rigidity. Complain, joke, or speculate as we may, the Cuban-American National Foundation on the one hand, and Fidel and the Central Committee on the other, still call the shots. The blockade has been tightened since the end of the Cold War, not loosened. In addition, the Mexican government has grown tired of providing a safe haven for Cubans in limbo; wanting neither an immigration nor a diplomatic crisis, it has curtailed entry by Cubans into Mexico, prompting many more to flee to Miami.

That a generational split distinguishes political and cultural sensibilities inside and outside Cuba is now indisputable; those involved in culture are just not waiting for political change to happen first. Many of the older, more established exiled intellectuals have either passed away or taken a back seat in cultural debates, yielding somewhat to the vitality and heterogeneity of perspectives brought by successive immigrations of younger Cubans to the U.S. What isn't always clearly recognized, however, is just how instrumental the voices of those marginalized by official discourses on both sides have been in keeping doors open all along. And among those who have consistently attempted to lessen the polarizations that have marked those discourses, many have been women. On the *comunidad* side, women such as Lourdes Casal, Dolores Prida, Ana María García, María Torres, and Nereida García Ferraz were key in the establishing of the Antonio Maceo Brigade, and in the initiation of the *Diálogo* that resulted in family reunification. Ana Mendieta broke ground by reestablishing links between artistic communities. Nina Menocal was the first to exhibit artists from both sides. The *cubanía* evoked by Cristina Garcia in her novel *Dreaming in Cuban* floats effortlessly across borders, as family members separated by geography, politics, and even death communicate with one another.

This is not to say that all Cuban women dissent from official points of view on Cuba. However, given that the areas that kept Cubans bound *despite* politics are primarily those of family and culture, and that women have traditionally been ascribed the role of their keepers, it doesn't surprise me that they would take the lead in these areas, or that they would cast a skeptical eye toward a political sphere that excluded them before the revolution, as well as outside it. Furthermore, while official channels of communication remain blocked or clogged by empty rhetoric, the kinds of exchange that have gone on across borders take forms usually associated with feminine discursive practices: home gatherings, letters, gossip, and other intimate forms of conversation. Long before Radio Martí transmitted news from abroad, *Radio Bemba* (word of mouth) was known to be the best source of information from within.

As more and more Cubans of all persuasions settle in Miami, the culture and the politics of exile will continue to change drastically. And if they do, where will the Mirandas go? Just yesterday, I bought a ticket to Miami to visit artists who have just defected, people who eight years ago could barely tolerate the sight of a foreigner. *We're reliving our childhood by watching them arrive*, a friend told me a few months ago. Another Miranda from the Midwest recently rented a pied-à-terre in *La Fla*, as we now call it, to be in the middle of it all. South Beach is beginning to feel like la Habana Vieja, complete with *jineteros* who peddle stolen goods at cut-rate prices right at your doorstep. Sometimes I jokingly tell friends that *la tortilla se va a virar*, and that Cuba will end up in Miami and Miami in Cuba. At the rate we're going, it could very easily happen.

MADELINE CÁMARA

THIRD OPTIONS: BEYOND THE BORDER

The point of view of this text is fluid. At times it turns to what the social sciences call "participant observation." Many of the attitudes and traits of the generation of Cuban intellectuals analyzed here were shared by the author, whether in conversation or through active participation. In addition, I have attempted to use personal memories, as well as information taken from recent publications, to recreate the historical and cultural context from which this generation emerged. I aim to elaborate a possible conceptual framework through speculative thought, along with a dose of subjectivity, for as a feminist I value the possibility of writing everyday life into theory, and vice versa. All this is said to caution against taking this essay either as a group's declaration of principles or as a theoretical platform. Rather, this is an account of the vicissitudes of this generation's birth and transfiguration.

Notes for a Genealogy of the Generation of the 80s

To some they are known as "The Children of William Tell," a term used in various artistic spheres by artists and critics.[1] They can be located chronologically (with important individual exceptions) as the so-called Generation of the 80s, or the fourth generation of the Revolution, made up of young intellectuals born and raised after 1959 but whose entry into Cuban culture occurred in the 1980s and 1990s. Of course, not all members of this generation have shared the experiences and concerns discussed here, but many studies agree that a representative majority have done so.[2]

The paradoxical relationship between culture and politics in Cuba has historically provided us with eras of necessary spiritual renewal that have acted as interstices between the country's periods of crisis and recovery. The ill-fated Mariel episode was followed by a period early in the decade called by some scholars "the golden age of the new vanguard." Havana was at the center of artistic activity that included music festivals, theater, film, ballet, art exhibits, literary colloquia, workshops for the discussion of social and cultural issues, seminars on philosophy, and the emergence of new publications. This fervor had the peculiar characteristic of enjoying a novel but relative autonomy from traditional ties to official institutions. The protagonists were young people, in addition to several important figures of our culture, some of whom had been erased from public recognition and were receiving renewed legitimation. In sum, we enjoyed an unusual degree of tolerance that benefited the arts significantly. It seemed as if the Mariel nightmare would be erased from our memory.

Within five years, however, reactionary forces had once again gained ground. This occurred at a time when the government was going through crises of loss of moral prestige and when increasing numbers of *balseros* were risking their lives to cross the Florida strait. All these conflicts and the anguish they engendered were reflected in the work of young artists. Osvaldo Sánchez, discussing the visual arts, comments, "Those in power were unable to understand how this political acidity of the young was the final gesture of legitimacy toward the revolution as a process of real participation."[3]

Even clearer proof of these artists' concern for the national situation came in the form of a document written by several members of "Paideia," a leading group in these alternative artistic practices, asking the ranking members of the government for changes in the country's political and economic development. The principal complaints of the Paideia Project can be summarized as follows:

1. ". . . there exists a contradiction between our proposed cultural politics and the practices of cultural institutions . . ."

2. ". . . the degree of ideological commitment demanded of intellectuals by political and cultural institutions is at odds with our activities, which are independent of the realm of politics . . ."

3. ". . . the concept of 'the people' being employed is reductionist and is applied embarrassingly in our culture . . ."

4. ". . . Cuban society fools itself if it replaces the real man with a concept of new man reducible to an ideological fiction . . ."

5. ". . . [the group] protests the spirit and practice of false consensus that in the name of political unity rejects the natural and historic multiplicity of Cuban culture . . ."[4]

The text was discussed with government officials at a meeting that young artists attending described as "sterile," where responses were entirely predictable. Many of their projects were disbanded almost simultaneously, in open response to the government's refusal to act on their demands. What followed will remain in the memory of many of us as a succession of lively fragments that were mutilated and torn out by force from their source of inspiration: closed exposi-tions, publications censured or withdrawn from circulation, forbid-den or repressed debates, personal humiliations, and intimidation.

This brief and anecdotal view cannot be concluded without refer-ence to an event that is crucial precisely because of its very few repercussions and its unfortunate outcome. After the Paideia Project was discussed, a radical response from some of the group's member-ship came with the formation of *Tercera Opción* (Third Option), an independent movement that sought to prepare a competing political program. Its members included, among others, César Mora, Omar Pérez, Rolando Prats, and Ernesto Hernández. The group's political activity was short-lived: Hernández left Cuba and has settled in Mexico, Prats aligned himself with the social-democratic current, from which he has since broken, and Omar Pérez and César Mora were called to compulsory military service, forcing their break with civil society. As far as we know, *Tercera Opción* ceased to exist as a political entity after a few fruitless attempts to ally the group with other dissident organizations.

What occurred was not unforeseeable. The cultural politics of the revolution, defined by the arbitrary motto, "EVERYTHING WITHIN THE REVOLUTION, NOTHING OUTSIDE OF THE REVOLUTION,"[5] was not prepared to accept that demonstration of independent thought.

Earlier in the 1980s a group of young painters in Mexico jokingly publicized their presence and activities with the phrase "The Cubans have arrived." With some art galleries opening their doors to them, the young artists began to file through, one by one. Not coincidentally, around the same time a literary critic in Mexico put together an anthology of young Cuban poets titled *Un grupo avanza silencioso*, "A group advances quietly." It was undoubtedly a boom for artists newly arriving in Mexico with the hope of continuing their professional development after the paths they forged as the vanguard of the 1980s were sealed off in Cuba.

To a lesser degree, this boom of Cuban artistic activity saw paral-lels in other Latin American capitals and, in one of history's para-doxes, in Madrid, Spain. I could enter into more detail about the scene in Mexico, where the greatest number of Cuban artists congregated, but I prefer to reflect on how all these centers were areas where the "third option" — unable to express itself within the borders of the nation — was flourishing nonetheless. These third countries do not offer residence but, rather, asylum. In a small number of specific cases, work permits or scholarships were offered by institutions or persons, and once the young intellectuals received permission to leave Cuba they found ways to prolong their stay, many times thanks to the "generous understanding" of the sponsoring entities.

I would not describe this situation as comfortable, given that the artists themselves do not enjoy absolute control over their own careers and personal interests. Often artists working in Mexico support their families in Cuba by sending much-needed dollars. An increasing number of persons try to bring their entire family to Mexico temporarily. Since this option is nearly impossible, at times because of the opposition of Cuban immigration authorities and at other times because of the policies of the country in question, the results are the dissolution of families and the formation of new kinds of personal ties in the foreign country.

Beyond Borders

Borders are not understood here to mean a land frontier but rather a point of separation, an area that serves to mark what is different as what is in opposition.

This is an era of exiles, in the sense of increasing transgressions of not only geographic but all kinds of repressive boundaries. To exercise the third option, then, is to seek exile from the way that Marxist-Leninist rationalism has justified political totalitarianism theoretically, and from ideological polarities and intellectual segregation. It is, at the same time, opting to understand knowledge as existing independently of the institutions of the State.

If artists have not been able to settle definitively in "third countries" and, as we have seen, structures within Cuba have not allowed for their integration, does the United States — offering them a warm welcome as political dissidents — become their Mecca? This is the belief of those who consider Miami — the capital of the Cuban exile community — territory of "Cuba Libre." Among my recent and fortunate lessons I have learned not to bring up polemical topics that refer to the Miami exiles, but I will state here that I do not agree with their self-image, and I will take on the responsibility of asserting that neither does the majority of artists to whom I am referring.

In the United States these artists and intellectuals are received with open arms and offered immediate political asylum in exchange for any anecdote they are willing to allow the media to broadcast. In a matter of hours they become political figures, unfortunately making them susceptible to new dangers, to new borders that threaten to limit and restrict their freedom of expression, their subversiveness. Accepting the rules of certain sectors of the Miami exile community works against this subversiveness under the false premise that once over here we are all united against a common enemy and that, therefore, strategies of confrontation and resistance have to become homogeneous to be effective. The most damaging consequence is readily apparent when nuance becomes conspicuously absent from the words of intellectuals who are obviously capable of subtle and profound criticism but who instead limit themselves to speaking in ways that Miami rewards — diatribes and overly personal analyses of the Cuban situation. The opaque character of the political discourse of the most reactionary sectors of the exile community is the perfect counterpart to the partisan litanies heard in Cuba. By accepting it a young artist or intellectual accepts his or her death as a dissident in a modern world.

I was shocked to learn how dissidence was conceptualised by a Cuban sociologist in an article published in a recent issue of the *Gaceta de Cuba* focusing on exile Cuban literature.[6] The article made pejorative reference to exiles as "mutants," silencing all possibility of change and opposition by classifying departures from the country as a betrayal of what is legitimate: Fidel's revolution. As I read the piece I thought that this manipulation of public opinion — which, surprisingly, permeates even the highest levels of sophisticated thought among intellectual Cuban elites who are clients of State institutions — gave the *Gaceta's* readers an image that is extremely disconnected from what today's international spheres consider to be dissident attitudes.

Those who tune into radio stations transmitting from the United States to the island, however, are no better informed, nor are those who read Miami's newspapers. In general, the tone of discussion is closed and permeated by exaggerations of the island's reality. News is often given with no contextualization, and the terminology of political analysis is aggressive and, at times, even tasteless. These kinds of exchanges, which extend to conversations, meetings, dinners, and other spaces of Miami's political and social life, make many of those who are just arriving avoid all discussions of Cuba. Once the necessary declarations are made to the immigration official who grants asylum, they gradually and voluntarily depoliticize their lives. Most new arrivals tend to work quietly at reconstructing a comfortable domestic space and material and emotional stability.

This behavior is understandable but unfortunate when it leads to isolation because Miami does offer more than its expressways and MacDonalds. What it offers is a space for us to reencounter the most typical customs of our culture, which have been lost on our island. Smells, tastes, linguistic variations, rituals of family life, and all those stories about Cuba's past that ordinary men and women insist on telling the most recent arrivals, are a kind of rite of passage. For those of us who have experienced this encounter, it becomes a way of retracing History in a Proustian manner, allowing things that were forgotten to rise to the surface again. In this way, we retrace a world that needs to be remembered and yet not idealized. The risk of idealization is not great, given the large doses of skepticism carried around by the "Children of William Tell."

Among the forces that most work against the project of seeking a "third option" is the negative view of our generation encapsulated in the phrase "velvet exile," used by U.S. exiles of an earlier generation to describe the lives of those who have settled in third countries and are able to travel to and from Cuba. This division points to ideological and even ethical differences but ignores the profound structural similarity between both kinds of ruptures with the mother country, the Cuba that shaped our imagination.

What is the most productive option within this generational crisis? I think that the great majority of these artists and intellectuals is seeking to create ties with colleagues in the U.S. and also with those living in other countries, including Cuba, ties that would allow for a critical understanding of the situation on the island. The second generation of Cuban exiles, those who flew with Peter Pan and others who left as children without knowing where they were going, have become professionals in U.S. society. Many of them are academics who have continued to reinvent their *patria* from within different disciplines and serve as useful guides because they have learned to function as intellectuals here without giving up their Cubanness or making concessions to nostalgia.

This second generation has also constructed a new vision of Cuba that is faithful to the culture but which also incorporates aspects atypical of the traditional Cuba that first generation exiles try to maintain and reproduce in Miami. Their meeting point with those artists and intellectuals seeking a third option is the same rejection of the idea of a monolithic and idealized vision of the island proposed by the Cuban government to its citizens as a way of preserving the nation. In this area of agreement there exists the possibility of dialogue about how to rescue that other history of our country hidden by the manipulations of political power. The varied positions that this second generation of exiles holds within a country as complex as the United States is perhaps what is most interesting about them to the intellectuals recently arrived from Cuba or "third countries."[7] Thus despite the diaspora, or even as a result of it, a generation that was born rebellious and felt expelled by the *patria*, as well as those from whom it was taken at an early age, can come together in what appears to be their historic mission, sung by the youth of Cuba: to remember William Tell, except we must put that apple on our own heads.

A Return to Origins

I want to close by taking the spiral full circle, to its origins. I want to speak of those living in Cuba, because it would be wrong to suggest that all those working for a "third option" have chosen to leave the country as the only route toward fulfilling their lives personally and professionally. Artistic and intellectual production continues to flourish on the island because, among other reasons, they are among the best ways of resisting the country's external and internal blockades. If I had to briefly characterize the focus of the work now being done on the island, I would say that it looks at the study of history and Cuban tradition, attempting to break down the "traps of faith" hidden in the books used by the educational system at all levels, including propaganda and everything written in support of official discourse. The result has been a kind of hermeneutics of suspicion that attempts to delve deeper than the simple chains of cause and effect that dominant ideology imposes on insular teleology. In literature we have seen the continuing enrichment of poetry as the genre of choice to reflect, at an individual level, on the crisis of the country and its inhabitants. This community of discourse has endured, demonstrating a desire to remain independent of official institutions which leave no doubt as to their disapproval of these oppositional cultural politics.[8]

Those who remain on the island have a privileged position from which to witness changing realities and interact with ordinary people, which always nourishes critical thought. Our counterparts in Cuba are indispensable to the redefinition of the collective project, and all contact made between them and us helps keep alive dialogue about Cubanness, conversations where national reconciliation and material and moral reconstruction of the country have become our key words.

NOTES

[1]It is the title of a song by the young Cuban singer Carlos Varela and a symbol in the poems of María Elena Cruz Varela. Critic Gerardo Mosquera also uses it to refer to young painters.

[2]See Osvaldo Sánchez, "Soñar con la espiral de Tatlin," in *Poliester*, No. 4 (Winter 1993), Mexico, DF.; Gerardo Mosquera, "Los hijos de Guillermo Tell," Ibid; and Liliana Martínez, *Intelectuales y poder político en Cuba*, Master's thesis, FLACSO, Mexico, D.F., June 1992.

[3]Osvaldo Sánchez, op.cit., 15.

[4]Liliana Martínez, op.cit., 110.

[5]The recent polemic in Cuba between the directors of the Mexican journal *Plural de Excelsior* and members of UNEAC was symptomatic of the debates concerning the amount of freedom of expression on which Cuban intellectuals can count. Once again Fidel's well-known phrase fixed the limits of the acceptable and clearly demonstrated how a policy that had stemmed from one era later became a regulatory axiom. The controversy stemmed from the journal's publication of a series of essays, written by members of the generation being discussed here, that were critical of the revolution.

[6]Rafael Hernández, "Mirar a Cuba," *La Gaceta de Cuba*, revista de la Unión de Escritores y Artistas de Cuba (UNEAC), September-October, 1993.

[7]The research and reflection about Cuba undertaken by the second generation of Cuban exiles, aiming for open communication with colleagues on the island, include the book of interviews and personal stories, *Contra viento y marea*, and an extensive number of essays and texts published as books, in anthologies or in cultural journals like *Linden Lane* and *Apuntes Posmodernos*. Some distinguished names in this field are: María de los Angeles Torres, Nereida García, Ruth Behar, Adriana Méndez-Rodena, José Antonio Solís, Antonio Vera-León, Román de la Campa, Marifeli Pérez-Stable, Ileana Fuentes, and Damían Fernández, all of them coming from the world of academia.

[8]I use the concept of a "society of discourse" in the sense that Michel Foucault applies it in "The Order of Discourse," as an alternative to the dissemination of truth outside of the regime that imposes it as doctrine. In this paper I am thinking of the communities of independent thought that have been created in Cuba around prominent figures like Moreno Fraginals, the late Zaira Rodríguez, Beatriz Maggi, and others, as well as debate societies founded by the *Instituto Superior del Arte*, literary

circles like the one sponsored by Reina María Rodríguez, and the group formed
around the recent creation of the journal *Proposiciones*, and the Lezama Lima
Chair.

Translated by Javier Morillo-Alicea

YANAI MANZOR

MY KEY

my key was held in the fingers of that man
bathed in the sweat of his fatigue

caressing itself
in your delicate fingertips

my key also hung from a ring of other keys

it touched the blood of certain wounds
on a Friday, volunteer labor,
on the machete, in the garden
of Loma and Thirty-ninth

held tight in a pocket
it felt the warmth of your thighs,
heard steps, light and nervous
smelled your dark pants

my key was held among your keys
and it could not open the lock
only be strung on a keychain
of some church or jail or deserted city.

Translated by David Frye

SONIA RIVERA-VALDÉS

GRANDMOTHER'S NIGHT

Exile
is living where no house
holds the memories
of our childhood

Lourdes Casal

and where we cannot visit
our grandmother's grave

It had been a bad day. I went to bed feeling like a rag doll empty of rags. My energy had left me after the absurd argument during morning coffee. I spent the entire day trying to recover it, but it wouldn't come back. Strangely for me, I went to bed feeling very sleepy.

I was falling asleep when all of a sudden I remembered my grandmother Estefanía, the only one of my grandparents I had ever met, my father's mother. I saw myself at the beach house in Santa Fe where I used to live, getting ready to travel to Fomento to see her. Someone had brought the news — Fanía had a stroke. I heard them speak in whispers so that the children wouldn't hear, heard the sad resonance of their voices and saw their faces, now unrecognizable, clouded in my memory. Only my father and I would go on this trip. She wanted to see me, her favorite grandchild. Besides, there wasn't enough money for my mother and brother to join us. I was so excited about the adventure of traveling by train, just me and my father, whom I seldom saw for more than two hours at a time. He spent little time at home.

Santa Clara was very far away, and Fomento even farther. I stood up and looked out the window for as long as I could stay awake. Everything was new to me.

Tía Caro's house was big. It had many rooms and a great patio in the center with flowers everywhere. To me she was the rich aunt, married to the son of a Spaniard who owned the only shoe store in town. My cousins Mesuka and Paquito, Fanía's kids, were there. They weren't there because of *la abuela*'s illness. They had been there for over a month, guests of Caro's who often invited them and at times even paid for their train fare. I think she invited them because they were her sister's kids, unlike my brother and I, who were her brother's kids and were never invited. Or maybe the problem was that everyone in the family thought my father was crazy, and that made a difference in the distribution of love and jealousy. My grandmother loved us the best, probably because she felt sorry for us. This brought on rivalries, and so the others loved us the least.

The kids ate before the adults did in Tía Caro's sunny dining room. And then they played. I didn't stop running around for days. How many were there? Three, four, a whole week? I still don't know. One of those days, in the afternoon, my cousins and I stopped our endless scurrying to climb the immense ceiba tree in the backyard. The adults took this very seriously. My grandmother called me into her room to ask me, in a voice I could hardly make out, to avoid dangerous games. She said if anything happened to me, then she would really die of a heart attack, and she wanted to live to see me all grown up. That never happened. She died a few days after my father and I returned to Havana.

The scent of aloe leaves filled my grandmother's room. She couldn't get up from bed because her left side was paralyzed. Her hair on the pillow caught my attention. It wasn't gathered in a bun, the way she usually fixed it, early in the morning, on the days she was at our house. When she was finished with her hair she would comb mine, but sometimes we traded places and I combed hers first. I braided it and tied bows on it, just like my own. Then I took her by the hand and showed her off to everyone in the house.

I slept most of the trip back to Havana, that's all I remember. A few days later someone brought the news that Estefanía had died. The sad whispers returned, this time with tears. Then they told me. I felt nothing, it didn't feel real. I returned to my game in the backyard. I was play-cooking, imitating her.

*   *   *

And now, as I lie half-asleep in my bed in New York, on this unusually cold night in March, I open my eyes and sit up in bed, terrified, thinking that my grandmother is buried in some cemetery in Santa Clara because she had a stroke while visiting my aunt Caro and I have never, never been to her grave. I have never seen the place where the only sane person in my family rests, the only one I didn't worry about, who combed my hair the way I asked her to, parted carefully in the middle, with four braids instead of two. The one who taught me to read when my parents didn't send me to school, who taught me to embroider little handkerchiefs and braid hair, plant flowers and tell the night-jessamines from the impatiens. The only one who told me family stories and knew how to cook my favorite soup with angel hair noodles, who applied mustard packs to my feet to bring down the fever from the throat infections I suffered throughout my childhood. The one who was proud that her brother had been a *mambí* and had fought in the war for independence, who taught me that Estrada Palma, no matter what anybody said, had not been a good president because he had handed Cuba over to the Americans.

I felt a long, deep ache in my chest when I thought that I had never, never placed a flower on her grave or gently wiped the dust from her tombstone, and now the family is scattered all over the world and God knows what state my grandmother's grave is in. Lost in the underbrush, covered by weeds as if no one knew her, and here she had left behind nine children and a bunch of grandchildren and great-grandchildren.

I cried late into the night, all the tears I had kept from crying since the day they told me she had died, when I was eight years old and went on pretending to cook in the backyard.

I fell asleep at dawn. When I woke up, my energy was back. And when I looked at the kitchen calendar I realized that it was the sixth of March, my grandmother Estefanía's birthday, born under the sign of Pisces in 1871, the year that the eight medical students had been executed in Havana by the colonial government, as she would always say to me.

Translated by Mirtha N. Quintanales and Vivian Otero

CARILDA OLIVER LABRA

SOIL

When my grandmother came
she brought along a bit of Spanish soil,
when my mother left
she took away a bit of Cuban soil.
I won't hold on to any bit of native land:
I want it all
upon my grave.

Translated by Ruth Behar

From *Ver La Palma Abriendo El Día*
   (Havana, Cuba: Ediciones Union, 1991)

AFTER PAPA . . .

After Papá celebrated his seventieth birthday
and he started speaking with an ear to the ground,
he told me he felt poor without his grandchildren
and I knew then that we had lost his shadow.

Afterwards the letters arrived
(he never forgot my birthday),
messages
telling me to keep up my spirits.
But between the lines
there was another world
draped in spider webs,
something always interfering with the phone calls,
something the size of a tear.

Papá, I asked,
How is your Parkinson's?
and he answered,
The girl has finished High School.
Papá, I asked,
Do you like the snow?
and he answered,
At last a boy was born to us.
Papá, I asked,
Can you live without the *yagruma* tree?
and he no longer answered.

In the photographs I saw him shrinking
like a lover's kiss.
And I remembering
the last time I saw him

wearing that very dark suit,
that was not as black
as his goodbye.

Time kept passing
— the time that doesn't fit inside a watch — ,
the letters grew more scarce,
the telephones let his voice slip away.
Toward the end he hardly spoke at all.
Then he just said: Cuba,
and they told me he was dead.

Translated by Ruth Behar

From *Ver La Palma Abriendo El Día*
     (Havana, Cuba: Ediciones Union, 1991)

CONTRADICTIONS, PLURALISM, AND DIALOGUE: AN INTERVIEW WITH RENÉ VÁZQUEZ DÍAZ

René Vázquez Díaz was born in Caibarién, Cuba, in 1952 and now lives in Sweden where he is a journalist. In addition to *La era imaginaria* (Montesinos 1987), *Querido traidor*, and *La isla del cundeamor* (forthcoming), Vázquez Díaz has published two books of stories, *La precocidad de los tiempos* and *Tambor de medianoche*. He has done a number of translations, among them *Viajes del sueño y la fantasía* (Montesinos 1989) of the Swedish writer Artur Lundkvist.

MARTÍNEZ: *La era imaginaria* includes many reflections upon the power of language and the relationship of language and ideologies. One of the characters points out: "We must call that language into question, we must bring to light the prejudices and values it carries along with it." I would like you to talk more about that idea.

VÁZQUEZ DÍAZ: I think that if there is anything common to all Cubans it is the fact that we talk a lot. Since I was a child I have observed the astounding ability of my neighbors, relatives, school classmates, friends, teachers, and myself to talk and talk "y hablar hasta por los codos," to exploit all the possibilities of the language, to the point that it loses its traditional, original, "normal" meaning and becomes *something else*. In Miami I have heard Martí's verses transformed by the daily talk. For instance, the famous Martí phrase "Sin Patria pero sin amo" is being transformed into "Sin Patria pero singamos." In Cuba we can observe the same thing; Martí's phrase "I have lived inside the monster [the U.S.] and I know his entrails" has been transformed into "I have lived inside the monster and how I miss him."

MARTÍNEZ: That is, the argument of your books is the equivalent of "we cannot stand to remain quiet."

VÁZQUEZ DÍAZ: A reserved Cuban, someone who does not talk much, is exotic and always gives rise to suspicion. The good Cuban always has something to say, she or he has an opinion about everything and a prescription for any illness. That's why there are so many bad Cuban journalists. Journalism is to let speak, as Jacobo Timmerman says. Cubans do not let each other speak even when it is a mandate of their profession. Among Cubans silence produces a certain anxiety, undefinable, unpleasant, a sense of social failure, that there is something not right. What is happening? Why is it that no one has anything to say? These people are really boring. Are they sleepy or is it that they don't like me? I went back to Cuba after ten years of absence with my wife who is Swedish and by nature keeps a trilingual silence: Finnish, Swedish and very Spanish. Because of linguistic differences she doesn't talk much. Well, people talked so much and so loudly that it seemed a joyful lynching to her. This is not always negative since the need to communicate in such a compulsive and loud manner creates an immediate intimacy and a wonderful oral tradition. Another of our impulses is that unstoppable need — very Iberic by the way and even more inexorable in Cuba — to impose one's ideas upon others at any price. That is why it is impossible to develop an idea through to completion within a group of Cubans; nobody is interested in listening, but rather all wish to express themselves as soon as possible, to state his or her idea although that implies interrupting and ignoring someone else. Notice that Fidel has always won or lost his battles not fighting, but rather, speaking. One of the reasons the revolution became stagnant is that the Comandante's discourse lost its magnetism and mystery. For me his speeches are objects of study not only because of what he says but the way he says it, that specialized, descriptive, demagogical and elliptic rhetoricism of an amazing inventiveness (especially when it comes to the definition of concepts in suggestive "sentencias" as well as labels and "nombretes" in his favor), but also the mysterious fact that so many people gather to hear what he has to say.

MARTÍNEZ: What is the reason for that?

VÁZQUEZ DÍAZ: That is explained, in part, by the fact that Castro continues to defend certain positions of unquestionable dignity. To deny that would be silly. Notice something: what really differentiates Fidel from his brother Raúl is that the first has the gift of language while the second is incapable of electrifying with the word. Another thing: the phenomenon of revolutionary slogans (nobody believes them but just as a rhythm like "guaguancó" they are repeated to the point of exhaustion; eventually, they replace reality) is also a very Cuban facet of the revolution: patriotic fervor, combative attitude and revolutionary intransigence. How much can a language take before it gets spoiled like milk? That is something that Cortázar pointed out but nobody paid attention to him in Cuba.

MARTÍNEZ: And in exile?

VÁZQUEZ DÍAZ: Miami radio stations are the most inquisitorial and "lengueteras" (long-tongued) of the entire world. There is gossip, persecution, lies, and the lowest politicking at a rhetorical level. In addition to that, the moment comes when they renounce responsibility. What is curious is that they think of themselves as different, "sublime," better than the propagandists of the Island. Going over Reinaldo Arenas's texts I was surprised and amazed at the silliness and the iniquities in his work. He was immersed in the imaginary era of the "rhetorical struggle" that prevails in and outside of Cuba.

MARTÍNEZ: All this has to do with what you said before: silence scares us.

VÁZQUEZ DÍAZ: Silence is considered an enemy of the Cubans. When we don't have anything to say, we sing. Notice how José Lezama Lima entitled one of his poetry collections *Enemigo rumor*. Do you see? Not even "rumor" is enough to fight back and exorcise the silence. We need to have noise, the endless bubbling of words because we have to fill the silence with anything, at any cost, with something silly or something genial, or as in literature, with long enumerations like Carpentier's: in a joke, a story, a "gritería," ten stories, funny remarks or remarks to make fun of others, and the erotic popular play that is made of looks, "miraditas," flirts, and touch, but above all, words that are attached in an ad hoc manner.

MARTÍNEZ: You are now exploring these ideas in the second part of a trilogy, *La isla del Cundeamor?*

VÁZQUEZ DÍAZ: In *La isla del Cundeamor* I consciously committed myself to explore the fact that each Cuban is an island surrounded by a lot of blah, blah, blah. And I wonder how come the sociologists, anthropologists, psychologists and even the psychiatrists have not studied the spontaneous and peculiar way in which we Cubans use the language against silence, that is, against death. I ask myself: Why do we express ourselves? What do we want to hide behind those manglers of words? What are the possibilities of a written language, a spoken language or even a language of dreams? I am telling you this because I have an uncle who does not remain quiet even in his sleep. . . .

MARTÍNEZ: In *La era imaginaria* and *La isla del Cundeamor*, in addition to the reflections about oral communication and Cuban psychology, the characters meditate upon other aspects of our culture from an anthropological, sociological, and psychological perspective. This is the case in your postulates on the status of women. When Nicotiano sees Violita washing clothes in *La era imaginaria*, he asks Federica if the chore is not a form of abuse. She responds: "Naturally. It is a nameless abuse. Girls' education consists of a habituation to the abuses they will have to endure when they become adults." I would like you to talk more about the situation of women in our culture.

VÁSQUEZ DÍAZ: In Cuban culture, as in Latin American culture in general, it is not enough to be male modestly and without exaggeration. One must be macho. There is a whole series of automatisms, beliefs, and rights associated with that concept. In popular language the homosexual is not a man, he is not even a human being. From women, the real man expects to be admired, to be pleased, to be obeyed and to be pampered. We are "chosen" by the grace of God. Women do not have balls, and great deeds require balls. We are good for prowess, heroism and risky actions, but we are reluctant to submit ourselves, with intensity and dedication, to a productive and monotonous task like daily work. What do we say about a woman that gets our admiration through a task that traditionally has been a male task? That woman has balls. I have always thought that the lack of respect received by Cuban writers — the Cuban bourgeoisie was particularly nasty about this, and later the revolution hurried to put a muzzle on its writers — has something to do with that subtle aspect of our machismo: books are not written with balls. Books are made with talent, solitude, discipline, and subtleties; that is why it is not an acceptable social task, it is rather suspicious, not necessary, it is non-lucrative, it is something that "comemierdas" or "faggots" would do. However, that does not mean that it is feminine work, because that would imply a lot of recognition for women. Female writers are not taken seriously. Why is it so difficult to accept that a female writer can be important and have influence over others? Recently the Cuban police, with an attitude of true thugs, mistreated the Cuban poet María Elena Cruz Varela because she thought she was entitled to say "I don't feel like it" ("No me da la gana"). I feel great admiration for female writers. Their sensibility allows them to explore different aspects and unsuspected facets of life. It is not by chance that one of the poetry collections of Reina María Rodríguez has the title *Cuando una mujer no duerme* (When a Woman Cannot Sleep). In the history of Cuban literature, from Avellaneda to our days, we could use Virginia Woolf's phrase that the history of woman's liberation is less eloquent than the history of male resistance to that liberation.

MARTÍNEZ: In your work, you often comment on the situation of women and the historical circumstances that have supported and maintained that oppression.

VÁZQUEZ DÍAZ: This situation of women's marginality is something that I have experienced since I was a child: my sister mopping the floors and I as a macho walking around with dirty shoes. Faced with the girl's protest, my mother defended me instead of my sister. It is astounding, this sacred maternal defense of the male's basic right to ignore the value of the work of women, a mission magically imposed by the same tradition that assigned me the streetwise role, adventurous and dominating. What kind of men are cooked in these spices? I don't know; probably, some sort of Mr. Wrong. In *La isla del Cundeamor* there is a character that pretends to be a lesbian, Alma Rosa, so the men will leave her alone, and she will be able to work among a group of machos. In the same novel, tía Ulalume, in spite of her feminism, doesn't hesitate to spy on her nephew's wife — it doesn't matter that she regrets doing that later — to see if she is having an affair with another man. There are things that Freud's followers should see. In Cuba there exists among couples a strange erotic relationship that reproduces the relationship of parents and children: "Kiss me, *mami.*" "Whatever you say, *papi.*" What does it mean to call a woman *mami*? I never could stand a woman who called me *papi.*

MARTÍNEZ: How do you see your novel *La era imaginaria* in reference to the literature produced in Cuba?

VÁZQUEZ DÍAZ: I do not think that the difference between *La era imaginaria* and the literature produced in Cuba is a matter of quality because my novel is neither a masterpiece nor is the literature produced in Cuba all mediocre. Unfortunately, they see those of us outside Cuba as a group of ghosts, traitors, sellouts, non-existents, non-Cubans. I have to repeat a phrase from *La era imaginaria*: "our grandmother is the same." I think that the project of a trilogy with the title *La era imaginaria* evokes Lezama Lima's idea of including the revolution within the imaginary eras. Eventually what differentiates my books from what is made in Cuba is the pluralistic acknowledgment that we Cubans, inside Cuba or outside, are all affected by history. But without adherence to official Cuban doctrine.

MARTÍNEZ: What are the elements of that official doctrine?

VÁZQUEZ DÍAZ: To avoid conflictive themes, to accept great silence zones, and not to put the finger on an open wound so as not to give weapons to the enemy. Those who stayed in Cuba are seen as the only representatives of Cuban culture while those of us who left are undefined, no one knows who we are. This does not mean that I accept and assimilate the doctrine of the exiled group, for whom everything is just the opposite but with a similar exaltation, passion, and blindness that makes them not only hide their own mistakes and deny the historical need for a revolution, but negate their own brothers and sisters, who in turn negate them through a belief in a different project for national development. I insist that it is necessary to talk things out — as Ernesto Cardenal says, we must light the candles and face one another.

MARTÍNEZ: That means that you do not accept the fact that ideologies can separate us.

VÁZQUEZ DÍAZ: Elena, ideology always separates us and it is inevitable, because it is not about anyone renouncing his or her principles and the voice of their conscience. However, we are united by a common culture and the desire to create a more just nation. When Fidel ceases to exist, the Virgen del Cobre will still be illuminating Cuba's sky and people will continue to dance the "conga" on the streets, even if some people oppose it. That does not mean that anti-imperialistic feelings will not gravitate above us like an imminent cyclone; that's a historical thing, a matter of elemental geography and national dignity. Nobody will convince me to repudiate Lam or Carpentier because they were in favor of the Communist government, and nobody will stop me from admiring Lydia Cabrera, Heberto Padilla or Severo Sarduy. Hell, I refuse! No! I defend the right to choose: you reject a writer because of your own literary criteria, as it is done everywhere else: because she or he is a bad writer, and instigator, but never because the writer is not loyal to the revolution. No! No political party can be the measure of everything. Observe how precarious and deceitful it is to silence a real artist: that was the case of Lezama Lima. It is like demanding that a ceiba tree not grow. Who were Lezama Lima's judges when he was declared "conflictive"? He was isolated in Cuba after the renowned

Padilla case. Soon after, the Cuban government had to rehabilitate Lezama. What an absurd story! Something unnecessary because a work of Lezama's excellence is like a tornado . . . you know it is there making the sky grey and you can look for shelter but you cannot stop it, you cannot control it. Rafael Alberti, whom I admire deeply as a friend, as a man and as a poet, went back to his country as an old man to realize that he was an immortal part of the most authentic Spanish tradition. The great cultural values of a country are not defined by the government nor by an ideology. They are chosen by the people, the new generations and the artists as they identify themselves with those values. What I do then is to find a place between both extremes and invent destinies that can evoke the contradictory currents of thought, the infamies, the fears, the lost hopes and those that cannot die, the patterns of behavior and the insanities of both groups. I would like to demonstrate how similar the two groups are: the Cubans outside and inside Cuba. And that cannot be done by the politickers; for them creation is part of a war, and all is fair in war, and the soldier must abstain, as a matter of fanaticism and also of survival, from showing understanding toward those on the other side.

MARTÍNEZ: However, this does not imply that your texts are apolitical, aseptic or neutral.

VÁZQUEZ DÍAZ: Not even medicine manuals are aseptic, and writing is like fighting: Voltaire said it, Strindberg said it. We know that to be the essence of Martí's legacy. The problem is that a novel is not a party manifesto but rather a reflection, a vision, an "espejismo," a series of images of human life in all its complexity. There are no immaculate lives. There are struggles, impulses, beliefs, principles, faults, virtues. The Communist Party is full of unscrupulous people and there are many degenerates in exile. However, on both sides there are many sincere and honest people. Then, no one is going to tell me stories. The creative work is not pure ("incólume") because if our reality is a bowl of beans rotting in the sun our books cannot be a shining gem. What we cannot do is take sides with either group; we must, rather, search for perspective and bring to light what the two parties cannot see. As my mentor Artur Lundkvist said, we should not fight something in such a passionate way that we become what we criticize.

MARTÍNEZ: As a writer and as a journalist you always attempt to analyze cultural manifestations. In your discourse there is always a pluralism filled with contradictions that do not echo either of the two sides.

VÁZQUEZ DÍAZ: I imagine that is how the contradictions that you see in my work arise. Everyone is right and everyone is wrong. I am included in that. That is the tragedy of the writer, she or he has to see in the dark and then choose the images. The writer must use his or her conscience. As Stanislaw Lem says, the only ones whose conscience is clean and transparent are those who never used it before.

MARTÍNEZ: In addition to writing poetry, short stories, novels and plays, you are a journalist. Would you talk about your work as a journalist?

VÁZQUEZ DÍAZ: I have been a cultural journalist. I have also been a literary critic and I have written many articles of opinion in Spanish and in Swedish. I do not think that a novelist can change the course of history nor influence political moments in a decisive way but his or her labor is to think and to contribute something by taking risks. Communism fell apart from within as it suffocated any attempt at criticism. Capitalism is a rapacious yet ingenious system: it allows criticism, it leaves a margin for people to think and to express themselves. In Communism people never know what is happening. What happened in Angola? What do we know about that war where so many Cubans died? How was it possible that the Department of the Interior got into that scandal about drugs and nobody knew anything about it? People get to know the savageries when it is too late because no one has the freedom to investigate things, to "fiscalize," to stir up the soup. What happens in Havana is not ventilated in the province of Oriente and the analysis is fearful and apologetic and the wounds are covered with a thin layer of diseased skin on the verge of gangrene. Those of us who are crazy and still believe that only some form of socialism can be the solution to the problems of humanity have to discuss these kinds of things. In Cuba writers and journalists became great sugar cane cutters. That's all very nice, but some sort of bad faith was attributed to them, some sort of destructiveness that removed from literature and the press any semblance of credibility. It could be that this is also part of our underdevelopment. Anyway, there is no human group that can put up with this, because it becomes stagnated and dies. Even within the family discussion is needed, criticism, conflict, tension. Once they are exposed to the light, not hidden, things can move ahead. On the other hand, to practice literary criticism in the press is a way of contributing to the development of society. In Sweden I have gotten into trouble with the cultural hierarchies, the police, etc. To give an opinion is to cause trouble and to expose oneself.

MARTÍNEZ: Is that ideological distance that I appreciate in your novel *La era imaginaria* possible because you live in Sweden instead of the United States? What does it mean to be a Cuban writer in Sweden?

VÁZQUEZ DÍAZ: In Sweden or in Jimaguayú, I will always be a Cuban. The more I assimilate into Swedish society, the more Cuban I feel. The more snow there is outside, the greener the countryside inside me. In Sweden I have suffered, I have lost and I have won. I feel grateful because there I found shelter, a place where I was able to pursue my literary vocation. In Sweden, my daughter was born, there I became a writer. However, it is very hard as a creator not to have access to the readers of your country; in Sweden I have a small group of readers and the publisher of my work, Bonniers Forlag, is the largest and most prestigious in the country. But in Cuba, nothing! That is very tragic. What kind of reception would my novels have in Cuba? What impact would they have on the conscience of the Cuban reader? Perhaps I will never know.

Bookmark, Ediciones Vigía.

SENEL PAZ

GOD DOESN'T HELP US

Sometimes it isn't just a little shower. It pours and thunders like the world doesn't have anything better to do, and the wind blows. The house doesn't know which way to tilt and it seems like there's lots of women dancing on the rooftop. If you cover and uncover your ears the rain says *guao, guao*, which is the name of a plant that makes you all itchy.

—I don't know the city, Elia, and I don't care. I've never left this province and I've never even gone as far as Santa Clara, but Estela is a peasant girl and a fool and anybody could trick her. She can't defend herself. How am I going to keep calm here knowing how far away she is, without anybody to take care of her? Don't insist, and don't get ideas in your head. She can't go to Havana.

—But Aunt, I live there and I know what's good and what's bad. I know my Havana from one end to the other. Besides, look, the lady I want her to work for is the best and noblest woman in the world, and she lives alone, there's no men there or anything.

As soon as the day starts to get dark and the air fills with the smell of earth, Grandmother can tell if the storm's going to be a big one and then she goes to the door making the sign of the cross with her hands and saying: I don't cut you with a knife, I don't cut you with a dagger, I cut you with the most holy sacrament of the altar. The storms she's driven off that way! And if not, me and my sisters sit on the stools with our feet up, without scissors in our hands, and every time it lightnings we say with Grandmother, quick, Blessed Saint Barbara, Lord protect us. But I like the lightning, because I see Grandmother with her prayers, and I don't see a thing, I see my sisters scrunched up on the stools, and I don't see a thing. It's like opening and closing your eyes, but without moving them.

—This woman is so good she's been without a maid for a whole month, just waiting for Estela. Now what am I supposed to tell her when I go back? You have to be polite. It's forty-five pesos free,

241

practically without working. You'd have to be crazy to pass it up, especially in the situation you are all in. Besides, like I said, I'm there, Aunt, I'll take care of Estela like a sister. Aren't we cousins?

— Look, Elia, don't get angry, but you've been raised different, you've got your way of thinking and I don't criticize you, because you always grew up apart from the family. How many years have you been living in that Havana all alone? Not Estela. Estela is something else. Estela is a fool.

— If the roof creaks when it rains and thunders like this, Grandmother warns us, You three run to Felamida's house, because it's the sturdiest; I'll run for the caimito tree. Once we were in one of these storms, Mamá was at work and cousin Elia was visiting, the daughter of Uncle Anastasio, when somebody knocked at the door: Tun, tun, tun.

— Oh, Aunt, let the girl defend herself.

Tun, tun, tun!

— No, because, besides, I'm blind, and how's she going to leave me? And if the war comes here, what do I do with these three children?

Tun! Tun! Tun! I went and opened the door.

— Oh, mister, what a scare! Who are you? Why do you have your heart on the outside?

— I am Jesus Christ. Go tell your grandmother.

— Grandmother, Jesus Christ is here.

— Boy! Don't you make fun of those things, especially when it's thundering out.

— He's here, Grandmother.

— Ma'am, — said Jesus Christ from the doorway.

Grandmother poked out her head.

— Oh, pardon me. I thought it was just this boy playing games. Jesus Christ smiled at her a little.

— Come in and have a seat, don't be ashamed. Don't look at the mess, every time it rains. . . . This is Elia, my niece. Well, you know that.

He sat down and drank the coffee that Elia brought him right away, in the unbroken cup.

— I'll just be here a minute, — he said.

Not a single drop of blood fell from his heart.

— Well, whatever you say, — said Grandmother. I'm really happy you came, you know? Without even calling you. Today is one of those days that there isn't a thing to eat, and the one who bills us for the electricity hasn't come because of the rain, but as soon as it lets up. . . . I'm going to set the dishes out on the table and you just fill them up for me with any old thing, it doesn't have to be fish or wine or anything out of this world, I've taught these children to eat anything, even kitchen lime, and a little milk for the boy, who's the frailest. And why not speak to don Genaro so he'll let us off paying the rent next month? You'll notice that I'm blind and I don't ask anything for myself. You have to be humble.

Translated by David Frye

ELÍAS MIGUEL MUÑOZ

STRANGE PLANET
Excerpts from *The Moviemaker*

We welcomed our Cuban guest with a Pinos Verdes feast: cholesterol-free scrambled eggs, high-fiber toast with margarine and sugar-free jelly, strips of imitation bacon, a tall glass of seedless orange juice and a cup of decaffeinated Mixwell sweetened with Ultrasweet.

"All this food for breakfast!" said Estela, as she nibbled at some of the offerings. "Cuánta comida!" she exclaimed after every other bite, eating to her heart's content.

My hungry grandmother, "Abuela," was here for one month; not enough time to show her the entire Southland, I thought, but we'd at least be able to explore the world-famous places.

I tried to describe to Abuela some of the tourist sites she'd get to visit. It wasn't easy; I had never described these places to anybody, much less in Spanish! Clumsily, I told her about The American Studios, where she'd see fantastic movie sets and special effects; The Movie Star Wax Museum, which was packed with the greatest stars of all time; Fantasyland, where she'd see ghosts and jungles and pirates and prehistoric creatures; Sea World, where she'd be able to pet a whale and talk to a mermaid. And there were the local hangouts: Gala Mall, which was a shopping paradise, and Ramosa Beach and the yogurt parlor and the Fifties Diner and the video arcade and. . . .

"Your grandmother needs to get some rest," Dad interrupted. "She should spend a few days just relaxing."

"I didn't come here to rest, Benito," Abuela protested. "Resting is for Galicians!"

I didn't know what Galicians she was referring to and I had no idea why they needed to rest, but the phrase sounded funny, *El descanso es pa' los gallegos.* Dad and I started laughing.

244

"Gina," said my mother, trying to spoil our fun, as usual, "you must keep in mind that Estela can't run around with you like a teenager."

"What is this?" asked Abuela. "You people talk as if I were ready to stretch out my paw already!"

Dad was laughing again, but I wasn't getting it. He deciphered the expression for me: "In Spanish you stretch your leg when you die. Your leg gets stiff. Get it?"

Got it: the first of many bits of Cuban wisdom that I'd gradually acquire from Abuela. People who died not only stretched their paws, I found out, but they also went out singing the "Peanut Vendor Song."

If you were called *mosquita muerta*, the little dead fly, that meant you were cunning, conniving, and hypocritical. (But how could a dead bug be so evil?) If you "played the corpse to see what kind of burial you get," that meant you didn't trust your friends. You'd be compared to La Gatica María, a pussycat, if you did something mean and then tried to cover up your act. María the pussycat, according to Cuban legend, went around defecating in people's gardens and then carefully hiding her crap.

You had to be assertive in life and always fight for your beliefs, said another one of Abuela's maxims, since "a baby who doesn't cry doesn't get milk." If you were not assertive and let people run all over you, you'd end up like "the shrimp that fell asleep and got swept away by the stream."

Old age, in Cuban culture, was the best time of life because you knew everything. After all, the devil knows more from being old than from being the devil. People who lived to be very old were bad bugs, *bichos malos*. Because a bad bug never ever dies.

*   *   *

There were surely more people at the mall than Abuela ever saw during carnival time in Cuba. Gala Mall was an indoor world with streets, stores, theaters, gyms, artificial sunshine and dense vegetation — real flowering vines and miniature palm trees — that grew in enclosed gardens.

Shoppers were transported from one floor to another in a cylindrical object made of glass. "They look so helpless in there!" remarked Abuela. No, she didn't want to travel in that "bubble" that went up and down incessantly. And she didn't care that the view from the elevator, once you reached the top floor, was spectacular.

There were at least five stories; each floor featured a large, stage-like platform where several dapper men and lovely blonde women stood, modeling clothes and makeup. "Are they human beings or mannequins?" Abuela couldn't tell. She noticed they breathed and moved in slow motion, smiling, winking, waving. There was something human about them. But how could those people—if they *were* people—just stand for hours, impersonating giant dolls? When and where and how did they do their "necessities"?

The mall had bakeries and candy shops and restaurants decorated to look like they belonged in the past or on another planet; boutiques where you could create your outfit on the spot, in a matter of seconds; rooms full of whirling lights and machines that simulated other machines. And there were soundproof rooms where you could record a song—your voice with an orchestra!—and fulfill your fantasy of being a famous *cantante.*

Gala Mall had impeccable restrooms; parks, playgrounds and even minizoos, places where animals were bred and raised and kept in cages for public viewing; where people went to buy—yes, *buy!*—dogs and cats and birds and monkeys and lizards and even snakes!

Abuela and I browsed through half the stores. I bought a full wardrobe for her, most of which she said she didn't need, and some clothes for my Cuban cousins. After a late lunch at Sir Burger (her first hamburger), we decided to head home. My grandmother was feeling overwhelmed and a little tired.

"You could spend all your time in here," I said, excited to have shared my favorite hangout with Abuela.

"Your entire life, yes," she replied. "But how do you keep track of reality in this place?" And I thought, What do you mean keep track? This *is* reality.

*   *   *

We went to Fantasyland on a weekday so we could avoid the lines. According to my mother, it shouldn't have made a difference to Abuela. "She must be used to waiting," scoffed Mamá.

Abuela found the singing dolls in the Tiny World attraction too plump and round, too perfect and unbearably childish. Yet she came out of the ride singing their song, which she loved, *Es un mundo de muñecas. . . .*

Mister Fantasyland sure had a talent for music, she said. My grandmother was deeply moved by Porky Lady, at the Big Pig Jubilee, when the female pig came down through a hole in the ceiling, wobbling on her swing, and sang her love ballad. Abuela couldn't understand a word of the song, but the melancholy tone of the animal's vibratos touched her.

"Americans are capable of making pigs sing!" she cried out, in awe.

We enjoyed the boat ride in the Pirates of the Tropical Sea attraction. We sat up front and, when the boat lurched downward into the bowels of the park, we were soaked to the skin. The vertigo was thrilling, but we didn't care for the rest of the ride. (I'd always hated it.) Why would anyone want to make a spectacle out of a town that's being pillaged and burned to the ground by savage men? Why would anyone want to witness such a tragedy? Battleships firing cannons in the middle of the ocean — the smell of gunpowder! — and beautiful homes being ransacked and women getting raped and filthy-looking drunkards wallowing in the mud of pigpens. You couldn't tell the men from the swine; they all had that same look of satiation and stupidity.

Abuela refused to go on The Jungle Voyage. "I've been to enough jungles in my life," she claimed. We also skipped The World of Dinosaurs because Abuela didn't care to see "those helpless monsters that were wiped out like ants."

In the Hawaiian Room, she was overcome by an attack of claustrophobia when the sunflowers started banging on the congas and the monkey-flowers went wild, making strange, angry sounds, and the rain started to fall.

"A mob of people trapped in here," she complained, "all of us listening to a concert of mechanical birds and as if that weren't enough, a storm just broke out, with lightning!"

She didn't fear the storm; she was used to bad weather in all its tropical forms: cyclones, hurricanes, thundersqualls. It was just that she couldn't understand what was "attractive" about this Hawaiian Room. Once outside, Abuela marveled at the cloudless skies. "This is truly magical," she said, finding it hard to believe that there wasn't a single drop of rain in sight.

The singing marble heads in the Ghost Mansion's cemetery fascinated her. "The way they play with your mind!" she shouted repeatedly as we rode through the haunted house, surrounded by whispering, moaning voices; as we watched the dancing spirits spin around the ballroom floor. "Even the smell is real," she remarked. "It reeks of death in this place."

She was tickled to discover a ghost sitting between her and me in the car. As the vehicle moved and swiveled down the rail toward the exit, it passed in front of a wall-size mirror. There we were, reflected, and there he was, the goofy-looking spirit of a young man.

"Look, Gina! He's so cute," Abuela said, giggling. "Qué chulo! Maybe you should ask him to be your boyfriend!"

No way! I thought. I knew much too well what male spirits were capable of doing. . . .

*   *   *

I'm filming her against her will. She dislikes my camera. She hates seeing herself *duplicada*, viewing that image of a woman who laughs and talks and looks just like her, Estela on the screen, a woman who is her and yet who isn't.

She's dressed like me, wearing faded blue jeans, with a wide black leather belt riding low on her hips; a pink tie-dyed T-shirt displaying the name of my favorite rock group, The Remedy, and black flats. Abuela faces her mirror reflection and discovers, incredulous, that she's turned into a replica of Gina.

"Qué bueno!" she says, laughing. "Now your little boyfriend won't be able to tell us apart."

My little boyfriend, that's what she always called Robby, my *noviecito*. She liked him. She praised his attempts to speak to her in Spanish. She accepted with a kiss the flowers he gave her when they first met and she even said, in a whisper, "Sank you, muchos sank you."

Robby and Abuela at the video arcade. He's eating up tiny mechanical demons with his magic wand. She's driving her sports car at full speed, avoiding the bumps, the potholes and the giant rocks along the road. Her tires screech as they burn down the freeway; her vehicle never explodes or goes up in flames.

"And I've never driven a car in my entire life!"

*   *   *

The Movie Star Wax Museum doesn't seem to impress her. She hasn't seen most of the movies represented by those magically made-up and dressed-up dummies. She does recognize, however, some of the stars behind the frozen masks: Chaplin, Bogart, Monroe.

"Imagine, Gina," she whispers, "having your image cooped up in here for eternity. . . . How sad."

Abuela at The American Studios. She doesn't "give a cucumber"—doesn't care—that prime-time shows and future box-office hits with megastars are being filmed a few feet away from us. The real thing! No wax dummies!

She's not impressed.

"You go to this place to have fun," she says of the Studios' Earth Tremor, "and they throw you in a hole, dígame usted! And they make the earth move around you until your guts are in your throat and your heart's coming out of your nose! There is nothing fun about that!"

"But it's good practice," I tell her, "for the Big One that's coming, the real earthquake. It'll hit before the end of the century for sure, eight on the Richter scale. And you have to know what to do, where to go to save your life."

I mention the earthquake alerts and the false alarms, the preparations: canned goods, stand in a doorway, etc. She turns pale. She doesn't believe me. "It's all true, Abuela! People have lost their lives in previous earthquakes. Thousands of people!"

She's been through one hundred cyclones and seventy-three hurricanes back in Cuba. But nothing prepared her for this potential catastrophe, this invisible monster that will jolt and agitate the ground when you least expect it. Nowhere to go; you can't escape its claws.

God willing, *si Dios quiere*, the monster will never show its ugly and omnipotent fangs. Hopefully she'll be back in her Cubita when it hits!

*   *   *

So few visual traces of her; a handful of clips. Yet I see a woman who looks and talks just like Estela. I hear that woman laughing while she cooks up a Cuban storm.

"I'll never learn my way around this maze!" she wails as she enters the kitchen. She doesn't like to use the microwave oven; the food placed in it for defrosting makes strange explosive noises, as if refusing to accept its fate. She never uses the icemaker, either. "When the machine makes the ice," she says, "it sounds like it's grinding your bones."

She hates the Mister PV coffee maker; it is the spitting image of a miniature spaceship and sounds just like one when it makes that awful, watered-down American version of *café*. She mistrusts the garbage disposal because it triggers an earthquake in the sink and can easily devour everything in sight. She's rescued five pitiful-looking spoons and two crooked knives from its clutches. And the horrendous racket it made trying to digest the silverware brought my mother to the scene of the crime, fuming.

"Estela! What catastrophe have you caused this time?!"

*   *   *

Abuela was bewildered by our waste products, the things we considered trash, *basura*. How could we throw away so many valuable objects? Bottles, plastic containers, cans, paper bags, all to waste! (Recycling was a concept my parents never took seriously, in spite of all my nagging sermons about saving the planet.)

I wish I'd kept that bundle of burger boxes that she had collected from our lunches at Sir Burger and arranged into a knicknack. "Isn't it pretty?" she said, slightly embarrassed, when I found her creation in one of the dresser drawers. I wish I'd saved the metal cookie box that she wanted to keep in case we ever needed a strong container. And the milk cartons and the cereal boxes and the twist ties that she liked to make into make-believe rings, *anillos de mentirita*.

"Are those the presents you're taking to your family back home, Estela?" Mamá would ask, sniggering, whenever she caught Abuela "saving" something.

My grandmother never took Mamá's cattiness seriously. She'd react to her daughter-in-law's snide remarks by first staring at her. Abuela would then ask her, "Are you feeling sick, Elisa?"

"No, I am not feeling sick," Mamá always responded. To which Abuela would say, "Are you sure?"

My mother would come back, glowering at Abuela, "Yes! I am sure!" To which Abuela added, "I don't know. You have that look of sickness again on your face, Elisa. Your nose and your lips are so contorted! Are you sure you don't have a pain in your stomach?"

The time my mother found us in her French living room, eating pizza and drinking milk shakes and getting oozing red stuff all over her untouchable furniture. "Dios mío!" she wailed. "What are you two doing to my Louis Quince?"

After hearing about the "distasteful incident" from Mamá, Dad talked to me and Abuela over breakfast. He reprimanded me, half jokingly, for feeding my grandma *basura*. Since when had I become a fast food junkie? I should know better, he said. And to his mother, "Eat all you want, mi vieja. That's one of the reasons you're here, no? So you can eat. But please don't let Gina feed you junk!

*   *   *

We're building a sand castle at Ramosa Beach. I'm showing Abuela the secret to perfect tanning, describing the Ramosa dudes that parade by us: the Surfer, the Yuppie, the Vato, the Neohippie, the Macho Latino, the Comecaca.

She complains about the gooey black stuff that got stuck on the soles of her feet when she walked down the shore. "It's the Blob, Abuela! El Blobo!" I tease her. But she doesn't know what I'm talking about. She never saw the movie.

Abuela reacts to the relentless waves. She feels assaulted, she fights them, tries to stay afloat but succumbs to them.

"No, Abuela, they won't stop. Believe me. This is not the Caribbean!"

She had never been to the beach until now, this trip. But she's always dreamed about the Mar Caribe. She has tried to imagine it and, yes, she could almost touch its peaceful waters, its sand white and fine like sugar. So vivid are her visions that she talks about *la playa cubana* as if she's actually been there, in Varadero; at "the most beautiful beach that human eyes have ever seen."

*   *   *

"These people have built a wall around their city," Abuela observed, as she and I strolled down the Pinos Verdes hill one evening. "They have tried to force the dark side of life out of their patios and swimming pools," she said, pointing to the homes we were passing. The mansions were hidden in the trees, protected by radar and powerful electronic devices. The Pinos Verdes people lived in a machine-like world disguised as nature. "Blind," she noted, "to anything beyond their houses and their sunshine."

Abuela told me of the village where she was born and raised, Piedrecita, which means "little rock." She talked of the big city where she lived now, Florida, province of Camagüey, which forms the belly of the lizard-island.

She said she loved and missed her home on the outskirts of town, Calle Egusquiza; her little house of white walls, the ceiba tree outside her window, the Cuban skies. And most of all she missed her neighbors, her *gente*, loud and spirited and driven to survive.

In this other world—Pinos Verdes, Ramosa, the South Bay—Abuela felt like a shrimp swept away by the stream. There was a wondrous civilization growing beyond her country's shores and she'd never known about it. This other world breathed and lived and thrived and most of all it consumed. It had such big needs! This other world existed, as did she, in a different dimension. Estela was out of her element. A stranger on my strange planet.

ROBERTO VALERO

AS IF IN A GAME

The lands of the sea were his name and his dreams were complicated tattoos. Once he discovered the clouds knitting letters but they were scattered, they couldn't say anything. He would have preferred that they had spelled the word love, or sadness, or the silly word poetry, but the clouds never went to school. That is why the road is his day, and no one knows the night. We are born alone and God takes us along in perpetual solitude. There is a first kiss that we will not remember,
        and the last good-bye,
           who suspects it?
      Who dares to decipher
          the furthest embrace?

Translated by Francisco Soto

LILLIAN MANZOR-COATS

PERFORMATIVE IDENTITIES:
SCENES BETWEEN TWO CUBAS

> Cuba is a peculiar exile, I think,
> an island-colony. We can reach it
> by a thirty minute charter flight
> . . . yet never reach it at all.
> (Cristina Garcia, *Dreaming in
> Cuban*)

Indeed, Cuba's "exile" is not only peculiar but rather anachronistic for this end of the twentieth century. Anachronistic, as well, are theories about a Cuban culture which has been and continues to be drastically split into two: the one produced "there," in the island, and the one produced "here" in the U.S. Cuban colony (la colonia "usano-cuabana").[1] In this essay I present an approximation to one aspect of that split cultural production: the theater or theaters of this island-colony. I will read two plays, *The Last Guantanamera* by California-based Elías Miguel Muñoz, and *La catedral del helado* (*The Ice Cream Cathedral*), a unipersonal theatrical piece based on a short story, *El lobo, el bosque y el hombre nuevo* (*The Wolf, The Forest and The New Man*) by Senel Paz—a Cuban writer residing in Havana. The focus of the reading will be the themes of gender and sexual/national identity. I will study, above all, the rearticulation of the aesthetics of camp, both gay camp and what I call "ethnic" camp or *picuencia* in its Cuban version, in these plays.

With this comparison I am attempting to create a bridge between the two theaters in order to question categories of culture and literary history based strictly on nationalist precepts. Although what separates the two Cuban communities geographically is a thirty minute flight, "dialogue" and bridges are automatically charged with economic and political tensions. Cuba is experiencing one of its most difficult moments in this century. Not only is collective survival of the chief values and accomplishments of the revolutionary process at stake, but also the physical survival of each individual who, for the first time in many years, has no means to acquire vital necessities. Within this daily "chaos" or "hell" of survival, the U.S. embargo acquires other dimensions. For the majority of U.S. Cubans who support the embargo for its supposedly political consequences, "dialogue" — even within civil society — means "to cooperate directly with the Castro regime." For some Cubans on the island, "dialogue" seems to mean "to turn the other cheek" so that "they can slap both."

In spite of these difficulties, there are many Cubans from both shores who take seriously the need for a dialogue and who believe in what I intend to undertake in this investigation: the necessity of exploring methodological alternatives for researching and historicizing "divided" or "dispersed" cultural productions. In other words, to explore in what way Cuban cultures are a part of the global currents and flows of "our America." This does not necessarily imply that I am endorsing a shift from national to transnational culture. I am emphasizing the insufficiencies of cultural and historiographical categorizations connected to a "modernist" concept of the nationstate. We know that this concept of nation-state excludes a great percentage of the world's population. We also know that a large part of this population is composed of exiles, refugees, temporary citizens, and other types of deterritorialized people. Furthermore, this construct of nation-state is related to systems of conventional signification which presuppose a unique national identity tied to a specific geographical location; that is, "national culture" presupposes a specific geographical space with well-marked and stable borders. However, displacements, physical border crossings, and cultural discontinuities force us to theorize "national identity" in another light, to disarticulate at the theoretical level what history has already separated: the anchoring of a "national culture" within one specific geographical space and within one linear history.

As a result of these geographical crossings, or parallel to them, Cuban visual artists became interested in the content of form, especially in what had been considered "bad taste" or *picuencia*, a Cuban version of kitsch. The *picúo*, according to these artists, refers to the extravagant vernacular decoration which, according to European aesthetic tenets, is considered outside of the realm of art. Artists such as Garciandía and the photographer Mayito adopt the *picúo* as their point of departure. They use popular elements familiar to many Cubans, in order to subvert socio-aesthetic hierarchies. Garciandía has a series of reliefs based on local sayings or witticisms. "Caballo regalao" ("Gift Horse") or "Mango bajito" ("Easy Picking"), for example, play with the literal meaning of the words and the images these sayings denote. Magdalena Campo visually eroticizes Cuban fruits whose names carry a double meaning. Playing with the sexual connotation of such tropical fruits as the papaya and the mamey, in her serigraphy series "A Taste of Cuba," she literalizes the erotic connotation that these fruits carry, in order to reconsider erotic relations between people.

Many of these plastic artists worked with playwrights and theater groups who, in the 1980s, also began to reconsider the relationship between theatrical language and content. With the "Teatro Buendía" and Victor Varela's "Teatro del Obstáculo," the theater became a public space where a series of possibilities were staged or rehearsed by and with an audience of young people who felt "marginalized." These young people, who have lived through the achievements of the revolution, demanded an expression in rhetorical forms different from the forms characteristic of the "official" voice of the revolution.[2] The heroic posture of the new man, a posture which had been instrumental for the revolution, began to be questioned. Thus, the cultural spheres of theater and visual arts became sites of critical rearticulation displacing the state. These proposals are important because they encourage us to rethink the relationship between center and margin, state and civil society. It is within this context that Senel Paz's story and the three theatrical adaptations take place.

Obviously, the relationships center/margin, hegemonic official cultures/subaltern popular cultures function in different ways in the United States and Cuba. Until very recently, U.S. Cuban literature had been analyzed within the category of exile literature. In these analyses, theater has generally remained outside the discussion or is simply mentioned in passing, as in Burunat y García's introduction to the anthology, *Veinte años de literatura cubanoamericana* [*Twenty Years of Cuban American Literature*].[3] In what little criticism exists regarding this literary production, two characteristics are usually emphasized: 1) this literature is written primarily in Spanish, and 2) this literature deals with the theme of "Cuban-ness" or the theme of exile. Burunat and García comment: "Although this literature shows us that the Cuban American has not assimilated linguistically or culturally to the United States, the structural assimi-

lation of many of them, that is, their economic success and participation in the financial and commercial activities in this country has
been almost total" (14). They continue their analysis: "Unlike Mexican American literature and Nuyorican literature, in Cuban American literature ethnicity is not defined as diversity and difference in
continuous clash with dominant culture, rather as attachment to its
forefathers and the traditions of country of origin" (14).

This characterization is quite deficient. In addition to the problematic use of the concept of "assimilation," the statement that
Cuban Americans have not linguistically assimilated to Anglo
culture — the assumption is that the Chicanos and Nuyoricans
have — is not completely true. It must be recognized that there are a
great number of works written only in English. Moreover, the use of
bilingualism, code switching, Chicano slang, etc., is very common
in all three literatures.

Returning to the part of Burunat and García's quote dealing with
the "Cuban American's" attachment to ancestral tradition, needless
to say, this attachment to the traditions of "our forefathers" is highly
problematic for some U.S. Cubans. With this legacy we also inherit
a construction of gender roles and a heterosexism which many writers are trying to combat. In the case of Caribbean culture in general,
and Cuban culture in particular, representations of masculinity and
femininity seem to be guided by a standard construction: to be male
equals being macho, macho meaning the excessive and extreme presence of masculinity or male dominance. Thus, maleness is culturally
coded as hypermaleness; the difference between macho and male
disappears. Constructs of femaleness seem to be more complicated.
Femininity is either culturally coded as the silenced, absent other (in
the form of virgin/mother, for example) or as excess (in the form of
whore or panicky, hysteric female).

In the 1970s, however, many Cubans in the United States began
to write as feminists and some as lesbians. They began to see themselves as different from what their community was supposedly
like — Cuban culture "here" — as well as different from the Anglo
community. As Eliana Rivero points out:

> We . . . began to be conscious of our being different from the
> dominant groups in the seventies, and internalized this difference
> as a first step in becoming members of one of the largest ethnic
> minorities in America. . . . We are consciously biculturals, and
> bilinguals in varying degrees. . . . Thematic richness for these

authors implies direct experiences of their ex-centric life; that is, an existence that is functional within the system but not at the center, and which the system — the anglo majority — can neither assimilate nor understand. It is at this juncture, I argue, that Cubans begin the process of becoming *Cuban Americans*. (167–68)

Elías Miguel Muñoz is a writer who belongs in this group. His work presents a critical attitude toward what it has meant to be Cuban, toward the idealized values of the pre-revolutionary Cuban culture, and toward the mythical vision or construction of pre-Castro Cuba.

For theater specifically, the differences in production between the Cuban communities in the U.S. and on the island are insurmountable. In Cuba, in spite of the ever-increasing scarcity of technical resources and state support to the theater — minimal though it may be nowadays — collective work among actors, playwrights, directors, and researchers has transformed the stage into a space of ritual. Especially nowadays with practically non-existing transportation and energy shortages, it is surprising to see the lines of people who actively take part in this ritual. As the Cuban critic Ileana Azor points out in another context: "The survival of rituals and cultural investigation, *mestizaje* [*métissage*] and a poetics of laboratory coexist in order to offer a space where rituals become true confrontations. Nationality does not disappear but it is put on trial by the creator's ingenuity and the instruments the actor's science can offer" (13).

I am interested in studying precisely how nationality, *lo cubano*, is being staged and reconsidered by Cuban playwrights in the U.S. and on the island. In the remainder of this essay I will concentrate on the rearticulation of *picúo*, that scandalous intermingling of objects and forms, in the plays previously mentioned: *The Last Guantanamera*, a play by Muñoz based on his novel *The Greatest Performance*, and *La catedral del helado*, a unipersonal composition by the director Sara María Cruz — one of the three dramatic versions of Paz's story.[4] *The Last Guantanamera* has not yet premiered. Cruz's adaptation of Paz's story was performed throughout 1993. In this essay I will be referring to the stage version I saw during the International Theater Festival in September, 1993.

The Last Guantanamera (TLG), written in English, portrays two U.S. Cubans as protagonists, Rosa and Mario, who are both gay. Together they travel to a world of memories and fantasies as they fabricate a story in which they used to be neighbors, friends, and adolescent accomplices in Guantánamo. The fantasy they invent, the anecdote of the Carnival Queen, serves as a unifying element between the two characters and is a recurring image in the play. This fantasy is staged as the two characters tell each other their secrets. During the play they reconstruct their personal and historic memory, the product of having lived alone in a repressive and homophobic culture.

The stage set of *TLG* exemplifies the aesthetic of bad taste. The stage is divided into three areas: a disco, Rosa's apartment, and a park at the beach. The apartment in Laguna Beach near the sea is decorated with modern furniture, art deco style, with posters of Cuba next to pictures by Georgia O'Keeffe and a hyper-realist nude portrait of Mario's lover. We see Mario and Rosa eating rice and beans with carrots as an appetizer and *mercocha* for dessert. The background music includes an instrumental version of "Guantana-mera", songs by Sara Montiel and Raphael, as well as Donna Summer and Bette Midler.

Like *TLG*, *The Ice Cream Cathedral* (*TICC*) is a play about friendship and intolerance; in Senel Paz's own words, it is a story about "intolerance toward those who are different, toward the minority, toward the weak. The story refers to the continuous intolerance in Cuba regarding sexuality, religion and culture." David, a young peasant, scholarship holder in Havana and a militant in the Union of Communist Youth, meets Diego, a homosexual, at Coppe-lia, a well-known ice cream parlor in Havana. During the course of the play, Diego and David become friends and discover that they have common interests in spite of the enormous differences that exist between them.

Diego's apartment, where most of the action takes place, is referred to as the hideout, the drawer, the closet, the alternative. The play's minimalist set consists of a stage covered with torn pieces of paper, a verbal carpet which during the play will be used as news, letters, and censored books. Eberto García Abreu sees these pieces of paper as "depository fragments of literary fiction, of the initial stim-ulus" (46). These pieces of paper have an analogous function to the use of photographs in *TLG*; the words or the visual images, traces of a historic and personal memory, violent in both cases, are trans-formed during the two plays into messages, objects, and theatrical points of connection and transition. On stage left there is a stool where the actor, Osmel Poveda, sits interpreting the role of Diego or

David. The stage and a portion of the audience are encompassed by smoke. The actor enters the indistinct and evanescent space of memory and from within this space the two characters begin to unfold.

Both performances pursue an access or entry into memory and from that point self-definitions begin. In *TLG*'s first scene, Rosa is dressed in a gray man's suit, white shirt, and a gold chain with a large Virgin around her neck; it is the Virgin of Charity, *La Virgen de la Caridad del Cobre,* patron saint of Cuba. She addresses the audience in the following manner:

> I used to think of myself as simply Cuban. But I've finally faced the fact that I'm here to stay. . . . It took me long enough! So now I'm a Young Urban Cuban-American, a YUCA. The 'yuca,' by the way, is a starchy root Cubans love to eat. . . . But I'm not just a YUCA; I'm a gay YUCA, a lesbian, a dyke, [cringing] a Tortillera! There, I said it. Tortillera. That word still makes me cringe. (7–8)

The axis of this self-definition is the discontinuity between ethnicity and nationality and its articulation with sexuality.

The historical and personal memory which makes Rosa cringe before she can utter the word *tortillera* or dyke is practically the same memory that makes David in *TICC* hesitate before talking about Diego and presenting him as "a . . . [pause] *maricón,* a queer friend of mine. And I say queer with affection because he would not like for me to say it any other way."[5] It is at this moment that through a short musical transition Poveda the actor gets up and gyrating histrionically across the stage changes from David into Diego. Standing stage right, Diego defines himself as a homosexual in opposition to queers and queens.

Diego makes this first entrance on stage without any of the markers of "effeminacy." Using gestures, Diego talks to David as if he were present on stage. But after this initial self-presentation, Diego begins to present the diction and gestures of the effeminate queer. He continues this long scene with the following speech:

> For example, if I'm standing in the balcony reading an essay by Fernando Ortiz and I see down there, on the street, the most beautiful mulatto of Havana, I go on with my essay. The belief that we can be blackmailed easily and that we are traitors by nature is completely erroneous and offensive. No siree, we are as patriotic and as strong as anybody else. And listen to me, [turning to the audience] Marxists and Christians won't get very far until they recognize that we are their allies; we do share the same

sensibility in relation to social needs. . . . If I have to choose between a dick and Cubanness, it is Cubanness of course. And listen [pause, to the audience] the decision ain't easy.

In this section of the monologue, the content of Diego's words appears to be in contradiction with his manner of delivery. By emphasizing his dedication to social duties and relegating desire to a secondary level, he destabilizes a homosexual identificatory process based solely on sexual preference.

The two instances in which Diego addresses the audience directly are important because they establish the kind of relation he will have with the audience for the rest of the play. In other words, they establish the erotic and political dynamics of this relation. The first one refers to the allusion to Marxists' and Christians' intolerance toward the homosexual. It is well known that in Cuba this intolerance resulted in serious excesses during the 1960s and 1970s. While the play only alludes to these excesses, the audience's laughter suggests that they can clearly read these allusions. During this "dark decade," homosexuals because of their "improper conduct" were equated with *gusanos* and counter-revolutionaries.[6] Obviously this ideological equation did not only occur in Cuba. In the U.S., for example, beginning with Eisenhower's administration, homosexuals were equated with spies and communists. This aside is important because it highlights the similarities between capitalism's and Marxism's heterosexist matrix.

The second instance in which Diego addresses the audience comes at the end of the quotation above when he apparently makes fun of what he previously took seriously. In other words, it is the moment of *choteo*, of mockery, in which the audience, through laughter, shares his irony. The Cuban philosopher Jorge Mañach was the first to analyze this phenomenon of *choteo*, of making fun of everything and everyone, as characteristic of the Cuban's "peculiar tropical psyche." He defined it as "a sign of independence which is exteriorized as mockery against all forms of authority" (71). This connection between *choteo* and the lack of respect toward authority is staged over and over again throughout the play.

In *TICC* the moments of *choteo* are connected to two authoritative and repressive aspects of official Cuban culture: ideological intolerance and homophobia. The last example of this *choteo* comes when Diego defines himself in the following fashion:

I am first, queer, second religious. Third, I have had problems with the system. They think that there's no place for me in this country but no way. I was born here; I am above all patriotic and Lezamian and I won't leave even if they kick me in the ass [gestures]. Fourth, I was incarcerated during the UMAP, Military Units to Assist Production [gesture].

For these four clarifications, Diego employs a highly histrionic diction and body language. In spite of the seriousness of what he is saying, his delivery suggests that he is trying to make the situation less important, as if it did not affect him too much. It was interesting to note the ways in which his hand gestures changed throughout. Initially, he held his two hands together, in front, in what is read as an "effeminate" posture; he then moved his hands to give the audience the finger while he slowly spelled out the words behind the infamous UMAP abbreviation.[7] The incongruency of this "obscene" gesture and the unnecessary clarification made the audience laugh even more.

This laughter brings to mind Mañach's analysis of laughter: "Laughter is something like a 'social gesture' of protest against the mechanization of life" (62). *Choteo* and its accompanying laughter are ways to undermine authority and they also serve as an escape mechanism. The important point here is not that *choteo* is essential or innate to Cuban character, rather that it arises from a specific collective experience. As Mañach explains: "Since its operation consists of reducing the importance of things, in other words, in stopping these things from affecting us too much, *choteo* arises in all situations where the Cuban spirit is affected by an . . . inflexible authority" (85). In the play, it is difficult to establish whether "history is assumed as a parabolic 'strategy' to refer to the present" (García Abreu 47). However, I believe that the audience's response privileges a reading of the play connected to the present, to contemporary Cuba.[8] Moreover, although the characters of Paz's story allude to "the events of the Revolution in those years," "to the situation and space of the 70s" (García Abreu 45), the theatrical and dramatic adaptation connects that moment to the present. In other words, the audience, according to my reading, responds through laughter to what it interprets as examples of "an inflexible authority" *now*, in 1993, not in the 1970s.

In *The Last Guantanamera* also the two central axes of the *choteo* are ideological intolerance, especially in the family setting, and homophobia. However, what is most prominently staged in this play are the performative aspects and theatricality of gender roles. Both Rosa and Mario try out a series of stylized and repetitive acts in which they question different ways of signifying *macho* and female, queer in its different roles, and dyke in its different roles. Through gestures, clothing, body language and movement, they put into question masculine and feminine roles within Cuban and Anglo culture. Moving from one role to another, both characters treat sexual identity outside of an essentialist paradigm in order to dramatically stage the role of Cuban *macho* or straight anglo, the woman queer as *tortillera* or *marimacha* or in its Anglo versions of *butch* and *femme*. In all of these versions, sexual identity is always qualified by ethnic identity so that all of these roles refer to their historical constitution and social context.

Music is used in both plays as a key element of their dramatic and theatrical development. The sound track of *The Ice Cream Cathedral*, created by Juan Piñera, utilizes the voice of Maria Callas singing arias from *La Traviata*. One would have to study how these arias are interwoven and interrelated within the development of the plot. In *The Last Guantanamera* one would also have to study not only the music of Sarita Montiel, Donna Summer, and Bette Midler, but also the ways in which Montiel's films figure as dramatic intertext. I would like to focus, however, on the theatrical aspect of the use of music in both plays. The preference for music by female entertainers and performers, Sarita Montiel in Muñoz's case, Maria Callas in Paz's and Piñera's, suggests these characters' identification with female characters who usually play the role of "women sexually wracked by inadequate males" (Jongh 68). This is by now a topos within the gay canon. From Tennessee Williams to Oscar Wilde in the Anglo tradition, and from Martín to Muñoz in the Latino tradition, many critics have pointed out that these women supply the writers and characters "a medium or mask that allows them to perform" (Newton 98). The gay male's identification with the "powerful" female star is an identification with woman as an emotional subject in a world in which man belongs to the space of action and woman to the space of emotion. Its "campy" reenactment, then, allows gays a space in which to perform the ornamentation and emotion, excess and exuberance characteristic of these divas and traditionally feminine performances.

In other words, I am suggesting that the theatricality of music in these two plays is a camp theatricality. Camp, as many have suggested, "defines a relationship between things, people, and activities or qualities, and homosexuality" (Newton 105). Camp is theatrical in its exaggerated, "stagey" style. As in theater, in order for camp to work there has to be an audience and a performer. Moreover, campy situations underscore this dramatic situation; that is, both performer and audience realize that each is playing a role. The underlying, unspoken subtext of this dramatic situation is society's heterosexual matrix. Camp's exaggerated, histrionic style is made visible through gestures. We have seen how the homosexuality of these characters, when it is staged, is signified through appearance, gestures, diction. All of these suggest different performative aspects of femininity and are contrasted with the behavior, appearance, and diction of the archetypal macho, David and his friends in *TICC*, the father in *TLG*.

The other quality of camp foregrounded in these examples is its humor. Camp is for fun and its aim is to make an audience laugh. Camp humor, in fact, is seen as a system of laughing at one's incongruous position (Newton 109). And the queen is probably the best example of camp's theatrical style and humorous strategy. The queen is the embodiment of the incongruities between an essentialized femininity and masculinity. More than anybody else, the queen demonstrates that there is no such thing as an authentic femininity, only representations of femininity which are socially and culturally redefined within specific historical moments. Thus, in *The Last Guantanamera*, Mario and Rosa, a queer and a dyke, rewrite throughout the play the recurrent image of the carnival queen, the drag queen. Neither one wants to play the gender role society has created for them and thus they decide to change roles at the end. However dangerous and limited, the contemporary U.S. allows for a space in which the queen can perform. In *The Ice Cream Cathedral* there is no such space. The name given in Cuban Spanish to the queens, *las locas* — the crazy ones — already suggests the role they occupy in society.

In these plays, camp style plays a role analogous to that of *picuencia* and *choteo* in Cuban culture. Camp is a strategy through which the performative aspects of genders and sexualities are foregrounded through theatricality and humor. Similarly, *picuencia* is a strategy in which the performative character of ethnicity or national identity is highlighted through exaggerated bad taste and humorous *choteo*. Camp speech, camp design, and camp costume in their consciously extravagant style are modes of dissociation from the conventional heterosexist matrix. But these characters' diction of artifice and exaggeration, the exaltation of style at the expense of content, the sense of life as role-play, which have emerged as a sign of camp sensibility in some of the key homosexual characters of the modern stage (Jongh 17), are intertwined and inseparable from *picuencia* and *choteo*. If camp functions to destabilize and transform the balance between sexual identities and gender roles, *picuencia* destabilizes the balance between a marginal ethnic culture and hegemonic official culture. Ethnic camp or *picuencia*, then, presents itself as bad taste with a vengeance and in good form. It is an aesthetics of inclusion within and against a society which privileges a monist and prohibitionist aesthetics of exclusion. As Rosa says in *The Last Guantanamera*, it is acting out and bringing to the forefront "the trashy memories of underdevelopment" (Muñoz 64).

It is within this context that one needs to read the ending of both plays. The last scene in *The Last Guantanamera* is titled "Rosamario." Both characters eventually end up nude. During the whole play, they have been looking at photographs of themselves in an album — the play suggests that these images be projected as slides on the kitchen wall. The only photographs absent from that album are those of Mario as the "carnival queen" with a pink fur coat, and Rosa dressed in a tuxedo as the queen's lover Amor. At the very end this photograph is projected and from the moment it goes up Mario will take off his fur coat and Rosa her tuxedo. Holding hands together, they walk toward the beach, as if they had been freed from clothes' identificatory weight, and they go back to their childhood, to that prelapsarian Guantanamo (suggested by the song). The only category that remains in place in that return is, utopically, friendship. Through a re-written and re-staged memory and within that space, Rosa is able to resuscitate Mario — he has died of AIDS — and both characters can become one, Rosamario.

This ending is at once different from and similar to the ending in *The Ice Cream Cathedral*. Diego leaves the country due to problems he had at work, caused by the intolerance of Cuban political culture. Although the play does not clarify the specific problems, the end result is clear. Diego utters his dramatic final words, "I'm leaving," and their tragic side is underscored once again by the music. The tragedy of those dramatic final words is of special relevance in present-day Cuba, especially in the artistic world.

I said that the two endings were different but, at the same time, similar. In *TICC* the differences between Diego and David also begin to be effaced. Although they never become one character, there are many instances, especially toward the end, in which we cannot tell dramatically nor gesturally who is who. As in *The Last Guantanamera*, it is in that emotional space where one mourns the absence of a loved one that the play ends and the recuperative ritual begins. In both plays, friendship and mutual comprehension and understanding are offered as the starting points for any utopic project. Similarly, the need to undress and to get rid of our repressive and homophobic monsters also seem to be a key prerequisite.

They are a prerequisite for that ritualized dramatic and theatrical encounter between Rosa and Mario, and between David and Diego. They are a prerequisite also for this intellectual and discursive encounter between our two dramaturgies born of the dispersion of the Cuban people.

NOTES

Funds for this research have come from the Organized Research Initiative on Hispanic Theaters, Focused Research Initiative on Woman and the Image, and Chicano/Latino Studies (SCR 43) at the University of California, Irvine. I would like to thank Pedro Monge-Rafuls and Elías Miguel Muñoz for their suggestions and cooperation; Polly Hodge for partial translations and editorial assistance; David McClemont for insightful comments and suggestions. I would also like to thank Rine Leal, Magaly Muguercia, Ileana Azor, Inés María Martiatu, Tomás González, Ileana Diéguez, and Pedro Oriols for the materials, time, and above all, the friendship they offered me during my stay in Cuba.

[1] *Usano* is a Spanish variation of Usonian, a term used by William Nericcio to playfully refer to citizens of the U.S. In Spanish, it is also a linguistic play on the word (g)usano, a pejorative term for Cuban exiles.

[2] I recognize that these brief paragraphs written from the outside are extremely schematic. This is not the place nor the moment to analyze in detail Cuban theater during the 1980s or that ambiguous and problematic concept "official voice of the Revolution." Boudet, for example, suggests that Cuban theater has never had an official line. Other playwrights, however, do refer to normative forms which seemed to have dictated creative as well as interpretative practices.

[3] For other analyses of Cuban theater in the U.S., see Escarpenter, and Manzor-Coats. See also the two anthologies edited by Arte Público Press and Bilingual Review Press.

[4] The other two versions are a monologue with the story's title directed by Rafael González, and *La catedral del helado*, a two-character adaptation by the director Tony Díaz.

[5] All translations of *The Ice Cream Cathedral* come from McClemont.

[6] Gusano literally means worm and it is the word used to refer to all those "slimy and dirt walking" individuals who left or wanted to leave Cuba. For a historical

analysis of homosexuality in Cuba and in the Cuban community in the U.S., see Argüelles and Rich.

[7]There is a similar scene in *TLG* where the actors make fun of the UMAP and the "witches hunt." In this play, Mario and Rosa talk about "the Raid" and "Las Barracas" (19–20).

[8]I am thinking, for example, of the way Paz's words are changed in the play when Diego talks about the ice cream he is eating in Coppelia. In Paz's story we read: "Delicious, isn't it? This is the only thing they do right in this country. Let's hope the Russians don't ask for the recipe in a whim because we'll lose it" (3). In the play, Diego says: "Delicious, isn't it? Let's hope *the Spaniards* don't ask for the recipe in a whim because we'll lose it." The shift alludes to the way the Russians were perceived to be in control of Cuba's economy just as the Spaniards are now with their joint economic ventures.

WORKS CITED

Argüelles, Lourdes and B. Ruby Rich. 1989. "Homosexuality, Homophobia, and Revolution: Notes Toward an Understanding of the Cuban Lesbian and Gay Male Experience." In Martin Duberman, et al, eds., 1991. *Hidden from History: Reclaiming the Gay and Lesbian Past*. New York: New American Library, 441–455.

Azor, Ileana. 1993. "Actor y ritualidad en el teatro latinoamericano." Paper presented at the symposium on "Teatralidad y Ritualidad," Machurrucutu, Cuba, September.

Boudet, Rosa Ileana. 1992. "Apuntes para una relectura crítica de los 80." *Gaceta de Cuba* (November-December): 10–12.

Escarpenter, José A. 1988. "*Las hetarias habaneras*: Una parodia cubana." Prologue to Corrales, José and Manuel Pereiras. *Las hetarias habaneras (una melotragedia cubana)*. Honolulu: Editorial Persona, Serie Teatro, 5–9.

García Abreu, Eberto. 1992. "La palabra al centro." *Tablas* 2: 44–47.

Jongh, Nicholas de. 1992. *Not in Front of the Audience: Homosexuality on Stage*. New York: Routledge.

Manzor-Coats, Lillian. 1991. "Who Are You, Anyways?: Gender, Racial and Linguistic Politics in U.S. Cuban Theater." *Gestos* 6.11 (abril): 163–174.

Manzor-Coats, Lillian. *Marginality Beyond Return: Gender, Racial and Linguistic Politics in U.S. Cuban Theater*. Manuscript in progress.

Mañach, Jorge. 1991. *La crisis de la alta cultura en Cuba e Indagación del choteo*. Miami: Ediciones Universal.

McClemont, David. 1992. *The Forest, The Wolf, and The New Man*. Unpublished translation.

Mosquera, Gerardo. 1986. "Bad Taste in Good Form." *Social Text* 15, 5.3: 54–64.

Muñoz, Elías Miguel. 1992. *The Greatest Performance*. Houston: Arte Público Press.

Muñoz, Elías Miguel. 1993. *The Last Guantanamera*. Unpublished play script.

Newton, Esther. 1979. *Mother Camp. Female Impersonators in America*. Chicago: The University of Chicago Press.

Paz, Senel. 1991. *El lobo, el bosque y el hombre nuevo*. La Habana: Edición Homenaje.

Rivero, Eliana S. 1990. "(Re)Writing Sugarcane Memories: Cuban Americans and Literature." *The Americas Review* 18.3–4: 164–82.

ROBERTO G. FERNÁNDEZ

RADISHES

Mrs. James B. beeped the horn of her 1956 Chevy, threw the shift in park, and turned off the engine. She flipped the radio dial and tuned in to the Mighty Voice of the Glades. The Country Hit Parade was on and she began tapping the wheel with her knuckles and the gas pedal with her foot to the rhythm of "Foolin' Around," sung by Buck Owens and The Buckaroos, as she waited for Nellie to appear on the front porch. She turned on the small battery fan that rested on top of the dashboard. The Chevy's windows were rolled all the way up to keep out the legions of nocturnal bugs that had descended on Belle Glade after the big flood. Old timers that had witnessed the hurricane of 1929 said firmly that back then there were lots of bugs but that at least they were local bugs and that this time they must have come from someplace else because they hadn't seen the likes of them before. The whole town smelled primordially putrid from the vapors given off by the muddy stew of decaying vegetation and carcasses of drowned animals. Thousands of years from this date, with a little heat and pressure, this same spot could be the site of a gigantic oil field.

"Shit, what's taking her so long? I hope she ain't in the john!" Mrs. James B. thought aloud as she turned the radio lever all the way left to the treble position.

The porch lit up and she heard the door slam. Nellie, clad in her work clothes, a yellow raincoat, a towel turban to cover her head, and a pair of her husband's socks to protect her hands, approached slowly.

Mrs. James B. cracked her window for a second and shouted, "Hurry up, woman! We ain't got the whole day!"

As she finished the last word, a squadron of palmetto bugs, buzzing in kamikaze formation, hovered ready to crash against the Chevy's high beams.

"Good morning, Mrs. James B. Oh, but what happened to your face? It's swollen."

"A bee got me this morning. But close that door quickly! Close itttt! I swear, sometimes I think you have a pea for a brain. What took you so long? Were you in the act?"

"Oh no. I don't act. But I played once the part of Genevieve de Brabant for the Ladies' Tennis Club Spring Festival of Plays."

"No kidding!"

"I can still recite all my lines," added a proud Nellie and then continued, "I know I took a little bit too long, but I have been so happy all this week. I am floating on pheasants' feathers."

"How can you be so chirpy when we lost our zoo? I swear this time it's really beyond me. Do you realize we're going back to our crappy job?"

"Oh, Mrs. James B., but I have great news! I saw a real live truffle when I took refuge on top of that tree. Do you know what that means? It means truffles never live alone. If you discover one, there are many more around. They bring such joy to me, memories of Rigoletto. . . ." She sighed slightly when she said his name.

"What in the hell is a truffle?"

"It's a delicacy. They grow in cool moist soil, under rocks or underground. My father said the name comes from the Latin 'trufera' which means tuber. They were so abundant in Mondovi. . . ."

"It sounds to me like one of them mushrooms. I hate them. I spend more time pulling them darn things out of my pizza than eating it, and I mean pulling out 'cause they get stuck in the cheese and I swear you need a shovel to dig them out."

"But, Mrs. James B., a truffle is not a mushroom. There is no comparison!" Nellie sounded politely indignant.

"Listen, Nellie, we better get moving, so leave your mushroom talk for later." Mrs. James B. turned on the ignition as she talked to her friend.

Crrrrr, crrrrrr, crrrr, the Chevy shook. Mrs. James B. kept turning the key, but the old heap stood its ground. The high beams flickered, losing power with each crank.

"Gummit! Do you know anything about cars?" She corrected herself as soon as she said it. "What a dumb thing to ask. Of course you don't."

"The air smells of gasoline," Nellie said. "When this happened to father's El Dorado he used to call Juan Benson, our gardener, so he could open the hood and check inside."

"Is that a fact!" a slightly sarcastic Mrs. James B. responded and then said aloud, but talking to herself, "I'm gonna let it cool for a while. Maybe the hot weather is making something stick."

"What do we do now?"

"We wait, Nellie. We twiddle our fingers!"

"I could call Nelson, but he doesn't know much about cars either."

"Air, air, air! I need to get out. I'm getting them hot flashes again. I need fresh air," screamed Mrs. James B. as she wiped the large drops of sweat that were breaking out on her forehead.

"But the insects. . . Mrs. James B., the insects. . .," Nellie reminded the torrid driver.

Mrs. James B. opened the door and rushed out, swatting at the flying critters. Once out in the open, she yelled at Nellie.

"C'mon, Nellie. C'mon out. You got your coat. They won't bother you! C'mon out and I'll teach you something to cool us down. I'm gonna teach you a cheer."

"OK," she said as she gracefully placed her right foot out and propelled herself with her left hand.

The teaching began.

"Repeat the words after me and move when I do. Is that clear? Do you follow me?"

Seeing that Nellie was attentive, she started. "Ready? Let's go: 'Lions, let's get to it, EM . OH . VEE . EE. Move it!' You have to shake your butt more when you say 'Move IT.' Like this," and she wiggled her buttocks.

"I think I know now, Mrs. James B. It's like a standing still tarantella."

Seeing that Nellie wasn't getting it, she walked behind her and, grabbing her rump, shook it, and said, "EM . OH . VEE . EE. Move it, Nellie, move it!"

They practiced five more times, and when Mrs. James B. thought Nellie had it, they coordinated a cheer, shaking their butts in unison. In her cheerfulness she hadn't noticed her arms covered with creeping things. When she saw them at the end of the last "move it," she screamed, and both women rushed inside the car. Mrs. James B. cranked it twice and when she was about to yell a louder "gummit," the frightened motor turned and roared. She floored it and they shrieked around the corner. A few seconds later they were cruising down Main Street. On their way to the packing house Mrs. James B. yawned a few times and decided to stop at Bertha's Big T truck stop to get a quick cup of coffee. She could have easily stopped at the

Dairy Queen, avoiding all those extra turns, but Mrs. James B. loved to see the truckers' heads craned around and feel their fixed stares as she sauntered to the counter.

"Kenny, a cup of coffee. Better make it a corn dawg and a cup of coffee," she ordered.

"For crying out loud, if it ain't Mrs. James B." He was happy to see her.

"The very same one, but make it snappy. I ain't got much time to socialize."

Before she got her order, Mrs. James B. tightened her belt two more notches to accentuate her imprisoned buttocks and further incite the truckers' lusty glances as she walked back to her car, her hips swaying in the night.

"Do it to me, baby!" the teamsters yelled in harmony, their tongues swollen with satyriasis.

Mrs. James B. stopped to smirk at them.

Inside the car, and while drinking her coffee, a beaming Mrs. James B. told Nellie what to say in case their fellow workers harassed them for their zoo fiasco. Mrs. James B. hadn't invited any of them for the ribbon-cutting ceremony. She thought she was about to become somebody, and somebodies don't have to hang around nobodies.

"You leave it up to me, Nellie. You keep quiet and let me handle it. When we get there, you walk nimbly like Jack."

"Jack the foreman?" asked a puzzled Nellie.

"No, no. The guy I read about when I was five. Didn't they teach you anything! And don't forget this time to please sit between myself and Naomi. I don't like her sitting next to me."

The foreman, Jack Jackson, was standing in front of the main entrance, and they could hear the monotonous sounds of the conveyor belt bringing in the produce. The other workers were already at their stations, their hands moving like a sideways millipede.

"Good afternoon," said a sarcastic Mr. Jackson. "A bit late, aren't we?"

"Beat it, Jack. We had car trouble, and you ain't paying us extra for getting up so early," answered back a sassy Mrs. J. B.

"You're lucky to have a job," Jack laughed balefully and plucked her by the sleeve on his way to answer the ringing phone.

"Good morning, gals," said the latecomers as they entered the nave's long corridor, illuminated by dim lights to save on electricity. Mr. Jackson pocketed the difference. "That bleach sure smells mean today," Mrs. James B. added when a whiff from the radishes' soaking tank reached her nostrils. Nellie walked a few paces behind her as was their custom, Nellie thinking it was a mark of distinction (as did Mrs. James B.).

In the dim light, ten women could be seen working in station five, counting the two new arrivals: Loly Espino, ex-wife of Senator Zubizarreta; Ana Maria Rey, wife of the poet laureate Lisander Perez; Pituca Josende, wife of Chief Justice Josende; Aida Lopez, the leading national contralto; Naomi Brown, nobody's wife anymore; Mirta Vergara, the freedom fighter; Maria Rosa García-Peña, daughter of the first President of the Ladies' Tennis Club, and Helen Valdes-Curl, wife of the late Pete Frey, the inventor of the improved muriatic acid.

The conveyor belt bringing the radishes was going at full speed, working to capacity as five trucks pulled into the rear parking lot bringing thousands more radishes to be unloaded, sorted, and packed. The belt was going so fast the drier didn't have a chance to do its work. Its task was to evaporate the bleach solution from the radishes that had been swimming in the soaking tank and the red dye tank that had made them redder, thus more appealing to color-conscious consumers.

"I think I am going to faint," said a dizzy, pale Loly.

"Don't look at the conveyor. Keep your eyes up, Loly."

"I can't, Ana Maria."

"Take your pearls off. I know how you start twisting the string around and counting the beads and that makes you dizzier. Take a break. I'll give you a hand. I'm fast!"

"Hey, ladies, stop the bantering and get your asses in gear!" shouted Mr. Jackson from his cubicle.

"It's OK, Ana. I am feeling much better," answered a slightly agitated Loly.

"He's so vulgar. He takes advantage of us because there isn't a man around. If I were to tell Lisander he would come and ask him to apologize to us or else he would ask him to choose his weapon and meet him at daybreak in the Winn Dixie parking lot. My husband is a gentleman. But I won't tell him because that beast might fire me, and we need the money. Lis is trying to find work, but it's not easy for a man of his caliber to find work suitable to his status. You know he's our poet laureate."

"I know the feeling. I am also a supporting beam in our home and for that we have to endure all sorts of rubbish around us. Before I forget, Ana, I heard a rumor that if someone in the family isn't working, the government comes and relocates the entire family to Montana. Then they make you work in buffalo farms where the women and the children have to milk the cows and the men have to make the cheese, and let me tell you that that place is as cold as Siberia and that. . .oh, excuse me!" Loly burped. She seemed bewildered by the prolonged sound that had come out of her mouth. "I am so sorry! I feel so humiliated! I have never burped in my life! Never. Not even as a child! I am so sorry! I am the first Espino to burp. What's becoming of us in this country! I am so sorry." With the last sorry she began to cry.

Ana held her hand, trying to console her as she continued sorting out the radishes with the other.

"Don't cry, Loly. It was a small burp. No one heard it," Ana smiled.

"Are you sure?" said Loly as she wiped the tears off her cheeks with her string of pearls.

"Yes, I am."

"I am very nervous, Ana. My brother Cioci and my sister Mely were arrested yesterday. You know how they go to different restaurants when we don't have the proper diet at home and they wait for the waiter to bring the basket with the bread and crackers and the butter squares and they start eating and when the waiter goes in to give their order to the kitchen they grab what remains in the basket and run out as fast as they can. But yesterday Cioci stumbled on a chair and they were apprehended. They were released on bail. It cost me this month's rent."

"Oh, Loly! Let me cheer you up with one of Lisander's latest poems. The one he wrote when our son Julian was born. It goes like this. Of course, when he says it, it sounds much better. I don't have his eloquence or his diction.

> A child from deep in his soul
> gave me such a sincere kiss
> that the day I meet my maker
> I will feel that kiss again.

"That's really beautiful," said Aida, the contralto, who was eavesdropping. "He should set it to music and I'd love to sing it."

The rest of station five nodded in approval, except for Naomi and Mrs. James B., who didn't understand what was going on, and Nellie, whose mind had flown to Mondovi.

"Whut she say?" asked Naomi to Pituca while wiping off the red dye on her apron.

"Is a poem her husband wrote for their son. Very nice, very nice." Pituca Josende strained her voice, struggling with the guttural sounds.

"Ah had uh hosband once tuh, but he left me wid four mouths tuh feed. He jus' took off one mornin'. He said he wuz goin' tuh de sugar mill tuh see if dey needed help and dat wuz de last time ah seen dat man."

"Losing a husband is nothing! The loss of your motherland is a weight that sinks your soul into the abyss of everlasting depression, forever damned to be a pariah," shouted Mirta, dressed in her camouflaged tight army pants. "But we shall return." This time, her voice echoed through the nave; then, in a lower tone, she added, "This is the struggle between civilization and barbarity. The hour has arrived to dislodge the sanguinary tyranny that has enveloped our beloved island. We must keep the pressure on. We mustn't be soft with the oppressors, for the tigers, scared by gunfire, return at night to their prey. We were that prey. The tigers approached on their velvet paws. We were relaxing, enjoying ourselves, with our guard down, asleep, and when we awoke and realized what had happened, the tigers were already upon us, devouring our flesh. We must go back and hunt the tigers! Why do I constantly incite you to struggle, to fight day and night at Pepe's Grocery, at Pituca's canasta parties, at work? I do it because I have known the pain of prison in my flesh. It's the hardest of pain. The most destroying of afflictions, that which murders the intelligence and withers the soul. But let me tell you something, women of our land, the absence of the motherland is worse than a prison cell. It's a loneliness that spreads like a cancer and is nourished by every somber sorrow, and finally wanders about, magnified by every scalding tear. If for some of you the concept of motherland is vague, think of your Xawa, especially you, Loly, you, Pituca, you, Nellie. . . ."

Nellie interrupted Mirta's patriotic harangue. "I'm not from there."

Mirta continued, ignoring Nellie's remarks.

"The motherland, Xawa, must be the altar on which we offer our lives, not a pedestal to lift us above. How many of you in this packing house are willing to take up arms, to become the paschal lambs on the altar of freedom?"

There was absolute silence.

"I know it's criminal to promote war when it can be avoided, but for us war is unavoidable. I know at the bottom of my heart that when life weighs less than the infamy in which it crawls, war is the most beautiful and respectable form of human sacrifice. Yes, war is frightening to those mediocre souls incapable of choosing perilous dignity over a useless life under oppression. I would like to ask each one of you if you are the type of woman who thinks more of yourselves than of your neighbors and detests the procedure of justice that can bring you risks or discomfort. I know you are not! I know you are women who love the certain benefits of a free motherland more than the dubious benefit of a never-ending exile, which will be the sole legacy to your children. I know you are ready like I am, willing to expose myself to death in order to enable our country to live. I am working in this place instead of training for the invasion because I am in need of cash to buy a machine gun. Now I want you to start your commitment to freedom by donating any amount, a quarter, a dime, a half dollar, to expedite the process of freedom by helping me to buy my weapon. Then you can rest assured that I will join the freedom fighters' training camp by the lake."

Mirta passed her military cap, but heard no metallic sounds. Her cloth plate returned empty. She said nothing and went back to work.

"Ah don't know nothin' 'bout yo' mama or whut yuh wuz sayin' about tigers and war but ah can tell yuh dat life ain't got no better after Johnny took off. Dere's another man goin' round muh place every night. Ah guess muh mama wuz right. She said ah wuz bad news 'cause ah gathered men 'round me lak ants to spilled sugar. Ah think dat man smells ah'm widout uh man and wants an easy piece, but ah ain't messin' round wid nobody. Ah might git me uh gun, not uh fancy one lak yo' want, but jus' uh plain old gun. Lawd, mah feet are sho killin' me today. How many chillums yuh have, Mirta?"

"I have no children. My children are the bullets I will put in my gun to bring freedom to my land!"

"We need a break, fast!"

"We sho do, Mrs. Pituca. De night is losin' flesh and blackness, but he ain't gon give us one 'til we finish dis load. Ah know dat man is uh sonuh uh bitch."

"No, no, no, Naomi. No bad words. Wash your mouse wis soap. Is no nice for a lady," Pituca scolded her, and went on saying, "My step-sister, a communist, says many bad words. I will not talk to her ever in my life again. If she has no food I will never give her nosin. Never!"

"Yuh have youngun, Pituca?" inquired Naomi.

"Eh?"

"Youngun, chillum, kids," she made a gesture with her free hand, indicating height.

"Jes, I have four."

"Oh, just lak me den." Naomi grinned.

"Change the station for just a second so we can listen to the news?" Mirta yelled to Mrs. James B. who was at the other end, rocking her hips to the rhythms of country tunes.

"I can't, Mirta. It's 'Foolin' Around,' my favorite song. Besides, the news brings bad luck," Mrs. James B. yelled back and continued to sing along the last refrain with the Buckaroos. "When you are tired of foolin' with two or three, c'mon home and fool around with me."

"Leave her with her music, Mirta," intervened Ana Maria. "I know that's her favorite song because she's always whistling it. It makes her happy, and you know how much she suffered during the flood."

"I'll be cow-kicked, Mrs. Perez, if you think you can bad mouth me. I ain't suffering a bit! But I'm pissed off 'cause I get to work with you pig-meats when I was about to piss on ice! I hate this rat hole as much as I hate the rain! So mind your own business or stick it where the sun ain't shining!"

Loly was going to say something to defend Ana, but the conveyor belt was churning, making its loud monotonous cries which drowned her soft voice. Mr. Jackson, who made his rounds to each station, making sure their socializing was kept to a minimum, turned up at station five. It was their turn. He got real close to some of the women, rubbing his dark regions against the unsuspecting backs, pretending to be checking on their quality control. Soon enough, the women realized what he was up to and warned each other of the impending lecher's attack.

There was silence now, each worker concentrating on the blemished radishes. Only the twinkling sounds of Ana's and Pituca's bracelets, heavy with charms, broke the silence as they swatted mosquitoes. The bracelets were loaded with big shiny medals commemorating their coming out parties, twenty dollar gold pieces, silvery crucifixes, tiny tennis rackets, diminutive cupids shooting arrows at unseen targets, and small green figures in the form of babies representing their offspring. Ana had two. Pituca had four. Neither woman had had the courage to pawn these treasures. Pituca had walked once to The Pawn Shop, but as she was about to knock on the door, she remembered her godmother who had given her some of the heirlooms, and, sighing heavily, turned around to leave. The following day she ended up at the packing house and at Mr. Jackson's mercy.

The sun was beginning to stir in the sky, its soft vermillion hues nearly blocked by the heavy fog that was rolling from the Big Lake. It settled so heavily inside the nave, it seemed that floating bodiless hands were toying with the produce. Then a cry of anguish was heard which awoke the workers from their zombie-like state. It was Loly.

"They are coming to get us! They want my pearls!" Loly's face was red and drops of perspiration stood out on it, like the morning's dew. She was looking at her fingers, now swollen and numb, peeling from the bleach and covered with tiny welts that had begun to bleed.

"Who's tryin' tuh git who?" asked a haggard Naomi.

"They." Loly pointed to the radishes.

"Girl, yuh crazy. Yuh afraid of dem radishes? Yuh crazy!"

"They're coming. They are coming to take me to Montana!" she said, running toward the next station, looking for a place to hide.

Some of the women rushed after Loly, trying to catch the fleeing Miss Espino and calm her down. Loly was too fast and eluded them, leaping like a frightened antelope. Mrs. James B., who had remained at her station listening to the end of the Country Hit Parade, got up and ran to the right of the soaking tank, sensing Loly's next move. Remembering one of Mr. James B.'s best tackles, she grabbed Loly by the ankles and brought her to the ground. Their collision knocked Loly out. When she came back to her senses, Naomi was wetting her forehead with a damp handkerchief.

Ana had stayed behind, working and reciting her husband's poems, oblivious to what had transpired.

"Hey, hey, hey, stop the ruckus and get back to work. I have someone new for your station. Maybe it will make you work harder. And you'll have to do that batch again. I swear you're like children, the minute I don't look you start goofing off. Her name is Dina Fabery."

"There ain't no ruckus here, Jack. She was upset because her hands are falling apart. You promised the new gloves would be here last week," said a sassy Mrs. James B.

"Get back to work! They'll come when they come. I ain't the factory that makes them!" He punctuated his sentence with a threatening gesture of his fist.

"I swear, if you touch me, you sissy, my husband will grind you into a fine powder," she yelled back as she swaggered back to the station.

Jack didn't answer her but showed Dina to her stool.

The fog was beginning to burn off and the conveyor belt had stopped churning. The women, taking advantage of their break, were now sitting on the floor eating honey buns and drinking rusty-tasting coffee from the dilapidated vending machines that sat across from Mr. Jackson's cubicle. Loly, who had borrowed Nellie's socks to protect her swollen hands, was completely calm.

"Ah didn't ketch yo' name," Naomi said. "Demita, right?"

"No, no, my name is Dina. In my country I was university professor of anatomy!" She punctuated her sentence by covering her tongue with the bubble gum she was chewing.

"Aw, is dat so. Ah'm Naomi Brown."

"Loly, are the socks helping any? I'm sorry they are not silk. I used to wrap Rigoletto's in pure Chinese silk," said Nellie as Loly kept gazing at a nail that protruded from the wall by the vending machine. "This would never have happened in Mondovi, never, never, never!"

"Dat where yuh from?" asked an inquisitive Naomi in a nasal-sounding voice. She spent the whole break or whenever she had a free hand pressing her nose between her thumb and index finger.

"Practically, yes. I was destined to be born in Mondovi but navigational problems prevented what was meant to be."

"Are y'all from de same place?"

"Yes and no, but let me tell you about Mondovi. It is paradise on earth where the truffles are as common as wild flowers. I can see in my mind my father talking to Sergio and Adriano, and Antonio Roasio shutting the door to his room in Albergo Tre Limoni D'Oro and walking down the Red Bridge della Madonnina and then crossing the Ponte Monumentale, heading for Besio's Clinic where his sister Franca Milano lies sick. After the visit he would stop at the Shrine of Our Lady of Mondovi and light two candles, one for his sick sister and the other for the soul of his friend Mario Trigari, who died during the Spanish civil war defending the Crown Prince of Spain, who was my father's personal friend, against the Reds."

"Who's de Reds? De Indians?"

"Oh, no, the communists."

"Yuh sho remember uh whole lot, Nellie. Ah wish ah remember dat much. Ah remember some when ah wuz growin' up up in Cordell livin' wid muh grandmama. Mah mama sent me to her when ah waz three and ah ain't never seen mah papa. Ah remember muh third grade teacher, Miss Hardee. She wuz white. She always made me sit in de front desk uh de second row. She said ah wuz tuh light tuh sit way tuh de back. She said, 'Naomi, yuh very light and if yuh press yo' nose everyday yuh gon do fine in dis world.' Ah always made better grades dan de real dark kids dat had tuh sit way in de back," she replied proudly.

"You made me remember a little verse my father wrote on his last visit to my meant-to-be-homeland. Pietrarca, a well-known poet, would probably say it has no literary value, but for me it's like my national anthem."

"Say it, girl."

"Do you sincerely want to hear it?" Nellie was moved by the request, her voice quivering.

"Say it, woman."

"It goes like this: 'Comme sei bell a o Mondovi, a chi giunge / nuovo a 'l tuo seno, e bella a chi ritorna / spronato dal desio che 'l cor gli punge!"

"Whut yuh say?"

"My father used to say that words that are like magic should never be rendered in another language. What I said is beautiful, believe me."

While the conversation between Nellie and Naomi centered on Mondovi and Naomi's native Cordell, Georgia, her children, and her missing husband, on the other side of the room the dialogue between Ana and Pituca Josende centered on their bracelets and was escalating to a scalding crescendo.

"Oh, Pituca, that's a beautiful jade figurine. Did your husband give it to you?"

"I beg to disagree with you," said Pituca. "This charm was given to me by my godmother on the occasion of the birth of my first-born son, Eurico. It's an authentic Colombian emerald in the form of a child."

"It looks more like a jade to me."

"An envious heart makes sightless eyes. Looks are deceiving to the untrained seer. I remember the day when my godmother gave it to me. We were horseback riding on our 40,000 acre recreational ranch. I was on a thoroughbred, and Goody was riding her Arabian stallion. We were riding side by side, and she told me to close my eyes and open my hands and deposited the precious stone in my palm."

"It must have been around the same time Lisander was courting me while we were canoeing in my family's private 150-mile river. He was a wonderful sailor, avoiding the rapids with the skill of a professional paddler. No wonder he represented us in the 1948 Olympic Games."

"A river, what is a river when you control the water sources?" responded Pituca with contempt. "My father, may he rest in peace, and I thank God each and every day of my life, until the day I die, for sparing him this diaspora and taking him in his sleep five years ago, controlled the waters. He possessed all springs seen and subterranean, the lakes, the rains, the hurricanes, the cold fronts and any other watering phenomena. If he had wanted he could have transformed your river into a dry bed."

"What is water, Pituca, in comparison to my family who owned all insects, amphibians and birds? We were sole proprietors by a Royal Decree of 1763, when one of my ancestors, Epaminondas Rey, bravely defended the capital against the English pirates. In gratitude for such valor the King of Spain himself bestowed upon the family for perpetuity all the 'aves,' 'amphibia' and 'insecta.' To put it simpler for you, like my Lisander would say, birds, frogs, and bugs. If we really had wanted we could have sent wave after wave of mosquitoes, gnats, wasps, bees, yellow jackets, fire ants, spiders, silverfish, aphids, whiteflies, mealybugs, torips, spider mites and scale crawlers, just to mention a few, and your silly father would have been forced to replenish our river in a hurry with all the water it needed. And I still say that charm is jade and not emerald."

The last words so offended Pituca that she tried to yank Ana's bracelet from her wrist.

"Help, help! She is trying to steal my bracelet," blared Ana in distress.

Loly, Helen, and Maria Rosa rushed in and were unable to quench the quarrel when Mirta stepped in and scolded the pugilists, pushing them aside and lecturing them on their obvious lack of patriotism, especially at a time when the motherland was mortally wounded by the red spear.

"In the memory of my late husband, Pete," Helen's voice quivered as she spoke to the combatants from behind the veil that had shrouded her countenance since her husband's abduction, "I beseech you not to debase yourselves by brawling."

"What's all the fuss?" asked a puzzled Mrs. James B. as she turned her radio down.

"Ah don't know whut dey were sayin' but ah think dey fightin' over jewlery," answered Naomi while pinching her nose.

"Nellie, Nellie," screamed Mrs. James B., pretending not to hear Naomi. "What's going on?"

"I didn't hear the whole argument, but I gathered Ana said Pituca's charm was made out of jade and not a true emerald and that her family was going to force Pituca's into filling up her river to the brim."

"All that fuss for that! Who gives a horse's patooty if it ain't a jade or no!"

"Mrs. James B.," replied Nellie, "The gem's origin is not really important, but the threat of sending those plagues is, because her family owned that array of insects and could have very well forced the Josendes into replenishing the river and if things got out of hand, even into serfdom."

"Hey, gals. The break is over. Get your asses back on them stools. You're a bad example to this Johnny-come-lately." He grabbed Dina by her left shoulder. She seemed to enjoy that extra attention. "One more thing. Reverend Fender will be talking to you tomorrow as you work. He has asked for my permission, so you make sure you show some respect to the Reverend."

There was no need to identify the thundering voice.

"Ah wish her family sic all dem bugs on Mr. Jackson," muttered Naomi as she walked back to work.

JUAN LEON

A CONNECTICUT YANKEE IN CUBAN MIAMI: REFLECTIONS ON THE MEANING OF UNDERDEVELOPMENT AND CULTURAL CHANGE

> It is good to open canals, to promote schools, to create steam-ship lines, to keep abreast of one's own time, to be on the side of the vanguard in the beautiful march of humanity. But in order not to falter because of a lack of spirit or the vanity of a false spirit, it is good also to nourish oneself through memory and admiration, through righteous study and loving compassion, on the fervent spirit of the natural surroundings in which one is born — a spirit matured and quickened by those of every race that issues from such surroundings and finds its final repose in them.
>
> José Martí

I

Perhaps nowhere more than in Miami do elements of developed and developing worlds so incongruously come together: skyscrapers and guavas, credit cards and Carnival. Miami is the cruise ship capital of the world and this nation's most active refugee center. It is a city of jubilant escapists, tragedies, and striking discrepancies: American blacks, indispensable to the modern foundations of Miami, continue to put in more hours working in the luxury liners and hotels than patronizing them. Haitians, citizens of the Western Hemisphere's poorest country, live close to the offices of American bankers. Cubans, heirs to the first socialist revolution in Latin America, happily consort with American capital.

Marketed as a colorful, "diverse," and exotic tropical paradise, the city has been embarrassed by African-American rebellion, political terrorism, the murder of tourists, and the corpses of refugees drowned at sea, overexposed bodies sometimes found curled on our tropical beach like dark question marks. Miami is indeed a place of tropical overexposure, where our modern fantasies intensively exploit the resources of tropical materials — geographical and human — even as they confront disturbing tropical realities. Extreme disproportions of wealth and power between North and South bring unwelcome and immediate immigration pressures. Latin American resistance to North American influence has brought fierce political struggles to the heart of Miami and nuclear missiles ninety miles from the Floridian coast.

From the perspective of contemporary cultural criticism, then, Miami can be a place of telling social interaction. There, deterritorialized Caribbean and Latin American peoples reclaim land. There, too, many of the new "invaders" rapidly succeed in the American style while other Americans both oppose and abet their integration. Post-colonials retaking an imperial resort — will they transform it? What are the stakes and opportunities? I would like to imagine that in Miami we can find or foster the sort of "communicative action" invoked by progressive social theorists like Jürgen Habermas, so that we might promote an open-ended, non-coercive, dialogical conversation among profoundly different groups and individuals which transforms the destructive, closely allied polarities of developed/underdeveloped, modern/primitive, Northern/Tropical. And yet the historical tendency of modernity has been to produce the reverse in manufacturing the underdeveloped, primitive, or Tropical supplement it simultaneously desires and disparages.

Writing of Habermas, Patrick Brantlinger echoes the commonly held concern that under modern conditions of rationalization and production, technocratic thought and action "come to seem the only legitimate types of thinking and acting" (190). If modernity is hegemonic, then an ideal speech situation is impossible down south. Tropical thought must appear "underdeveloped," either oxymoronic or second-rate. What is more, tropical thought remains necessarily in the camp of difference because it is only of interest in its subordinate and distant location. As Marianna Torgovnick has explored and documented, modern thought demands its primitive counterpart. (It will be most helpful in this essay, I think, to roughly identify rather than distinguish the primitive and the tropical or underdeveloped, though the terms, of course, have their distinct connotations.) Torgovnick argues that modernism and, especially, postmodernism find in "the primitive" a physicality and spirituality, a holism and sense of cultural rootedness, that modernity seems to lack (245).

Thus the primitive is both modern fantasy and post-modern symptom. Can there be room in Miami and in our modernity, for a tropical underdevelopment, a primitivism, that is radically transforming rather than merely a temporary relief for us, a drawn-out struggle for the people caught up in our uncertain but overwhelming social development?

II

This diary is useless. Underdevelopment and Civilization. Never learn.

Inconsolable Memories

Miami was built in the twentieth century as an American playground, a supplementary location that modern living somehow required, a place of recreation, rejuvenation, and retirement, the payoff and the tropical compensation for the task of Northern development. Miami never had an industrial base or strategic importance. The city came into being as a cultural, not economic or military, necessity. Still a resort and a haven for retirees, Miami now thrives as a post-modern "transactional" and multinational borderland where money, information, goods, persons, and ways of life are interchanged and reconfigured across the great North/South divide. These two major aspects of the city give rise to the most powerful themes of its literature and assure that in recent years the meanings of Miami have had as much to do with the extraterritorial as with the local.

Note the work of important interpreters in this regard: Guillermo J. Grenier, Alejandro Portes, and Alex Stepick III retell the history of the city's immigrant groups with sociological care (*Miami Now!*, Grenier and Stepick, 1992, and *Miami: City on the Edge*, Portes and Stepick, 1993). Joan Didion (*Miami*, 1987) and David Rieff (*Going to Miami*, 1987; *The Exiles*, 1993) interpret for American ears the lives of Cubans in Florida. T. D. Allman descants upon the city as a kind of futuristic cyber-space, quoting Wallace Stevens and Borges (*Miami: City of the Future*, 1987). And there are also serious, purely fictional, accounts: Christine Bell's charming, sad novel, *The Perez Family* (1990), Russell Banks's wrenching *Continental Drift* (1985), and, especially, Roberto G. Fernández's brilliant satire of American and Cuban-American life, *Raining Backwards* (1988).

These resources provide more than sufficient material for an exploration of the city's meanings—and I will return to *Raining Backwards*—but I would like to consider two other novels first in order to pose certain questions of "development." Admittedly, it may be that only a Cuban-American schooled too long in the Northeast would find it necessary to reflect upon development and cultural change in Miami through texts so far beyond the city's boundaries as Mark Twain's *A Connecticut Yankee at King Arthur's Court* (1889) and Edmundo Desnoes's *Inconsolable Memories* (1967) (best known in the film adaptation, *Memorias del subdesarollo* or *Memories of Underdevelopment*). Twain's novel is of a distant time and place, Desnoes's story is set in Havana of 1962, not present-day Miami.

Nevertheless, in the character of Hank Morgan, Twain develops a remarkably precocious theorist and practitioner of Western development, one who seeks to nearly single-handedly modernize the English of the sixth century. A self-proclaimed Yankee of Yankees, Hank is a classic American developer critically assessed through Twain's double-edged satire. Hank, the foreman of a nineteenth-century arms factory in Hartford, takes a violent blow to the head, and awakens miraculously in a romantically imagined Middle Ages. Twain makes use of the scenario to satirize the industrial and chivalric excesses, respectively, of the American North and South. He is also quite self-consciously thinking of the relations of the modernizing West to non-modern societies. Thus Hank begins his rapid rise to power by modeling himself on imperial conquerors, making use of his knowledge of natural science as they did:

> It came into my mind, in the nick of time, how Columbus, or Cortez, or one of those people, played an eclipse as a saving trump once, on some savages, and I saw my chance. (66)

"The Boss" comes to see himself as an enlightened revolutionary, but he is tragically short-sighted and conflicted, an at times gushingly sentimental man who protests that he is without feeling or poetry, an infuriatingly thoughtless man who keeps a secret diary, a recklessly self-aggrandizing egalitarian, a writer who composes a life story he has good reason to believe no one will ever read. Hank realizes his mechanical prowess but doesn't fully understand his personal motives. He teaches, but only to those that are loyal to him. He "Hankers" after the presidency in his new Republic. He never shares his power, destroying his machinery rather than lose control over it.

In his final days, Hank sits down to turn his diary entries into a long confession (the manuscript of which we read as the bulk of *A Connecticut Yankee*) even as he makes preparations for a peculiarly modern form of genocide, the "clean" kill at a distance. Watching knights die against his high-tension fencing in flashes of electrical light, he considers, for a moment, the inhumanity of that extermination: "One terrible thing about this thing was the absence of human voices; there were no cheers; no war cries. . ." (403). The modern separation of body and soul culminates in this moment of death. Hank's followers, an ill-fated few, die in the pestilential stench of rotting corpses produced by Hank's defenses, and Medievalism returns to England.

Granted, Twain delights in mocking Arthurian legend as he has the pragmatic Hank fall into an England conceived not in history but in Malory, but the American humorist is also pursuing a searching critique of the arrogance and revolutionary pervasiveness of modern development. Unable to compromise, negotiate with, or find any salvageable value in the non-modern society he sets out to systematically destroy, Hank is gruesomely undone by the high-tech slaughter he engineers, the resistance of the locals, and the magic he ridiculed and considered impotent. (After being wounded by a fallen knight, Hank is mesmerized by Merlin, who has disguised himself as an old woman. He sleeps for thirteen centuries.) Obsessed with confrontation, hierarchy, and technological progress, driven by passions he denies or misunderstands, convinced (most of the time) that he acts in the best interests of the locals, Hank is the classic modern, white, male, imperialist developer. As for the Medieval society he leaves behind, it is not a happy collective of feminized anarcho-primitivists. It is Camelot, not Herland. The most pressing issue may not be one of better or worse societies, however, but of power. Twain chooses to have Hank win the final battle and lose the war — an ambiguous rewriting of modern history. The ending of the novel demonstrates Hank's power and recounts its complete self-destruction. Outside the bounds of fiction Hank's power, the military and social force of modern development, has nevertheless been historically overwhelming.

Modern development in Hank's tradition does not present any constructive form of cultural interaction between developer and the "underdeveloped." Instead, development has fabricated the underdeveloped subject. Hank, the enlightened developer, gives rise to Sergio, the "unenlightened" person of underdevelopment. Both are preoccupied with power, but only one must fear the brunt of it. Desnoes's central character, Sergio Malabre, writes throughout the weeks leading up to the Cuban missile crisis of October, 1962. Unlike Hank's sworn enemies, Sergio is an ambivalent man. He is simultaneously attracted to and repelled by modern development, respectful and resentful of it. And he fears its power. When Sergio's family and friends flee to the United States, he chooses to stay in Havana, and yet Sergio has little that is good to say about the Cuban revolution or the society and culture he has, in effect, sided with. At times he seems sympathetic to them, but that feeling remains largely inarticulate as his personal identity, never very secure, falls apart to the point of silence.

Sergio finds himself lost in a no man's land between the developed world of the United States (most immediately represented by Miami) and underdeveloped Cuba. It is odd that he chooses to remain "in underdevelopment" when he is so frequently contemptuous of it, that he stays on the island though he cannot articulate the reason for his decision. And yet this is the classic position of the "underdeveloped" subject who lives in a crisis of identity and dislocation, who inhabits the gap between home and the foreign language in which that home might be described. As each day passes, and more of the old order disintegrates, the island seems to increasingly reveal its distasteful underdevelopment. Its people, Sergio reflects, pay too much attention to the present. They make too few demands upon themselves and are satisfied with so little. They are too much given to merriment: "Cubans can't endure suffering for long without laughing" (131).

An aesthete and intellectual, Sergio admires the elaborately artificial, the intricately planned and technologically advanced. For Sergio, French novels always call to mind Cuban social and psychological backwardness while every new American product, as it appeared on the market, would remind him of Cuban scientific and industrial inconsequence. Thus the island appears to him at times as merely an agglomeration of unskilled laborers and thoughtless consumers of things American, "a sweatshop, a country of parasites" (141). Waste, incapacity, and misdirection—the tragedy of underdevelopment in Cuba, for Sergio, is that the bourgeoisie, with the resources to modernize the island, spent themselves in efforts to give the appearance of development, a costly display he sometimes participates in.

At other times Sergio urges "genuine" development, but he does so in darkly ironic commentary, employing the language of imperial tourism and lacing it with several levels of cutting irony:

> I insisted that they had to modernize the country: put an end to all those thatched huts and all the Cuban rhythm and primitive gaiety and force everybody to study mathematics. Nothing. All wasted. (121–122)

Caught up in this complex linguistic game, he is in some ways very much the modern Caliban of the Caribbean. Sergio is the colonized subject who finds that he can only articulate his reality in the language of the master. On the other hand, Sergio appears strikingly obtuse, a white, Cuban, middle-class mediator who can neither find a cultural or political middle ground nor "see through" his post-colonial thinking. It is not uncommon for post-colonial writers to abrogate imperial languages, to reappropriate them in interlanguage, syntactic fusion, code-switching, and refusals to translate, but Sergio doesn't do any of this. Heir to the Creole syncretisms of Guillén, Lam, and Carpentier, of Caribbean and Latin American culture more widely, Sergio reads Montaigne and Lao-Tzu. Thus when Roberto Fernández Retamar speaks reverentially of the spirit of the Cuban *mambí*, the rebellious black slave, he invokes a figure alien to Sergio (16). Sergio is a defanged Caliban, without the biting tongue or dangerous monstrosity, and yet it may be as much his knowledge as his ignorance that undoes him.

Sergio does carry revolutionary anger, or its inklings. He resents Russian tourists who, like other colonizers, make of Cuba a place for fulfilling their instinctive drives, for hunting, fishing, sunbathing, and the life of the senses. When in these moods he fearfully admires Fidel's defiance of the Yankees. Still, he remains convinced that there is no opposing Yankee weaponry, the highly-developed fist. At best, one can only hope for a painless death. As Sergio awaits nuclear annihilation in the final pages of the novella, he fantasizes about his imminent extinction. Neither a revolutionary, a hero, nor a martyr, Sergio doesn't want a slow and bloody death, a torn body. If he must be a victim he would rather go quickly:

> Dying at the center of a clean bomb, as Eisenhower, I think, called it first. . .; it's a stupendous solution, a clean death, artificial, without pain or blood; a clean bomb without much fallout. (171)

The island, then, is a trap. Cuba is a nation too poor and too little for the "touch of greatness" that fighting the United States might convey. "I would rather go on being underdeveloped," he remarks (174). Sergio can only regard himself as a contemptible, mediocre creature, a coward, a cockroach, a modern man. He imagines the "clean" death almost with relief.

If even when awaiting death Sergio is an aesthete, striking Kafka-esque poses and searching for one delicious, inconsolable memory, I think he also sees himself as a realist, one for whom further writing is pointless. Americans, whom he mostly associates with modern development, have "imposed their way of life upon the world" (132). Sergio doesn't expect that anything will change that, let alone his ruminations. Americans have the bomb and the American smell: "It's the smell of nylon, toothpaste, lipstick, deodorant, detergent. . .," explains one of his women friends (134). America possesses the military force that can extinguish him, as well as the products that attract him. It seems inevitable to Sergio that Cubans will either waste their efforts in misguided attempts at development or that modern America will seduce, belittle, bully, or blow apart his island and its underdeveloped culture.

III

"Hey, Mr. González, I was born here, and you know what my national anthem says: 'to make enough money, to have a Trans Am, that is to live.' Who's playing next?"

"We are lost, Count Pepe."

"Mr. González, don't take it so hard. The world keeps on turning. . ."

Raining Backwards

Twain remarks in the guise of the narrator/tourist who stumbles across the aged Hank that his interlocutor's conversation was surprisingly restful: Hank, a mass murderer, did all the talking. Sergio's confused and fearful thoughts come to a dead end, but they underscore for us, I would suggest, the seductions and the potentially deadly powers of Hank's modernity. Neither Twain's nor Desnoes's texts leave much room for us to imagine the cultural or historical survival of the non-modern, of the primitive, underdeveloped, or Tropical. It is impossible to use the terms themselves without awkwardness. Will we be able to find in the case of Miami, or elsewhere, a location where modernity allows for or is transformed by alternative cultures it does not ignore or denigrate?

In Miami, the distance of the modern "clean kill" becomes nearly impossible. Bodies wash up on the shore. Displaced tropical people move among us. Perhaps Miami's difference, then, can become the city's most dangerous substance. Perhaps it is already the most carefully controlled, both profitably marketed and generally feared. Miami is already exotic. Will it bring underdevelopment northward or take development down south? Will Cubans in the city become more like Americans or Americans more Cuban? Will we find Hank, the *mambí*, or someone else on the streets, a mestizo?

Cuban-Americans in Miami are often showcased as models of both immigrant success and cultural survival (much like the Jewish people, in this sense). Long familiar with U.S. customs even as islanders, beneficiaries (until recently) of generous U.S. support as refugees, and unified by exile, these Cubans formed a powerful "ethnic enclave" in South Florida which promoted both economic prosperity, assimilation, and, paradoxically, cultural conservation. Cubans in Miami tend to be frank admirers of many things they consider quintessentially American: multi-party democracy, free market capitalism, and sophisticated weapons systems. They intermarry with Anglos relatively freely. And yet these Cubans rarely view themselves as simply "American." Nor do Anglos think of them as American. Cubans remain uncertainly foreign, their culture something of another land.

We might then consider the language of Roberto Fernández's satiric account of cultural life in Miami as much from the perspective of post-colonial literary theory as from that of American literary history. In a scene from *Raining Backwards*, his extravagant fictional documentary/murder mystery, a radio reporter working for the Florida Department of Tourism visits Little Havana. The representation moves from the stereotypically "Spanish" to the comically primitive. Beautiful senoritas and gay caballeros stroll Eighth Street. Soon a corner market is imaginatively transported to a "thirdworld" setting where shoppers haggle over prices, disputing the quality of roosters. Monkeys chatter. Men and women carry great wicker baskets. Cubans themselves are similarly reported as underdeveloped, childlike:

> I have noticed that they are fond of bright colors, of music and of flowers. These people love praise and are sensitive to criticism.

They're naturally quick to learn and gentle, but like people of warm climates, generally, they're passionate and resentful. (135)

At the same time the text is full of language that reappropriates Cuban culture and articulates a Cuban-American mixture of cultures. Untranslated Spanish marks difference. Both Spanish and English are transformed in an "interlanguage," Spanglish, that suggests a developing interculture (on the widespread use of interlanguage in post-colonial writing see Ashcroft, Griffiths, and Tiffin, *The Empire Writes Back*).

Drug runners, Everglade revolutionaries, plantain chip magnates, and politically obsessed patriarchs, Cubans in Fernández's caricature are presented as fantastically different from suburban Americans. They occupy another world, and, in so doing, sometimes encounter stiff resistance. Jimmy Olsen (Superman's sidekick reincarnated) is bewildered and outraged to discover that he must use a shotgun to keep superstitious Cuban worshipers away from his apparently miraculous ceiba tree. The "Tongue Brigade" (promoters of the "English-Only" ordinance) manage to have Spanish speaking labeled a form of mental illness.

Despite their differences, real and imaginary, no more than Sergio can these characters make use of a coherent nomenclature — Spanish, English, or Spanglish — for articulating their separateness from the modern "Americanos," for speaking of their own virtues. Instead, Cuban characters distinguish themselves and their ways of life by repeatedly remarking upon American behavior, setting it apart, and incompatibilities in these observations suggest curious, at times deadly, gaps in the modern system. The "gringos" are said to "know everything," but the gringos cannot be sure which of the bottles of medicine on the drug store rack may have been anonymously poisoned. Their Cola is refreshing, but the diet soda causes cancer. God must be from the United States, but only the Cubans have religious visions. Americans never turn off the television.

In this way the Cuban characters of *Raining Backwards* distinguish themselves from Americans by implied antitheses. Thinking backwards. Americans place their parents in old folks' homes. ("We don't," remains the unstated assumption.) Not an articulated cultural alternative, barely a statement about intergenerational bonds, but a stand-off in which all sides, through Fernández's lampooning, appear ridiculous. At the same time these characters fear that America scatters and changes people, that their cultural differences will vanish as the young become increasingly American. Cultural continuity breaking down, love of homeland gives way to love of sports cars and material excess.

Perhaps what is needed is a different kind of writing. I am sympathetic with those critics who suggest that alternatives to modernity will survive only through a new kind of literacy, a technological know-how that allows its practitioners to turn the system against itself (see, especially, *Technoculture*). Cuban and Cuban-American hackers holding illicit conversations in the INTERNET? Haitian techno-saboteurs? Perhaps modernity will yet produce, in these interstices, the kinds of renewing conversations among equally respected participants that Habermas has envisioned. Perhaps a simple fear of self-destruction will demand alternatives. But I am also skeptical. E-mail has a flattening quality. The use of high-tech systems seems always to bring dependency upon them.

More fundamentally, I suspect that writers like Lori Gruen, Chaia Heller, and others are right in saying that only a revolt against "control, power, production, and competition in all of their manifestations" will disempower oppression in its modern forms, will take the wind out of Hank Morgan (*Ecofeminism* 84). They are right to challenge the presumed necessity of power relationships. Perhaps Hank is not necessary, but in the modern world we seem for the most part to have decided that we like his conveniences, need his power, and fear his bomb. Culturally and personally, we work with him or must fear him. Much more likely than world revolution, then, is world modernization, a future in which we will indeed meet at a round table in an ideal speech situation, only to find ourselves saying the same things and escaping, for a short while, to the same factitious tropical resorts.

WORKS CITED

Ashcroft, Bill, Gareth Griffiths, and Helen Triffin. *The Empire Writes Back: Theory and Practice in Post-colonial Literatures*. New York: Routledge, 1989.

Brantlinger, Patrick. *Crusoe's Footprints: Cultural Studies in Britain and America*. New York: Routledge, 1990.

Desnoes, Edmundo. *Inconsolable Memories* (1967). In *Memories of Underdevelopment*. Rutgers Films in Print Series. New Brunswick: 1990.

Fernández, Robert G. *Raining Backwards*. Houston: Arte Publico Press, 1988.

Fernández Retamar, Roberto. *Caliban and Other Essays*. Translated by Edward Baker. Minneapolis: University of Minnesota Press, 1989.

Gaard, Greta (editor). *Ecofeminism: Women, Animals, Nature.* Philadelphia: Temple University Press, 1993.
Penley, Constance, and Andrew Ross (editors). *Technoculture.* Minneapolis: The University of Minnesota Press, 1991.
Torgovnick, Marianna. *Gone Primitive: Savage Intellects, Modern Lives.* Chicago: The University of Chicago Press, 1990.
Twain, Mark. *A Connecticut Yankee at King Arthur's Court* (1889). New York: Penguin Classics, 1987.

CARLOTA CAULFIELD

LANDSCAPES OF THE MIND

My house is a music box
and the calm there
is a tunnel of almond blossoms.

I am nostalgic today:
summer is bordering my house
and I roam the world
in my memory.

I spent ten years collecting dreams
and forgetting the coastland of my country.

I am now bordering the domain of a shadow.

SUNDAY

Love set them going, our mothers,
tiny little wind-up toys
as shiny and urgent as pearls;
later dull and slow, like late model cars,
something bloated about their design.

Love set them going, directed
their noses to the clean cosmetic,
the innocent films.
They married one man;
they made love only once.

It was love that gave them careers,
new wares, made them
dark-haired girls sifting rice,
checking magazines for quick tests titled:
"Do you know your lover?"
"Is your marriage happy?"
Every day the air of nitrous oxide.

They never told the fathers about us,
the daughters standing with arms akimbo.
We were the open secret,
as beautiful and repellent as tattoos.

Now they see themselves the snail on the tank.
We are stone nymphs come to life,
brilliant betas,
too many things at once.

I tell you, if you whisper to me, woman,
it goes no further.
Pain or peace, I cannot take it to them.
If you touch me, your albuminous kiss,
that is between you and me.

It is love, casuist love, a twisted Gabriel
who turns them away:
Our mothers, black veils, votive, orthodox,
gravely whispering to men
misdemeanor sins.

They light dripless, traceless,
invisible candles for penance,
sing prayers like insurance,
dream crashes in station wagons, family cars.
Year after year, the missal for breakfast.

When we become them, a little taller perhaps,
buddha women late in life,
will we be like them,
with our steeples and postulates,
trembling?

Tell me, here, with a tremor of a different sort,
our eyes lidless, your breath cool,
about our mortality.

RITA MARTÍN

ELISA, OR THE PRICE OF DREAMS

She already knew the reason for everything. The house stood among the various hills. The house. The hills. Hills of the ancestors. She: the youngest daughter of the eldest. The sister: I will look after her. The others: we want to play. The reddish-brown curls, almost blond, came together in rhythmic locks receiving her laughter. The air: the only real substance even if one were sure of the earth. Three neighbors: Petrona, Petrila, and Petronila:

Let her be beautiful.
Let her be good.
Let her be worthy.
Let her be herself.
Let her be alive.
Let her not die.

How long had she endured like this, given over to levitation? Her gaze shifted toward the woods that rose between cotton fields which offered still another day. Contour of the waters. Pines gathered in their roots with modesty. In the branches the singing nests rose up. Leaves speckled the profound oval of the heights. With caution, Elisa breathed the eternal perfume of the place. Inevitably, whichever way she turned, a similar sensation accompanied her. Gardens of begonias and agonies, tuberose, butterflies, sorrows, lilies, joys. They respected and greeted her passing. It was night and she ought to return.

The way had been long. Behind her tired feet an enormous wound. A star weighed heavily in her hands. Placing it on the rock she preferred to rest a while, and for the first time in so many years she closed her eyes.

Awake Awake Awake
Awake

The minstrels:

> We will quickly narrate
> while you invent a dream
> and unite the body with dance
> you will arrive, arrive
>
> It is the woods:
> The woods upon us.

SILENCE

Beneath the spurs of the moon the horsemen suffered. The murmur of the mockingbird had been extinguished. In songs neither the blue mantle nor the black border. Dust was inundating the river, bordered in red. Waters overran storms, they became one. A drop fell thick and serene into a crack. Elisa hurried to find the inhabitants of the town.

In the darkness she distinguished the walled-in dwellings. The village was deserted. At the end of a narrow lane a dying light announced one survivor. The stooped man received her:

"Tell me, Sir, what is going on?"

"Just now, at this moment, nothing."

"I don't understand."

"You fled this place, you must understand. You are dethroned."

"Exiled, Sir, be precise."

"As you may suppose, your men are my property."

"I never had property rights over any man whatever. They must not be the same ones."

Enraged he ordered her to go on.

Elisa no longer listened. A preoccupation overcame her. She should arrive home early. She might leave for months and years but she had never returned late. Slipping, she arrived. The door creaked lightly. A tiny bird fluttered about above the floor. She opened the window and, taking the animal in her palm, urged it to fly.

"No, just give me an hour. They have contaminated our air."

As if in gentle labor the young woman gathered some stems and dried grass. She cuddled her gentle singer. The arrangement complete, she decisively entered the room.

In the house the body of a man levitated. Elisa's beloved bore a deep wound in his side. Sweating, he opened his eyes in order to be heard:

"Come, come here."

"Wait, I will heal you."

"Don't do it. It's a trap."

"What are you saying?"

"The hour has arrived for proving that only your presence has the power to restore me. Now you must proceed as has been resolved."

She headed for the river. The waters had not yet come up to their usual level. Without hesitation, and recalling a future past, she began the rite. First she stripped off her blouse. Her skirt was almost torn to pieces by the grass. The last step: the enormous weight of her shoes. She always did the same. She was naked. She touched herself to be sure that nothing remained hidden, and, like a girl, entered.

Through her white skin bounded a vein. She spent all night rinsing her hair down to her feet with the fluid that gave way as soon as she took it up in her adolescent fingertips. With the coming of light the inflowing water turned back into the old window pane. The hummingbird flew and Elisa raised her voice:

"Make in every cup the nest that is required."

They arrived, carefully dressed. They went to their daily tasks. The canal abutted the center. No one could ignore the spectacle.

"Yes, she's an exhibitionist."

"A brazen woman."

"Doesn't even answer. A common whore."

"Could she be crazy?"

"She's sure not from here."

"Call the police, come on, call the police."

"Look, don't do anything," said the boy, "look how she has fire all around her and she doesn't burn."

"It's true, she doesn't burn. She doesn't burn."

SHE DOESN'T BURN

"If it's a matter of nature, let her be."

Late in the morning, around the time that becomes confused with midday just before the afternoon, the lover carried the wound and, softly, asked for her lips. Arm in arm, the young woman's hand ran over his back and neck at the same time her narrow waist was run through by her lover's sharp iron. They were powerfully one. Slowly the waters moved and the rhythm of precise harmony made their bodies. When the whirlpool grew gigantic around the two figures a great blast pierced through the very center of the waterspout. At that moment Elisa sobbed, while he opened his mouth as if to cry out. Both opened their eyes tired and content they slowly observed each other.

They did not return to the circle. Men and women who had been waiting there cried. A bird carried an egg in its plumage. Taking it with the highest respect, it was placed between breast and breast.

One of the villagers:

"The truth is I never knew anyone but I existed."

"What'll we do? That man with the dead-end street prohibits everything."

And then the most knowing:

"There is a legend. The books say that we were to be saved by a woman. That this woman, one that had never been seen by us, would present herself nude and in a youthful body would display the most ancient of wounds."

The boy:

"And the woman at the river?"

THE WOMAN AT THE RIVER.

"Who's seen her before?"

"Isn't she naked?"

"Could she have the wound? Could she?"

Lady: tell us if you bear the wound, of all wounds, the immemorial.

She did not respond. She separated her body from that of her lover and before the curious ones displayed the strange rectangular wound, deep, red, in which could be glimpsed, smiling and healthy, the old muscle.

It's her.

IT'S HER.

HER.

Regarding the boy, she began to dress. And she threw into the air the egg that suddenly burst into wings. Over there in the narrows day broke and a bolt of lightning split the dirty lamp in two.

Several months later, Elisa was feeling sad. She sent for her friends and begged for the best horses for a journey. Her sweet lover kissed her and whispered in her ear: Go. Elisa came out into a kind of opening before she arrived. She remembered the words of the neighbors and the judgment of the elder. She went to the woods and sprinkled the honey with perfume. Unforeseeably, she hid herself away in a village lane and warded off a hundred thousand men. She placed the rose in her fine lips and bid farewell with a sigh.

Today they still ask the beloved: "Do you know when Elisa will return?"

He smiles, and with the answer he will give every day of his life explains: "Why get worked up? She just left today, at dawn."

Translated by Juan Leon

From Salvador Redonet, ed., *Los últimos serán los primeros* (La Habana and Madrid: Editorial Letras Cubanas, 1993).

LINA DE FERIA

POEM FOR THE WOMAN WHO TALKS TO
HERSELF IN THE PARK

in your umbrella filled with holes there are no rumors
only histories of all those losing cities
the sites where nothing remained but ruins
where it often seemed nothing was worth saving
and you longed for so many improbable hands
that you became a torn branch on the ground.
you spoke in order to believe
and now you don't believe in parks
you don't believe men
you don't believe yourself
your incoherence grows as if you'd been struck
like something from which one must turn away
or turn red with disdain for tradition
in the face of nothingness, what is left
someone derailed your margins
and now you uproot us from your time
leaving us to be shadows you don't respect
stripped of a body before you
although you are right
and if criticism is worth anything
if my denunciation is nothing else
than the instinct to feel you are our animal
                    a species of ours
                    our possibility and goal
(you were as logical as anyone and now solitude crushes you
and no one detains you and no one could detain you)
what were you before,
mother, concert-player, prostitute,

she whom tedium held, the alienated one, the one who loved
    platonically,
the asexual one, the clumsy one, the one who remained
    unfinished?
you are pathetic and extraordinary
if you lie you lie with your truth
and that's how some of us see you with your bench and your
    umbrella
with your lips edged with a trembling line
telling stories no one remembers
               and eternal as a picture
I'm sure they'll know how to hear me if I say
you're a character out of antonioni or buñuel
you'd be an absolute for dostoyevski
and your hands are for chagall
you're close to them in a way
as you are to me in our common life
woman that speaks like a hammer
no one will speak of you but you'll stay
the shame again singing the song
that's definitely out of style
facing the theater of Calzada and D Street.

Translated by Ruth Behar

From Lina de Feria, *La casa que no existía* (Havana: Cuadernos Union,
1967)

MARÍA ELENA CRUZ VARELA

THE WALL

To the East. To the Northeast. Insolent. Abrupt. Uncontainable.
Double-edged blade running from ground to sky to wall.
And there, a woman. Debating with herself.
The rocks dispute how she inherited her silks.
The padding of her suits. And that pain
stabbing at her ribs. The sword and her innocence
draw a furrow of bitterness on her flesh. The woman.
And the sword. And the wall. And the ravine. And the silks.
And the mud. At her feet, a jug. Broken
from the trips to the spring. The spring that has gone dry
because of the madness of her moons. To the North. To the South.
The wall. The wall and her imperturbable silence.
The certainty of her silence feeds the ivy. The woman
and her clothes torn to shreds by the trip. Before her eyes, the
wall.
At her back, the sword. At her feet, the ravine.
Impossible to advance. To turn back. Impossible
to scurry away on her side. A glance to the sky.
Blue without understanding. The woman debating with herself.
    The woman
and her sword. The woman and her wall. The woman.
Her ravine and her broken shoes. And her twitching face
choosing the emptiness. A leap. An endpoint. The wall.
The muteness. And nothing.

Translated by Ruth Behar

From María Elena Cruz Varela, *El angel agotado* (Miami: Ediciones Palen-
que, 1991).

RECENT CUBAN ART
A PORTFOLIO

Antonia Eiriz, *Entre Lineas* (Between the Lines), 1993. Oil on canvas.

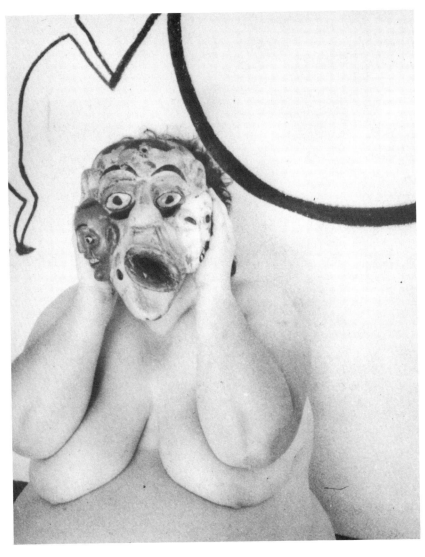

Cecilia Portal, *Tiempo, Pecado y Muerte* (Time, Sin and Death), 1990. Palladium print.

Yovani Bauta, *Ideología* (Ideology), 1990. Mixed techniques on paper.

Consuelo Castañeda, *Perugino-Barbara Kruger*, 1992. Oil on canvas.

Natalia Raphael, *Crucifixion II*, 1993. Clay, sand, pigment on wood. Photo by Warren Patterson.

Ernesto Pujol, *suitcase # 1, cribs*, 1994. Acrylic and dye on vintage vinyl.

Ernesto Pujol, *suitcase # 4*, Cuba, 1994. Acrylic and dye on vintage vinyl.

Osvaldo Mesa, *Dreams of Big Black Kisses* (detail), 1989. Installation.

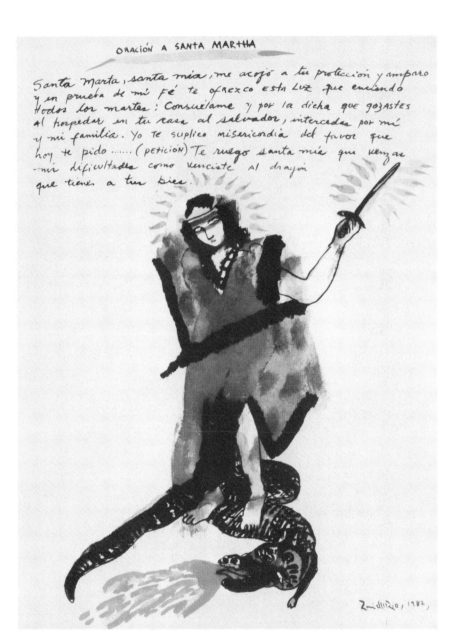

Zaida del Río, *Oración a Santa Martha*, 1987. Mixed techniques on board.

Yolanda Fundora, *Yemaya*, 1992. Oil enamel on masonite.

José Franco, *Eternal Return*, 1992. Ink on paper.

Humberto Castro, *La Primera Palabra* (The First Word), 1991. Oil on canvas.

Quiqueya Henríquez, *Retorno* (Return), 1991. Wood.

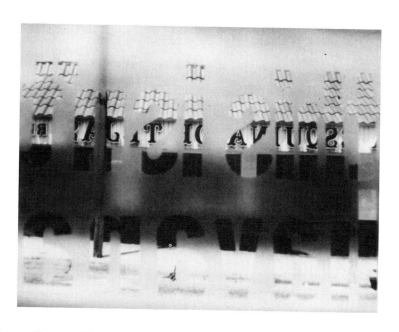

Arturo Cuenca, *This Isn't Havana*, 1991. Hand-colored photograph.

Ricardo Estanislao Zulueta, *Humane Society VI*, 1992. Photo-performance.

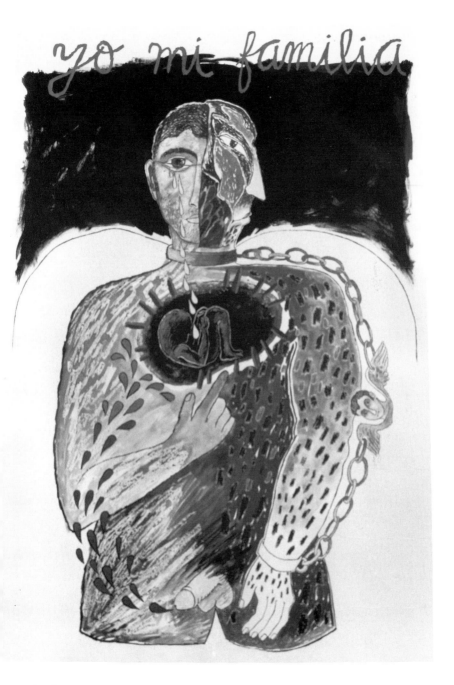

Rolando Estévez, *Yo mi familia* (*Me My Family*), 1994. Ink on paper.

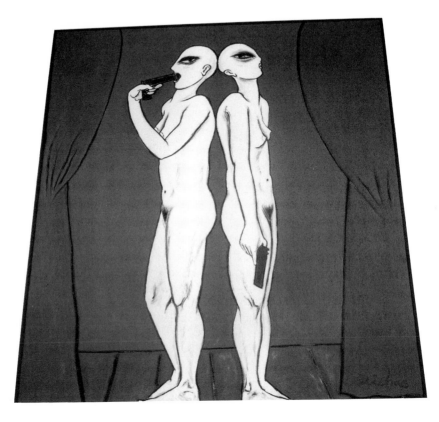

Rocío García, *Geishas,* 1994. Oil on canvas.

PART 3 Remembering / Recuerdos

Dulce María Loynaz
del libro *Poemas sin nombre*
-1953-

XV
Hay en ti la fatiga
de un ala mucho tiempo
tensa.

ROLANDO ESTÉVEZ
EDICIONES VIGÍA, MATANZAS, CUBA.

ABILIO ESTÉVEZ

BETWEEN NIGHTFALL AND VENGEANCE: REMEMBERING REINALDO ARENAS

When I first met Reinaldo Arenas, one afternoon toward the end of 1976, I had not yet read his work. I seem to remember a classmate of mine from the University of Havana taking me to Arenas's room in the Hotel Monserrate. The hotel stood (and stands) on the street of the same name, behind the Havana Institute of Secondary Education (where Martí had studied), near the Capitolio and Central Park, in the boisterous and crazy heart of the city. The hotel was in a deplorable state, yet you could tell it had known more sumptuous days, with its wrought-iron elevator, marble staircases, and the stubborn dignity that *habanero* buildings never seem to lose despite the erosion of time and history.

It made no difference that he was barely thirty-four or that a categorical and official silence surrounded his work; he was already a celebrity. Among us, the young people of the time, he had an aura of irreverence and mystery, a tropical François Villon, famous in Paris and New York, even more sacred because we had no way of reading him: any attempt to obtain one of his books was all but condemned to failure. Literary tradition has proved—examples abound—that prohibition is the first step on the way to fame.

In those 1970s, years of my first dazzlements, the myth of Reinaldo Arenas had already begun. It was said, for example, that he had arrived in Havana with a manuscript full of mistakes and spelling errors which was, apart from all that (or because of all that?), an extraordinary novel, *Celestino antes del alba* (*Celestino before the Dawn*).[1] He had already been in prison and, it was added, he lived a very dissolute, almost marginal life. He was recognized as a literary mystic.

To complete the myth, José Lezama Lima and Virgilio Piñera had paid attention to him. The former, to elevate Arenas with one of his lapidary phrases: "The spirit of genius has no limits, it can even reach a shepherd from Holguín." The latter, setting aside his customary slander, to add in pontifical tones: "There has been no other storyteller in Cuba since Lezama, until Reinaldo Arenas." This he told me one day when he was getting ready to take up one of his famous collections for the writer in disgrace.

The room in the Hotel Monserrate was minimal. A few centimeters less and no one would have been able to live there. Narrow old bed, table, typewriter, a few books. Very few.

Reinaldo was lying down and he begged our pardon, said he had a fever, a throat infection; the night before he had been delirious from fever and had tried to get up to describe his delirium. As a result a new novel was taking shape within the head of the tireless writer.

The first thing that impressed me was his sweet, measured tone of speech, so inappropriate for the diabolical character that they had undertaken to describe to us. He was extremely delicate, exquisite, asking us about our own writing, counseling us, before going on to describe his own work methods, that of course there was no one method that could be taken as a model.

The second thing that impressed me — and still impresses me — was the way he lived *in* and *for* literature, tried to live *from* literature, turning everything into words, even the ravings of his fever. It was not that this was something unknown for me, given that Virgilio Piñera was my teacher at the time, and there was no one like him for living *in terms of literature.* What was truly marvelous in Arenas's case was meeting a literary mystic when one expected to find a pleasure-seeking *vividor*, a hedonist, with all of the good and the dreadful that phrase encloses.

Reinaldo, man-literature, for whom reality served only as a pretext, including those splendid adolescents with whom he enjoyed surrounding himself.

After that visit I began to read him. Piñera himself loaned me a copy of *Celestino antes del alba* from the library of God knows who. Later on, *El mundo alucinante (The Hallucinatory World)*,[2] Abelardo Estorino's copy; on the first page I read a dedication written in an almost illiterate hand: "For Estorino, playwright and martyr, with affection from Reinaldo." A hand which let you know it was familiar with Sartre and Genet.

Piñera, who could not hide his admiration for Arenas, narrated for me the vicissitudes of the UNEAC[3] competition when he tried to award *El mundo alucinante* a prize against Alejo Carpentier's fierce opposition. I pressed him about this arbitrary act from a man who had written no less than *El siglo de las luces*, a novelist whom I admired and whom I believed (I was still in my twenties) to have passed beyond good and evil. Virgilio smiled wisely and quickly replied, "Alejo has an excellent nose for approaching danger."

It goes without saying that after I read these novels I shared my teacher's admiration. You didn't have to be terribly sensitive to be perturbed by this writer of the lineage of Carlos Montenegro and of Piñera himself, irreverent, spoilsport, with the rare gift of turning the most trivial incident into a literary act or trivializing the most important, with a narrative vigor that went beyond errors or corrections. As with Chesterton, all the demons lived in the heart of Reinaldo Arenas. And all the angels, I would add.

Afterwards no prohibition, veiled or explicit, mattered. Just as his absence became an unimportant detail (from the literary point of view, of course). We read him and we continue to admire him. Secretly or not. In Havana or in New York, Arenas, that symbol, that Celestino awaiting the dawn of his hallucinatory world in a palace of white skunks,[4] has stayed with us.

Now he returns in the pages of *Antes que anochezca* (*Before Night Falls*). In all his magnificent horror and wonder. His love-hate, his anguish and despair more obvious than ever. Now he returns from exile (like someone who has finished doing time in hell), inscribing himself — above the ephemeral ups and downs of politics — in the long and illustrious list of writers exiled from this Island-mother who expels us and gathers us in. Here, once more, excessive and brilliant, that we may admire and pity him, which is in the last instance to pity ourselves.

The book has passed from hand to hand. The copies of the carefully produced Tusquets edition of scarcely two years ago are already falling to pieces, covers torn off, pages crumpled from use.

It has been much discussed. There are those who deny that it is an autobiography and adduce that everything it narrates is pure fiction, that it is novelized, that Reinaldo exaggerates where he does not lie, that more than a book of reminiscences we face an act of vengeance, or as José Rodríguez Feo brilliantly expressed it when he loaned me a copy: "Here you go, a masterpiece of slander."

Autobiography? Yes. There can be no doubt. Delirious, exaggerated, lying; but who can deny that he is there, in full-length portrait? If it is not the Reinaldo Arenas who was, at least it is the one

Book cover of the Spanish edition of Reinaldo Arenas, *Antes Que Anochezca*
(Before Night Falls), Barcelona: Tusquets, 1992.

he wished to be. The character he preferred for himself. What memoir, what autobiography corresponds exactly to reality? Where, for
an author, does reality begin and end? Arenas simply did what any
author proposes to do when he wrote his life: he mystified it. Here
the mystification takes on the proportions of delirium, true. He
wanted to be delirious, just as André Gide *wanted* to be sincere. Yet
I suspect that sincerity is one thing, and truth something else. From
this point of view, I do not doubt Arenas's sincerity — even though
his pages at times fall short of the truth.

What does it matter, for instance, that when he narrates the
burial of Virgilio Piñera he speaks of how "a multitude of people and
even boys, mounted on skates and bicycles, followed the corpse"?
There was no such multitude on bikes and skates: I was at the
funeral. But the *character* Piñera could be followed by a multitude
of *characters* on skates and bikes, coming out of his own *Concilio y
discurso*. There was no multitude: there should have been. The fact
took place, in effect, thanks to literature.

In this sense, *Before Night Falls* reveals an author loyal to his
obsession. If in previous books we saw him draw his characters from
himself, here we see him elaborate himself through them, creating
his own character through fiction.

Any man is a mystery. No book reveals the mystery that a man is.
At most, we can only try to discover him in the truth/falsity of
writing. And what we discover from it, in the end, will not be the
man as he is or was, but as we imagine him.

There is no noticeable difference between Celestino, Fray Servando, Arturo, or Reinaldo. They are identical, one and the same
mystery for our inexhaustible delight of discovery — the morbid pleasure of finding a truth which always escapes.

For quite a while, since long before his exile (the first of his
deaths), Reinaldo was no longer a being of flesh and bone but an
entity of fiction, one more among the great dramatic personas of our
literature. He did not oblige his characters to become persons,
rather he carried out the sole legitimate act: to turn his own person
into a character.

The relation, as of connecting vessels, between this tragic adventure with the subtitle "Autobiography" and the preceding books is
evident. Like the others, the book seems to follow an epigraph from
Being and Nothingness: "My original fall is the existence of the
Other." Better yet, "Hell is the Other." The Other as the center of
our lives, the torturer/observer who brings us unfailingly to self-

torture and self-observation. The pitiless Other who makes us piti-less toward ourselves. In this case, the narrative goes from the realm of the family to that of history; from the unknown/runaway father to the mother/tyrant-by-abnegation-and-sweetness (classical scheme, delightful Freudian greys); from the other father who betrays him (the ruler) to the other mother (the Cuban Revolution) which is also a tyrant because it is maternal, thinks it has all the keys and imposes them, assumes the power to determine good and evil.

Before Night Falls could also be titled *The Lost Illusions*. The illusions lost here are not like those of Lucien de Rubempré. They are of a stable family and of a stable world in which to live. Terra firma: the nostalgia for utopia. The Dantesque terms in which Reinaldo tells his life within revolutionary Cuba are prefigured in the first pages, in which he describes the nightmare of his childhood. A bad end couldn't square with a good beginning. His death is foreseen in one of the first and most beautiful sentences in *Before Night Falls*: "The first taste I remember is the taste of earth." Those closest to him say that long before he left Cuba, and before AIDS had been inscribed in the history of our horror, Reinaldo already spoke of suicide as a certainty soon after he passed the threshold of forty years.

There is, then, an initial nonconformity. The nonconformity which makes a writer of the most unlikely man is here carried to the point of delirium: born into the humblest family, with no education, in the Cuban backwoods; raised fatherless; with a frustrated mother who took refuge in being single; an avowed homosexual in a hostile environment; having a subtle sensibility in the closed universe of a severe society; conscious of "being different" in an Island where that is a crime and where all differences were supposed to be abolished.

This horror could give birth to anguish. But would that be enough? The anguish one senses in Arenas's book is greater, reminis-cent of Kierkegaard. Something more profound brings us to an exis-tential problem. For him, as for Camus, suicide is the only truly serious philosophical problem: knowing whether or not life is worth being lived. Unlike the author of *The Myth of Sisyphus*, Arenas gave legitimacy to suicide. We know his answer.

From this feeling of estrangement, this awareness of separation, you could only expect a man disposed toward dissent. Inadmissible that he respect the lineaments of social and political life. Even set-ting aside the indubitable truth that to write is to disagree, that the essence of the writer in any country and age is to say "No," in Arenas that became his only meaning. Perhaps, as some would like to think, this wrenching, against-the-clock struggle damaged the poise of his literature. But that is unimportant. We have the example of his struggle, his despair, his irreverence, his lack of self-control, which he raises to the level of morality. By this I mean the example of his faith.

Reading *Before Night Falls* is, in the long run, an exercise in unmasking, catharsis. As much as he tries to fool us, Reinaldo Arenas reveals himself in the end as a moralist.

This is a morality in the guise of antagonism. Among my papers I have a clipping from a French newspaper—I don't know which, it doesn't have a title or date—in support, apparently, of the French edition of *El mundo alucinante*. After describing the inhuman conditions under which he was writing, Arenas writes a revelatory phrase: "The world and I are at war." Here's the key, not only to *Before Night Falls* but to his entire literary production. Yes, it's true, even in the most inoffensive writer there is a certain animosity against the world; enmity is one of the fundamental motives for anyone to sit down and try to mend the world, as Goethe would say. It is no less true, though, that for Arenas animosity took on a monstrous tinge. It was the only meaning of his literature, consciously and with *ostinato rigore*.

Very early on he took note of the battle; he enlisted, of course, on the side of those who fought alone. And he brooked no truce. His life—which we can unfortunately now look at in its entirety— exhibits a perennial calling for struggles for the word: defamation and vengeance as method. Defamation and vengeance which serve us, the readers, as cures. I don't know if he suspected his capacity for saving us. If he had, I suppose he would have changed his method right away.

Hatred, rancor, corrosive humor would mask his fragility. Apart from enmity, we see a vulnerable man who doesn't know what to do with love. Somewhere in *A la recherche du temps perdu* Proust says that he who loves most is he who is most alone, and the one who worries most about his fellow men is the one who runs away in fear of hearing a word of disdain where he hoped for a caress.

Take as an example one of the great themes of this book. The obsessive erotic charge reflects the terrifying solitude that traverses it. The sense of separation takes on a pathetic tone. Love can never be fulfilled. The Other can only be encountered at the level of the senses. Maybe we should listen to Oscar Wilde, who declared that lust is the mother of melancholy. In *Before Night Falls* lust is the daughter of despair. And testimony to isolation, exile, the hopelessness of searching. There is no truce for generosity, for fulfilling what Ortega y Gasset proposed when he wrote that "Love, more than an instinct, is a creation." Here, everything is desire, simple desire, without support; that is, abandon, preaching in the desert. The one we are looking for never shows up to compliment us. We are alone, condemned to the borderland of the skin, to failure. Lack of love is supplanted then by destructive erotic adventures.

At this point I would like to stop for a moment to refute an observation by the Cuban novelist Manuel Pereyra. Referring to *Before Night Falls*, Pereyra asks, in an article published in the Spanish journal *Quimera*, how it is possible to speak of the repression of homosexuals in a country where the author confesses to having had sexual relations with more than five thousand men. I do not know if this is an ingenuous question, if Pereyra is ignorant of the *characteristics of insular eroticism*. Disregarding the fact that the number cited is surely exaggerated, there is no contradiction between repression and promiscuity. Quite the contrary: we know of the "good family man" who runs furtively to some bucolic hideaway; of the "respectable gentleman" who abandons his wife for a while in search of an anonymous hand and mouth; of the "disciplined military officer" who satiates himself at night with the one he will ridicule the next day.

Reinaldo Arenas took on the role of enemy long before he knew where or even who the enemies really were. He equipped himself for combat and he combated to the end with all the arms he had: imagination and a marvelous capacity for storytelling. He thought he saw the enemy in every shadow, even in the harmless and eternal windmills.

We cannot overlook the fact that this was not a simple matter of choice. His life was made difficult. He had to live through the worst type of political intolerance in the Cuban 1970s and to suffer the hardships of exile, which no one deserves. He was harassed, persecuted, and watched. Like so many others, he was expelled from the country that was his by right. The result: suicide, the ultimate heresy. And a body of work which we cannot disregard if we wish to understand this terrible Island at all.

Like it or not, we Cubans have *Before Night Falls*. What does this book mean for "the Cubans of the Island"? The same as for "the Cubans outside," I imagine: a shout in the middle of the night, when we were hoping to enjoy our placid Edenic dreams. A shout that removes us from the torpor of "there" and "here." Hangman halting at the foot of the bed to execute himself executing us. Showing his own horror and the horror of a world that surrounds him in such a way that we cannot remain indifferent, eyes closed, inhaling aromas which do not exist.

We won't worry about grammatical mistakes or simplicities. Reading a book written against death (the ultimate antagonist), it would be stupid or wicked to waste time on such trivia. Apart from mistakes it has an extraordinary "power of reflection," as Proust would have it.

True or false, exaggerated or not, we have here the autobiography of a man in despair, the testimony of a martyr we can no longer overlook. The book of a great storyteller, one of those who do not allow a moment of truce.

Reinaldo Arenas damns us and we come to love him, as we love the demon who saves us by showing us the frightful sight of our own lives.

Havana, 17 March 1994

NOTES

[1]Published in English as *Singing from the Well*, translated by Andrew Hurley (New York: Viking, 1987).

[2]Published in English as *Hallucinations; Being an Account of the Life and Adventures of Friar Servando Teresa de Mier*, translated by Gordon Brotherston (New York: Harper & Row, 1971).

[3]Unión de Escritores y Artistas de Cuba, the Cuban writers' and artists' union.

[4]Referring to Arenas's *El palacio de las blanquísimas mofetas*, published in English as *The Palace of the White Skunks*, translated by Andrew Hurley (New York: Viking, 1990).

Translated by David Frye

JOSÉ KOZER

LUNCH

I'm from the back country. I can't say I'm from the back country,
  this is a poem.
Fact: a few years now I've lived in the big city. Can't say it like
  that. This is (still) a poem.
Should I start? Background music, Zauberflöte (not bad) (well, not
  that I know, what do I know about music): music, in the
  background. Do I hear?
Vineyards, chirimoya fields, must be Aguadulce or Arroyo
  Naranjo: it can't be that what I see way over there from this
  lofty spot (a thousand meters off) (and over there, the sea; a
  Mediterranean sea; what light; and in the middle of winter:
  not even in Cuba) here: not here; a poem.
We shall be. With Papageno, Pamina. Alright, alright, let's not get
  carried away; I eat. I drink and piss. Health? So-so. And I'm
  sharper than a tack, I'm not in debt, the place, a bit cramped.
What do you mean they're calling? Put in here, they're gone. Left.
  Put it here, I'll cough it up; after all, I owe you naught
  (learned reference), this life I lead is the life I lead,
  tautolowhatsit? Toma chocolate, paga lo que debes.
Learned it from my father. Social class: peasantry. Turns out they
  changed everything, we got worried, we left: I was born in
  the midst of the loftiest middle bourgeoisie in the city
  (Papageno?) of Havana: and with the way the world turns
  and all of its bickering and squabbles,
there was white (Christians) rice, beans (Moors), a salad (what they
  give you, when they give it), two glasses of beer, and I'll add
(even if it's a poem) a bit of chocolate to allay the need for dessert,
  an infusion.

Translated by David Frye

314

The cover of *La Revista del Vigía*, a journal produced in Cuba by artisans dedicated to the craft of book and journal publishing by independent means: "an act of faith in the utter necessity of the cultural arts, without which life itself would become impoverished."

MARÍA EUGENIA ALEGRÍA, ROLANDO ESTÉVEZ,
AND ALFREDO ZALDÍVAR

VIGÍA: THE ENDLESS PUBLICATIONS
OF MATANZAS

With few resources, almost no official sponsorship, without funds, and almost without paper, a new editorial house has surfaced in the city of Matanzas. On the banks of the San Juan River, across from the old Plaza de Armas, on the second floor of an old colonial house in the city's Vigía plaza, is this wonder of Cuban publishing. The center of activity is a vast tiled room; the only things serving as decor are a couple of tables, two enormous antique barometers hanging from the walls, clippings of paper once discarded after being used for commercial or industrial purposes, scissors, glue, a primitive mimeograph machine, a pile of photocopies, strips of cloth, textiles, drawings, and, above all, the tireless hands of the poet-printers who cut, paste, sew, draw, and write.

From here, beginning in 1985, some peculiar volumes that define the "activities" of *La Casa del Escritor* (the House of the Writer), an institution tied to the Ministry of Culture,[1] are printed with the aim of encouraging literary expression. In Matanzas, the director of *La Casa del Escritor* is Alfredo Zaldívar, a young poet with a fighting spirit who for years worked his way through the leaden cultural bureaucracy of the city. Only half of the job falls on Zaldívar's shoulders because his obvious talent in the field of cultural production and as an organizer of restless young artists has joined forces with the creative genius of poet and painter Rolando Estévez, who became the graphic designer of the early volumes and later of the journal. Estévez had been a designer for the stage, and it is to him that Vigía owes its image, its reputation as a work of art, and the quality of the issues — especially of the journal *La Revista del Vigía*.

ZALDÍVAR: In 1985 *Ediciones Vigía* emerged out of the need of a group of artists of the city to see their work, which they valued as

316

literature, in print. We did not have a preconceived idea about what the volumes would look like. Our resources were scarce: a mimeograph machine that someone from a press was able to lend us, and a typewriter — also borrowed — because we owned neither. These are the only two machines we have used in the history of Vigía. More than anything, we use our hands and our imagination.

ESTÉVEZ: Vigía's beginnings were very rudimentary, but this was so as an aesthetic choice made on principle, because we were fascinated by the possibilities of working with stencil, and little by little we learned its secrets. To the stencil we later added watercolors, then to writing by hand on each issue we added gluing things, tearing things, allowing texts to remain as manuscripts.

In the mid 1980s, when Vigía was beginning, Cuban publishing had already passed its golden era of the 1970s — specifically the books of *Casa*, some of *Unión*, the first books of *Letras cubanas*. By the 1980s editorial possibilities decreased, and books became uglier, much less interesting. We wanted to encourage the professional development of young artists and writers from the provinces, who faced enormous difficulties trying to get published by national presses. The city already had *Ediciones Matanzas*, but it was conceptually limited and aesthetically flat in its printing and design. For these reasons Vigía emerged at a time when Cuba was publishing a fair number of books but nonetheless was in need of beautiful books, books that themselves would be works of art.

ALEGRÍA: *Ediciones Vigía* emerges at a time (1985–86) of ample editorial opportunity in the country. Does this not mean, then, that the choices made for it were not only for aesthetic reasons but also because it sought independence by keeping costs low and achieving self-management? This independence meant that after the main publishing houses closed during the *período especial*, *La Revista del Vigía* not only remained as the only literary journal edited in Cuba with its own funds, but also has kept printing new issues.

ESTÉVEZ: You say that Vigía emerges at a time of ample editorial possibilities, which I think is debatable, because they were indeed ample — but for whom? The selection criteria of large editorial houses has been very faulty, with books lacking wide appeal receiving large first printings, while other titles that were of interest to certain sectors were not published. Promoting the work of young artists in this atmosphere is very difficult. What we must stress and repeat is that Vigía's editorial aesthetic was not chosen in 1985 out of material need or because there existed no other possibilities. I insist that Vigía emerges out of aesthetic necessities.

Why self-management? Well, because it was very difficult to ask MINCULT for little pieces of cloth. It was easier to go to a workshop and find pieces of textile or to go to the newspaper *Girón* and ask for two reels of paper — although these days it is, of course, more difficult. Our intention was, from the beginning, to produce books that were works of art, and as a result Vigía now publishes the only interesting Cuban literary journal printed in the country. Because *Unión* is published in Mexico and *La Gaceta* has a limited circulation consisting solely of members of the UNEAC and is published with foreign resources. And I do not include *Casa de las Américas* because it is an international journal.[2] Vigía survives because independence has always been a priority. We always knew we wanted to do something that depended solely on us. We saw in self-management the spirit of artisanry, the spirit of art itself, in addition to the fact that it allowed for complete autonomy.

ZALDÍVAR: While there were more books and materials than there are now and large printings, there was also an enormous number of books not being published because they were backed up in the publishing bureaucracy. Printing was at a peak, in the sense that publishers were putting out 25,000 copies of books for the educational system, but editorial criteria were extremely narrow. Because we had taken on modest printing goals with low-cost materials, we were able to survive the crisis and continue putting out volumes. With printings of only 200 copies we have never lacked paper, for we make do with what we have. We have been affected by material conditions, but not as much as *Ediciones Matanzas*, which has not published a single book this year. We have already finished nineteen and hope by the end of the year to have met our editorial goals, including putting out the three journals.

ALEGRÍA: *Ediciones Vigía* is subordinate to the MINCULT because it was established at *La Casa del Escritor,* which is an official cultural institution. When culture in Cuba was institutionalized with the creation of the MINCULT in 1976, a pyramidal structure was created whereby all artistic production in one way or another became tied to an official institution which takes care of its material, financial, and organizational problems.

ZALDÍVAR: When I started working as the director of *La Casa del Escritor* I was also municipal president of the *Asociación Hermanos Sainz,* which was subordinate to the *Unión de Jóvenes Comunistas*

(Union of Young Communists) but nonetheless enjoyed a degree of autonomy. But there is no official imprimatur. We are an official institution that wants to do unprecedented things, and so we have to seek out the means ourselves. We are also a very poor institution that depends on another very poor entity, the *Dirección Municipal de Cultura* (Municipal Administration of Culture). The fact that we have salaries and an office does not mean that all our material needs are supplied. After five years we have a mimeograph machine thanks to the good will of some members of the *Dirección*, who at times supply us with paper, ink, and stencils. Estévez is someone who works here because he believes in Vigía, but he hasn't received a cent in eight years. Nor have any of the designers, painters, or writers. We receive our materials through personal effort and with the help of collaborators. We are an official institution, like all institutions in Cuba, but we remain self-run because we believe in this work and want to do it. In addition, from an editorial perspective, nobody interferes with us. We decide what we want to publish.

ALEGRÍA: Do you think this self-management guarantees editorial independence?

ZALDÍVAR: No, because you can be as self-sufficient as you want, but if you write something against the revolution or socialism you can't publish it.

ALEGRÍA: But you are allowed to publish work by Octavio Paz and Gastón Baquero, who are considered enemies or detractors.

ZALDÍVAR: I don't know if I am allowed to or not, because no one has ever said anything to me either way. Our editorial decisions are based on artistic, literary criteria. We consider that although Gastón Baquero and Severo Sarduy decided to live in Madrid and Paris, they are very Cuban, and the Cubanness of their writing is more distinctive than a lot of the work written here. We believe they are assets to Cuban literature, and that is how we defend them. You also have to keep in mind that our circulation is not massive, that about 200 copies are printed and they go to libraries, institutions, and persons interested in literature. They are exclusive editions; to own a Vigía volume is somewhat of a privilege. I don't think the government is unaware of what we do, but we publish work not generally circulated in Cuba for a sector that is already familiar with it.

ALEGRÍA: Zaldívar was saying that you have always been editorially independent, that you've never had government officials interfere or suggest anything.

ESTÉVEZ: Total independence. Vigía has always published what it wanted; the people directing it and its achievements have always been respected.

ALEGRÍA: Do you not relate this, on the one hand, to the general openness of the visual arts in the early 1980s that sought to break the monotonous rhetoric that pervaded all representations of national life, and, on the other hand, to the editorial openness of the last five or six years, when things never before published have begun to circulate? A kind of cultural and ideological openness — slow, subtle, and even a bit disguised?

ESTÉVEZ: Disguised is the key word here. That it has happened is unquestionable. There have been times when Vigía's art has been considered bold, due to the questions it has raised. We also publish texts that problematize our situation, that do not praise the revolution. The dynamic and thoughtful art of the 1980s came from an openness in which Vigía participated.

ALEGRÍA: Now that we have talked about Vigía, let us move on to *La Revista del Vigía*, the true wonder of the publishing house. Following a rich tradition of Iberoamerican literary journals, frequently associated with groups of writers and poets who many times come to be considered a "generation," the journal has special significance. Its graphic presentation stems from an aesthetic that defines the text itself as a work of art. From its beginning text and image have been inextricably linked. It became a refreshing and creative way of making available literary novelties that were being produced with great difficulty. *La Revista del Vigía* has documented practically all of the country's recent literary history by publishing the work of young poets from all over Cuba, in plaquettes, anthologies, and individual volumes. With the success of the journal, editorial criteria have become more rigorous, and a delicate balance needs to be maintained between presentations of the best Matanzas poetry and that of Cuban work in general, as well as internationally recognized literature.

ESTÉVEZ: *La Revista del Vigía* also comes out of a need for a new forum, because there was a need for a cultural space where things that the Cuban press was not valuing could be valued. For example, José Gorostiza's work has not been published in Cuba, and so there is a need to give José Gorostiza a space in Cuban literature. This is also the case with Martínez Rivas. The journal has a section titled *El pergamino* (The Parchment), which in every issue is dedicated to a single author. There the author's work is critically introduced and a sample of it is published.

ALEGRÍA: Let's return to Vigía's design and aesthetic, especially that of the journal.

ESTÉVEZ: don't think Vigía would have been the same without its image. I remember that we asked Perla María Pinedo to illustrate the first edition of the journal, and those illustrations were precisely what we needed. Zaldívar has always been very good at knowing which painter is best for each edition. For the issue in honor of Mme. Blavastki we asked Yovani Bauta to do the illustrations. His paintings at the time were very mystical, with hard, broken lines, which fit her perfectly. Only an editorial house with complete independence can do this in Cuba.[3] Going to a butcher shop to find paper—that is as independent as going out to find Yovani to illustrate Blavastki.

ALEGRÍA: The artistry of these volumes is so linked with the final meaning of the text that a curious fetishism has been created with splendid issues like *Pronóstico del Gris*, on the Matanzas poet Carilda Oliver Labra. There you used pieces of cloth and sequins taken from one of the poet's evening gowns, with the end result being a small, beautiful volume worthy of one of twentieth-century Cuba's great women writers of mythopoetic, sexual poetry.

ESTÉVEZ: This is the sense in which Vigía's aesthetic is postmodernist, because it expresses a kind of thinking that gives special emphasis to concepts, and turns form into content. That same aesthetic gives an extremely individualistic character to each book and gives the written material an image that corresponds with its content. Even the materials used make the journal a postmodernist phenomenon. It is one of a kind in Cuba.

ZALDÍVAR: At Vigía we are determined not to renounce the traditional ways of printing, like the mimeograph machine. This is our aesthetic and we want to defend it and continue issuing printings of 200 or less. In the near future sales will probably raise Vigía's income, which will improve the quality of the printing, the paper, and the ink. Perhaps more elaborate methods will be used, salaries will go up, and working conditions will improve. But basically the same Vigía will be maintained. I think we are prepared to continue, despite the fact that most major Cuban publications have ceased production.

NOTES

[1]Hereafter abbreviated as MINCULT.

[2]*La Gaceta de Cuba*, a publication of the Union of Writers and Artists of Cuba (UNEAC — Unión de Escritores y Artistas de Cuba), Casa de las Américas, literary journal published by the research center of the same name.

[3]He is referring to the rigid structure of publishing in Cuba, which is run by a group of employees. Each person is charged with a specific, specialized task — design, photography, etc., thus preventing the hiring of independent contractors who might be more qualified for a given project.

Translated by Javier Morillo-Alicea

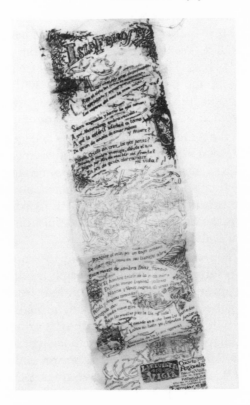

Scroll of "Isla Famosa," poem by José Martí, with drawing by Sigfredo Ariel, for Vigía magazine.

GUSTAVO PÉREZ FIRMAT

THREE MAMBOS AND A *SON MONTUNO*

Mambo #1

"Lost in translation": take it literally, turn phrase to fact, transform the commonplace into a place. Then try to imagine where you end up if you get lost in translation.

When I try to visualize such a place, I see myself, on a given Saturday afternoon, in the summer, somewhere in Miami. Since I'm thirsty, I go into a store called Love Juices, which specializes in nothing more salacious or salubrious than mild shakes made from tropical fruits. Having quenched my thirst, I head for a boutique called Mr. Trapus, whose name — *trapo* — is actually the Spanish word for an old rag. Undaunted by the consumerist frenzy that has possessed me, I enter another store called Cachi Bachi — a name that, in spite of its chichi sound, is a slang word for junk, *cachivache*. And then for dinner I go to the Versailles of Eighth Street, a restaurant where I feast on something called Tropical Soup, the American name for the traditional Cuban stew, *ajiaco*. My choice for dessert is Tropical Snow, which is Miamian for *arroz con leche*; and to finish off the meal, of course, I sip some Cuban-American Espresso (don't go home without it). In this way I spend my entire afternoon lost in translation — and loving every minute.

Translation is a place, an uncommonly common place, my place (or yours). I was lost and now I'm found — in translation.

Mambo #2

Some years ago a Cuban radio station in Miami aired an advertisement promoting an airline's reduced fares: "Piedmont Airlines quiere limpiar el aire sobre sus bajas tarifas." "Limpiar el aire"? "Clean the air"? This sentence is ungrammatical in two languages. First mistake:

323

perhaps influenced by the Spanish "poner en limpio," "to clean up," the author of the ad must have thought that the English idiom was "clean the air" rather than "clear the air." Second mistake: he then decided that "clean the air" could be translated word for word into Spanish. Third mistake: he rendered "about" as "sobre," which in context sounds too much like "over" or "above." Hence: "Piedmont Airlines wants to clean the air above its low fares." But this sentence does have a certain flighty logic, especially considering that it went out over the airwaves. Piedmont's clean-air act is an interlingual utterance that remains up in the air, that cannot make up its mind whether to land in that domain of Spanish or English.

Another comedy of grammatical errors will bring us back to earth: there is a Cuban-owned pizza chain in Miami called Casino's Pizza. When Casino's was launched (or lunched) a few years ago, its publicity campaign included a bilingual brochure. I quote the first sentence of the Spanish text: "Su primera mirada, su primer olor, su primer gusto le dirá que usted descubrió La Pizza Ultima." Since "La Pizza Ultima" ["the last pizza"] doesn't make much sense in Spanish (it should have been "la última pizza" anyway), upon first reading this anglicized sentence I had the impression that the final phrase was an incompletely digested translation of "the ultimate pizza." In order to check out my hunch (if not my lunch), I went to the English text: "Your first sight, your first smell, your first taste will tell you that you've discovered La Pizza Ultima."

So what happened to my hypothetical Ultimate Pizza? It seems to have been eaten in translation. The same phrase that sounds like an anglicism in Spanish is offered as a hispanism in English! Food for thought: the English phrase presupposes a Spanish phrase that presupposes an English phrase that doesn't exist.

What Casino's is selling is paradox-lovers pizza, the one that gets consumed in the cracks between languages. Like the Piedmont ad, "La Pizza Ultima" refuses to be English but cannot be Spanish. If Beny Moré was the "bárbaro del ritmo," the authors of the ad must be *bárbaro* of barbarism, bards with a barb.

Sometimes the American dream is written in Spanglish.

Mambo #3

One of the landmarks of Cuban Miami is a restaurant called Versailles, which has been located on Eighth Street and 35th Avenue for many years. About the only thing this Versailles shares with its French namesake is that it has lots of mirrors on its walls. One goes to the Versailles not only to be seen, but to be multiplied. This quaint, kitschy, noisy restaurant that serves basic Cuban food is a paradise for the self-absorbed: the Nirvana of Little Havana. Because of the bright lights, even the windows reflect. The Versailles is a Cuban panoptikon: you can lunch, but you can't hide. Who goes there wants to be the stuff of visions. Who goes there wants to make a spectacle of himself (or herself). All the *ajiaco* you can eat plus all the jewelry you can wear multiplied by the number of reflecting planes — and to top it off a waitress who calls you *mi vida*.

Across the street at La Carreta, another popular restaurant, the food is the same (both establishments are owned by the same man) but the feel is different. Instead of mirrors La Carreta has booths. There you can ensconce yourself in a booth and not be faced with multiple images of yourself. But at the Versailles there is no choice but to bask in self-reflective glory.

For years I have harbored the fantasy that those mirrors retain the blurred image of everyone who has paraded before them. I think the mirrors have a memory, as when one turns off the TV and the shadowy figures remain on the screen. Every Cuban who has lived or set foot in Miami over the last three decades has, at one time or another, seen himself or herself reflected in those shiny surfaces. It's no coincidence that the Versailles sits only two blocks away from the Woodlawn Cemetery, which contains the remains of many Cuban notables, including Desi Arnaz's father, whose remains occupy a niche right above Gerardo Machado's. Has anybody ever counted the number of Cubans who have *died* in Miami? Miami is a Cuban city not only because of the number of Cubans who live there but also because of the number who have died there.

The Versailles is a glistening mausoleum. The history of Little Havana — tragic, comic, tragi-comic — is written on those spectacular specular walls. This may have been why, when the mirrors came down in 1991, there was such an uproar that some of them had to be put back. The hall of mirrors is also a house of spirits. When the time comes for me to consume my last tropical soup, I intend to disappear into one of the mirrors (I would prefer the one on the right, just above the espresso machine). My idea of immortality is to become a mirror image at the Versailles.

Son Montuno

Back in the mid-eighties there was a popular Latin discotheque in Miami called the Banana Boat. "El plantanito de Kendall," as it was sometimes called, featured live music by many of the exponents of the so-called Miami Sound. One night I was there to hear Willie Chirino, a popular Cuban-American singer who is something like the Billy Joel of the YUCAS. In addition to going through his repertoire of hits, Chirino played a traditional *son montuno* by Miguel Matamoros called "El son de la loma." Now this song is really an inquiry into the essence of *cubanía*, an inquiry that takes the form of a question about the birthplace of the members of the Matamoros trio. In the opening lines a young girl asks her mother where the singers, *los cantantes*, come from, "Mamá yo quiero saber, de dónde son los cantantes." The punning answer is that the singers hail from the hills but sing on the plain, "son de la loma y canta en llano." "Llano" means both "plain" and a way of singing, and "son" means both "they are" and the name of the music in which the reply is framed.

One of the people in the audience that night was José Fajardo, a gifted flutist who in the fifties led Fajardo y Sus Estrellas, a Cuban *charanga* second only to the Orquesta Aragón in quality and acclaim. When Chirino began to play, Fajardo went up on the stage, took out his wooden flute, and—*sin estrellas pero brillante*—joined in the *son*. What then followed was a *montuno* memorable for the extended counterpoint between Chirino's American keyboard and Fajardo's Cuban flute. Given that this musical mix was taking place only a few blocks from a strip mall called Loehman's Plaza, in my mind the "Son de la loma" became the "Song of Loehman's," and as such a moving, melodious emblem of the acts of translation that make up Cuban-American culture. Acts of translation: *loma* and Loehmann's *son* and song; Havana beats and Banana Boats. It was remarkable enough to hear the "Son de la loma" in a Banana Boat; but to hear it played in tandem by Chirino and Fajardo seemed little short of marvelous.

That night I realized where the *son* went when it left Cuba: to Kendall.

VIRGIL SUAREZ

FROM *GOING UNDER:*
A CUBAN-AMERICAN FABLE

XAVIER CUEVAS found himself stuck in bumper-to-bumper expressway traffic. The lunch time rush hour in Miami. Exasperated, he changed lanes, taking chances in his 240GL Volvo. An accident, he suspected, cutting to the right-hand lane where the dense traffic moved at a faster pace. *Coagulate*, the word came to his mind. *Undo this coagulation!*

Xavier, the young-urban Cuban-American. The YUCA, the equivalent of yuppie. Business at hand at all times. In haste, no time to waste. Twenty-four hours a day not being enough time. Seven days a week. No time to rest, for in this magic city of Miami, The Sun Capital, there were many deals to be made, and whoever struck first struck big by making the money.

Into the center lane. Behind an eighteen-wheel Mobil Oil rig. Nobody budged to let him in. Nobody gave him a chance. Couldn't they see he was in a hurry? Stuck indeed. Caught. Missing in action in Miami. Driving had become too hectic. A time-consuming chore. Traffic, he thought, so much of it on the streets these days . . . going nowhere.

Traffic was being funneled to the only lane open on the right. Why must traffic always slow down to a halt on both sides of the expressway for an accident?

Nosy people. Either that or bored.

Time, Xavier had come to understand the hard way, equaled money. It was that simple formula this country was founded upon. He remembered his high school history teacher telling the class: "The business of America is making money!"

"*Of All The Things I've Lost,*" read one bumper sticker on the car in front of him, "*I Miss My Mind The Most.*" So many cars. Where was everybody going?

327

HE IS HERE! read another bumper sticker.

The accident up ahead looked serious. A yellow Ryder van had turned on its side and burst into flames. Black smoke mushroomed over the long line of traffic. When your number came up, it was time to go. Thinking of death and dying made Xavier shudder, so to forget about it he reached for his cellular phone and dialed his office number.

It rang three times. The answering machine came on: "You have reached the insurance office of Xavier Cuevas." Darleen, his secretary, sounded scratchy on the tape. She had stepped out for lunch. The machine beeped, but he didn't leave a message. He pressed a code number to check for messages. While the machine rewound, he noted the time. He'd been stuck in traffic now for thirty-five minutes. So many things I need to do, he thought.

Lately his memory failed. His concentration waned. He constantly wrote little memos to himself to remember things. Sometimes he didn't remember them until Sarah, his wife, showed the crumpled pieces of paper to him before putting his clothes in the washing machine. Was this important? was what she always asked. By then it was too late, the need to remember specific things had passed. Sarah had gotten him one of those writing tablets that stick to the windshield and rest on the dashboard.

The machine whirred and clicked. Beeped.

A woman's husky voice came on. She needed quotes on the cheapest auto insurance. "If it's too expensive," she said, "I'll pay only P.I.P."

Xavier wrote *NO MONEY IN IT* on the tablet, then crossed it out.

The next message was a long silence. Xavier waited for a voice to speak, but no one did. Then the line clicked. Somebody'd been doing that a lot lately, calling his number and not leaving messages. Dead silence.

Next on was a client who was unhappy with his group health insurance premiums. The voice sounded familiar, and Xavier tried to figure out who he might be. The man said, "I am tired of leaving messages. Get back to me please, or I'm afraid I'll have to take my business someplace else!"

FAMILIAR VOICE.

Another beep.

Then Eloisa, a client from way back when he had started to sell insurance, said, "Xavier—" she always pronounced his name with a

"J" for Javier—"Izquierdo is not well. Not at all." There was a pause during which the faint sound of Eloisa's sobbing became audible. She continued, *"De malo a peor!* He wants to see you as soon as you can—" Then she hung up.

Izquierdo was dying of throat cancer from his sixty years of smoking cigars. Xavier made a note to make time to go by. Izquierdo and Eloisa lived in a condo in Kendall, which was in the opposite direction.

The last message was from Xavier's mother.

"Cariño," his mother said, "I need to talk to you. Come by if you can."

The machine clicked and whirred and beeped five times, signaling the end of all the messages.

As he returned the phone to its cradle between the front seats, Xavier noticed the driver in a beat-up Ford Pinto making strange gestures at him with his hands. What Xavier had done wrong, he didn't know. The man looked terribly upset; he flipped Xavier the middle finger.

"Same to you buddy," Xavier said.

Once the opportunity opened, the Pinto cut in front of Xavier. The Pinto had New York plates.

Suddenly, the man in the Pinto stepped on the brakes and stopped. Xavier wasn't paying attention and when he realized he was going to crash he slammed his foot on the brake. Then, almost voluntarily, the steering wheel moved under his hands and turned. His car swerved to the right missing the fender of the Pinto. Close call, Xavier thought and took a deep breath. His heart beat in his throat. There was a throbbing at his temple.

Up ahead the lights of the police cars, ambulance, rescue units and fire truck flashed. Firefighters doused the flames with a foam spray. Traffic gridlocked.

Finally, when his turn to pass the accident arrived, he turned to look at the foam frothing from the truck's charred and mangled chassis, and stepped on the gas. In the rear view mirror he noticed that the flames had been extinguished. It didn't look like the driver of the truck had made it. Hell, driving in this much traffic was too dangerous, but he, Xavier, like everyone else, had to do it.

Welcome to the hustle and bustle of Miami's daily life.

Northbound on the 826 expressway, getting ready to engage in some heavy-duty cross-lane cutting, Xavier wondered about his mother's call. She sounded worried on the machine. On his way to see a prospective client, he decided to make a pit stop in Hialeah to find out what his mother wanted to talk to him about.

It was twelve minutes past one on a Monday afternoon. Blues Monday. Back-To-The-Grind Monday. He hadn't eaten lunch. His stomach felt hollow. It growled. He'd been on the move since morning, taking care of business. Dropped off an insurance health application, answered calls, checked over the mail merge list Darleen had been compiling on the word processor. Pumped gas.

Calls and errands, no time for much else—such was his life.

Most of his clients were Latinos and often, too often in fact, he couldn't help but feel like an inadequate go-between: an ill-equipped translator between two cultures, one which he worked hard to serve and understand and the other the source of his livelihood, which he needed to protect and respect.

As soon as he exited the expressway, traffic once again stopped. This time it was for a funeral caravan. A long string of cars with their headlights on were escorted by policemen on motorcycles. Traffic was stopped at a green light to let all the funeral cars pass. Xavier thought: they only let you run red lights when you're dead. What good was it then?

The funeral procession passed and traffic moved again. The phone rang and he picked it up.

"Hey, X," Wilfredo, his office partner, said.

"Where are you?"

"Esplain later," Wilfredo said. It bothered Xavier that his partner spoke with such a thick accent when he was capable of speaking without one. They had grown up together, gone to the same schools, learned the same language from the same teachers. Whenever Xavier mentioned the accent, Wilfredo called him an *arrepentido*, embarrassed to be Cuban. Wilfredo believed he was as much Cuban as he was American, fitting right in the middle where the hyphen separated the two worlds.

"I've been running around like a chicken with its head chopped off," Xavier said.

Xavier stopped at a red light. **WELCOME TO HIALEAH, The City of the Future**, the sign on the median read. Cube city, U.S.A. *Bienvenidos a Hialeah, la ciudad que progresa y tropiesa*, the city that progressed and stumbled. This was the city where he had grown up when his family moved here from Cuba in 1960, when he was a year old.

"Monday is not my day," Wilfredo was saying.

"What day of the week is, pal?"

The light turned green and Xavier made a right turn on to 49th Avenue where the fruit, peanut, and flower vendors were out in full force, wearing tattered straw hats, weaving among the stopped cars.

"Where are you?" Wilfredo asked.

"On my way to see my mother."

"Say hi to her." Then, "You want me to meet you at the office?"

"I don't have the slightest clue when I'll be back." There was a client in Miami Lakes he had to see at two-thirty. That gave him enough time to wait out the lunch traffic at his mother's.

A Trans Am with tinted windows cut in front of the Volvo. It was the kind of fast car Wilfredo called a Cuban Ferrari. Wilfredo drove a Camaro, which he called a Cuban Porsche.

"Can't believe this. Fucking traffic!" he said to Wilfredo. "Driving in Hialeah's like entering the Indianapolis 500 on horseback."

Wilfredo laughed.

A short, skinny man approached the Volvo and tapped on the window.

"Hold on," Xavier said.

The instant Xavier rolled down the window, the man slipped in a piece of paper which fell on Xavier's lap. The man walked away quickly. Xavier read the three by five index card aloud: "Phone call, while you were out. Re: personal. Hi lover; I hear you're an adventurous guy who really likes a good time. Call me. I have a personal message just for you . . . My number is: 976–3231. Signed, The Foxx."

"Save that number," Wilfredo said.

"Two dollars for the first minute, fifty cents for each additional minute. Can you believe it, some jerk is making money with this crap?"

"Sex sells," Wilfredo said. "It's in the Constitution."

Xavier tsk-tsked.

"Hey, X," said Wilfredo, his voice full of excitement. Then he switched to Spanish: "*Si vieras la gringa que ligue anoche?*" Xavier should see the woman Wilfredo picked up last night. "Hot, hot, hot. She's a marine biologist."

Wilfredo was so predictable, or was it because Xavier had known his partner for so long? "A couple of days ago it was an aerobics instructor."

"She told me this incredible story about how octopi mate."

"How *what* mates?"

"Octopus," he said. "You know, the sea creature with all the *tenta-culos.*"

"Tentacles, that's the word."

"Listen. The female octopus has her vagina in her nose. If she's not in the mood, you know, and the male tries anything funny, she bites it off."

"Painful stuff."

"Thing is he's got eight penises. Eight tries, then he's out."

"I'd be more careful," he said to Wilfredo, making a note: *All the cars and they all need to be insured.*

"I think I'm in love."

"Same thing you said last week."

"This time it's the real thing."

Xavier fought a strong urge to preach to him about the all too real risks of sleeping around. AIDS lurked behind every smiling face at bars and clubs—places Wilfredo frequented—and he was playing Russian roulette with five bullets in the barrel.

"Hey, bro, I better let you go," Wilfredo suggested.

Good idea, Xavier thought, then said, "Got to mom's."

"See you later, alley gator," Wilfredo told him. "I'm going to have my hands full right now, if you know what I mean."

"Watch out for hernias."

"Noses, *Cubiche*, it's noses I should worry about—"

The line clicked.

Xavier hung up and smiled. He couldn't believe his partner's energy—if he only had it for the business.

He turned the corner and pulled up behind his mother's blue Thunderbird in the driveway.

The house was in need of paint—rust and mildew turned the walls orange and green where the spray from the sprinklers hit. How many times had he offered to hire and pay someone to paint the house? Since his parents' divorce, his mother let the outside of the house go. The lawn needed to be mowed and the hedges trimmed. The roses by the fence had dropped their petals and now the ground was speckled with them.

Before climbing out of the car, Xavier removed his beeper from the sun visor and hooked it to his belt. Switching the vibration buzzer on, he stepped out of the air-conditioned cocoon to the humid, choking heat of the driveway.

Lizards scurried out of the way and hid as Xavier approached the front porch of the house he grew up in. He rang the doorbell but there was no answer. He should have tried to reach her on the phone before driving out. Maybe she had called from work. Perhaps she was on the phone or taking a shower.

His childhood was spent on these streets. He had lost track of how many years his parents had owned the house, having bought it in the early sixties.

He rang again, then he heard his mother's footsteps.

Opening the door, she said, "Got my message. Good."

She'd been cleaning. Her hair smelled of detergent and her skin, when he greeted her with a kiss, was moist with perspiration.

"I always get your messages," he said as he entered the house. "I didn't know whether to call you here or at work."

"Took the day off," she said. "Sometimes you've got to do that."

She worked as a buyer for the Burdines department store in Westland Mall.

As she led the way to the kitchen, she said, "I don't know why I take days off. I always end up doing work."

"Welcome to the club," he said. "I've been at it since early this morning."

From the rear of the house came the sound of music, a tune Xavier thought he knew because he had been hearing it most of his life. His mother was playing her old Cuban records, her prized possessions.

Mirna Alarcón was in her late fifties, tall and pretty, though her age showed in the wrinkled skin beneath her almond-colored eyes.

In the kitchen he could hear the music better; it was the sound of *congas* going *tuc-tuc, tac, tac/truc-truc, truc-trac.*

A wet mop leaned against the refrigerator in the corner of the kitchen. Soapsuds came up in the sink. The Windex and 409 spray bottles sat on top of the stove.

He told her about the impossible traffic and from habit opened the pantry.

"Are you hungry?" his mother asked.

"Hungry's not the word," he admitted, closing the sliding door.

"I ate lunch a while ago," she said. "I can fix you some leftovers."

"I'll pick up something on the way," he said and sat down on a stool behind the kitchen counter. "I don't want to trouble—"

"Nonsense. Shouldn't eat junk food. All that cholesterol."

He didn't want to ask her point-blank why she had asked him to come over. Obviously she was fine. There was something different about her appearance. It took him a couple of glances to figure it out. A new hair style, cropped short on the sides, bobbed in the back. It made her look very young.

"All I have to do," she said, "is heat it up."

She took the chicken and yellow rice and fried plantain leftovers in tupperware containers from the refrigerator, spooned them into a plate, and placed them in the microwave oven.

Since the divorce, his mother tried hard to lead an activity-filled lifestyle. She went on cruises to the Caribbean with her friends. Away to watch the musicals on Broadway. Always came back and talked incessantly about the stuff she had seen in New York.

"How—" his mother stopped to press the START button. "How are Sarah and the children?" She sat on the stepladder on the other side of the counter.

"They're fine, mother. Lindy wants to have her ears pierced. She watched how it's done on television."

"Bring her by the store. I'll get someone in jewelry to pierce them for her," she told him.

"Sarah wants to wait until she's older."

Mirna gave him a look of disapproval, then said, "The longer she waits—" Again she stopped. "And you, how are you doing? How many policies did you sell last week?"

"Not enough."

"*La avaricia rompe el saco*," she said in her clear and soft-spoken Spanish. Avarice corrupts.

"Sink or swim," Xavier told her. "It's the nature of the business. I have to stay afloat or else."

Sink or swim. That was precisely the way he'd been living for the last few years. Always in a hurry, but never enough time. He felt the tugs and wondered if his time to sink had come.

"I suppose you want to know why I asked you to come?" she said.

Xavier flashed her a what-could-be-so-urgent? look.

"I have good news."

At least someone did.

"I wanted to tell you before. But I had to wait for the right time."

"Did something happen?" he asked, checking the time on the kitchen clock and his watch. He was synchronized.

"Ready?"

"Ready."

"I'm getting married," she said.

He didn't know what to say. He was dumbfounded. *His mother getting married?* Why not?

She started to say something but paused. "Well, I've been thinking it over."

"To whom?" he asked. He wondered what kind of expression he had on his face since his mother was looking at him so strangely.

"This is really difficult for me, *hijo*." She placed a doily in front of him. From the cabinet drawer she pulled silverware, then she went down into the florida room and turned off the music.

"I am happy for you," he said finally. Why shouldn't she marry again? "Who is he?"

"I've always been honest with you, haven't I?" She returned to the kitchen, set the silverware down in front of him, then grabbed a glass from the cupboard and put ice in it.

He agreed.

The food's aroma filled the kitchen with a thick cumin-cilantro-and-chicken-in-yellow-rice smell.

"Well?" he asked.

"I told your father. We had lunch the other day."

"What did he say?" Xavier didn't know his parents still had lunch together.

She smiled. "You know how he is." She walked to the microwave to check the food. It was ready. Steam rose from the plate and swirled in front of him. Succumbing to its influence, he felt hungrier than ever.

"Really, what did he say to you? What does he think?" His father was living with a "friend," as Mirna put it, in Miami Beach, and Xavier didn't want to think about these living arrangements either.

"There's an avocado," she told him. "I can cut it and make you a salad."

Xavier told her not to bother. "Tell me what he said, for Christsakes!"

She got him a Diet Pepsi. She brought him a napkin. The pepper and salt were already on the counter. Xavier missed his mother's attention. Why didn't he come over more often?

"He wished me good luck," his mother said, returning to the fold-out step ladder. "He said to me, 'Why spend the rest of your life alone?' So I told him he was absolutely right."

"That's nice of him."

She smiled the way his children smiled when they had a trick up their sleeves or a secret. "Your father's become an understanding man," she said, sarcasm thick in her voice. "We get along fine now that he understands himself better, now that he is—"

"You'll be happy now," Xavier interrupted her.

"Aren't *you* happy for me?" she asked.

"Of course I am."

"I want you to meet him."

"Tell me who he is," he said.

"You'll like him."

"How can I like him if you don't tell me who he is?"

"He styles my hair at the salon."

This caught Xavier off guard. "Your hair dresser? You are marrying your hair dresser?"

"Hair stylist."

Same thing. He grew quiet. His mood changed, plummeting to murky depths. He put the fork and knife down.

"What's the matter?" she asked.

"I've got to go, mother," he said.

"I thought you were hungry?"

"I'm late for an appointment," he lied. He was upset but he didn't feel like explaining why. Besides, he didn't want to ruin his mother's mood.

It wasn't that he had anything against hair dressers/stylists. No, it wasn't anything like that. It was the idea of her getting married. After all these years. . . .

"How about a *cafecito*?" she asked.

"No thanks."

Silence, then she looked at him and said, "Maybe it's my turn to have a middle-age crisis. You must promise me not to talk to your father about this."

"I thought you had told him."

"I have," she said, "but I don't want him to talk behind my back."

"Does he know who you are marrying?"

"It's none of his business."

"You are right," Xavier said and stood up.

"This man cares about me. Loves me."

His lunch was beginning to sour in his stomach already. He went to the bathroom, washed his hands, splashed cold water on his face, rinsed his mouth, and combed his hair in front of the medicine cabinet mirror. His was a tired face, tired eyes, and a mouth tired from talking. Why don't people ever stop talking? he wondered as he stared at his bloodshot eyes. Sometimes he wished he didn't have to speak.

His mother's toiletries had taken over the bathroom completely. There was a bottle of Pierre Cardin men's cologne next to the toothbrushes. Was it his? Probably. Was he spending nights here?

What's going to happen to this house? Would she live here among so many old memories and make her new marriage work?

Let her marry who she wanted, it was none of his business. His, nor his father's. It was her happiness. He thought he could make himself understand.

Once again in the kitchen, he thanked his mother for the lunch and congratulated her. It isn't every day your mother announces an engagement.

"Will you be there?" she asked.

"Where?"

"At the wedding."

"When is it?"

"We haven't decided yet, but it'll be soon."

"Am I invited?"

She hugged and kissed him. "Don't be silly. Who do you think is giving me away?"

"Be serious, mother."

"I am."

Xavier moved to the front door. She followed him there and put her hand on his arm as if to stop him.

She said, "I still care about your father. But I don't want to spend the rest of my life alone."

"You're not alone," Xavier said.

She's an adult, Xavier admitted to himself as a way to form some sort of rationale, and she has a right to do as she sees fit. But what could she and this man have in common? He tried to imagine them sitting around, relaxing, and the man doing her hair all the time. Checking it. Combing it. Fiddling with it. Saying, "I've got to get it perfect. Look at your hair. Your hair's the reason why I married you, darling."

Xavier realized the unfairness of the stereotype.

"Goodbye, mother."

"Keep in touch," she said. "I'll send you and Sarah an invitation."

Outside, the harsh mid-day sunshine made him squint. He got in the car. Putting on his shades, he pulled out of the driveway, waved to his mother, and drove on. He couldn't believe it, his mother getting married, and she wanted him to give her away. He wrote down: *MOTHER'S MARRIAGE.*

Warm air mixed with faint exhaust smells that came out of the Volvo's air vents. He loosened his tie and removed the beeper, hooking it to the usual place on the visor.

DATE?

Twenty minutes to get to Miami Lakes to see his new client. At the corner of 60th Street and 12th Avenue he made a left and headed westward. School zones in this area slowed down traffic. No, sir, this city wasn't traffic friendly. But his appointments had to be kept, calls answered, errands run, and the bills for living paid.

A WEDDING GIFT FOR MOTHER?

Sarah would know what to buy.

He turned the radio on, searched for easy listening music. Without words. He scanned the stations. No luck. He changed his mind. Turned off the radio. Silence, he said to himself, was more gratifying.

Xavier leaned his head back against the headrest. A tension headache started behind his eyes, heartburn in his chest.

He was back in traffic.

ELIANA S. RIVERO

"FRONTERISLEÑA," BORDER ISLANDER

(A Marifeli, amiga siempre)

I remember one day in the summer of 1979 gazing out my kitchen window in Sierra Vista, Arizona, and looking clearly across the border. Around this part of the country, where light shines down perpendicular and blinding, one can literally see forever on a clear day. As I watched the landscape across my back yard, I could see the Cerro San José and the little white houses and tilled fields perched on its foothills: this was Naco, Sonora, on the windy and dusty border across from Naco, Arizona, a loose collection of homes and businesses lodged on the invisible line between northern Mexico and the southwestern U.S. lands. Here I was, Cuban to the souls [sic] of my feet, with a couple of bottles of Havana Club rum in my cupboard and some black beans bubbling on the stove, looking at the northernmost reaches of Latin America from a border town in which I felt out of sorts, at the margins of life. I was navigating through the rough waters of a marital separation, and had just returned from a trip to Cuba. I was literally looking at life from *la margen* (the bank, the shore).

I have always wanted to use the feminine gender form of margin in Spanish, the irregular line where land meets water, rather than the masculine one, which is an irrevocably peripheral band of terrain, edges outside the body of words on a page. *Los márgenes* are white and square and usually, in my profession, have red marks on them. *Las márgenes*, on the other hand, are loose and imprecise, and point to the ebb and flow of tides. Could it be that there is no way in my mother tongue to distinguish and delimit those two types of marginality? Be that as it may, I insist on grammatically engendering my borders, not precisely to make them fluid (mythically female?) but rather—more importantly—to have them evoke the

339

coastline of an island, where ocean meets land. That is the space of my original identity: I grew up on a narrow strip of land encased by liquid borders, the narrowest portion of the island of Cuba, in the Pinar del Río province, only forty kilometers wide between Mariel on the north and Majana on the south.[1]

If truth be told, fifteen years ago I did not conceptualize "marginal" as much as I experienced it. I had few clues about how other people who wrote and studied Latino literature felt at the time. But my own feeling was, most vividly, one of being definitely out of synch. Even though I had been living in the United States since 1961, earned my college degrees here, married and started a family in this country, I still saw myself as quite "different." On the border, looking in and out — and this was now a reality as well as a metaphor.

Little did I know then that in a short while I would begin lecturing about the works of Mexican American authors which are now considered classics. Miguel Méndez, author of *Peregrinos de Aztlán*, and born in Bisbee, Arizona, was my friend and had given me a copy of the original 1974 edition of his landmark novel. I had met Alurista (*Floricanto en Aztlán*) and Bernice Zamora (*Restless Serpents*) at the home of a Cuban-American-Hawaiian (!) professor in Calexico, California, in 1976, and had spent long nights listening to Chicano authors read. In Tucson, I had befriended Margarita Cota Cárdenas, Miriam Bornstein, Marina Rivera, and Aristeo Brito, who were my students and colleagues, and who had just begun publishing in the mid-seventies.[2] The pioneering Chicana artist and poet from San Antonio, Angela de Hoyos (*Chicano Poems for the Barrio*) had introduced me to the works of U.S. Cuban Mireya Robles (*Tiempo artesano*) in 1978; Mireya would go on to live and teach in South Africa, and to publish her great novel *Hagiografía de Narcisa la Bella* in 1985. In Houston and New York I had spent long hours listening to Rolando Hinojosa (*Estampas del Valle*) and Miguel Algarín (*Mongo Affair*). I had read Piri Thomas (*Down These Mean Streets*) and Pedro Pietri (*Puerto Rican Obituary*), and when I met the latter at a party in San Diego I greeted him as "the great Nuyorican poet!" (He burst into laughter at my remark, while we both sipped rum and Cokes.) Stan Steiner's *Borinquen* and Luis Valdez's *Aztlan* were prominent paperbacks on my shelves; but all I had to show yet for my "CubanAmericanness" were exile texts of nostalgia about a lost island, or parodies of Cuban street life mixed in with *santería* images, written by fellow immigrants such as Ana

Rosa Núñez or José Sánchez Boudy. What a (comic) relief it would be, two years later, to read Roberto Fernández's satire about the Miami Cuban cosmos, *La vida es un special!*[3]
I had lived through the Chicano cultural renaissance and met its main protagonists; I had read and enjoyed the works of U.S. Puerto Ricans. It would take half a decade, however, for me to complete an academic "crossover" into Latino studies (this field did not even have a name then). Precisely in 1979, during that crucial first trip back to Cuba, I met Lourdes Casal and Dolores Prida in Havana; the writings by these two women, my compatriots and fellow "community members," would have a profound effect on my psyche and on my construction of self. However, it would take me a few more years, until 1983 to be precise, to begin formally compiling and studying the writings of Chicana, U.S. Puerto Rican, and Cuban American women in a comparative manner. My choice of women authors was not accidental: in reading their texts I had recognized in them the same quest for identity and similar affirmations of "being other" that had become an integral part of my American *vivencia,* or "lived" experience.[4]

Fifteen years ago, Latinos and Latinas were marginal to the main academic fields. Some in my generation of immigrant students and writers had spoken of ourselves as *puentes,* bridges, with one foot in one identity (the Latin American) and one functional foothold in the Anglo American mainstream. In other words, we felt defined by the hybrid cultural identity that Cuban Americans shared with other ethnic minorities, but at least here — in Arizona, in the Southwest, in this new field of research — we could begin to be at home by expressing the bilingual and bicultural idiosyncracies that were our lot. In addition, we — the women scholars and teachers who studied many of these works, and began introducing them in the humanities curricula around the country — were also frequently connected to the new enterprises that consolidated into women's studies programs, research centers, and feminist publications. In this sense, we were people dreaming, hollering, and dancing at the borders of academia and society at large, insisting on our right to be let in, but most of all, on using our voices to tell our own stories.[5]

However, when I stood at my kitchen window in 1979, I was even out of my "normal" personal space: out of love, out of luck, and back from that faraway, original home that I had just recovered (or had I?). The trip to Cuba had indeed been a journey to my roots, which I had suppressed for a long time. Like many of my fellow immigrants, I had undergone a process of "decubanization" in the sixties, as I moved away from the cultural enclave of Miami and out to the larger territory of the U.S. mainstream (whatever that meant). My contemplation of identity had included the metaphorizing of cultural experience as that of an alien from another planet: it had taken me nine or ten years to walk into a room of English-speaking, very Anglo-looking people and not feel like a Martian ("Cuba. Planet Cuba. Where the hell is that?" — Cristina Garcia, *Dreaming in Cuban*). To counter that feeling, I had dived headlong into assimilation; not into a wild *sueño* of crossover fantasies, but into a neutral soup of *latinismo*. I absorbed whatever accent I was around, ended up sounding Chilean for years, Mexican American bilingual for even longer, Cuban only when I traveled to the island (even with my speech sprinkled with American slang words) or drove to Tucson to see my parents.

I had felt the rejection of English-speaking citizens of this country when encountering my linguistic and cultural otherness ("Speak American! You are in America now!" — yelled at me at a bus stop in Florida). I had suffered the consequences of subtle demographic clashes when I was suddenly immersed in the Mexican American communities of southern Arizona, and Chicano colleagues thought me "cute" and made fun of my Caribbean variety of Spanish. I was a token Latina in an academic environment, "too white" to really represent a minority group; too upper middle class to suit the taste of several Latino colleagues. I had the wrong color, the wrong ethnic origin in this part of the country, and even exhibited traces of a radicalized "other gender" persuasion. I was politically incorrect within a marriage that had harbored expectations of traditionalism; and most certainly I was ideologically anomalous, indeed rebellious, within a reactionary exile culture which was assumed to inform my views and my world vision.[6] I was a living bridge, arching over land and over water, and at this point with a sinking feeling of impassability. My roads led nowhere but to isolation. Ironically, I was also "other" when I returned to Cuba, although I had carefully kept internal files of cultural and affective memories that survived in language, in literature, in music, in family rituals.[7]

I have come to understand that we U.S. Cubans are border people and border entities, in the spiritual and social sense of the term: within the national political panorama, within the U.S. Latino cultural landscape, and some even within our own ethnonational subgroup — more so those of us who are female, a condition which adds its own marginality. Some Cuban Americans are ideological islands, some others live as continental add-ons, yet others inhabit peninsulas of their own, connected to the mainland by functional roads, but mostly out there by themselves, tenuously holding on. All of these geographic metaphors point to off-center psychospaces, to hybrid cultural identities that we share with other ethnic minorities. Fortunately, we seem to be able to claim a collective identity, both existential and public, that can benefit from our very hybridism, and not be narrowly framed by limitations of how we are perceived by society at large or by other subgroups.

In addition, many of us can still recover, as part of our family history, the memories of other border inhabitants and islanders who were our grand- and great-grand ancestors, as they migrated to Cuba from different parts of Europe. My own grandfather and great-uncles and aunts came to Pinar del Río from the Canary Islands and from southern Spain, those terminal reaches of the Bourbon Empire that sent quite a good number of their population across the Atlantic in search of better fortunes. They were "fronterizos" as well as pioneers, and I learned from them a certain sense of "portability," and no small amount of adaptability, that has allowed me to construct my own center of meaning.

Over the last decade I have fully traveled the road back to "recubanization," emerging from the neutrality of Hispanismo and Latinismo to a full-blown consciousness — rather a full-fledged affirmation — of hybridity as well as of Cubanness. Yes, I am Cuban by origin and culture (should I say temperament or is this too emotional?), *but I have lived elsewhere most of my life.* For me, this is now a very positive affirmation. I am a hybrid, a *puente*, a being of two places at once, but also of *one* place which is dual and fluid and rich. The anguish is gone; a sense of wholeness now presides over the process. I can recognize the nostalgia that I indulged in some years ago as part of the becoming; I can also see that I am what I am (*soy*) where I am (*estoy*) — *soy lo que soy donde estoy.*

In my daily life I notice how the music that I enjoy playing on the keyboards is much more Cuban American than in the eighties. Am I falling prey to the spell cast by Gloria Stefan in *Mi Tierra*? (What a great answer to our own local Linda Ronstadt and her *Canciones de mi padre*; *montuno* versus *mariachi*.) Or is it that electronic instruments now available produce better sounding *salsa*?

No matter: I think the porous borders of my islander identity are

made more penetrable by the sand particles (of sound and images) of
the desert where I live.

NOTES

[1]This was the historically famous Trocha, the Spanish enemy line that General
Antonio Maceo and his invading troops, coming from the Eastern provinces, had to
cross in order to bring the revolution to the West during the Cuban War of Independence (1895–1898).

[2]Margarita (*Noches despertando inconsciencias*) and I became the editors of a
small anthology, *Siete Poetas*, that collected poetry by three Cubans, three Chicanas,
and one Latina/Peruvian. The project was sponsored by a grant from the National
Endowment for the Arts, which funded our editorial efforts (Tucson, Scorpion Press)
in 1977. *Siete Poetas* preceded a larger anthology brought out in 1986 by Bilingual
Press, *Nosotras: Latina Literatura Today* (some of us were also included in the larger
collection).

[3]Miami: Ediciones Universal, 1981. I draw a clear distinction between *Cuban*
texts written in the U.S. and Cuban *American* writing: the first belongs to what is
widely termed "exile literature," while the second is part of the growing body of
ethnic American literatures known as "Latino Lit," ideologically and culturally
related to the bilingual/bicultural texts of Chicanos, Nuyoricans, or U.S. Colombians
and Central Americans. For more precise definitions of these terms, see my
"(Re)Writing Sugarcane Memories: Cuban Americans and Literature," in Fernando
Alegría and Jorge Ruffinelli, eds, *Paradise Lost or Gained? The Literature of Hispanic Exile* (Houston: Arte Público Press, 1990), 164–182.

[4]This work would not lead to some significant results until much later: *Infinite
Divisions: An Anthology of Chicana Literature* (University of Arizona Press, 1993,
coedited with Tey Diana Rebolledo). My first academic reflections about the "Cuban
condition" and its relation to Latino identity appeared under the title "Hispanic
Literatures in the U.S.: Self-Image and Conflict," *Revista Chicano-Riqueña* 13 (Fall-
Winter 1985): 173–192.

[5]These images were inspired by the titles of three great books and one classic
scholarly work: Cristina Garcia's *Dreaming in Cuban* (New York: Alfred Knopf,
1992), Sandra Cisneros's *Woman Hollering Creek and Other Stories* (New York:
Random House, 1991), Sandra María Esteves's *Bluestown Mockingbird Mambo*
(Houston: Arte Público Press, 1990), and Annette Kolodny's "Dancing Through the
Minefield: Some Observations on the Theory, Practice and Politics of a Feminist
Literary Criticism," *Feminist Studies* 6 (Spring 1980): 1–25.

[6]Ironically, I am possibly one of the very few Cuban Americans targeted for a
"mitin de repudio" in the Southwest: namely, a specially convened meeting of the
Cuban Society of Tucson in 1979 to plan a vocal, public censure of what were
perceived to be my "communist sympathies." The other people who were so "honored" by local groups were the members of the Cuban National Basketball Team
when they came to play in a Phoenix sports arena in 1980.

[7]I had actually returned to Cuba as part of a group of people involved with the
Círculo de Cultura Cubana, *Areíto*, and the Brigada Antonio Maceo, with all of
whom I would share political convictions, friendships, and committee work for
several years to come. This connection became for me a lifeline to all things Cuban
while I continued to live in the Southwest.

CUBANS AND AIRPORTS

I confess! I suffer from a terrible compulsion. For a long time I have refused to see the signs and all the while my malady has grown more intense. Now I cannot deny the awful truth. Please, allow me to explain.

After I arrived in the United States, I soon began to realize how airports are always crowded with Cubans and other Latin Americans. If a relative or friend is flying away on vacation, even if it is just for a week or two, usually from the New York metropolitan area to Miami, it does not matter if he or she is flying off at an awkward date or hour, the family and friends of the traveler cancel their appointments or work obligations and promptly plan a well-organized expedition to the airport. Assorted grandparents and retired old friends, children, babies, distant relatives, a friend of a friend, even total unknowns travel to the airport in caravans, three or four packed cars to accompany one single traveler in a glorious and rousing sendoff. Cubans and other Latins account for the daily congestion in the parking lots of New York airports.

Once they arrive at the airline terminal, they mass in the most improper places, blocking some door or standing in the middle of the way with perverse ubiquity. On cue they all begin to speak at the same time, doubtlessly at the top of their voice. This is done with the aim of accustoming their relative or friend to the noise of the airplane. At the same time, they slap, pinch, and manhandle the suffering vacationer as much as their energies allow. It has been argued that Cubans go on vacation just to recover from airport farewells. Of course, there are also invariably three or four relatives with their Instamatics and movie cameras, blinding with their flashes everyone who comes nearby. These photos, I am convinced, are shot without film since I have yet to see a print with anyone I know in it.

As the weary traveler walks to his departure gate, his cortege tries to mix with the other passengers until they are detained by the

security controls. They press against the glass walls, wave their arms
frantically, bang with their fists on the glass, throw kisses, and all in
all make absolute fools of themselves. As soon as their relative disappears from sight, a mad rush begins to the observation deck or any
window which might offer a view of the plane. Here they argue
vehemently.

"Look, there he is, waving back. Don't you see him?"

"No, I don't."

The poor fellow has probably collapsed in his seat.

In 1972, I was traveling to Europe for a few months on a research
trip. Already well aware of the problems, I took leave of my wife
and children in Princeton and proceeded to Kennedy airport on my
own. When I stepped out of the bus at the terminal, arrayed in full
battle gear were seventeen of my relatives, ranging in age from
sixty-two to three years old. I was hit by a barrage of flash lights,
temporarily blinding me. All the Americans looked at me in amaze-
ment, trying to discover if I was some famous Latin American celebrity. My male relatives fought among themselves for the right to
carry my bags, while their female counterparts savagely elbowed
each other in an attempt to monopolize my attention.

After an excruciating wait—I had lost all sense of time and
place—the passengers were called to board the plane. Those were
the days of lax security, and my mother and mother-in-law, holding
me by my arms, engaged in a fierce dispute to be the last one to say
good-bye. Pushing and shoving other passengers, they reached the
door of the airplane itself. There stood (a good eight inches taller
than myself) an Icelandic stewardess-goddess who with cold blue
eyes looked with scorn at this Latin face. I was already graying at
the temples, and there I was held like a moron by these two old
women. My mother and mother-in-law shouted their advice on how
to brush my teeth, and what to eat. My Icelandic nemesis ordered
me in her most sarcastic tone to take my seat. I humbly obeyed, all
the while entertaining the idea of hiding in the lavatory for the
entire flight.

Returning is no bargain either. Since most Cubans take the late,
inexpensive flights back from Miami, they arrive in the New York
area around 1:30 a.m. There the family waits. Alas! I well remember returning from my honeymoon, a mere week in Miami, to find
my parents waiting at the airport at 2:30 a.m.!

And yet, in spite of my dim view of this behavior, I cannot hear a
friend, even an acquaintance mention his or her impending flight,

before, unable to control myself, I offer my services. It doesn't matter how busy I may be, or how utterly inconvenient the trip. I plead, threaten, do anything in my power to drive my friend to the airport. Americans often mount stiff resistance.

"Come on, Teo," they say, "you know I can easily take a taxi or a bus."

I will accept no excuses and slowly, with persistence and inexorable logic, melt away their objections. I have driven friends to the airport more than four hundred times! I am possessed by my Cuban compulsion to take people to airports, to have them all for myself, to say the last good-bye.

ERNESTO SANTANA

KNOTS IN THE HANDKERCHIEF

They told me that this way I wouldn't forget.
  Seeing the knot, I'd remember immediately what I wasn't supposed to forget.
  Today, my only handkerchief is a knot of knots that doesn't mean anything.
  As always, I start by undoing a knot, and then it's as if I realize, finally, why I left that mark.
  When the handkerchief is all unknotted, wrinkled but flat, I stare uncertainly at it for a while in my hand, as if it were a strange bird that knows something I don't know but which will never be able to tell me what it is.

Translated by Ruth Behar

From Ernesto Santana, *Nudos en el pañuelo* (Havana: Casa Editora Abril, 1993).

GEORGINA HERRERA

Yolanda Fundora, *The Poet Georgina Herrera*, 1994.

IN THE WAY OF FORTUNE

My two children, remember this:
The Treacherous One, Mistress of the Clever
    Dream,
does not rest in her pursuit. I fear
not to be, suddenly, one day,
this loving animal whose owner
primarily you are,
and then successively of the rainbow,
of the afternoons like this, of the river,
of the lightning. . .

When
She Who Plays with Me and Always Wins
comes at last, cry with all your heart.
I have suffered
from a hopeless love for life.
And now, in the way of fortune,
grains of sun and moon, intermingled,
for the most beautiful of sunsets, I leave you.

Translated by Yolanda V. Fundora

From Georgina Herrera, *Granos de sol y luna* (Havana: UNEAC, 1977). These translations will form part of a book in progress edited by Sonia Rivera-Valdés, *El proceso creador de las escritoras de Cuba durante los últimos treinta y cinco años: Historias íntimas y antología.*

SEA'S PATH

Her belly is in the waters of the sea
warm and elegant it irrigates the earth
    the garden of her children
and the precise conjuration of her grain fields
    colors the work with love
Yemaya opens her skirt like the salty surface
of the waves saturating the roads of men
next to her purple skin are born new epochs
and in the measure of her song comes the sweet
  flowing plenty of her root.
Mother of currents
    in the humid amphora
insolence drinks the broth of your ire
to break bread there is no resting in your silence
and the secrets of the fertile, multiplied earth
wind themselves in the warmth of your stars
    The way of Olokum is deaf.
Let no one clamor for him in their petitions
    and at the terrible hour
    do not look at him.
His visage in the ferocity of a rock
    deep in the deepest sea
and in his violent dagger perish the exposed in the abyss.
There is no crossroad for his form
    that astonishes and inclines
the sweet bliss of Yemaya.

Translated by Juan Leon

From Minerva Salado, *Palabra en el espejo* (Havana: Ediciones Union, 1987).

PILGRIMS OF THE DAWN

To the crew of the "Sirene" (1836)

Stranger, you who have not seen the hanged,
grandparents, fathers, sometimes hallucinating, builders
of marble in Ifé or Benin, princes of walled towns
You who cannot imagine this sea filled with dead
This country an obscene lagoon
a threshold of malicious memories
I want you to know the godless yoke
Feel shame as well
at the blood spilled here
In the name of my white ancestors
I speak to you
In the name of Canoon, the slaver:
"When we weighed anchor the sea was so great it was lost
       to my sight. After six months of sailing
       we reached a coast close-set with trees
       like savage stakes. We carried little stones
       of purple and reams of taffeta which later
       were traded for a tremendous batch of
       black men full of body and black women guaranteed
       to breed. . . ."

Now think of the crossing,
those black heads, those polished arms
eaten by malaria and typhus
Think of the fierce breakers,
the yellow skulls down under

Walk down any street in my city
and you will hear the drums calling to prayer

and a god, half thunder half palm
speaking through the conchshells

Listen, stranger
Be my stroke of luck
Give these eyes a rest
This remorse, salvation
Stay with me until daybreak
You will be amazed at the solitude of this island,
these pilgrims always unveiling the dawn

Translated by David Frye

From Miguel Barnet, *Con Pies de Gato* (Havana: Ediciones Union, 1993)

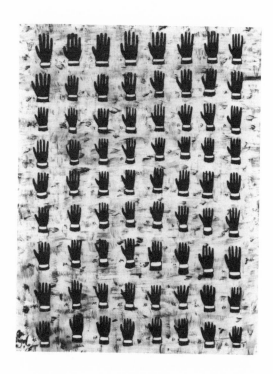

Ernesto Pujol, *black hands bound*, 1993. Oil
on canvas.

CARNAVAL

Carnaval is a work in progress. Book and lyrics by Carmelita Tropicana and Uzi Parnes. Music by Fernando Rivas. *Carnaval* was presented at Performance Space 122 and at INTAR as a staged reading with funding from NEA in March 1993. The following is an excerpt.

PROLOGUE

Carmelita Tropicana, a low rent Carmen Miranda, is in New York City's lower east side, in a basement with a boiler. She is sitting at a table, dejected, imitating Goya's lithograph: *The Sleep of Reason Produces Monsters.* Her speech is underscored by flamenco music.

CARMELITA

It is the best of times; it is the worst of times
Que vida tan amarga — Donde esta la miel para mis labios
Where is the honey for my lips?
Oh monstrous reason!
Or is it the sleep of reason produces monsters
[Speaking to the audience] No, I am not the beautiful Nefertiti
These days I don't feel very witty
Mira, que tengo angst, angst, angst
Once life it was sweet in the land of the Queens
Jack, Charles, Ethyl — three giants who pranced
Oh how we sang and danced
Art flourished; we were nourished
And now it is gone
And I suffering
Pulling my hair out like Jocasta, Electra, Medea
I am Carmelita, once a fun-loving chiquita
Beauty queen, nightclub entertainer

Head priestess of the Carmelita sisters in the Church
Of the Born Again Virgins
Superintendent, performance artist
In short, I am everywoman
A prisoner of her time
Bitter like a lime
Oh woe is me
To suffer modern urban rape
Homelessness, drugs, crime, AIDS, bashing of gays
And so much racial hate.
Ai, ai, ai
Guns and knives
A ubiquitous sight
And the innocent victims'
Blood spills on the pavement
I look and oh my back it turns into one big knot
No acupuncture, chiropractor or treatment of moximbustion
Can undo this lump, cure my spirit, soothe my rage
I cry to the heavens
No más, no más, no more
Estoy adolorida, atolondrada, atormentada
Tragame tierra — swallow me earth
I have to escape this modern day hell
But how?
No, not alcohol, drugs, or even caffeine
Perchance the boiler time machine
[She goes to touch the boiler] Oh yes. Oh boiler time machine
Give me a little respite
Once again, I want the hope of the newborn babe
Send me to another time, another space
A place where there is untainted sun and air
An ocean breeze where people don't wheeze
Instead of ugly subway stares, cold cement
And gouging rents
I want a little green grass, a picket fence
A place where people smile and say "hello"
And orange framboyan trees that smell
And where the bell is not a death knell
But the ringing of a ding a ling a ling
Of a pushcart of ice cream
Oh boiler time machine
Into thy womb, thy chambers of aquastat and gauge

I entering
Because any time, any place, any yesterday
Gotta be better than this rotten miserable
Modern day hell

Music ends.

Oh that this too mortal flesh
Carne que se va—
Carne—carnaval—
Carnaval! That's what I need
But not of today
Of yesteryear
I'll give myself
One day in carnaval
A lot can happen in a day
I synchronize my watch
For surely in such time
I will eschew my angst
And cleanse my soul of all this rotten, negative stuff
My body holds
I'll walk again with sternum high
And behold a world full of love
Free of hate!

Carmelita enters the boiler time machine.

Blackout

SCENE 1

Havana Harbor, 1939

Lights come up on Rachel, a young, German-Jewish refugee who stands on the deck of the SS St. Louis. She waves enthusiastically at the people on shore and begins to sing.

CARIBBEAN WATERS
SO WARM AND SO GENTLE
NOT LIKE THE ROUGH OCEANS
I HAVE KNOWN
CARIBBEAN WATERS
YOU BRING ME TO FREEDOM

YOU GIVE ME THE HOPE
I'VE NEVER KNOWN BEFORE
CARIBBEAN WATERS
SO WARM AND SO GENTLE
YOU GIVE ME THE CHANCE TO FIND
A NEW TOMORROW TODAY
CARIBBEAN WATERS
YOU BRING ME SALVATION
YOU GIVE US THE CHANCE TO GET AWAY
FROM OUR OLD WORLD
WITH ALL ITS HATE AND ALL ITS CRIMES
AND ALL ITS BIGOTRY
CARIBBEAN WATERS
PLEASE TAKE ME TO FREEDOM
TO THAT NEW AND PROMISED LAND
WHERE I SHALL LIVE AGAIN

Lights up on Otto Dick, German officer of the ship and spy who is speaking into a microphone.

OTTO

Ladies and gentlemen, please return to your cabins. I repeat, return to your cabins. The ship will not be allowed to disembark.

RACHEL

[Desperately] Caribbean waters, please be my salvation, but if I die, let me not die in vain.

Rachel jumps overboard.

Blackout.

SCENE 3

Casa Marina — Havana's most notorious bordello

Bonito, Head of Cuban Immigration (played by Carmelita Tropicana), is in bed kneeling in a white shirt with boxer shorts. He has a big gold ring. He holds a cigar in one hand and in the other a glass. He is listening to lovemaking noises through the wall.

BONITO

Fast. Too fast. Must be American. Little finesse, no concentration.

He burps and scratches.

Negrita ven aca.

Cleopatra enters and sits by him. She seems serious.

BONITO

Que pasa, tienes el moco caido?

CLEOPATRA

You know, it's been a year.

BONITO

That long. How time flies.

CLEOPATRA

It was carnaval. The moon was out. Maybe that's what did it.

BONITO

What are you talking about?

CLEOPATRA

The first time we met. Remember? I was in the parlor waiting.

BONITO

Que guajira, dust all over you, broken-down shoes, hair a mess.

CLEOPATRA

Didn't stop you. You asked Madame for me. The look on your face when she said I was not for hire, just the cook and cleaning lady. That night in the kitchen I was making chicken fricasse and the sound of those onions frying, the moon above made me feel like things could be different for me in Havana.

(Cleopatra sings *Moonlight Over Havana* and dances while Bonito chomps on his cigar)

MOONLIGHT OVER HAVANA
CARNAVAL MAGIC GLOWS IN THE NIGHT
MOONLIGHT OVER HAVANA
RHYTHM AND MUSIC AND LOVE WHAT A DELIGHT

MOONLIGHT OVER HAVANA
BRINGS THE SPARKLING LIGHT OUT IN YOUR EYES
MOONLIGHT OVER HAVANA
PLEASE SAY YOU LOVE ME, BUT DON'T TELL ME LIES

MOONLIGHT AND MUSIC AND YOU
IS ALL THAT IT TAKES TO MAKE MY DREAMS COME
    TRUE
IN THIS CITY SO FULL OF ROMANCE
FATE HAS BROUGHT US TOGETHER IN THIS DANCE OF
    LOVE
OH, MOONLIGHT AND MUSIC IT'S TRUE
WITH YOU NEAR ME I'LL NEVER BE BLUE
DARLING YOU MAKE ME FEEL SO GAY
IN MY HEART AND MY SOUL FOREVER YOU WILL STAY

MOONLIGHT OVER HAVANA
CARNAVAL MAGIC GLOWS IN THE NIGHT
MOONLIGHT OVER HAVANA
RHYTHM AND MUSIC AND LOVE WHAT A DELIGHT

MOONLIGHT AND MUSIC AND LOVE
AND THOSE CUBAN STARS SHINING ABOVE
MOONLIGHT AND MUSIC AND YOU
IS ALL THAT IT TAKES TO MAKE MY DREAMS COME
    TRUE
IN THIS CITY SO FULL OF ROMANCE
FATE HAS BROUGHT US TOGETHER IN THIS DANCE OF
    LOVE
OH, MOONLIGHT AND MUSIC IT'S TRUE
WITH YOU NEAR ME I'LL NEVER BE BLUE
DARLING YOU MAKE ME FEEL SO GAY
IN MY HEART AND SOUL FOREVER YOU WILL STAY

MOONLIGHT OVER HAVANA
MOONLIGHT OVER HAVANA
MOONLIGHT AND YOU

(At the end of the song Bonito smacks her rump and when she gets his pants a card falls out of his pocket)

BONITO

Get me my pants.

CLEOPATRA

[Looking at a card] What's this?

BONITO

What are you doing poking around?

CLEOPATRA

I wasn't poking, it fell.

BONITO

[Handing it to her] Read it. Oh, I forgot you can't read. It's an invitation to the Yacht Club.

CLEOPATRA

I wish I was her.

BONITO

Who?

CLEOPATRA

Your wife. She gets to go to the Baile de Carnaval del Yacht Club.

BONITO

Cleopatra, you would hate it. Stuffy, boring people. It's not like the carnaval on the streets. I go because it's necessary. To do what's necessary is important in life. I married a woman whose most important feature. . . .

Getting close

No, it's not her beautiful brown eyes like yours. Or her full ripe mouth like guayaba fruit or a sumptuous and promontory rump like yours . . . it's her papá, the Senator. If it wasn't for her papá, she would be very unattractive. Walks like a chicken. But I did it. I married a chicken. Because it was necessary. Face facts, Cleo. Some things you can't change. Even if you wanted to. Like going to the Yacht Club. You're a beautiful color but the wrong one. We'd have to talcum powder you from head to toe. You know the ex-President couldn't even get in and he's even a shade lighter than you. Hard to believe. But true. The President of the Republic and he couldn't get in. What we got together is paradise. Look at the fine specimen of a man you got.

He snaps his finger and she gets him his sombrero.

You could be stuck with a beer-belly Americano or worse an Anacleto with eczema and a toupé.

Carnaval music is heard outside.

Mira, mira el carnaval pa que llorar, pa que llorar.

CLEOPATRA

Es hora de cantar
Es hora de bailar
Un meneito pa ca
Un meneito pa lla

Together

Sueltate baby, que la conga pasa ya
Y arrollando va.

BONITO

That's my girl.

He kisses her cheek and leaves through Madame's parlor.

SCENE 4

Otto Dick, spy and officer of the SS St. Louis (played by a woman), sits reading a newspaper at the El Dorado Cafe. His monologue is underscored with music.

OTTO

Oh news, news, news
I love the news!
In this land mit nomen Cuba
The propaganda machine is working full steam
The headline of the Havana Post
Who are these Jews?
An editorial reads: these undesirables, criminals
They must not be allowed to disembark
Send them back
Cuba's economy is in stagnation
We cannot allow more immigration
It's perfect these news
I love the news
Why there's even a photo of that Jew Herr Goldstein
Handsome devil with shaved head and deep-set eyes
He does look evil
A criminal or an animal
Wouldn't want him meeting a muchacha or fraulein
In a dark street at night
Nein, nein, nein.
Photos in the news
It's the truth
Who can argue with that
It's a fact
The populace never knows
Hidden agendas
Those that control
Linked arm and arm with the mighty sword
Is the mighty pen
As Mein Kampf has disclosed
The populace is unaware
Of what they are sold
The truth goes by the name of News
Otto Dick knows that news, news, news
With respect to the news

It's "Caveat Emptor" — buyer beware
I tell you the truth is clear
Nations all gather
Claiming morality and goals humane
Oh poor refugees, a space must be made
The U. S. A. says: "Ethiopia, Angola, Central Africa would be
      nice
Italy's Mussolini declares the open areas of Russia would be fine
The USSR thinks — Oh, no, no. Icy Alaska would be divine.
It's all very clear
As the ship the St. Louis
To the world will soon prove
Nobody wants these creatures called Jews.

Music fades

The German mind, that of the Third Reich outshines especially
    that of Otto Dick [Salutes] [Señor]

Heil Hitler.

SCENE 5

Lights up on Bonito, who is reading a newspaper and smoking a
cigar en route to the Cafe El Dorado.

BONITO

Reading

El Bonito declares we must let these people in . . . in the name of
humanity. Yes, a humanitarian. That's me. I signed all those landing cards, about 1,000 of them. What a cramp I got! But when I
figure the money the pain goes away. How to make more, that's
the name of my game. The waters are getting very murky. It looks
like a tempest is coming. The locals I can handle . . . I've been
swimming in this political swamp for the past fifteen years.
Favors, bribes, botellas . . . I know it all. I know my swamp. I can
differentiate the different genus and species, the crocodile from
the alligator. The problem is the swamp is invaded by the international set: Los Yankees de New York and the Germans from
Deutschland. Las cosa estan revueltas.

Continues to read

The President declares decree 937 must be enforced and furthermore, the status of tourists cannot be accorded to the passengers of
the St. Louis.

Upset

Not tourists! Desgraciado! I thought I could get that in. Well, I
tried. I know the President wants a cut. But we'll see. Batista put
us both in. We will wait for him to tell us which way the wind
blows. Unless El Presidente wants to go solo, independent. And
forget that Batista once put him in. Not Bonito. I'm loyal. The
military and police Batista commands. That man knows just how
to wear his pants. Let's see. If the Yankee from New York, Mr.
Seersucker, can provide us with a bigger bond . . . then we can all
get along. Maybe Otto Dick will go for that. Let's see.

He exits

SCENE 6

Outside the El Dorado Otto Dick sits waiting for Bonito drinking a
beer and smoking a cigarette while reading a newspaper. Bonito
enters and sits next to him.

BONITO

Dick, can I offer you Havana's finest? Once you have Cuban
tobacco you'll never smoke anything else.

Smelling and enjoying the cigar sensuously

As beautiful as a naked woman.

OTTO

I enjoy cigarettes.

Enjoying the cigarette similarly

You have this burning sensation in the tongue that flows from your
mouth into the esophagus and settles deeply into the recessed cavi-
ties of your lungs. I detest American cigarettes, weak, tasteless.

Carmelita's grandmother, owner of the Cafe El Dorado, goes to the
table and eavesdrops throughout their conversation.

ABUELA

Señor Bonito, the usual?

BONITO

Si señora, un cafecito bien negrito. I see you are drinking our beer.

OTTO

Yes, but it cannot compare with our German beer. Piels Bitte, the best.

BONITO

At this hour I like a strong coffee. I like my coffee like I like my girls . . . dark and sweet.

OTTO

I prefer weiss und blond.

BONITO

Weiss?

OTTO

White.

BONITO

Each to his own. That's why colors were invented. I missed you the other day at Casa Marina. Madame was expecting you with a special treat.

OTTO

The Captain of the ship has been under stress. He cancelled all shore leave yesterday. For the time being he gives the orders . . . stupid as he may be. Bonito, let's get on with business. I have several matters to attend to and one of them concerns you.

He takes out an envelope and hands it to him.

Another Jew jumped overboard, a girl by the name of Rachel
Siberishe.

BONITO

Dios mío! Not another one.

OTTO

This is her dossier and photo.

Carmelita's grandmother comes in with coffee and removes the
photo on the table to put the coffee down and stays with it, looking
at it.

OTTO

Madame, Please.

He takes the photo from her.

Her father is an important scientist. I want you to find her and
when you do, deliver her to me.

BONITO

This is costing me. In five days that's two suicides and two who
have jumped overboard. That throws my figures off for my meeting with Mr. Seersucker, the American lawyer. The bond has to be
higher.

He takes out a pad and pencil.

Let's see, that's 985 Jews times $970, converted to pesos, minus
15% for the Chief of Police and 2% for . . . can't you talk to the
Captain? Can't he lock these people in their cabins? I can't afford
more suicides or Polacos jumping overboard.

OTTO

These are not Polacks. They are Jews. As head of Immigration you
should know this.

BONITO

Polacos is just a slang word we use for Jews.

OTTO

Such inaccuracies.

BONITO

Dick, you want this girl and you want to conduct your affairs in this island. I hear a lot about a German restaurant, Die Blutwurst Haus.

ABUELA

Terrible heavy food. Greasy.

BONITO

There is a lot of foreign activity there. I do not interfere. I will cooperate but I have my price. I want these Jews.

OTTO

This may be beyond our control. From what I read in the newspapers it seems public opinion in your country is averse to this situation. The President favors decree 937 prohibiting further immigration.

BONITO

There is still time, the President may be convinced by the Chief of Police. I'm hoping to count on you. You can exert pressure on your government. My figures are not added up yet. A bigger bond can make us all very happy. Dick, because it's carnaval let's take off our masks . . . what's your price?

OTTO

Price. Deutsche Marks, Cuban Pesos, American Dollars. Money is just a tool. A means to achieve. Money is crude if not attached to values, to a philosophy, a grander view and scheme. You, Bonito, are too narrow-minded to see what I mean. You suffer from an island mentality. I am European. My mind is continental. The world is ruled by the continent, our continent. Our continent has new leadership, borders are changing. A new Europe is upon us.

Take off your mask . . . take off your blinders, Bonito. The new age is now.

Clicking his heels

Deliver the girl, Rachel Siberishe to me, then we talk. Guten tag.

He exits.

BONITO

That's some Herr Dick. The snake of the swamp rears its head. I must be careful. A snake can strike like lightning. It's true I signed papers, forged a date. I use but I don't abuse. Not Otto. He has a taste for blood. The best part of the hunt for him is the kill. Not me. I don't play rough, strictly white collar stuff. Let Otto keep his continent. I'll stick to my island and the Americans. After all the U. S .A. is only 90 miles away.

The carnaval comes through.

LOURDES GIL

PILGRIMAGE TO FRANCE:
THE CUBAN PAINTERS

Human beings have always felt the need to read signs in the coarse surface of rocks or in the spirals of clouds, such as the vertical clouds often seen in the Caribbean. Ramón Alejandro calls them Solomonic columns; he envisions them laden with knowledge as well as moisture, the imaginary support of a celestial vault.[1]

We are stirred by the hidden meaning of unexpected affinities, by the multiple times and places converging on an unseen point. And it may be that to interpret the capricious arrangements of numbers or recurring dreams, to ascribe an ominous significance to the cyclical patterns of history, is to carve out an alternate route in the proverbial pilgrimage to the truth, to outline the search for the ontological reason of our existence.

"There are pathways in the sky and in the ocean for the birds and the fish that the eyes of a man cannot perceive, yet the eye of a buddha can," writes Alejandro. And so we ask, what is the eye of a buddha and where is it found? Who can discern the hidden lines that pierce the sky and the sea? How do birds and fish learn their invisible orbit, how do they pursue the trails that we cannot see?

The compelling power of this image springs from its inherent mystery, the absence of all logic. Its metaphor inscribes itself in the realm of myth, like a catalyst driving us to a parallel code, a registry where an unearthed text translates into a lucid, up to then submerged, language. The vocabulary *avant la lettre* may not reveal the desired treasure map of the islands, but on Alejandro's cosmology of signs we behold the serpent's ring and the incubation of Eros. We enter the space where allegories unravel.

In the early decades of this century, Amelia Peláez and Lydia Cabrera were disciples of the same art teacher in Paris. Like them a foreigner in the French capital, Constructivist Alexandra Exter was a White Russian émigrée who had fled the October Revolution.[2] In those post-Armistice days the city exuded the dissolute, carefree climate that permeated the West at the end of the Great War — perhaps as a premonition of the impending second version. This was the Paris of Gide and Cocteau, of Picasso and Utrillo, Braque and Léger, Hemingway, Céline, and Malraux.

Yet these three exceptional women came from lands far removed from the epicenter of the recently extinguished conflagration — which was, in spite of its high-sounding name, a European dispute. Exter had fled the fratricidal struggle that divided and subdivided her native Russia, the microcosmic battleground where the various ideologies which would eventually modify the Eurocentric balance of power in the world began their conflict.

For their part, Lydia Cabrera and Amelia Peláez had come from a country as young as they were. A new republic, barely awakening from its own warring nightmare, was now shedding the weight of a colonial past and anxiously tracing the outlines of its national identity. Both Lydia and Amelia, in their efforts to retrieve primeval Cuban myths and expose the human and natural landscape of a hybrid culture, were pioneers in the rediscovery of this heritage: Amelia in the emblematic abstractions of her art; Lydia in the anthropographic vindication of her research and tales.

Together with the other prominent Cubans of their time, they embarked on the mission of peeling away the layers of four hundred years of colonialism and historical distortion in an attempt to uncover the true face of the nation. Yet they were not tracing on a blank canvas. The search for what has been called "lo cubano," "la cubanidad," the innermost essence of "Cubanness" (terms given to the national consciousness as a definition of identity) had constituted one of the fundamental ethical pursuits of previous generations of artists and intellectuals. The theoretical debate over "lo cubano" became a consistent element, present in every effort to transform Cuban society, up to the present day.

This crucial quest frequently began as a journey, a metaphor for what was to become a time-honored Cuban tradition in the island's difficult history. The pilgrimage to the sanctuary of another country initially occurred in the aftermath of Spain's domination of the island. The first territorial displacements began late in the eighteenth century, gravitating toward Spain, Paris, Mexico, Caracas, and New York as the preferred nuclei. These early émigrées were invariably "criollos," the Cuban-born children of Spaniards, an educated elite craving autonomy and seeking influential allies for their cause in the metropolis.

As greater numbers became actively involved in the struggle for independence toward the end of the nineteenth century, a quick getaway to a nearby haven seemed more expedient. Exiles headed for Key West and Tampa to settle, with their families, in what they regarded as a temporary, albeit indefinite, arrangement.

Ironically, it was within the framework of these successive migrations, these constant movements from and back to the island during the last two centuries, that the Cuban national identity evolved. The sense of loss and the elegiac tone found in Cuban art and literature were rooted in the recurring displacements of the country's history.

Meanwhile, the seemingly fortuitous encounter of Peláez, Cabrera, and Exter in Paris during the 1930s affirmed in them a profound sense of the artist's mysterious path. They had entered a distinct private space, a site of incubation inhabited by that rare confluence of the historical past and a hypothesis for the future. It engulfed them in the language of myth.

What unseen reality was about to unravel in this *mise-en-scène?* What predisposition in the psyche of the three led to the uncharted region of their sojourn? What inner landscapes were shared, what cluster of images evoked, what pleasures sought? What precarious mist had they stepped into that would determine their destiny?

One cannot help but wonder what these formidable women discussed at their periodic gatherings. For although absorbed by aesthetic concerns, they were still aware of the pitfalls of history and its confused jargon. If one could only untie the Gordian knot that bound these three Graces, these new Fates in their undaunted Parisian rendezvous. They briefly had in their possession the convoluted, tenuous cord that would entangle the globe, the fuse-line leading to the implosion of our age.

Yet innumerable and persistent signs beckoned at the shores of the incipient republic. "We were an anomaly," wrote José Martí in 1891, "with the chest of an athlete, the hands of a dandy and the brain of a child."[3] Shunning the temptation to repeat this parody, Amelia Peláez sought to define the symbols of our culture by creating a Cuban pictorial language. "We were as a masque, with English breeches, Parisian vest, North American jacket and Spanish cap," Martí wrote. Lydia Cabrera exposed the porous disjunctions implanted in the

Amelia Peláez (1896–1968), *Interior con Columnas* (Interior with Columns), 1951. Tempera.

Wifredo Lam (1902–1982), *La Silla* (The Chair), 1943. Oil.

Cuban soil and assembled the deep-set roots of our African components, which many sectors in our society preferred to dismiss.

But to discard the mask outlined by Martí and scrub the smudges from the insular chin required an artistic instruction that Alexandra Exter was unable to convey in her lessons. It was impossible for Exter to transmit to her students any predictions of a revolution, or to prophesy the legacy of an exile that has not yet reached its final stage.

The Russian artist could impart no more knowledge than a gesture of precognition, since she was the inadvertent custodian of an implausible reality. Her painter's brush doubled as a magic wand, with which she encoded the cell formed by the three women into an enduring metaphor, open to future revelations. The women proceeded through that French interlude between wars like a thread going through the eye of a needle, until the pieces began to assemble at the upheaval of 1959.

Ramón Alejandro referred to Paris as "the empirical mind, the target point of the Universe."[4] He saw the rest of the world as a mere appendage, the limbs to the whole body — a partial truth, the hues and sounds of an unfinished rhapsody. "You are not in France here: you are on this planet. Other lands seem as distant as the people who inhabit them. From here humanity was conceived as a concept, such as Marcus Aurelius or Hadrian conceived it."

Trying to define whether Alejandro paints in a state of rapture or from the most coldly calculated logarithm, is to approach his art and enter his world through a blind alley leading nowhere. Equally futile is to attribute Alejandro's luminosity, the translucent intact light in his painting, to either his native Cuba or his adoptive France. To trace the ineffable radiance of his landscapes to the tonality indigenous to the Adriatic or the Peloponnesus — where his visions first erupted onto canvas — is once again to stumble upon a mirage.

"It's disconcerting to interpret every sunbeam that results in a turquoise blue here or a tangerine there," warns Alejandro, "particularly in the case of the Cuban people, a complex and irregular prism producing a proportionally distorted rainbow. Yet therein lies the source of our riches." Then he muses: "Are my roots planted in La Víbora[5] and my wings extended over Montmartre? Root and wing belong to the earth and the air. But where do the other elements, fire and water, come from?"

Other notable Cubans went to live in Paris a century ago — the philosopher José Antonio Saco, the composer José White, writers Enrique Piñeyro and the Countess of Merlin, scientist and poet Felipe Poey, artist Guillermo Collazo. Marta Abreu, a patroness of the arts through her personal fortune, bestowed the Maison Cuba on the Cité Universitaire. Abreu's influence is still visible today in the magnificent structure bearing her name and fashioned after El Escorial.

Yet a migration in the opposite direction would prove more significant to the country's future. French-born muralist Jean-Baptiste Vermay, for instance, left Paris to establish the Academia de San Alejandro in Havana in 1818. It was to become the fountainhead of Cuban art for many generations. The structural system for the as-yet-uncharted plethora of collective images, the lines and colors of the native landscape, as well as the coherent imagery of the nation, was laid out at San Alejandro.

France's role as a catalyst for Cuban imagination and thought continued into the twentieth century with Wifredo Lam and Victor Manuel, Nicolás Guillén and Alejo Carpentier, among others. It has been strengthened in our day through the massive exodus brought on by the revolution of 1959, which generated the more permanent displacements of artists Jorge Camacho, Gina Pellón, Ramón Alejandro, Guido Llinás, and Agustín Cárdenas; writers Severo Sarduy and Nivaria Tejera; playwrights José Triana and Eduardo Manet. Most of their work has been produced beyond the Cuban territorial space.

But France has not acted as sole conduit for Cuban aesthetic and literary discourses. In a historical continuum dictated by the undercurrents of political turmoil, other arteries have carried the flow from the Cuban heartland. Spain, Mexico, Venezuela and the United States became the terminus to the Cuban axis. And comparable to the Jewish nation, which cannot be contained within its geographical boundaries, Cuba swells and spills; it scatters only to gather again; is disjointed and later conjoined, ever present in the multiple spaces it inhabits. "The island is an echo box, a resonant vault punctured with images that came from Europe, from Africa, from China and North America. . . ." Alejandro emphasizes. In its meager dimensions, the island inhales the discordant breezes of the larger nations that have

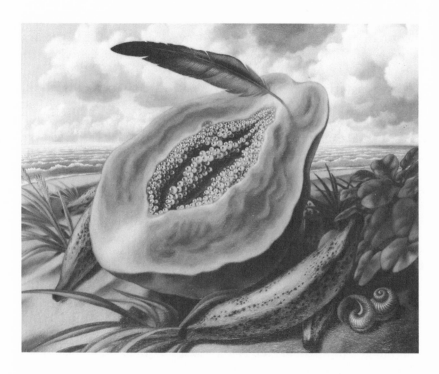

Ramón Alejandro (1943–), *L'Appel Du Large* (The Call of the Sea), 1991. Oil on canvas.

nurtured its children. It chokes and spits, reaches out in vain, unable to seize the cosmos. It grows grotesque tentacles that adhere to every land it touches. Like its ailing people, a wound in the gut of the Americas, it lies as a petrified bubble undulating sensuously atop the submerged plateau of the Gulf. Perhaps the embryonic, curved petal sketched by Amelia and Alejandro will still find a passage over the ocean, among the marlin and the hummingbird.

NOTES

[1]Alejandro (born 1943) is a prominent Cuban artist living in Paris. He left his native Havana in 1960 and attended the Escuela de Bellas Artes in Buenos Aires. In 1963 he settled in France to study at Friedlander's studio. His first solo exhibitions were highly acclaimed by French critics. Roland Barthes, Severo Sarduy, Bernard Noel, and Cabrera Infante, among others, have written catalogue introductions to his exhibitions.

[2]Amelia Peláez (1896–1968), one of Cuba's major artists, lived in Paris from 1927 to 1934 and returned briefly after the war in 1948. After she attended the Academy of San Alejandro in Havana, she and Lydia Cabrera studied at the Ecole du Louvre and in Fernand Léger's Académie Contemporaine, where they became students of Alexandra Exter. Amelia's contribution to Cuban art lies in the rediscovery of Cuban flora and colonial architecture ("mamparas," "mediopuntos," arches). She is among the principal founders of Cuban modernism.

Lydia Cabrera (1900–1991), one of Cuba's most respected writers, played a leading role in the compilation of Cuba's African folk tales, proverbs, and traditions. Her research brought the attention of renowned anthropologists such as Alfred Métraux to Cuba's still undiluted pockets of African languages and cultures. Although she cultivated fiction, she is better known for *El monte* (The Mount), a study of Afro-Cuban religions.

Russian Constructivist painter Alexandra Exter lived in exile in Paris until her death in 1950. Amelia Peláez owed much of her technical knowledge, as well as the planning of Amelia's first vernissage in Paris, which Lydia Cabrera organized in 1933, to Exter's influence. The three women remained friends, although they lost contact during World War II. Amelia finally located Exter in 1948, living in poverty outside Paris. After her return, Amelia sent her food and clothing regularly from Cuba.

[3]"Our America," José Martí's most famous essay, was published simultaneously in *El Partido Liberal* (Mexico) and *La Revista Ilustrada* (New York) in 1891. All quotations are from *Our America: By José Martí*, translated by Elinor Randall and edited by Philip S. Foner (New York and London: Monthly Review Press, 1977), 91.

[4]All quotations are from Alejandro's personal correspondence with the author (1991–1992).

[5]A somewhat removed and traditional neighborhood of Havana. Built in the second half of the last century, the architectural and ornamental motifs (stained glass and iron window grilles, columns with decorated capitals and friezes, ceramic floors, stucco balustrades) give the area a distinctly old-fashioned flavor. Both Alejandro and Peláez come from La Víbora.

MIRTHA N. QUINTANALES

MOVING

NOVEMBER 1983

I traveled in a cardboard box
packed between my books and
the old kitchen dishes.
My traveling companions:
the typewriter
the unfinished thesis
and the other manuscript, which also threatens
to remain without end.
In this strange new place I now
face serious decisions:
how to clean a rug
with so much history,
where to place the threadbare
sitting couch,
which wall to cover with
this or that other painting.
With each dish that I take
from each cardboard box,
I reread the news from the *Village Voice*
or the *New York Times*
from last week,
from two years ago.
And in the midst of this chore
so often repeated,
phantom kisses caress me,
hands without prints
glide over my body
reaching for the point of weeping.
From one sob to the next

from one tear to the next
I keep a careful count:
too many strange places
too many cardboard boxes
and unending chores.
Too many loves existing
only in my imagination.

Translated by David Frye

"De espaldas a tu cabeza" (With my back to you).
Drawing by Zaida del Río.

ALAN WEST

MY LIFE WITH FIDEL CASTRO: A SOAP OPERA WITHOUT TRANSMITTER

It is strange that one comes closer to the truth only in words that one no longer fully believes. Truth is a reanimation of dying words.

Elias Canetti

Episode One: Innocence Lasts Shorter Than Expected

The presence of some people can fade with repetition.
Not so with Fidel Castro.
I saw him for the first time when he triumphantly entered Havana in January of 1959, and, truth be told, I've never seen a multitude so given over to happiness as on that day.
Better for you to choose the word: joy, jubilation, exaltation, boisterous frolic, ecstasy, rapt enjoyment, delirium.
It was a moment of supreme celebration, but no one suspected it would also be a moment of supreme definition.
It was to be the beginning of an event that would mark me the rest of my life, this man who hadn't even shaken my hand.
Afterwards, I saw him many times on TV, during the first year of the revolution, but my memory of those occasions is faint.
I was brought up hating him, hearing jokes, insults, calumnies, betrayals, stories, letdowns. Of Raúl I won't even mention. "I, too, fought in the mountains but later, when it went bad . . ." as if communism were a pork chop decomposing out in the sun. "Chico, I believed in Fidel, but when he started to take our kids away to the Soviet Union. . . ."
And so on.
What's the point in going on?

Of course, with such a supreme example of Evil, in the long run I had to become fascinated by it. And so I surrendered to "Evil."

Episode Two: The Plot Thickens as I Look for Trouble

But before proceeding with Fidel, I must admit that my fascination with Evil started with a true example: Hitler. And let's make things clear. Even though Fidel Castro has some major defects, to compare him to Hitler is of such scant political value and historical credibility that I'm not going to waste time refuting it. Mother certainly never held back from wanting to make Fidel into the Prince of Darkness. Curiously, however, he was never mentioned by name. Either a pronoun was used, insults (grime ball, son-of-a-b, that crazy man, shameless bastard), or in the majority of cases, nothing was said. As if invoking silence were a way to dissolve him from history; or a way of invoking the *mirabile duellum* of theology that would put him under the rule of God. Catholicism has always been excessively verbal in attacking sin and evil. Let's not forget that devil in Greek (*diabolos*) means to slander or defame. Silence or a refusal to name him was maybe a ruse to avoid committing slander or being bedeviled by rage; and yet at the same time, it was a way of expressing my mother's grief, her uprootedness, the desolation of exile, her way of "saying" that this condition was unnameable, cast in shadow, removed from the sphere of humans and equally distant from language.

But I'm digressing. I'm not sure exactly when my opinion of Fidel changed and if it was due to any analogies between our lives: I too studied with the Jesuits and played basketball as an adolescent. What I do know is that I arrived at Fidel through his alter ego, Che Guevara. I read a collection of his writings and speeches edited by Grove Press with a Paul Davis poster on the cover that still retains its mystique from the 1960s, although I prefer the more "pop" versions by Raúl Martínez, because of their freshness and candor mixed in with a subtle irony that is always demystifying.

With Che I began to understand that socialism was not so vile, that it was imbued with generous impulses of human solidarity which moved me. But by some intricate maneuver that never ceases to surprise me, I saw Fidel and Che as socialists and not as communists. I understood them to be two different things (well, they are!) and that on the one hand socialism was good and communism, hmm. . ., that was something else. I know I spoke about these subjects with my parents, but I can imagine that the logic I used would have been more twisted than trying to explain a virgin birth. I'd give anything to listen to myself again, because it would provoke endless laughter nowadays. (Maybe I opted for this distinction out of self-preservation, because to use the "C" word without expressing disgust was dangerous in Cuban exile circles).

Episode Three: The Bad Guy Becomes the Good Guy

The end result was that my image of Fidel changed to being positive: I liked his anti-imperialism, his support for the Vietnamese struggle, his vision of Latin America, where he saw the need to wage a second war of independence against the tyranny of Capital, and his defense of Puerto Rico's right to independence. And let's not forget his reckless honesty: he was the first Latin American politician in power who told the *yanquis* who they were unambiguously and sent them to hell. (More importantly, they didn't blow his head off, though not for lack of trying). It matters little what your ideological inclinations are or how you might judge Fidel's historical trajectory after 1962. As a people we have one thing to thank him for: he gave us back a little of that dignity of what it is to be a Latin American. There's still a lot of that dignity left to be recovered.

Sure, it was the sign of the times: the student unrest, Che in Bolivia, guerrilla movements in Guatemala and Venezuela, the Tupamaros, the independence of many African countries, Vietnam, the Beatles, Roy Brown, Viglietti, the Cuban new song movement with the likes of Silvio Rodríguez and Pablo Milanés. And yes, of course, there was the Soviet invasion of Czechoslovakia, which depressed me for a long time and had an impact on me, I imagine, similar to that of the XX Congress on many militants of the 1950s. Except I had no years of militancy, I was fifteen. The invasion taught me one thing early on: that the foreign policy of the Soviet Union was not going to coincide with the advances of world revolutionary movements. Cuba was another reality and it didn't necessarily have to follow the Soviets in their stupidities. Even so, Fidel backed the invasion, an unacceptable position for me, although he managed to harshly criticize the Soviet Union in the same speech. My position was closer to that of Mario Benedetti, though I couldn't articulate it as elegantly as he did. Seeing things in the wider context of what was going on in Latin America, there was no need to be alarmed, he observed. The danger for us never had been Soviet interventions, but those of the United States. I say it is still truer today after the implosion of the so-called socialist bloc.

From there I went on to read Fidel's speeches (not all of them, I've only one lifetime) and they impressed me. They were not typical of a Latin American politician, not loaded with demagoguery and empty phrasing, that I would hear from the guardians of colonialism in Puerto Rico. I'm not saying Fidel was exempt from being demagogic, only that he handled his discourse with more vision and honesty than most politicians I had been exposed to up until then. The length of his orations would sometimes worry me because it's not easy to listen to someone speak for three, four, or five hours (the record, I think, was nine). Certainly Joseph Beuy's description of Marcel Duchamp would never apply to Fidel: "His silence is quite overrated." But I'm not interested in his oratorical abilities, his deft use of language and metaphor, his skillful didactic manner, his enormous persuasive powers. That's been discussed by García Márquez, Cardenal and others quite evocatively.

It would perhaps be more useful to see Fidel as icon, as image. It was in fashion after the revolution to sell fake beards everywhere and my parents must have somewhere a photo of me on the front steps of my grandfather's house. I'm wearing the fake beard, a toy rifle, and an olive green fatigue cap. The iconography of the *barbudo* (the guerrillas who sported beards in the mountains) captured not only the imagination of Cubans but of the entire globe. Among non-Cuban youth of the time, beards were in. I had one for eight years, but I don't know if was the influence of my childhood photo or for other reasons. Julio Cortázar, Tolstoy, Nietzsche, George Bernard Shaw, and Valle-Inclán used beards so I wasn't in such bad company.

Episode Four: History as Image, The Image of History

Revolutionary photos of Fidel always bring out the positive side of his character: his intelligence, his humor, his athletic abilities or his firmness against the blackmail of the U.S. government. There are two in particular that stand out: one where he is with Che, another with Camilo. The one with Che is interesting because Fidel is not talking, but listening. His left arm is on Che's right shoulder and he's leaning toward him to hear some words said in a low voice. Although you see Fidel in profile he exhibits curiosity, interest; he's absorbed by what Che is saying. There is also a note of tiredness and seriousness, but, above all, an intimate tone between two friends and brothers in struggle who have been through it all. In his left hand Fidel has a lighter so maybe he was about to light a cigar and mix in smoke from a good Montecristo with words and friendship. They both have beards, of course, they're dressed in olive green and Che has on his ever-present beret. A frozen moment, where history/ myth and human intimacy come together. And though it captures two great Latin American figures, there's nothing heroic, grandiose, or theatrical in the moment depicted.

The photo with Camilo Cienfuegos is legendary. Fidel is up on the podium with his left hand touching the microphone. He's in the middle of a speech and there are two doves, one on the podium, the other on his shoulder. To his right is Camilo, who seems to be looking at a distant point, with the eyes of a mystic. Fidel is captured in profile, again, and you notice his large nose and his hand, delicate and beautiful. It is a moment where he seems to be at a loss for words — a rare occasion for him — maybe because he has just become

Photograph of Fidel Castro and Che Guevara.

aware of the doves. His gift for oratory has yielded for a second to something that seems crafted by divine providence. The warrior, in the thick of speech, in the middle of his exhortations, with the thunder of his words and the vehemence of his convictions, is being visited by the messengers of peace. The photo irradiates exaltation and at the same time it's bathed in a harmonious and enigmatic tranquility. The rational world of politics is devoured by an irrationality that seems religious, but goes beyond it. Or maybe it illustrates Harold Laswell's celebrated phrase: "Politics is the process by which the irrational bases of society are brought out into the open."

Perhaps that irrationality is what helps to define the emotional charge of charismatic leadership which this photo (and many others) typifies. Even if not totally extinct, we are living in the twilight of the world of charismatic leaders. Khomeini recently expired, as have Churchill, Roosevelt, Mao, and Hitler. There are some still around, like Gadaffi, Walesa, Kim Il Sung and Fidel. Outside of Fidel, none of the others has a world-wide impact, which is not to say the others are not universally known.

The positive aspect of charisma is evident: it fills a political vacuum and in periods of great changes (i.e., a revolution), external crisis (military intervention by another country), or internal crisis (civil war), it is a unifying force which brings together a nation in order to overcome fear and apathy and thus be enabled to enact change, establish peace, or repel an invader. Canetti (in *Crowds and Power*) has insightfully pointed out that being in a multitude helps us to conquer a distance. That distance is fear of the unknown, of being touched or transgressed by others and at the same time, the tenacity of solitude. And not just the solitariness of the loner, but the kind of alienation produced by a society where there is a "war of all against all," as Hobbes said. This distance is annulled in the multitude, in that moment that Canetti calls the discharge, and that is where those beings in the crowd feel that their differences with other humans disappear and equality reigns. Class, race and sexual distinctions vanish and in their place "the people" arise, a combative instrument for achieving the necessary tasks: production, defense, social change.

A charismatic leader is extremely efficient in eliciting from a group of people that moment of discharge so that they become "the people." But this also harbors a great danger, sometimes of catastrophic proportions: a crowd can become a herd. When that happens, people hand over their capacity for independent thinking to the leader because he (or she) has arisen from a powerful collective dream, from the need that people have to elaborate myths of social reconciliation. When the thin line between confidence and adulation is crossed, then a people begins to trade in democracy for the vision or whim of one person. It engenders the worst confusions: the unity of consensus becomes a blind impulse for monolithic unanimity, criticism is interpreted as treason, a certain independence of spirit is viewed with suspicion and, in the worst of cases, collective paranoia may reign.

I offer these two dimensions of charismatic leadership because usually either the negative or positive side is brought out, according to the ideology of the person making the observation. I want to highlight both because they are inseparable and because they give a more complex view of what Cuba is and the nature of Fidel's leadership. The revolution is the literacy campaign, defeating the invasion at Playa Girón (Bay of Pigs), the Second Declaration of Havana, the elimination of hunger as it is known in the rest of Latin America (although since 1990 there have been severe food shortages), the defense of Angola against South Africa, and the sending of doctors to Ethiopia, Nicaragua and Mozambique. The Revolution is also the backing of the invasion of Czechoslovakia, censorship, the UMAP (internment camps in the mid-'60s), Mariel, and the Ochoa trial and execution.

Despite the revolution's failures the iconographic stamina of Fidel continues unabated, though a bit tarnished by recent events. His charisma is multifaceted to a degree rare with Latin American icons. We see many sides to Fidel: the sportsman, the avid reader, the economist, the politician, the passionate orator and conversationalist, the agronomist, the excellent cook, the investigator with a scientific curiosity. He projects a sense of humor, and displays the kind of audacity that Danton called for. (He was obsessed for many years in trying to find and breed a new strain of cattle for Cuba — maybe he's a cowmunist instead). There's one negative note: Fidel shows a very un-Cuban trait, he doesn't dance well. Could it be that his orisha has strayed from him?

But maybe this staying power is explained by nationalism, in his ability to embody the history and values of Cuban nationalism. In recent years we have seen how powerful both nationalism and religion can be, imbued as they are with such fierce irrationality, even though discursively they can often appeal to reason. Gorbachev learned it in a cruel manner, but Cuba is not beset by the same dilemma. Its nationalism is not internal in that it threatens to break up the territorial boundaries of the nation. On the contrary, it is a unifying force. But nationalism has its traps: when it becomes deformed, it elevates the particular into a universal that is abstract and rigid, without recognizing that people (a nation) evolve like an individual and that being Cuban is not something static (ecstatic, maybe) and eternal. You hear it said in Cuba that "We are not communists but Fidelistas," an unfortunate phrase since it belies an historical blindness, an analytical void and a metaphysical emptiness. It also is a startling admission of the failure to create an institutional framework for a democratic society. To have a true effectiveness, nationalism has to establish itself, fiercely construct its identity, but to avoid falling into an idealist illusion, it has to prepare its own disappearance. And there, the image of the icon and his role has to change, construct a new type of subjectivity, and not just retrench into the deformed identity that has resulted out of an endless struggle with Goliath.

A corollary of this irrationality (of nationalism joined to bureaucratic collectivism) is proclaiming the law to be superior to the human beings whose life it is supposed to govern. The movement of History or the tenets of the Class Struggle are what take precedence. It is impossible to distinguish between what is permissible and what is prohibited. Politics borders on theology. In a recent statement Fidel said: "If something dies [communism], it can also revive. Lazarus died and Christ said 'Rise up and walk'. Perhaps communism needs someone to say 'Rise up and walk'." Resurrection leads to insurrection. St. Augustine meets Rosa Luxemburg.

Episode Five: Good Guy Becomes Real and Tragedy Sets In

The majority of graphic representations of Fidel in Cuba show him as a hero, as a leader of mythic proportions. Raúl Martínez was one of the first who drew him as a pop icon, as he did with Che, and now there is a new generation of artists taking the images, symbols, and slogans of the Revolution and giving them new twists or criticizing them openly.

Carlos Rodríguez Cárdenas comes to mind. He is barely thirty, an artist born and raised in the revolution. His painting "Construir el cielo" (Building Heaven) from 1989 is a work that takes apart and recomposes one of the most famous slogans of the revolution. Its elements are simple: three hills or green mountains, an immense step-like, aqua-colored brick wall and a black background or sky. The wall is much bigger than the mountains. The slogan, in white letters, is over the black. The letters are like those of a cheap computer or calculator. There is an unrelenting play and commentary on nature and society, on utopia and conformity, the universal and the particular, on thought and action. It is a fertile, suggestive and polemical piece.

Or take Flavio Garciandía, with his installation that questions the hammer and sickle as sign. He submits it to various interpretations: decorative, blasphemous, symbolic, and thus he examines the relationship between the esthetic image and the political image and the danger of having both become empty and docile.

"Construir el cielo" (Building heaven) by Carlos Rodríguez Cardenas, 1989.

Another artist, Alejandro Aguilera, has an installation with photos of Fidel when he was a prisoner on the Isle of Pines (after the aborted Moncada Barracks attack). Underneath the photos you see his prisoner number. Aguilera skillfully touches on the question of power, demystifying Fidel (as figure of power) in a way that reminds me of Nicolás Guillén's poem "I Said I Was Not a Pure Man." Rejecting the "purity" of clerics, grammarians, academics, and those who don't like to get their hands dirty. Guillén speaks about being a frail creature, one who likes to drink rum and fornicate on a full stomach; Aguilera, in showing us Fidel Castro as a political prisoner, beams back an astonishing reversal: someone who now wields such great power was at one time persecuted, suffering at the hands of a vile and corrupt government. Nothing is more humble or humiliating than being a prisoner. Aguilera has given us a flesh and blood Fidel, an "impure" man, as Guillén would say.

Here we can say that the image of Fidel starts to embody the idea of tragedy as Raymond Williams defined it in *Modern Tragedy*: as something linked to social crisis, to revolution. It is born to redeem humanity, but it is also born of pity and terror. And "it is born in the actual suffering of real men thus exposed, and in all the consequences of this suffering: degeneration, brutalization, fear, hatred, envy. It is born in an experience of evil made the more intolerable by the conviction that it is not inevitable, but is the result of particular actions and choices." The revolution has to be seen in its totality, i.e., the aspect of liberation and that of terror, and neither one cancels the other one out. They are inseparably linked and the fact that they *are linked* is what is incurably tragic.

This tragedy has manifested itself harshly with writers. This isn't the moment to go into detail about what has happened to people like Virgilio Piñera, Reinaldo Arenas, Heberto Padilla, and more recently to María Elena Cruz Varela and Jesús Díaz. In a talk given recently, Chilean fiction writer José Donoso commented on the erratic nature of censorship under a rightist-military regime, referring to his native country under Pinochet (1973–1990). He attributed it to the fact that since they were not intelligent, they despised anything artistic. In their zeal to maintain order, they attempt to flee the ideological realm by trying to abolish politics (it's a fantasy). On the other hand, communist regimes place great value on the cultural. Perhaps it's because they are hyper-ideologized societies (everything is political). Vaclav Havel underlines the importance of ideology since it is a bridge between reality (social and individual)

Images of Fidel. Top: Carlos Rodríguez Cardenas, "Las ideas llegan más lejos que la luz" (Ideas go farther than light), 1989. Bottom: a tabloid tribute to his revolutionary charisma, 1993.

and the needs of the system. As time goes by, the abyss between the two grows greater. Ideology functions as an element of legitimation and continuity in the lives of its citizens. Its importance grows even greater and its inflated value creates an absurdity: instead of ideology serving power, the opposite happens. One inhabits a world of appearances. That's why words become so important: they are used to quiet or tranquilize the population or they become thunderbolts, because telling the truth puts into question and shakes the whole apparatus, even the state. The word goes back to its origins: to found, create, name and liberate.

Episode Six: The Set is Turned Off

And if we journey to the source we understand that the incarnation of this tragedy is Ogún, orisha of war, employment and hospitals. He is the protector of those who work with iron (the militia), surgeons, and he is also supreme symbol of justice and overlooks all acts of violence and crime. For a period he lived in the forest (fed up with human folly and bloodshed) and it was Oshún, with her sensuality and ability to dance, who brought him out of the woods. In the case of Cuba, it was History that took on the form of Oshún. Maybe she has to bring out a different orisha now, hopefully Obatalá, creator of earth, sculptor of humans. She/he is said to rule the head, both thoughts and dreams, and procures harmony and peace. Obatalá is always sought out to resolve disputes because of his purity, her ability to mediate.

But the source, the seed, is traveled to from exile, another pole of tragedy brought on by revolution. Exile is a state of basic and insuperable sadness: it is an ontological, metaphysical, emotional distance and rarely will it be discharged into a crowd. But curiously, as Cioran said: "The more we are dispossessed, the more intense our appetites and illusions become." It heightens the senses to the point where it shatters boundaries.

It also affects your vision. In your adopted land the contours of everything become unreal, which only its crushing familiarity can ameliorate. The options are not enticing: nostalgia is an exercise in freezing time (only possible through the amorous embrace) where you can remain in an endless state of grief. Sooner or later this leads you to desperation or idiocy. Forgetting is a little more pleasant than self-mutilation and, in time, will spill over or burst, spraying about with even greater cruelty all the little pieces of a fragmented self. And there's the state of permanent translation, which sounds more like some kind of linguistic Trotskyism, which quivers between panic and a kind of hunger that devours itself in mirages. What is to be done? Invent, as Rushdie says, imaginary homelands, with scraps of what we're left with: memories, smells, streets which go on endlessly, winds which blow over scar and scorn like a voice made of smoke and resurrections?

Wallace Stevens used to say that exile was a spiritual state like winter: the passionate memory of summer and fall and the hope that comes with spring are always near, but unreachable. Exile doesn't have the rhythm of the seasons, but in another dimension: myth, pain, distance, and image.

But there is something positive to be gained: a consciousness of counterpoint (but not of tobacco and sugar); a fugue starts to be crafted with several cultures, more than one kind of dream, with a wider vision. Maybe that's why I can imagine Fidel as painted by Portocarrero (birds and flowers coming out of his beard), or Mendive (a huge cowrie shell with Changó's hatchet), or Miró (his face and uniform turned into squiggly lines), or Botero (a ponderous Fidel holding a lobster in his hand). As I mold him into shapes and colors I see him as persecuted and prosecutor, as hope and desperation, as rigidity and flexibility, as myth and history. That is, I can cipher and decipher Fidel Castro much easier than I can myself, because he is the image of that distance that I recreate and try to abolish with words, like Obatalá scratching life into clumps of earth with a snail.

Lejanía means distance, expanse, remoteness, with a dose of longing. *Lejaniá* is looking at the sweet movement of the *mariwó* skirt of Ogún, and knowing that movement is a counterpoint: a constant remembering and a suppressing of what can't be said. And to know that it is a mask that gnaws and digests shipwrecks and reconquests; that it is a change in the tide that brings hidden cowrie shells and not a delirium of monuments.

José Martí said that poetry was *lejanía*. It's important to add that poetry might be one of the few ways of mending that distance, a different kind of discharge that evolves into a kind of constellation which would recover that collapsing star of mutilated bodies that overcrowd history.

Lejaniá could be the beginning of a bridge, even if it flows into the intoxication of solitude or art. *Lejanía* always sings like a pine tree in the night.

REINA MARÍA RODRÍGUEZ

THE ISLANDS

watch and don't be careless with them.
islands are apparent worlds.
cut out from the sea
they live the solitude of lands without roots.
in the silence of the water a stain
from having dropped anchor only that time
and left behind the wreckage of tempests and squalls
on the waves.
here the cemeteries are lovely and small
and ceremonies forsaken.
I've been bathing and now sit on the grass
this is the foggy zone
where there are mirages
and I smile again.
are you here or am I in danger
I begin to be free within those interchangeable limits:
the dawn will return.
islands are apparent worlds
bedspreads of weariness covering those who'd bring calmness
I know that my own thoughts were all that was real
an interval between two times
cut out from the sea
I'm the spear thrust toward a more tenuous place
where girls grow young again
disregarding the wisdom and rigidity of those who've aged
unaware of the movements and contortions of the sea
islands are apparent worlds salt stains
another woman I don't know thrusting herself at me

only a minor life
the gratitude that never hurries of the islands in me.

From Arsenio Cicero Cristobal, ed., Poemas Transitorios: *Antología de
Nuevos Poetas Cubanos* (Mérida, Spain: Ediciones Mucuglifo, 1992).

LETTER TO A WOMAN FRIEND

Marilyn   in this city there are lots of men
infinite numbers of men   colossal
magnificent   giant.   we have them made of stone
and also   of course   of flesh.
I don't know how to look at them and they don't see me
they don't even suspect that I touch them
undress them   but
they've got cars   suitcases
or they're in a hurry.
they don't know how much I suffer
because the one I want might get confused
and pass by forever   unnoticed.
don't laugh   I'm going to step out with a sign
discreetly   in various languages
I'll hang it from my heart
with serpents and lights:
THE WOMAN YOU SEARCH FOR IS ME
(a peddler of watches
in the middle of the desert).

Translated by Ruth Behar

From Reina María Rodríguez, *Para un cordero blanco* (Havana: Casa de las
Américas, 1984)

AMANDO FERNÁNDEZ

EL FUEGO

A glare enters through the window.
Es un Fuego. There is a fire.
The houses around you are burning.
The neighborhood burns.

Escuchas unos gritos. Sales a observar.

You hear screams coming closer.
You come out the door to observe.

A man brings a child in his arms.
He leaves him in your front steps; and flees.
Another man comes out from a blazing building.
After some confused steps, he falls.

Un hombre trae a un niño.

A woman passes by.
She covers her eyes with her hand.
Una mujer pasa. No quiere ver.
She doesn't want to see.

You call her name; but she does not answer.

The fire reaches some nearby trees.
It consumes them.
The wind blows and makes swirls.
It drags the ashes.

Some men approach.
They are dressed in brilliant colors.

They grab the child's body
and enter your house.
There, they place it over a table.
They cut it into pieces.

Lo cortan en pedazos.

One of the men turns to you.
He offers you a bleeding fragment
of the child and tells you:
"Come; es su carne."
Without a doubt, you eat.

The taste in your mouth is sweet.
Then, you swallow it
and it turns bitter in your entrails.
It burns you.

Es amargo, y te quema;

Outside, the fire explodes. You hear its fury.
It reaches your house and engulfs it.
Te envuelve.

You think of the island.

Ah, tú piensas en la isla.

"Woman Who Waits," overlooking plaza where Jewish peddlers used to sell in Old Havana, December, 1991. Photo by Ruth Behar.

RUTH BEHAR

QUEER TIMES IN CUBA

Niurka takes my sweaty palm into her own beautifully manicured hands and together the two of us push through the crowd. Gracefully, she weaves us both around to the center of the Cine Chaplin and we leap upon two perfect seats facing the screen. In the blink of an eye, every seat around us fills up. Suddenly, someone yells, "Get up, old guy, don't you see that seat isn't yours?" Hundreds of people stop their conversations to watch and listen. "¡Mira, una bronca!" someone says. The man in the seat refuses to budge. "He took the girlfriend's seat! What nerve! Look at the poor woman standing there," a vehement voice exclaims.

"The show has already begun," Niurka says to me, laughing. The audience becomes an instant jury and concludes that the man has unjustly claimed his seat. "Stand up! Stand up! That seat isn't yours!" people yell out to him from all over the theater. A policeman arrives on the scene and before he's had a chance to say a word, the man reluctantly gets up. People applaud. There's a sense of giddy excitement in the air that feels as wild as kids getting out of a long day at school. Niurka and I also feel liberated. We've both left behind our husbands and children. Rey, the owner of a cerulean blue 1956 Chevy with red upholstered seating, whom I've hired with dollars to drive me around Havana, waits for us outside the theater. When the movie is out, he'll return us to our families, waiting in Niurka's neighborhood in Miramar.

While we wait for the film to begin, I realize how strange are the turns of destiny, immigration, and reunion which have brought me, a white Cuban-born woman, and Niurka, a black Cuban-born woman, together to the movies. Niurka is the daughter-in-law of Caro, the black woman who was nanny to my brother and me until we left Cuba in 1961 when I was four and a half years old. When I first returned to Cuba in 1979, I feared that Caro would not want to see me, that she'd view me as a middle-class white girl to whom she'd turn her back in a gesture of defiant revolutionary pride. Instead, Caro welcomed me and told her entire Miramar neighborhood about me. In that once posh neighborhood of suburban houses and three-storey apartment buildings, where today blacks and whites live next door to one another, I am known as *la hija de Caro*, as Caro's daughter. Caro's twin sons Paco and Paquín and her daughter Adriana, who are only a few years younger than me, also treat me with affection. Our mutual trust transcends race and class boundaries, even if we don't forget that those boundaries have everything to do with my position as the one who comes and goes and their position as the ones who wait for me to return. Thanks to Caro and her family, returning to Cuba has become for me an act of faith in the possibilities of spiritual kinship. Since none of my blood relatives remain in Cuba, Caro's family is my only family on the island now.

Being with Caro and her family I come to understand that what I lost in being exiled from Cuba as a child was the everyday contact with black Cubans. Like other white Cubans who came to the United States as young children, I grew up with a raceless image of Cuban culture, a bleached-out version of the culture, listening to Beny Moré, Pérez Prado, and Celia Cruz, but not knowing they were black. I grew up not being able to have intellectual discussions with black Cubans like Paco and Paquín, who spend much of their time arguing heatedly about the pros and cons of capitalism and communism.

With Niurka, a lawyer and committed Communist Party member, there is the deep bond that comes from feeling you have found a soul sister you never expected to find. I first met Niurka in 1991 on the day she returned from a two-week stint doing volunteer labor gathering tomatoes in the countryside. I'd heard she was a Party member and imagined she'd be grim and humorless, attired in baggy pants and shapeless workshirt. Niurka, it turned out, was stunningly beautiful and vivacious. She wore a tight tee-shirt and very short shorts. In her hands she carried a bunch of ripe fruity tomatoes, which she happily passed around, as if she were distributing party favors. Her long nails were painted bright pink. She didn't despise me, as I'd feared she would. From the start, she engaged me in intense conversation. That very same night, while we talked and compared notes about our lives, she sat in the patio of her neighbor's house having her hair dyed black because she said she'd gotten too much sun out in the fields. Like me, Niurka is a vain woman, an ambitious woman. Like me, she has chosen to only have one child. Like me, she thought nothing of telling her husband to watch their child as we took off for the movies.

It is December 11, 1993, the last day of the Latin American Film Festival in Havana, and we are about to see *Fresa y chocolate* ("Strawberry and Chocolate"). Directed by Tomás Gutiérrez Alea, who in the early 1960s defined another key moment in Cuban history with his film *Memorias del subdesarrollo* (Memories of Underdevelopment), and Juan Carlos Tabío, *Fresa y chocolate* has drawn huge crowds and won a string of prizes, including best film, at the Festival. The writer Senel Paz, on whose prize-winning story "The Wolf, the Forest, and the New Man" (1991) the film is based, has also written the screenplay, which portrays the unlikely friendship of two men — Diego, an outspoken gay art critic, and David, a young, sexually repressed, Communist activist.

As the film begins, Niurka squeezes my elbow. "That's a *posada*," she explains. "Where couples go to have sex. They pay by the hour. People don't have enough privacy in their own houses, so they go there." David is with his girlfriend, who chastises him for bringing her to such a rundown place. "Sex is all you want from me," she says. While she goes to the bathroom, sweet-faced David looks through a peephole in the room and sees a woman screaming as she reaches her climax. His girlfriend returns, naked and ready, but he tells her he'll wait until they're married. Next scene we see her getting married, but not to David. Niurka whispers into my ear, "She's chosen a bureaucrat, someone who will make it possible for her to live well and to travel. She's not marrying for love." Disappointed, David looks on, reduced once again to being a voyeur. It is after this failed heterosexual romance that Diego enters David's life.

"Look, that's Coppelia," Niurka tells me, as the film moves to the famous ice-cream parlor in the park in the Vedado section of Havana. Diego and Germán, a gay artist friend, decide to play a joke on David. Diego flamboyantly joins David at his table and when David stands up to leave he discovers that the only other available table has been taken by Germán. With disgust, David watches as Diego savors his strawberry ice-cream, which he's chosen over chocolate. Seductively, Diego tells David about the books, including some that are forbidden and unavailable (by Vargas Llosa and Cabrera Infante), which he could lend him at his apartment. David follows along, mainly out of a sense of revolutionary duty. He finds Diego a politically suspicious character and plans to gather more facts to be able to report on him.

Instead, as the story unfolds, David finds himself increasingly attracted to Diego as a friend and mentor. David, from a rural *campesino* background, feels he owes the privilege of his Havana education to the revolution. But it is Diego who truly teaches him about his own Cubanness, introducing him to such classical figures of Cuban literary and artistic culture as the writer José Lezama Lima and the composer Ernesto Lecuona (both of whom were gay), as well as to the popular Catholicism and Santería that became taboo in a secular Communist state. David gradually comes to understand Diego's gayness and to appreciate and even admire his political outspokenness. For, indeed, Diego's gender subversion is inseparable from his political subversion. Diego, in turn, who'd made a bet with his friend Germán that he would get David into his bed, ceases to view David as merely the object of his frustrated desire and begins to love him enough that he fears he has tarnished the innocence of his once homophobic friend. As the movie comes to a close, Diego, who kept from David the knowledge of his decision to leave Cuba, finally announces, "I can't stay, there's nothing left for me here," and asks David to please hug him goodbye. A hug representing no demands of any kind; a hug of forgiveness, friendship, redemption, and hope.

With that last hug, the audience of the Cine Chaplin rises and applauds. As we leave the theater, no one pushes anymore. Outside, Niurka and I find Rey just waking up from his nap in the backseat. "How was it?" he asks. "Excellent," Niurka responds. "It was full of truths that needed to be expressed." Rey nods his head. "Exactly what my wife said."

*

Fresa y chocolate is an end-of-century Cuban film responding to the way manhood and nationhood, in the figure of the revolutionary hero, became inextricably connected after the 1959 triumph of the revolution. In his *Education and the New Man*, Che Guevara wrote of the revolutionary as a man guided by the sentiment of love for the people, a man dedicated entirely to the revolutionary cause, a man who wouldn't allow his mind to be distracted by trivial matters, such as whether his children had holes in their shoes. There is only one specific mention of women in El Che's text, and it is cast in the language of abjection—women's role, he says, ought to be one of sacrifice to help the revolution come to fruition.

Cuba, as a colony of the United States, was an emasculated nation. Redeeming the Cuban nation required the creation not so much of a new woman but a new man. Nothing threatened the utopia of new men more than homosexuality. As they left the port of Mariel in 1980, gay men were shouted down with the words, *"¡Que se vaya la escoria, que se vayan los homosexuales!"* (Leave scum, leave homosexuals!) And yet because this homophobia was so terribly conscious, so terribly out of the closet, it also left deep scars in the revolutionary psyche.

Fresa y chocolate is a meditation on the cruel cultural dynamics that defined that historical moment, opening the door for necessary, and cathartic, remembering. Given the legacy of the manhood-nationhood equation, it is no accident that *Fresa y chocolate* focuses on the complexities of male identity as they emerge in the friendship of a gay critic of the revolution and a young revolutionary. Racial exclusions are revealed by the fact that the two key male protagonists are white, and that the only black character in the film is a *santero* who remains speechless. The gay critic and the revolutionary are imagined as separate, not as one and the same person, and their male-to-male reconciliation, to the virtual exclusion of women and blacks (definitely so in the original story version, partially so in the film version), is presented as the central reconciliation needed to heal the wounds of the divided nation. Ultimately, too, Diego leaves, suggesting there is not yet a place for the outspoken queer in the Cuban nation. Lesbianism, an even more taboo subject in Cuba, is not even alluded to in the film.

Despite these limitations, Diego and David are so humanely evoked that other identifications become possible, so that I, seeing the film with Niurka, come to understand how the two of us represent another kind of dyad: the white bourgeois Cuban-American woman who returns searching for bridges to her native land with dollars in her pocket, the black revolutionary Cuban woman who takes it upon herself to reassure the girl-child whose parents took her out of Cuba that she can still return to the home she left behind.

*

While the acceptance of homosexuality is the central theme of *Fresa y chocolate*, both Tomás Gutiérrez Alea and Senel Paz have declared that they didn't intend to make a gay film. As films like *Paris is Burning*, *The Crying Game*, and *Farewell My Concubine* have lately shown, homosexuality has become a favored window for revealing the tensions of social, historical, and national transformations in a new, "queer," way. By making a socially rejected gay man a popular hero, Gutiérrez Alea and Paz seek to create, they say, a new awareness about the need for greater tolerance of difference on all levels of Cuban society. But why, I wonder, do they insist on emphasizing that they are approaching queerness as a metaphor rather than a reality?

I, also a heterosexual, was pondering this question on the eve of the new year as I made my way to the feminist, lesbian, and gay bookstore in Ann Arbor. For days I'd been feeling "queer," as I always do when I return from Cuba, at seeing once again the lavish overabundance of goods in supermarkets, shopping malls, and store windows. In Cuba I handed out gifts of Ivory soap and economy-size bottles of shampoo, Bic pens and pads of yellow legal paper, aspirin and vitamins, blouses and underwear, and Barbie dolls (bought by my mother) for the daughters of Niurka and Adriana. I'd played the Santa Claus role that intellectuals on the island find so reprehensible. But I selfishly hoarded a box of saltine crackers, just in case some unforeseeable shortage struck, and ended up bringing it home, unopened. Now I couldn't eat a single cracker from that box.

Something drew me to want to end the year at Common Language Bookstore, gazing at the shelves of books on gay and lesbian history, literature, and erotica, and the field called "queer theory." To my surprise (I almost felt as if I were entering the movie set of an Ann Arbor-based "Strawberry and Chocolate"), on top of the shelf of gay and lesbian poetry I spotted two loose paperback copies of Fidel Castro's recent speeches in English translation. The bookstore owners hadn't figured out yet in what category they belonged. What would Fidel think, I wondered, of the company his speeches were keeping?

Making my purchases of poetry and fiction books, I wanted to say something to the owner to acknowledge my appreciation for her bookstore, but couldn't find the words. She handed me the books and wished me a happy new year and I wished her the same. Stepping out the front door, I looked back wistfully. I think I wanted to find Diego.

*

Actually, *Fresa y chocolate* has made me realize that in the United States I know a Diego, a painter I met in Cuba who left the island via Spain a year ago and now lives in Miami. Back home, his parents, committed members of the Communist party, continue to tell people their son is in Spain and expects to return. This Diego tells me about going to Disneyland with some friends and finding himself the only one in the crowd unable to play along and shake Mickey Mouse's hand. He says he just stood there, analyzing Mickey Mouse as a figure of the capitalist system and wishing his fantasy life were not so controlled by Marxist criticism. And yet later, in a more rhapsodical mood, he says he misses the *pobreza repartida*, the shared poverty, among his friends in Cuba, which gave them the time and the space to spend nights together lost in conversation, drinking tea made from garden herbs. In Miami, everyone is always rushing somewhere, always comparing notes to see who's exhibiting in the best galleries and who's not making it. Paints are available in every imaginable color, he tells me, if you can afford them. He's having trouble selling his work and peddles jewelry part-time to make ends meet, news which he hopes will never find its way back to Cuba. At least he's not hungry, he says, remembering how in Spain he had to be rushed to the hospital the first time he ate a large meal. Here he's put on thirty pounds. . . . How quickly, he says sadly, the reality of Cuba starts to fade and becomes memory. From Cuba a friend writes him a letter coated with wax drippings from the candle he uses to light up his house during blackouts. After a while, the letter becomes unintelligible, unreadable, a cryptic work of art.

But there are Diegos, too, who have the opportunity to leave Cuba and choose to stay. Looking out over the foggy port city from the circle of windows on the 25th floor of La Habana Libre Hotel (recently purchased by a Spaniard and renamed Guitart), I'm having breakfast with Abilio Estévez, a talented writer of my generation. "This," he says, "this amazing city is what I came back for." I dig into a thick cheese omelette made on the spot by a short-order cook. My friend only eats a little bread and a banana, fearing that overly rich food will upset his stomach, which has grown accustomed to the leaner diet of the "special period," as this time of economic crisis is officially known in Cuba. But he prefers to speak of a more profound crisis, the crisis of social values that tourism, prostitution, and the quest for dollars have engendered as the government scrambles for hard currency in the wake of the dissolution of the Soviet Union. Still, he says he doesn't want to live anywhere but in Havana. He's too old, he adds with a chuckle, to start over as a Latino in the United States.

While in the United States last year on a speaking tour, some of his contacts became furious when he declared he wasn't planning to defect. They told him they'd worked hard to get the invitation for him and found his desire to return to the island absurd. It seemed absurd to him, in turn, that the condition for his visiting the United States was for him not to return to Cuba. "Wouldn't you be shocked," he asked me, "if I invited you to present your work here and then said, thank you very much, you're here to stay?" (I nodded but didn't tell him that this, precisely, is the paranoid fear that obsesses Cuban-Americans who return to visit the island.) His most heartbreaking moment, he recalls, was meeting a gay Cuban-American writer in New York who's not been able to secure a visa to return to the island for a visit. The man cried at their first encounter, repeating over and over that he wished he'd never left Cuba.

At the same time, my friend speaks of the other exile, the exile of those who stay in the island, watching as everyone departs. After a while, he says, your wrist gets tired of waving goodbye. And writing, at a time of blackouts and shortages, is nothing less than heroic. He lives in a small wooden house with his mother and sister's family. Although they accept his gay identity and gay friends, the only space he can call his own is his bedroom, which also functions as his study, where a Mona Lisa sign cautions, "Sadness is Prohibited." He writes on the back of manuscript pages rejected by Cuban publishers. "But I'll stay. I won't abandon this country. No matter how hard it gets." He pauses and peers into my eyes through his wire-rimmed glasses. "This country is you and me sitting here. You left as a child because your parents made the decision to leave. I stayed because my parents made the decision to remain. The only difference between us is that you have dollars and I don't, so I can't invite you to breakfast."

*

Cinema in Cuba after the revolution became a touchstone for public discourse, and there is no question that the mutual recognition of Diego and David represents the possibility of many reconciliations, including national reconciliation between those who left and those who stayed. The current joke about *gusanos*, the exiles who were called "worms" because they abandoned the revolution, is that they're no longer *traidores* ("traitors") but *traedólares* ("dollarbringers"). With the growing dependence on dollars as the primary form of currency in Cuba, immigrants in the United States who send money to their relatives back on the island could potentially boost, even bolster, the economy, as is the case with remunerations sent home by Overseas Chinese or Mexican-Americans. According to *Newsweek*, remittances from abroad exceed $500 million, about one fourth of all the hard currency Cuba will earn this year. Dollars now bear the nickname "Elegguá," after the Santería god that opens paths.

A special dispensation has always been granted those of us who left the island as children and returned in search of political engagement while holding back our criticisms. But lately the attitude toward adults who left in the early years of the Revolution, and even as late as the Mariel boatlift, has also softened. When I returned to Cuba in February the plane was full of "Marielitos," and more than a few Diegos, most of whom left as young men just hitting their twenties and haven't seen their families since; many of those returning had eggs thrown at them when they left in 1980. One of the Diegos I spoke to, who now owns a Mexican restaurant in Chicago, says he refuses to be bitter, life is too short, and Cuba is more than its politics. He'd packed his bags with nail polish and lipstick for his sister, toys for her children, whom he didn't yet know, and clothes for his mother. For himself, he'd only brought two tee-shirts and the pair of pants he was wearing. "I'm not going to show off with my own family," he said.

From the island side, the desperate need for dollars to reinforce a faltering economy has a good deal to do with the acceptance of those million of us who now make up the Cuban diaspora and aren't openly hostile. But only the worst cynic would argue that dollars are the only reason that everyone in Cuba is reaching out toward exiles. During this "Strawberry and Chocolate" time, Cubans on the island are needing to redefine who they (and we on the outside) are as a people, and in the process their sense of nationhood is shifting and expanding. They want to make room for Diego. And for many others whom they once rejected. It is a moment of opportunism, yes. But also of vulnerability. Of tenderness.

While I'm in Havana in December I receive a late-night phone call from a man who went to school with my father. He's just heard from his brother that I'm visiting and wants to meet me. Could he come over immediately to the hotel lobby? I say yes and find myself a few minutes later in the company of a tall, thin, soft-spoken man in a fine wool yellow cardigan. He refuses to allow me to buy him a drink, though half way into our conversation he says he's very embarrassed but could I get him a pack of cigarettes? Like my father, he's of Turkish Sephardic background and had to go to night school so he could work days to support his family. After the revolution, he became an economist and has traveled widely, including to Vietnam, as an agricultural expert. He remembers he got his first hangover at my father's bachelor party. And he remembers how a few years later he attended a meeting of the Sephardic community at the Union Hebrea Chevet Ahim, where there were three categories of people — those who had fixed their date of departure, those who had their visas but didn't yet know when they'd be leaving, and those who had just filed their immigration papers. He said he'd never felt so alone. He'd decided to stay in Cuba because he believed the revolution would better people's lives. Was that such a futile hope? Is that a reason to feel sorry for himself?

Stopping to puff on a Marlboro, he catches my eye and tells me I have the same profile as my father's sister. "You know," he says, "Years ago, when I saw all those people leaving, I thought I'd never want to see any of them again. And then I heard you were here, the daughter of Alberto Behar, and I couldn't help myself, I needed to see you right away." His eyes start to water. "Tell me about your father. What's he been up to?" I tell him he works as a Latin American representative for a textile company in New York. That he's successful. That he's traveled a lot. That he's been a tourist in Hong Kong, Athens, Cancun, Istanbul, and even Leningrad. That he and my mother don't really like the fact that I visit Cuba. That they tell me there's no reason for me to want to go back. That my father is often at odds with me. That we often argue about Cuba. That he often won't talk to me. . . . But tell me, I say, what message would he like me to relay to my father? He smiles. "Tell him to come for a visit. To come on a tourist package." He's shocked when I tell him that because of the blockade it's illegal in the United States to visit Cuba as a tourist. "Well, then, tell him to come however he can. Tell your father we're not going to eat him."

*

The Coppelia ice-cream parlor of *Fresa y chocolate* takes on a poignant set of meanings for me when I learn that our neighbors in the Vedado apartment building where we used to live are having a couple of scoops of ice-cream for breakfast every day for lack of milk. Despite the hard times, they insist on preparing a fancy dinner for us. But you have to let us know a day in advance, okay? So we can get everything. What do you prefer, pork chops or lobster? I tell them that rice and beans are really fine, that at home we eat neither pork nor lobster. They don't believe me. That can't be true. They insist I choose. So I take the lobster. Are you sure this won't be too much of a sacrifice, I ask, a few too many times. I'd be happy to take everyone out to dinner, I say. Her green eyes ablaze, Consuelito responds, "So it's alright for you to sacrifice yourself to come here and we're not allowed to reciprocate?" To remember is to live, she says, and gives me the swizzle sticks she's saved from the 1959 New Year's party at the Hotel Riviera. Keep two for yourself and give two to your mother. Ask her if she remembers how happily we spent that night. . . . Christie, my counterpart, a white woman like me of middle-class origins, puts a topaz stone into my hand when she learns that we share the same astrological sign. Make a ring for yourself, Rutie, she says, so you'll remember me. . . . In the two-bedroom apartment with the pink bathroom tiles that is a mirror image of the one I grew up in, I eat lobster in a creole sauce with rice and fried green bananas. It all tastes strangely delicious. The lobster is a touch salty, seasoned with old memories and farewell tears.

*

Hoping it would offer me a way to reconcile my Cuban and Jewish identity, I went to the island in December with a group organized by Eddy Levy of Miami, who founded Jewish Solidarity to bring humanitarian aid to the remaining one-thousand Jews of Cuba. Most of the fifteen thousand Jews who fled Cuba after the revolution and settled in New York and Miami had never challenged the dominant don't-look-back attitude toward Cuba. Although they prospered in the United States, they lacked the courage to send even one box of matzoh to Cuba. Judaism has been kept alive in Cuba through the efforts of Jews in Canada, Mexico, and Argentina.

Yet Eddy Levy's plea for help for the remaining Jews of Cuba touched a nerve in the Jewish Cuban-American community. Oddly, it took a man gone blind from retinitis to offer a more generous vision of the possibilities for connection among those Jews who left and those who stayed in Cuba. Jewish solidarity took off in Miami this past October with Xiomara Levy, Eddy's wife, overseeing all the legal and business aspects. When we departed on December 8 donations had been obtained to bring a ton of powdered milk to the Jews of Cuba as well as canned foods, medicine, office supplies, and Hebrew books. Boxloads of toys were collected both for pediatric hospitals in Havana and for Hanukkah celebrations. Many Jewish Cuban-Americans in Miami gave generously, though quietly, toward this relief effort. Each box he lifted, said Eddy Levy, reminded him of his immigrant Sephardic father, a peddler of whom he had been ashamed as a young boy.

Among those who formed part of the twenty-five member group were several Jewish Cuban-American women returning to the island for the first time. Some of these women left behind husbands in Miami who still feel wary about setting foot in the island that North American journalists like to dub Castro's Cuba. In returning to Cuba, they had to confront, as do all immigrants who go home again, their traumas about having left behind a part of themselves, of their lives, which they will never again recover. At the same time, they had to confront the reality of contemporary Cuba and the fact that they are now foreigners in their own country; at best, they are kindly "cousins" trying to aid their poorer Jewish kinfolk, many of whom are part-Jewish, or married to non-Jews, or recently converted.

On its five-day visit, the group was torn between the desire to remember the dead and the need to understand the plight of the living. Our first morning we climbed into an air-conditioned bus, and were led by a Havanatur guide to the Ashkenazi and Sephardic cemeteries, located just outside of Havana in the rural town of Guanabacoa. One Sephardic woman draped herself over the graves of her parents and cried herself dry; her trip to Cuba began and ended at the cemetery.

The second morning we squeezed into a tourist van and made a series of visits to the homes of elderly Jews living in the crumbling old section of Havana. Upon opening the door, each received a plastic bag with a bar of soap, a roll of toilet paper, a bottle of shampoo, and a container of dried milk. For several members of the group, such charity seemed pitifully negligent, and when they saw that these visits were also being filmed, they chose not to leave the van. I was among those who gave in to anthropological curiosity and went to every house. Undoubtedly, our most disturbing encounter was with a disoriented old man who lives in a corner walk-up. He wore a grimy shirt and a banana hung from his pocket. Blinded by cataracts, he shuffled aimlessly around the house. As we said goodbye, he asked if Yom Kippur, the Jewish holiday of atonement celebrated in September, had already passed. For one of the women in the group, this was the epiphany of the trip.

For yet another woman, the most significant thing we did was join a Hanukkah party with the children at the Patronato synogague. Yet even then, there were uncomfortable moments. When the trays appeared filled with plates bearing one latke, a scoop of macaroni salad, a piece of matzoh, and a sliver of cake, people grabbed at them eagerly, only to be told that the members of our humanitarian group would be served first. Later, some of the congregants asked members of our group for money. Giving charity to those who'd swallowed their pride enough to beg, the group members came to realize just how much the Patronato as a symbol had changed. With its immense St. Louis style arch and lush velvet-seat auditorium, the Patronato had once been a symbol, for the rich Ashkenazi Jews who built it in the 1950s, of their success in establishing a secure and prosperous home in their New World island. They engraved their names in gold on placards, not knowing they were leaving behind memorials to their exile.

For years the Patronato was in a state of near abandonment, the pigeons praying for the thousands of Jews who'd left. But in the last three years the Patronato has been enjoying a renaissance. Judaism is being revived on the island just as American Jews begin to take notice of the existence of Cuban Jews. I'm continually hearing of another research or movie project about the remaining thousand Jews of the island. They've become a kind of exotic artifact — Castro's Jews, as they were dubbed in a *Hadassah Magazine* article. Yet the revival of Judaism has to be understood in the context of the growing tolerance of all religious practice in Cuba, made possible by the recent official acknowledgment that revolutionary commitment and religious observance can coexist in the same person without contradiction — just what Diego, amidst crucifixes and Santería offerings, told David.

*

As the Jewish Solidarity trip came to a close, arguments arose among the group members. An emergency meeting was called by Eddy and Xiomara Levy. There, in the splendidly renovated Hotel Sevilla, with its Andalucian courtyard and handpainted tiles, as the air-conditioning hummed and Xiomara Levy's hair conditioners stood quietly at attention on the dresser, people argued: What should be the first priority of Jewish Solidarity? Repair the cemeteries? Create a retirement home for the aged? Teach the children? It was impossible to reach a consensus. Most made vows simply to return. . . .

*

On their last night in Havana the Jewish Solidarity group went to the Tropicana Club. Was it snobby of me not to go? I understand that a free drink was also included in our tourist package.

*

My cousin Alma, a wealthy interior designer in Miami, was in the group too. Besides wanting to demonstrate her solidarity with her Jewish brethren on the island, she had another mission in going to Cuba. She needed to visit Tere. Tere, Caro's older sister, worked at the home of my aunt and uncle, caring for Alma until she left Cuba at the age of eighteen. Tere turned down marriage to stay beside Alma's brother Henry when he was dying of leukemia. After Henry's death, when my aunt steeped herself in volunteer work to forget her pain, it was Tere who mothered Alma. And after our family left for the United States, it was Tere who continued to visit Henry's grave at the Jewish cemetery in Guanabacoa.

Tere, a lean wisp of a woman, cried when she saw Alma. Baby blonde and plump-cheeked Alma didn't know how to begin to thank Tere. She gave Tere money, she gave Tere clothes, she gave Tere chocolate. Alma tried to describe her life in the United States — how she eats frozen yogurt for a midnight snack, rather than ice-cream, not to put on weight. Tere listened attentively. Then she asked questions about the entire family. There was no cousin, however distant, that Tere didn't remember. When Alma said goodbye, Tere said that seeing her again had been the biggest joy of her life.

*

When I returned to Havana for a week in February to participate in the International Book Fair, Christie insisted I accept three hundred Cuban pesos she'd saved up for me to buy books. How could I accept *her* money? It's a gift, she said, and though I know it's not worth anything compared to your dollars, I want you to have it. So I put Christie's money in my wallet. How odd I felt, carrying around those multicolored bills bearing pictures of José Martí, Camilo Cienfuegos, and Che Guevara. Sure enough, at the fair, they were selling books for pesos. You had to stand on long lines for them — especially to get books by recently vindicated writers like José Lezama Lima, Virgilio Piñera, and Severo Sarduy, or the newly reprinted works of Rómulo Lachatañeré on Santería and Afro-Cuban folklore (for which, later, some *santeros* were offering four and five times the price for them at the fair). They were selling books in dollars too. There was no line to get them. For Christie's sake I stood on two (not very long) lines to buy books in pesos, but afterwards I began to hear Ben Franklin shouting in my ear, "Time is money!" and bought in dollars. Bought time, not books, stuffing my woven cloth bag with all the hours and days I'd never recover in Cuba, no matter how often I returned.

*

Caro, Paco, Paquín, Niurka, and several of their neighbors come to hear me read at the book fair (Tere stayed behind to guard the house and the dollars Alma gave her). Few things have given me more joy than catching Caro's eye as I read aloud. She'd nod and smile and glance back lovingly. But when I finished she scolded me, because I'd cut the reading short, fearing I was taking too much time. Why did you rush, she said, no one was in a hurry. . . .

Niurka organized a neighborhood party for me, and there was food and cake and rum and music and dancing under the stars shining urgently in the long darkness of the night. I arranged transportation so that Consuelito could come with Christie and her husband. That was when I learned that Consuelito and Caro hadn't seen each other in decades. Our apartment across from Consuelito's, which my parents left to Caro, was taken from her almost immediately and she fought bitterly to get it back. Defeated and angry, Caro vowed never again to set foot in our old building in El Vedado. But that night Caro stood before Consuelito, the two of them forced to confront the pain of a past they preferred to forget, all because I'd returned, searching for a bridge, not content to leave well enough alone.

*

In late April I am again on a plane to Havana. So many trips to Cuba, my mother says, are you sure you won't get into trouble? I try not to absorb her nervousness; I have enough with my own nerves. I'm on my way to the conference on "La Nación y la Emigración," a dialogue organized by the Cuban government to discuss Cuba's relation to its diaspora and, many of us hope, open the way for the normalization of travel and cultural exchange in both directions. I'm nervous about going to Cuba on an expressly political mission. One critic calls the event "a fiesta with the tyrant." My name, along with those of other Cuban-American participants, has been printed in the *Miami Herald*, and when Alma tells me people have called to let her know that *they know* I'm going, I feel as if I've been outed. No more quiet bridging between the two sides. No more not quite here, not quite there. Mona Lisa smiles and from her mouth another bubble spurts, "Ambivalence is Prohibited."

In the short space of the half-hour plane flight, we're shown a skillfully-edited color video. There's the Hotel Comodoro in Miramar, where the 219 diaspora participants will be staying. There are the four male leaders with whom we'll have our dialogue. There are the convention facilities and the restaurant where we'll choose our meals from a deluxe buffet. There are the lush waterfalls, where bikini-clad women relax among the palm trees. There's a singer dressed all in white except for a red sash; she crosses herself before the Virgin and sings, *"Para todos los cubanos, que viva Changó!"* As the video winds down, I begin to understand that we're not returning to help build the revolution, as was true of the Antonio Maceo brigades in the late 1970s and early 1980s. We're coming back, those of us who have succeeded in business, politics and academics in the United States, for another kind of engagement with the island, where at best maybe we'll be a cross between tourist, folklorist, and capitalist with a conscience.

On our way to the hotel in an air-conditioned tour bus, we stop for a red light and end up side by side with a *tren-bus*, a truck pulling an extra long trailer, a grim Havana invention to deal with the gas shortages of this queer time. Everyone is squeezed together on the *tren-bus*. From my window I can see the beads of sweat forming on the brows of passengers. For a moment, stopped in traffic, the nation looks into the eyes of the diaspora as if into a mirror. An eternal moment, an ocean, separating us.

*

When we register for the conference, we're each given a name tag and a travel bag filled with tourist brochures that are populated by so many blonde white folks that you'd think Cuba was a Nordic country. At the start of the conference, Roberto Robaina, Cuba's minister of foreign relations and our host, announces that he's aware that some people question their use of the term "immigrant" to speak of those of us in the diaspora. In Miami, to call yourself an "immigrant" rather than an "exile" is to throw in the towel, not only in the sense of announcing that you think the current regime in Cuba is acceptable, but that you don't expect to ever return and form part of the Cuban nation. Robaina says they're using the term "immigrant" because they think it defines more accurately the status of a Cuban diaspora scattered among twenty-seven countries. Indeed, Cubans have come from far and wide for this conference, not only from all over the United States and Latin America, but from Russia, Rumania, Spain, Zimbabwe, and even Australia. Nevertheless, as María de los Angeles Torres noted in a *Miami Herald* essay this past May, the denial of the existence of "exiles" was quite a loaded political strategy.

Inside the convention hall, each of the four leaders speaks at length about the justice system, reconciliation, Cuban culture, the economy. All are adamant about the need to salvage, in the midst of the crisis, the social project of the revolution. Ricardo Alarcón, president of the Cuban National Assembly, holds up a copy of the Sunday magazine of the *Miami Herald*, the cover of which shows a homeless woman holding up a sign, "I will work for food." This, he says, is what Cuba will become if we fail to save the country. As his speech meanders to a close, he recounts a conversation with a farmer. Alarcón told the farmer he'd be speaking at this conference and asked if there was any message the farmer wanted him to relay to us. Just tell them, the farmer said, that I hope we'll never again have to use a banana plantation as our bathroom.

After each speech, there is time for questions and comments from the floor. A few people ask questions, but most of the "immigrants" are obsessed with the need to assert the strength of their bond with this nation in which they no longer reside. They are, by turns, eloquent, righteous, apologetic, bombastic, and sentimental. Many of the respondents take up, in one way or another, the point made by Alarcón's farmer. Says one Cuban-American, "We don't want to return as *conquistadores*, to auction off the island. No one's planning to send anyone to the banana planations." Another says, "You tell that farmer that all of us present here, even though we live abroad, have never been able to forget this island, and that none of us want anyone here to return to how things were in the past." A Cuban living in Argentina says, "I don't come to drink a *mojito* in a comfortable hotel. We want to be part of the changes taking place in this country. We want to know how we can be useful. We've not come here to exhibit our dollars!" The Cuban-American daughter of two illustrious exiled Cuban families says, "I want to know how I can become a member of the Cuban Communist Party! Fatherland or Death — and that's not for sale in any tourist shop!" A Cuban living in Romania says, "The Cuban people have never gotten down on their knees and never will!" A Cuban living in Zimbabwe says, "It would be better to stop being, than to stop being Cuban!" And most heartbreakingly, there is the Cuban, I don't know from where, who says, "We've had enough wars and hatreds. I come in the name of my son Ariel. 'Papá, I don't want to leave,' he said. No sooner did we arrive in the new country than our boy was killed in a motorcycle accident. He'd only just turned five. . . ."

Throughout all of this, when we think he's not there, Fidel, they say, is watching us on video from the Palace of the Revolution.

*

The day before the conference began was the birthday of the twins, Paco and Paquín. I hadn't remembered. But on this visit, fortunately, I'd decided to leave behind the vitamins and bring Pepperidge Farm cookies, so I was able to give each of them a package of chocolate cookies as a birthday gift. And then, as if life were a movie, Caro offered me strawberries — tiny, bruised ones that she'd brought back from her hometown south of Havana. How strange. Just two days before I'd sat in my Ann Arbor kitchen with my son Gabriel eating obese, watery strawberries from our local supermarket. I'd noted how huge yet tasteless they were. Caro's strawberries were so tart they stung my tongue. I could only eat two of them. When I was done, Caro took the stems from my hand to her hand.

*

In April, Consuelito is sad. Her granddaughter, Mónica, has just been told that even though her grades are good, there are only six positions available for those who want to study at the University of Havana. Her choices are to study chemistry at a school far away in the countryside, and only be able to come home once a month, or study gastronomy or tourism in the city. Mónica decides to try gastronomy. When she returns home, Consuelito asks Mónica what she learned. Mónica says she learned how to set tables and fold napkins. The next day, at the Hotel Comodoro, I notice how neatly the tables are set and the napkins folded, and how quickly, almost maniacally, the waiters jump to fix things when they've been disturbed. Raising a napkin to my mouth, I leave a kiss for Mónica's lost illusions. (And three months later I learn, happily, that she's going to study chemistry, after all).

*

In April, Abilio is also sad. He's recently turned forty and broken up with his young partner. But that's not what's making him sad. He's writing, he says, writing incessantly, but something is missing. He no longer knows what he's looking forward to. He still says he'll never leave Havana, no matter what, but he needs to get out for just a month or two, to come up for air. There's a nervous twitch low in his gut, he tells me, and it won't go away. This time, at breakfast at the Hotel Comodoro, he eats more lavishly than he did in December, and doesn't object when I pack up a few pastries from the buffet for him to bring home to his mother.

*

On the last afternoon of the three-day conference, the moderator announces that El Comandante will host a reception for us at the national palace. Although most of the participants start clapping and cheering, I can't believe how queasy I start to feel. Can I go, will I go, shake hands with Him, plant a kiss on His cheek? I haven't yet made up my mind when, at lunch, a friend asks me point-blank if I'm going. Buoyantly, I reply that I want nothing more than to be able to go as an anthropologist and with detachment look into the eye of this man, this myth of a man. But—and as my voice breaks I remember how terrible my arguments with my authoritarian father have always been and how much worse things have gotten between us, as I struggle even now, a woman who in two years will turn forty, to assert my independence, and I think, can I give my hand, my lips, to a yet more stern Father? But those words don't come out of my mouth. I hear myself saying, instead, "Out of respect for my parents, I can't go. . . ." For my parents, yes. For my father, too. All the tears I've been holding back are eddying fiercely in my eyes, but I only allow one drop, a crystal sharp as glass, to fall into my palm.

*

It isn't until I return to Miami three days later and receive police escort to disembark the plane that I learn about the video. My first reaction, though, at seeing the muscular policemen is to panic and think my mother is right, the FBI has finally caught up with me.

The morning after the conference someone in Castro's inner circle, with or without permission, released a twelve-minute video excerpt of what had been a two-hour-long reception. At first it sold for $700, then the price came down. Immediately, those twelve minutes, showing exiles, as Miami journalist Liz Balmaseda put it, "groveling before Castro," were beamed on Miami TV. Over and over and over, the clips were shown, until they became a maddening litany, unleashing hatred and rancor in the exile community against those who'd gone to the conference.

Nothing in the days and weeks following the conference commanded as much obsessive media attention as the sight of Miami attorney Magda Montiel Davis kissing Fidel Castro, coquettishly shimmying her shoulders, and saying, "Thank you for what you've done for my people. You have been a great teacher for me." There, according to Liz Balmaseda, "in a Havana-to-Miami TV minute," all hopes for the dialogue were dashed.

Certainly what was dashed was Magda Montiel's political career. She'd been lobbying the United States government to show greater openness to Cuba and lift the blockade. And she'd aspired to get to Congress on the Democratic ticket. Not only did her entire staff quit after the revelation that their boss had engaged in devil worship, but Montiel was harassed, threatened, and publicly repudiated by hardliners in the exile community. But the kiss and Montiel Davis's words also shocked and angered a wide sector of the exile community, for whom her odd daughterly devotion represented an outrageous betrayal.

For my part, I realized how easily I might have fallen into the Magda role — unconsciously being flirtatious in an effort to catch Father Fidel's attention. For no matter how strong and conflicted our emotions about Fidel may be, there is an erotics to his domination. Women deny it at their peril. Men, too, but in a different way, not daring to admit they could be seduced by a more macho man.

Eddy and Xiomara Levy, in turn, appeared on the video chatting amiably with Fidel. By the next morning the Jewish Cuban-Americans in Miami who'd formed part of our group in December dissociated themselves from Jewish Solidarity. My cousin Alma said to me, "Eddy and Xiomara betrayed us. They told us Jewish Solidarity had nothing to do with politics."

Betrayal: to lead astray, seduce, to fail or desert, to disclose in violation of confidence. Betrayal: of the revolution, the reason given why Marifeli Pérez-Stable, Carmen Díaz, and María Cristina Herrera, key Cuban-American women of the preceding 1978 Diálogo, were not invited to the Nation and Immigration Conference. Betrayal: the word on too many Cuban-American lips after the video.

Did Magda Montiel betray the exile community? Or was Magda Montiel betrayed by the Father of her abandoned homeland, the King Lear of the country with which she was seeking to reconcile? Suddenly, because of that TV minute, the whole of the Nation and Immigration conference came to revolve, in Miami representations, around a highly gendered image of an *"encuentro amoroso"* — a "lovefest" — between Fidel Castro and the Cuban-Americans who attended the conference. A cartoon in the *Miami Herald* showed a starry-eyed Fidel, his face, hat, and shoulders covered with lipstick kisses, and from his mouth a bubble saying, "It's always so nice to speak with the opposition." The video of the reception with Castro became an inverted *Fresa y chocolate*, in which female Diegos, like Magda Montiel, returned to pay homage to the Cuban Revolutionary only to discover the devastating implications of their act.

Sadly, tragically, the absent daughter of Cuban patriarchy was reinserted into this heterosexual version of *Fresa y chocolate* and cruelly manipulated by the Miami media in collusion with the most hard-line elements of the Cuban power structure. To what end? To make it difficult for women, especially Cuban American women, to be taken seriously in any effort to inscribe themselves into the narrative of Cuban national identity. To make it painfully difficult, even as it becomes ever more necessary, to keep speaking of building a bridge between the diaspora and the island.

*

Too much is unravelling too rapidly. José Horta, the director of the Havana Film Festival for the last sixteen years, left Cuba at the end of June and is seeking political asylum in the United States. Some of his recent troubles with Cuban authorities, Horta declares, are connected to the screening of *Fresa y chocolate* at the festival. In the meantime, Miramax Films has bought the film and it will be released in the United States next January. It has already been shown to enthusiastic audiences at Miami-Dade Community College, despite accusations that the film is twisted propaganda intended to trick innocent viewers into thinking there is true freedom of speech on the island. Film companies in France, Japan, Argentina, and Germany, among others, have also acquired *Fresa y chocolate*.

I wish Senel Paz all the success in the world with his story. I still want so much to believe in David and Diego.

*

Just before I left Havana in December, *Fresa y chocolate* moved to the Yara theater, directly across from the Coppelia ice-cream parlor and a block away from my hotel. In the mornings, as I headed for the breakfast buffet on the 25th floor of La Habana Libre Hotel, I'd watch the crowds forming in front of the theater. By nightfall the lines would extend for many long blocks. My heart rose to my throat, seeing the number of people in Havana — estimated at a million — who in the midst of a staggering crisis were willing to wait hours to witness for themselves the possibility of friendship between Diego and David. Like Diego, I longed for a hug goodbye because I knew I was leaving.

Bookmark, Ediciones Vigía.

ZAIDA DEL RÍO

TWO FIGURES ON A BRIDGE

All I have
is the fine edge of the table
where I work and sustain myself.
As a child I'd ask my father
why though still awake
he closed his eyes.
He'd tell me it was so
his eyes could rest.
A bridge over this world.
A few planks for two insomniacs
bumping into each other.

Translated by Ruth Behar

"The Woman-Bridge."
Drawing by Zaida del Río.

AUTHORS

María Eugenia Alegría is a literary critic, translator, and member of the editorial collective of *Vigía* in Matanzas. She lives in Varadero, Cuba.

Maria de los Angeles Torres is Assistant Professor of Political Science at DePaul University in Chicago. She has recently completed a manuscript, *In the Land of Mirrors: Cuban Exile Politics.*

Jorge Luis Arcos is the author of several critical works on José Lezama Lima and a book of poems, *Conversación con un rostro nevada.* He edits the magazine *Unión* of the National Union of Writers and Artists of Cuba.

Miguel Barnet, poet, ethnologist, and novelist, is the author of *Autobiography of a Runaway Slave* and *Rachel's Song.* He is currently a director of the Fernando Ortiz Foundation in Havana.

Jésus J. Barquet is the author of three books of poetry, most recently *El libro del desterrado* (1994), and has been awarded the Letras de Oro Prize in Essay for *Consagración de la Habana* (1992). He teaches at New Mexico State University in Las Cruces.

Ruth Behar is Professor of Anthropology at the University of Michigan. She is the author of *Translated Woman: Crossing the Border with Esperanza's Story* and co-editor of *Women Writing Culture.* She is currently at work on a memoir.

Emilio Bejel, poet and critic, teaches at the University of Colorado at Boulder. Among his poetry collections are *Huellas/Footprints, Casas deshabitadas,* and *El libro regalado.*

Marilyn Bobes is a journalist and poet who works as a poetry editor for the Letras Cubanas publishing house in Havana. Her poems are collected in *Hallar el modo* and in anthologies.

Patricia Boero is a Cuban-Uruguayan filmmaker and journalist. She lived in Cuba from 1985 to 1990, working for TV Latina and BBC radio, and now works at the John D. and Catherine T. MacArthur Foundation as Program Officer for media.

Madeline Cámara is a graduate student at the State University of New York, Stony Brook, where she specializes in Latin American literature. She has written widely on feminist cultural issues, and in Cuba she edited *Letras Cubanas.*

Lourdes Casal, one of the major writers of modern Cuban-American literature, is profiled in the introduction.

Carlota Caulfield, Assistant Professor of Hispanic Studies at Mills College, is the author of several books of poems, including *Angel Dust, Visual Games for Words & Sounds,* and *Hyperpoems.*

María Elena Cruz Varela has won numerous prizes and honors for her poetry and her human rights advocacy in Cuba. She is the author of three books of poetry; Ecco Press will publish an English edition next year. In 1992 she was a candidate for the Nobel Peace Prize. She currently lives in Puerto Rico.

Abilio Estévez is a poet, playwright, and essayist who lives in Havana. He is the author of a book of prose poems, *Manual de las tentaciones,* and several plays. In 1994 he won the Tirso de Molina award in Spain for his play *La Noche.*

Lina de Feria's books of poetry include *La casa que no existe* and *A mansalva de los años.* She lives in Havana.

Amando Fernández, who died in 1994 in Miami, was the author of several books of poetry, including *El ruiseñor y la espada, Los siete círculos,* and *Antología personal.*

Pablo Armando Fernández is the author of *Aprendiendo a morir* and *El vientre del pez,* among many other works of poetry and fiction. He is the editor of *Unión,* the literary and arts magazine of the National Union of Writers and Artists of Cuba.

Roberto G. Fernández is the author of *Raining Backwards* and *La vida es un special.* He teaches Spanish literature at Florida State University at Tallahassee.

Victor Fowler Calzada is the director of publications at the Escuela Internacional de Cine y Television at San Antonio de los Baños, Cuba. He has published *Estudios de cerámica griega,* a book of poems, and is the editor of forthcoming anthologies on young Cuban women poets and on erotic Cuban poetry from the nineteenth century to the present.

Coco Fusco is a New York–based writer and artist. She is the author of *English Is Broken Here* and currently teaches in the School of Art at Temple University.

Lourdes Gil, born in Havana and now living in New Jersey, is the author of *Empieza la ciudad* (1993), as well as several collections of poetry. Another book of critical essays, *Voyage through the Temperate Zones: The Art and Literature of Cuban Extraterritoriality,* is forthcoming.

Flora González Mandri teaches in the Humanities department at Emerson College, in Boston. Her book, *José Donoso's House of Fiction,* is forthcoming.

Georgina Herrera is a poet who lives in Havana. She is the author of *Gentes y cosas* and *Granos de sol y luna.*

José Kozer's latest book of poems is *De donde oscilan los seres en sus proporciones* (Spain, 1991). He teaches in the Department of Romance Languages at Queens College, in New York.

Juan Leon currently teaches English and American Literature at Kyoto University in Japan.

Iraida López directs the Caribbean Exchange Program at Hunter College, in New York.

Rosa Lowinger specializes in art conservation and restoration and is also a playwright. She lives in Los Angeles.

Lillian Manzor-Coats teaches comparative literature, women's studies, and Latino studies at the University of Miami. She is the author of *CoBrA/Cobra: Un encuentro posmoderno, Borges/Escher* (Editorial Pliegos, forthcoming), as well as essays on Latin America and Latino cultures in *World Literature Today, Gestos, Latin American Literary Review,* and *Ollantay Theater Magazine.*

Yanai Manzor, a poet, graduated with a degree in cybernetics from the University of Havana. She currently lives in Miami.

Teresa Marrero is Associate Professor of Spanish at Tarrant County Junior College. She lives in Fort Worth, Texas. Her stories have appeared in *Linden Lane Magazine.*

Rita Martín is a writer currently living in Miami.

Elena M. Martínez is Assistant Professor of Spanish at Baruch College, CUNY. Recently, she published a book on the works of Juan Carlos Onetti.

Raquel (Kaki) Mendieta Costa taught Cuban cultural studies at the Instituto Superior de Arte for eighteen years in Havana. She is the author of *Cultura: Lucha de clases y conflicto racial, 1878–1895* and writes frequently on contemporary Cuban cultural and art movements. She currently resides in Chicago.

Nancy Morejón is a poet, editor, and literary critic who lives in Havana. She is profiled in our double interview.

Elías Miguel Muñoz is a Cuban-American author of three novels and two books of poetry, as well as two books of literary criticism. He has recently completed his second play, *The Last Guantanamera*.

Achy Obejas is a poet, journalist, and fiction writer. She is the author, most recently, of a collection of stories, *We Came All the Way from Cuba So You Could Dress Like This?*

Carilda Oliver Labra is the author of *Sonetos, Antología poética,* and *Ver la palma abriendo el día*. Her new poems are forthcoming in *Se me ha perdido un hombre*. She lives in Matanzas, Cuba.

Senel Paz is the author of *El niño aquel,* a collection of short stories, *Un rey en el jardín,* a novel, *El lobo, el bosque, y el hombre nuevo,* a novella, and the screenplay for the film *Fresa y chocolate (Strawberry and Chocolate)*. He lives in Havana.

Gustavo Pérez Firmat, a poet, literary critic, and Professor of Spanish at Duke University, is the author of *The Cuban Condition* and *Next Year in Cuba*.

Louis A. Pérez teaches history at the University of South Florida in Tampa. He is the author of *Cuba: Between Reform and Revolution,* among many other books on Cuban history.

Mirtha N. Quintanales is an anthropologist employed as faculty member and coordinator of the Latin American and Caribbean Studies Program at Jersey City State College, Jersey City, New Jersey. She was born in Cuba and immigrated to the United States in 1962, when she was thirteen years old.

Zaida del Río is an artist, engraver, ceramics decorator, and illustrator who lives in Havana. Her work has been exhibited internationally and published in *Herencia Clásica*.

Flavio Risech teaches in the School of Social Science at Hampshire College, in Amherst, Massachusetts. He has written widely on the subjects of class and identity politics in Latin America and the United States.

Sonia Rivera-Valdés was born and grew up in Havana. She now lives in New York City, has a Ph.D. in Spanish, and teaches at York College. The story in this issue is excerpted from her work in progress, *El libro de los aniversarios*.

Eliana S. Rivero teaches Spanish literature at the University of Arizona. She is coeditor of *Infinite Divisions: An Anthology of Chicana Literature*.

Reina María Rodríguez is the author of several books of poetry, including *Cuando una mujer no duerme, Para un cordero blanco,* and *En la arena de Padua*. She lives in Havana.

Teofilo F. Ruiz is the author of *Crisis and Continuity: Land and Town in Late Medieval Castile* (University of Pennsylvania Press, 1994). He teaches history at Brooklyn College (CUNY).

Minerva Salado is the author of several poetry collections, including *Al cierre, Tema para un paseo,* and *Palabra en el espejo.* She currently lives in Mexico City.

Excilia Saldaña is a poet, critic, and children's writer. She directs the book program for children and young people of the Association of Cuban Writers in Havana. Her publications include *Kele, Kele, Poemas de la noche,* and *Mi nombre.*

Ernesto Santana is a poet who lives in Havana.

Ester Rebeca Shapiro Rok, aka Ester R. Shapiro, Ph.D., was born in Havana in 1952. She is Assistant Professor in Psychology and Research Associate at the Mauricio Gaston Institute, University of Massachusetts at Boston. Her published work includes the co-edited *Tradition and Innovation in Psychoanalytic Education* and *Grief as a Family Process.*

Lucía Suárez is a graduate student at Duke University in the field of Latin American literature and culture.

Virgil Suarez was born in Cuba in 1962. He is the author of three books of fiction on the Cuban-American experience: *The Cutter, Latin Jazz,* and *Welcome to the Oasis.* He teaches creative writing at Florida State University in Tallahassee.

Carmelita Tropicana, a Cuban-American writer and performance artist, has been collaborating since 1984 with **Uzi Parnes,** writer and director of experimental theater, film, and video.

Roberto Valero, who died in 1994 in Washington, D.C., was born in Cuba in 1955. He published six books and won the Letras de Oro Literary Prize for essay. He taught at the George Washington University in Washington, D.C.

Alan West (b. Havana, 1953) is a poet, essayist, narrator, critic, and translator. He is the author of two children's books on Roberto Clemente and José Martí. His recent book of bilingual poetry is *Dar nombres a lluvia—Finding Voices in the Rain* and forthcoming is a book of essays on Cuban culture and literature, *Tropics of History.*

Alfredo Zaldivar, a poet, is the founder of *Vigía,* a cultural arts magazine and publishing house based in Matanzas, Cuba.

ARTISTS

Eduardo Aparicio (b. Guanabacoa, 1956) holds a B.S. in Linguistics and French from Georgetown University and an M.A. in Photography from Columbia College, Chicago. He recently moved to southern Florida after living in Chicago for fifteen years.

Yovani Bauta, originally from Matanzas, is a painter now living in Miami.

Consuelo Castañeda, an experimental painter who taught at the Instituto Superior de Arte in Havana, now lives in Miami.

Humberto Castro, a painter, lives in Paris.

Arturo Cuenca, a photo-collage artist, lives in New York.

Antonia Eiriz, one of the major figures of twentieth-century Cuban art, died in Miami in 1994 while working on her last canvas.

Rolando Estévez, a poet, designer of *Vigía* magazine, and artist, lives in Matanzas, Cuba. His work is featured on the pages separating the three parts of this book and on our back cover.

José Franco, a painter, lives in Buenos Aires.

Yolanda Fundora, a designer and artist, lives in New Jersey.

Roció García, a painter who received her artistic training in St. Petersburg, Russia, lives in Havana.

Nereida García Ferraz is a Cuban American artist and photographer who has lived in Chicago since 1971. She has received two NEA fellowships for painting, and her work has been exhibited in Mexico, Italy, and the United States.

Florencio Gelabert Soto, a sculptor, lives in Miami.

Quisqueya Henríquez, a conceptual artist, lives in Miami.

Tony Mendoza is the author of *Ernie: A Photographer's Memoir* and *Stories*. He was the recipient of photography fellowships from the Guggenheim Foundation and the National Endowment for the Arts. He lives in Ohio.

Osvaldo Mesa, an artist, lives in Baltimore.

Cecilia Portal, a photo-collage artist who learned the craft of photography in Mexico City, now lives in New Mexico.

Ernesto Pujol, a painter and artist who recently exhibited his work in Havana, lives in New York.

Natalia Raphael, an artist and sculptor whose work has been exhibited in Matanzas, lives in Boston.

Zaida del Río, a painter and poet, lives in Havana.

Ricardo Estanislao Zulueta, an artist who specializes in photo-performance, lives in New York.

6384